RETHINKING MAO

Explorations in Mao Zedong's Thought

NICK KNIGHT

LEXINGTON BOOKS

A division of
ROWMAN & LITTLEFIELD PUBLISHERS, INC.
Lanham • Boulder • New York • Toronto • Plymouth, UK

LEXINGTON BOOKS

A division of Rowman & Littlefield Publishers, Inc.
A wholly owned subsidary of The Rowman & Littlefield Publishing Group, Inc.
4501 Forbes Boulevard, Suite 200
Lanham, MD 20706

Estover Road
Plymouth PL6 7PY
United Kingdom

British Library Cataloguing in Publication Information Available

Library of Congress Cataloging-in-Publication Data

Knight, Nick, 1947–
    Rethinking Mao : explorations in Mao Zedong's thought / Nick Knight.
        p. cm.
    Includes bibliographical references.
    ISBN-13: 978-0-7391-1706-4 (cloth : alk. paper)
    ISBN-10: 0-7391-1706-8 (cloth : alk. paper)
    ISBN-13: 978-0-7391-1707-1 (pbk. : alk. paper)
    ISBN-10: 0-7391-1707-6 (pbk. : alk. paper)
    1. Mao, Zedong, 1893–1976—Philosophy. 2. Mao, Zedong, 1893–1976—
Political and social views. I. Title.
    DS778.M3K65 2007
    335.43'45—dc22   2006100665

Printed in the United States of America

♾™ The paper used in this publication meets the minimum requirements of American
National Standard for Information Sciences—Permanence of Paper for Printed Library
Materials, ANSI/NISO Z39.48–1992.

Contents

Acknowledgments

I FIRST BECAME INTERESTED in Mao Zedong's thought in 1971. At that time, I was an undergraduate student at the University of Queensland, majoring in political science. I was fortunate enough to be taught Chinese politics by Dr. C. L. Chiou, himself a Mao scholar. Chiou possessed the happy knack of communicating to his students his enthusiasm for his subject, and I became fascinated with the challenge of understanding how Marxism had been understood and used by Marxists in China, particularly as it was then being used in the late stage of the Cultural Revolution.

The interest sparked by Chiou carried forward into my doctoral studies at the University of London's School of Oriental and African Studies, where I was supervised by Professor Stuart Schram, without doubt the foremost Mao scholar in the West. While Professor Schram and I disagreed, and continue to disagree, on many issues of interpretation, he communicated to me a very important lesson: the importance of grounding the interpretation of Mao and his thought on detailed analysis of the Mao texts. Schram rightly had no patience with the cavalier disregard of conventional rules of evidence so patently obvious in much that was written on Mao. His own interpretations of Mao's thought never strayed far from the Mao texts, and this represented a salutary lesson in a field of study into which ideology unavoidably intrudes. Schram also communicated to me the importance of making the Mao texts available in scholarly English editions, although my contributions in this area nowhere near approach his enormous contribution. His *Mao's Road to Power* series, in particular, represents a phenomenal achievement, one that makes accessible to the Anglophone world all known Mao texts to 1949. This series makes informed debate on

Mao and his thought much easier, and all those interested in this subject are very much in his debt.

These two scholars were a major influence on my early study of Mao Zedong's thought, and I gratefully acknowledge their inspiration and assistance. I also express my sincere gratitude to the following: Dr. Wang Yuping of Griffith University's School of Languages and Applied Linguistics has for nearly two decades helped me with the Chinese language. Professor Arif Dirlik, formerly of Duke University and now semi-retired, has consistently supported my research and has read much that I have written. Professor Michael Dutton of London University and Dr. Paul Healy of the University of New England were a significant theoretical influence at a stage in my research when I needed it most. Many Mao scholars in China, too numerous to list individually, have assisted my research. While I thank them all, three stand out. Professor Ran Changuang and Professor Li Yongtai of Sichuan University, and Professor Bi Jianheng of the Sichuan Academy of Social Science, gave me an astonishing amount of help when I was wrestling with the philosophical dimensions of Mao's thought.

A number of teaching colleagues have supported my research in material ways. Professor Colin Mackerras was a wonderful mentor and collaborator in both teaching and research. How fortunate I was to have Colin as head of the School of Modern Asian studies when I joined it in 1981! I also acknowledge the help of Associate Professor John Butcher, a truly inspirational teacher and colleague, and Doug Smith for his prodigious feats in both library and classroom on my behalf. My sincere thanks go also to my research assistant of recent years, Dr. Liu Xian.

As ever, my greatest debt is to Jill Kenny, my partner for the best part of three decades. Her love and support have allowed me to achieve my goals in teaching and research. No words can be found to thank her adequately.

The chapters in this book draw on the following publications, which in each case have been thoroughly revised, updated, and expanded: "The Form of Mao Zedong's 'Sinification of Marxism'," *The Australian Journal of Chinese Affairs* 9 (January 1983): 17–34; "Mao and History: Who Judges and How?" *The Australian Journal of Chinese Affairs* 13 (January 1985): 121–36; "Mao Zedong and the Chinese Road to Socialism," in *Marxism in Asia*, eds. Colin Mackerras and Nick Knight (London and Sydney: Croom Helm, 1985), chapter 4; "The Marxism of Mao Zedong: Empiricism and Discourse in the Field of Mao Studies," *The Australian Journal of Chinese Affairs* 16 (July 1986): 7–22; "*On Contradiction* and *On New De-*

mocracy: Contrasting Perspectives on Causation and Social Change in the Thought of Mao Zedong," *Bulletin of Concerned Asian Scholars* 22, no. 2 (April–June 1990): 18–34; "Politics and Vision: Historical Time and the Future in Mao Zedong's Thought, 1936–1945," *Journal of Oriental Studies* 29, no. 2 (1991): 139–71; "From Harmony to Struggle, From Perpetual Peace to Cultural Revolution: Changing Futures in Mao Zedong's Thought," *China Information* 11, nos. 2/3 (Autumn/Winter 1996): 176–95; "Mao Zedong and Working Class Leadership of the Chinese Revolution, 1927–1930," *China Information* 12, no. 3 (Winter 1997–1998): 28–45; "Working Class Power and State Formation in Mao Zedong's Thought, 1931–1934," *Journal of Contemporary Asia* 32, no. 1 (2002): 29–46. I am grateful to the editors and publishers of these publications for permission to use copyright material.

Chapter 4 draws on "Mao Zedong and the Peasants: Class and Power in the Formation of a Revolutionary Strategy," which was originally published in *China Report* 40, no. 1 (January–March 2004): 49–76. Copyright Centre for the Study of Developing Societies, Delhi, 2004. All rights reserved. Reproduced with permission of the copyright holders and the publishers, Sage Publications, India Pvt. Ltd., New Delhi.

Introduction: Rethinking Mao **1**

THERE ARE A NUMBER OF REASONS WHY it is necessary, some thirty years after his death, to rethink Mao. First, the Chinese authorities have over the last three decades made available an enormous number of previously unknown or little known texts by Mao. The publication and widespread dissemination of these documents within China, and their elaboration in the Chinese media and scholarly journals, have not been without ulterior political motive, something I will comment on below. Regardless of the motivation for their release, ready access to these Mao texts has not only radically expanded the textual terrain on which the study of Mao and his thought is based, it has altered the contours of that terrain so dramatically that some conventional interpretations have been called into question and earlier debates shown to be in need of reopening. For these texts bear new witness to many themes—literary, philosophical, ideological, military, political, economic, and personal—central to Mao's thought. The new texts stand as a challenge to interpretation, for they appear as uncharted territory, in need of exploration.

Second, and at the expense of stating the obvious, the world has turned many times since Mao stood upon it. With its turning have come profound changes, both in China and internationally, that inevitably impact on the way in which we think about Mao. During the later years of his life, one could still speak of an international communist movement, even though there were bitter divisions within it. The Soviet Union existed, as did the international tensions generated by the Cold War. China remained under Mao's sway, and the ideas that were later to underpin the radical reforms of the 1980s and 1990s had been condemned as heresy and were in full retreat under the onslaught of the Cultural Revolution. Yet, within a few

short years the Cultural Revolution's heresy had become the new orthodoxy, bringing a transformation to China's economic and social fabric as
dramatic, if not more so, than any of Mao's ambitious political campaigns.
The changes in China in the direction of capitalism and the weakening and
eventual collapse of the Soviet Union in 1991 accompanied and in part facilitated the virtual demise of the Left in the West, with the disappearance
of communist parties in many countries. The victory of China's reform
agenda, with its retreat from socialism, has been echoed in Western countries with the triumph of neo-conservatism, whose economic rationalist
credo has justified a sustained attack on the public culture and a large-scale
renunciation of the responsibilities of the state for the welfare of its citi-
zens. In both China and the West, confidence in the potential of conscious
political action to achieve human equality has been severely eroded. It has
consequently become very much more difficult to comprehend, let alone
justify, the egalitarian socialist ideals of earlier generations, and particularly
those of Mao's generation who sought to achieve socialism through revolutionary means. The word "socialism," once a potent ideological signifier,
now assumes a rather dated air. The erosion of socialism as a political movement and the apparent exhaustion of its ideological appeal have altered not
only the empirical sense in which the word is used, but also the value status (good/bad, rational/irrational, relevant/irrelevant) which the concept
attracts. And yet, the socialist values that motivated Mao and the revolutionary generation to which he belonged were as tangible to them, and as
apparently realizable, as the very different values that have motivated subsequent generations.

However, it is evident that many commentators on Mao's life and
thought are no longer willing to take seriously his professed belief in
Marxism and socialism. The constraints of the present, including values
and forms of consciousness at variance with those of earlier generations,
have served to inhibit recognition of the explanatory value of a worldview
so different from that prevailing at the moment; for if Marxism and socialism make no sense *now*, how could they have *then*? The interpretation of
Mao's thought inevitably requires the use of many concepts, such as "socialism," whose meanings and values alter and fluctuate over time. For the
scholar who now takes seriously Mao's commitment to socialism and
Marxism, there is thus the burden, additional to the very demanding challenge of achieving a reasonable familiarity with the Mao texts, of swim-
ming against the tide of contemporary opinion and of asserting that,
despite all that has transpired over the last three decades, socialism remains
a category relevant to the understanding of Mao ideas and actions.

The present and recent past thus create the prism through which Mao's life and thought are refracted. As the prism changes, so too do the images that appear. The study of Mao and his thought has no immunity from the influence of successive contemporary contexts; the temporal vantage points Mao scholars occupy inevitably shape and color their perspectives and interpretations. Given the constantly changing political and intellectual environment within which the study of Mao proceeds, closure of debates on Mao's life and thought is not possible. Conclusions asserted as axiomatically correct in one historical context lose their appeal in another; the academic fashions of one era, with their commitment to particular values and perspectives, lose their gloss as they are superseded by other intellectual fashions. Assessments of Mao are, in this sense, always preliminary, always awaiting further rethinking.

Nowhere is this phenomenon of Mao studies as a process, one that reflects the dominant values of a particular historical context, more evident than in post-Mao China. Following the proclamation of the 1981 "Resolution on certain questions in the history of our Party since the founding of the People's Republic of China,"[1] which attempted a balanced view of Mao's achievements and failings, Chinese scholars and Communist Party theorists moved to examine aspects of Mao's life and thought previously off-limits; but they did so in a manner that clearly reflected perspectives and values of an emerging "regime of truth."[2] Deng Xiaoping's theory, which incorporated a broad agenda for economic and social reform as well as an authoritative reinterpretation of the Chinese Communist Party's history and Mao's role in it, unambiguously established the framework and limits within which explication and critique of the Mao texts could proceed. By and large, Chinese scholars and Party theorists have conducted themselves and their scholarship appropriately; they have absorbed the prevailing orthodoxy and it has found its way, often quite unconsciously, into their scholarship.[3] One can espy in the vast discourse of Mao studies in post-Mao China a general observance of Deng's dictum that Mao's "contribution to the Chinese revolution far outweigh his mistakes" and his "merits are primary and his errors secondary." Dimensions of Mao's thought and policies criticized in the "Resolution" have been accepted as legitimate targets of critical scholarship; but the overwhelming tenor of the very large body of scholarly literature generated in the 1980s and 1990s was overwhelmingly positive.[4] Thus, while the general atmosphere in which the study of Mao in post-Mao China occurs is more open and critical than previously, the constraints remain, constraints that derive from the prevailing political ethos.

Similarly, the study of Mao in the West has altered as the political and social climate has changed. Most notable has been the dramatic decline of interest in Mao, as scholars have turned their attention to seemingly more topical issues. The flood of scholarly publications during the 1970s and early 1980s has reduced to a trickle, with interest in Mao kept alive by a handful of die-hard scholars, including myself, who remain convinced of the scholarly significance of Mao's thought, policies, and historical position. The task of such scholars has been made the more difficult with the publication in both China and the West of a large number of memoirs and biographies of Mao that are either salacious or denunciatory or both.[5] These warts-and-all studies usually paint an extremely negative portrait that appears to render nugatory any serious scholarly study of Mao. Stories of Mao's sexual peccadilloes, vengeful personality, and eccentric behavior are taken as a general detraction from the significance of his life and thought and role in Chinese and world history. While this obviously need not be the case, such *ad hominem* attacks have had their effect. Whether true or not, balanced or unbalanced (and most are the latter), such accounts of Mao's personality and personal life have contributed to a climate in which the demonization of Mao is assumed the only appropriate object of interest.

This book is founded firmly on a rejection of this current of opinion. It commences from the assumption that the scholarly study of Mao's thought remains significant. An understanding of the sources, conceptual structure, and development of his ideas can contribute to an understanding of his actions in the political realm; it can also provide a window through which can be glimpsed the worldview of the revolutionary intellectuals who influenced and were in turn inspired by him; it is also essential for a comprehension of the ideological and intellectual world within the Chinese Communist Party (CCP) and the People's Republic of China during the Mao era. These are surely not insignificant issues. Moreover, discussion of themes in Mao's thought is relevant to debates on other issues in twentieth-century Chinese history. An example is the role of the peasantry in the Chinese Revolution; another is the nature and effectiveness of socialist construction in China during the 1950s and 1960s; still another is the influence on China's intellectual world of Marxism and other European bodies of thought in the first half of the twentieth century. There are others. Without a tradition of the study of Mao's thought, which implies as necessary a study of the intellectual, political, and cultural world that shaped him and which he in turn shaped, other debates on the history of modern China would be the poorer.

Moreover, not only is an understanding of Mao's thought significant for an understanding of China's past, it is relevant too for comprehension of China today. While the intellectual, ideological, and political environments in China have changed dramatically since Mao's death in 1976, his influence has in no way been expunged. China's historians and political scientists still operate within an intellectual context that owes much to the past; their frameworks for understanding, including their epistemological approach, have not fully shed the ideological and political influence of China's revolutionary and socialist history. Ideologically, the CCP still operates within the framework of the 1981 "Resolution" that, while criticizing Mao's failings, accords Mao enormous credit for the victory of the Chinese Revolution and the successes of the early phase of socialist construction. The CCP has certainly not abandoned Mao and his thought, and Party theorists continue to struggle with the almost insurmountable problem of reconciling Mao's revolutionary Marxism with the current Party leadership's opening of China to capitalism and globalization.[6] Mao's ideology continues to resonate, sometimes strongly, sometimes less so, in the Party's ideological pronouncements, but particularly in its insistence that China remains a "socialist" country. Politically, Mao's influence is evident in the CCP's internal structures and organizational practices, which bear the hallmarks of Mao's understanding of the Leninist theory of party-building. In each of these realms—intellectual, ideological, political—Mao continues to cast a long shadow.

But it is not just in the corridors of power and halls of academe that Mao casts a long shadow. "Mao revivals" occur at various intervals among the Chinese people and indicate the continuing presence of Mao in the popular consciousness. One of the most significant of these revivals occurred at the time of official celebrations in 1993 to mark the centenary of Mao's birth. This particular "Mao revival" occurred at a number of levels. Its most superficial and evident manifestation was a lively trade in Mao memorabilia (Mao Zedong cigarette lighters that play the "East is Red," Mao Zedong emblems hung like St. Christopher medals in taxis, Mao calendars and badges).[7] A more substantial manifestation was the outpouring of books and essays on Mao's life, some of which disclosed intimate tidbits about his personal and sexual life.[8] Alongside the official celebration of Mao's centenary (conferences, academic publications, exhibitions, and films) there thus ran a populist current of nostalgia for the former leader. This nostalgia was an outward expression of a range of emotions. At its simplest, it expressed little more than mere curiosity in the antics of a famous leader; at a deeper level, it expressed the insecurity felt by many Chinese about the pace and direction of change; it was indicative too of a yearning for the imagined certainties of the past. This unofficial Mao revival thus represented an inchoate but nonetheless tangible expression of opposition to the Party's reform agenda and for this reason was perceived by China's leadership as something of a threat.[9] The oblique criticism of the reform process implied by the Mao revival was not readily controllable and placed China's leaders in an invidious position, for they were bound by the prescriptions of the 1981 "Resolution" to speak of Mao as a flawed leader whose positive contributions nevertheless far outweighed his errors. Popular interest in and reverence for Mao could not be proscribed without simultaneously calling into question both the legitimacy of the post-Mao leadership and the coherence of the Party's ideology, which was built on and inextricably intertwined with Mao's ideology.

The 1993 "Mao revival" has not entirely subsided, and popular interest in Mao has ebbed and flowed in the years since. This phenomenon is a timely reminder that Mao left a complex and volatile legacy, one not readily constrained by the approved framework for understanding his life and thought contained in the 1981 "Resolution." Mao represents different things to different Chinese, and their varied understandings are mobilized to achieve different effects. These may range from the simple (hanging a Mao calendar for decorative effect) to the complex (invoking Mao's name to mobilize support in the struggle against corruption). These constructions and uses of Mao and his thought vary, not only because the texts written by and about Mao are numerous, diverse, and complex, but also because the concerns which motivate interest in Mao are themselves diverse and subject to change.

The continued influence of Mao and his thought in China and elsewhere (witness the upsurge of Maoist revolutionary activity in Nepal) thus adds weight to the case for a continued study of Mao's thought. But how *is* Mao's thought to be studied; how *do* we approach such a complex task? As I demonstrate in chapters 2 and 3, Mao scholars have responded to these questions in quite diverse ways; they have mobilized different values and methodologies, and posed different questions. The conclusions they have reached have inevitably varied, and it is evident that there is no uncontested approach. In my own study of Mao's thought, I have been guided by certain ways of thinking. The first involves what might be described as a cartographic approach, one that conceptualizes the vast body of Mao texts (the "work" [oeuvre], as Michel Foucault describes it) as a terrain.[10] Like physical terrains, this particular terrain has boundaries, contours, and identifying landmarks. It alters as new texts and information come to light, or as texts are occasionally removed from the register.[11] It thus periodically requires remapping. Many scholars have explored this terrain, although the maps they have drawn provide different and sometimes contradictory perspectives, guided as they are by divergent objectives. It is a terrain I have been traversing for some thirty-five years, and in that time its landscape has changed significantly. Some areas I had explored and "mapped" now appear different, and I have been obliged to revise the conclusions I had reached; other areas appear largely undisturbed.

Second, conceptualizing the Mao texts as a terrain awaiting exploration suggests the need for a "compass." Without a clear sense of the direction in which to proceed, the journey can have no clear outcome. What is required is an articulate framework that provides the questions with which to interrogate the texts. My own explorations in Mao Zedong's thought have been grounded in and guided by an interest in the history of Marxist and socialist ideologies, and the process through which these were introduced to China, adopted by Chinese intellectuals and political activists (particularly in the 1920s and 1930s), and elaborated, developed, and applied in the context of the Chinese Revolution and socialist construction after 1949. My interests are thus those of a historian of ideas concerned to understand how a radical ideological tradition that emerged first in Europe has evolved in a different historical and cultural setting. My inclination has been to accept at face value professions of conversion and adherence to Marxism on the part of Chinese revolutionaries and intellectuals. This has certainly not been a universal tendency amongst those who have studied the thought of Mao and Chinese revolutionary intellectuals; indeed, there has been an unfortunate tendency in the opposite direction, of either rejecting or belittling claims to belief in Marxism. The grounds for this dismissive treatment are various, but a commonly encountered perspective is a refusal to accept that Chinese could really understand a European intellectual system of thought. Still another is based on a political premise: Because Marxist ideas have been used in China in ways deemed inappropriate, then the commitment and level of understanding of those advocating such ideas are not to be taken seriously. I reject both of these approaches. I accept that many revolutionaries and intellectuals who happened to be Chinese did make a genuine intellectual and political commitment to Marxism; they struggled with the complex concepts and forms of reasoning characteristic of that ideology, and many became conversant with it. This does not, of course, imply any necessary acceptance of the ideas and values that emerged on the basis of this engagement with Marxism; still less does it imply acceptance of the political actions supposedly motivated by those ideas and values. But it does accept the validity of attempting to comprehend the ways in which Chinese Marxist intellectuals explained their understanding of the influential system of thought they advocated. To engage with their ideas on their terms appears to me to be a basic premise of the historian of ideas, and yet it is certainly not one widely shared in the study of Mao's thought and Marxism in China.[12]

One of the reasons for the disinclination to take seriously assertions of belief in Marxism on the part of Marxists in China is, in my view, a rather threadbare knowledge of Marxism on the part of scholars making judgments about Marxism in China. The lack of anything approaching an adequate understanding of Marxist theory has not prevented some scholars from making the most egregious assertions, often in the form of throwaway lines, about the inadequacy of Mao's comprehension of Marxism.[13] I discovered, rather to my surprise, that my familiarity with the history, theory, and texts of Marxism has given me a perspective on the history of Marxism in China not shared, or widely shared, by fellow Mao scholars.[14] I had assumed that a basic requirement of the study of Mao, who repeatedly claimed to be a Marxist and whose texts are full of references to Marxism, would be a reasonable familiarity with Marxist theory. But the history of Mao studies does not confirm that this is the case.

My explorations of the terrain of the Mao texts have thus more often than not been prompted by a search for landmarks indicating the Marxist and socialist dimensions of Mao's thought, but I have not ignored the influence of the Chinese intellectual tradition. Analysis of Mao's philosophy of history during the Yan'an period revealed only too clearly that his perception of historical time and the future drew on utopian themes in both the Chinese and Marxist traditions. However, it is instructive that utopianism is not a major theme in the Chinese tradition, as it is in the Western tradition, and that it was to this theme that Mao turned when attempting to situate the Chinese Revolution and the Anti-Japanese War in the broad sweep of history. It was this forward-looking and optimistic dimension of the Chinese tradition, rather than its dominant tendency to revere the past and perceive history as moving in cycles, that drew Mao's attention, for it seemed to complement the teleological theme in Marxism that perceived as inevitable a future of peace, equality, and abundance, historical objectives that he so ardently desired. His attempted synthesis of these themes drawn from the Chinese and Marxist traditions was only partly successful, and there remained tensions that did not so much resolve themselves as become irrelevant as his own utopianism declined in the 1950s and 1960s (see chapters 5 and 9).

The themes considered in this book are thus largely concerned with the Marxist and socialist dimensions of Mao's thought, but not entirely so. In each case, I have attempted to "rethink" Mao by subjecting his texts to fresh scrutiny, paying particular attention to the evidence contained in documents recently become available. They are themes central to Mao's thought, and analysis of them provides insights into the mind that, more than any other, influenced the course of the Chinese Revolution and the period of socialist construction after 1949. For example, central to his revolutionary strategy, from the 1920s to the 1940s, was a particular perception of the role of the working class and peasantry and the position of each class relative to the other. Mao's understanding of this class relationship, as I demonstrate in chapter 4, has been frequently misunderstood in commentaries on his thought. Rather than a peasant revolutionary, Mao thought of himself as a Marxist who invested the working class with the leading role in the revolution; and in line with Marxism, he believed that the peasants, while enormously important, were not able to assume that leadership role as a result of limitations imposed by their class conditions of existence. There is abundant evidence to support this view. There is evidence too to support the suggestion that Mao would not have abandoned the cities so completely and "gone up to the mountains" had not the crisis of 1927 dictated a strategic retreat into the countryside. In the event, Mao was obliged to rely on the peasantry and to develop a strategy for rural-based revolution, but he never lost sight of the fact that China's future lay in the cities. The future was a socialist and industrial future, and it was the working class rather than the peasantry that held the key to that future.

Similarly, Mao's understanding of the Marxist theory of social change has frequently been misrepresented. It is often suggested that Mao turned his back on the materialist philosophy of Marxism, glorifying rather the capacity of ideas to transform society. He is thus depicted as an "idealist" or "voluntarist," one who regarded the ideological-political superstructure of society and struggles within it as the primary source of social change; the economic base, which Marx had attributed with this role, became in Mao's mind pliantly malleable to pressures for change from the superstructure. Yet, a careful exploration of this dimension of his thought does not bear out this interpretation. While his views on the capacity of politics, ideology, and culture to contribute to social change did go beyond that of a mechanical and reductionist materialism and did vary, his general perspective remained an economistic one; he continued to regard the economic foundation of society—forces and relations of production—as the ultimately determining factor in history. The interpretation offered in chapter 6 demonstrates that, during the early Yan'an period, various perspectives on social change emerged in Mao's thought. While it is clear that Mao was searching for a formulation that could provide a clear conception of the historical role of politics, ideology, and culture, his various discussions of social change were invariably underpinned by an acknowledgment of the primacy of economic forces. In this respect, the Mao of the Yan'an period remained safely within the bounds of Marxist orthodoxy.

Another theme central to Mao's thought is the manner in which he understood the process through which Marxism could be applied in China. This process, which he referred to as the "Sinification of Marxism," has been interpreted by some commentators as an attempt to subordinate the universality of Marxism to the specific characteristics of China's culture and history, and the contemporary realities of the Chinese Revolution. From this perspective, Marxism in China becomes Chinese Marxism, an exotic and orientalised offshoot of a European ideology, one that is by definition heterodox. Mao was, it is true, extremely concerned to ensure that Marxism was applied effectively in the Chinese context to enhance the capacity of the CCP to achieve its revolutionary objectives; he was also insistent that CCP intellectuals and cadres base their actions on a firm grasp of Chinese history and culture. He had no patience with those who spouted Marxist formulas and made no effort to investigate and understand Chinese reality. However, he was insistent that this process of coming to know and change Chinese realities had to be founded on a methodology that ensured the universality of Marxism would not be compromised. In logical terms, this is a difficult task, for it speaks to a fundamental problem in the philosophy of science that contemplates the way in which universal laws can be derived from observations of particular instances. Mao certainly did not resolve this problem, but then he was not in any strict sense a philosopher of science. Yet, he did arrive at a formula that allowed him to assert with confidence that the integration of Marxism's universal laws with the concrete realities of the Chinese Revolution could be achieved without detracting from Marxism's universality. The rather tortuous logic underpinning Mao's "Sinification of Marxism" is reconstructed in chapter 7, and the conceptual difficulties of his attempt to integrate the universal and particular explored.

One of the problems that Mao, along with other leaders of newly emergent socialist nations, had to confront was just how a socialist society could be established and then consolidated to the extent that a transition to communism would be possible. When Mao guided the Chinese Revolution to victory in 1949, he recognised that the seizure of state power represented only the first stage in a long and arduous struggle to transform the very essence of society. How was this struggle to be prosecuted, and what were its goals? In this area, at least, the writings of Karl Marx could offer little concrete advice, for his focus had been the dynamics of nineteenth-century industrial capitalism in the European context. While Marx did consider at length the historical development of precapitalist economic formations, he was virtually silent on what policies a socialist government of a largely feudal society should implement. While at a very general level Marx's philosophy of history, particularly its teleology, could inspire a particular orientation to the construction of socialism in such a society, Mao was obliged to look elsewhere for practical guidance. The most obvious source was the Soviet Union, and in the early years of the People's Republic of China, Mao and his colleagues assiduously applied many of its experiences, although his own experience of state-building garnered during the Yan'an period was never far below the surface. By the mid-1950s, however, Mao was becoming increasingly impatient with the shortcomings of the Soviet model and at a theoretical level began to consider a road to socialism that would more effectively conform to the particular characteristics of the Chinese context and exploit its potentialities. In this, Mao was guided by the imperative, recognized and acted on during the Yan'an period, to "Sinify" Marxism. To persist with a foreign model for socialist construction, as the Soviet model increasingly appeared to be, could only retard progress towards the consolidation of socialism in China. In Mao's mind thus emerged the possibility of a "Chinese road to socialism," one inspired at a general level by Marxism but guided in practical detail by China's characteristics. The major themes in the "Chinese road to socialism" are explored in chapter 8, and its dramatic manifestations in the form of the Great Leap Forward and Cultural Revolution explained from the perspective of Mao's own thinking.

The onset of the Cultural Revolution is often explained by reference to Mao's "utopianism," which in this context usually implies a gross divorce from reality and the attempt to achieve quite unrealizable goals. I approach Mao's "utopianism" quite differently. I argue, in chapter 9, that it was in fact the decline of Mao's utopianism, evident throughout the 1950s but accelerating in the 1960s, that contributed to his decision to initiate such a wide-scale and damaging political campaign. By the mid-1960s, Mao had abandoned any possibility of an imminent transition to communism; the imperative now was to defend the gains of the revolution from the depredations of influential "capitalist roaders" within the CCP itself. He could envisage the Chinese road leading not to socialism but to a capitalist restoration, and his preoccupation became the prevention of such an eventuality. Toward the end of his life, his vision of the future thus veered away from the utopian to a bleak assessment of humanity's long-term future.

These, then, are the themes that I have addressed in this attempt to rethink Mao. They represent significant dimensions of his thought but there are others just as significant not explored here. Of these, the philosophical dimension of Mao's thought is the most obvious. I have omitted consideration of this here as I have explored it in considerable detail elsewhere; indeed, this theme is so important that justice could hardly be done it within the confines of a single chapter.[15] This volume thus does not offer a comprehensive history of Mao's thought. Its purpose is rather more modest, being to recount a series of explorations in Mao's thought based on a close reading of the Mao texts. Writing the book represented an opportunity to rethink Mao, and I offer it to the reader in the same spirit: as an opportunity to rethink their own position on the thought of one of the twentieth century's most influential figures.

In the following two chapters, I contemplate methodological issues that confront the study of Mao and his thought. This exercise provides a critical introduction to the field of Mao studies that will help contextualize the explorations in Mao Zedong's thought that follow.

Notes

1. *Resolution on CPC History (1949–81)* (Beijing: Foreign Languages Press, 1981).

2. For Foucault's concept of a "regime of truth," see Paul Rabinow (ed.) *The Foucault Reader* (New York: Pantheon Books, 1984), 72–75.

3. For analysis of the field of Mao studies in China during the 1980s, see Nick Knight, ed., *The Philosophical Thought of Mao Zedong: Studies from China, 1981–1989* (Armonk, New York: M. E. Sharpe, *Chinese Studies in Philosophy, 1992*), introduction.

4. See Nick Knight, "Mao Studies in China: A Review of *Research on Mao Zedong Thought*," *CCP Research Newsletter* 2 (Spring 1989): 13–16.

5. See, for example, Jung Chang and Jon Halliday, *Mao: The Unknown Story* (London: Jonathan Cape, 2005); Li Zhisui, *The Private Life of Chairman Mao* (London: Random House, 1996).

6. Nick Knight, "Contemporary Chinese Marxism and the Marxist Tradition: Globalisation, Socialism and the Search for Ideological Coherence," *Asian Studies Review* 30, no. 1 (March 2006): 19–39.

7. For a discussion of this phenomenon, see Melissa Schrift, *Biography of a Chairman Mao Badge: The Creation and Mass Consumption of a Personality Cult* (New

Brunswick: Rutgers University Press, 2001); see also Michael Dutton, *Streetlife China* (Melbourne: Cambridge University Press, 1998), 242–71.

8. See, for example, Fan Hao, *Mao Zedong he ta de guwen* [Mao Zedong and his adviser] (Beijing: Renmin chubanshe, 1993); Li Zhanping and Li Shuqin, *Mao Zedong lixianji* [A chronicle of dangers experienced by Mao Zedong] (Beijing: Zhongguo shuji chubanshe, 1993); Pang Xianzhi, *Mao Zedong he tade mishu Tian Jiaying* [Mao Zedong and his secretary Tan Jiaying] (Beijing: Zhongguo wenxian chubanshe, 1989); Zheng Yi and Jia Mei, eds., *Mao Zedong shenghuo shilu* [Records of Mao Zedong's life] (Nanjing: Jiangsu wenyi chubanshe, 1989). For a review of some of this literature see Thomas Scharping, "The Man, the Myth, the Message—New Trends in Mao-Literature from China," *China Quarterly* 137 (March 1994): 168–79.

9. See the "introduction" to the 1993 edition of Ross Terrill, *Mao: A Biography* (New York: Touchstone, Simon and Schuster, 1980, 1993), 18–23.

10. See Michel Foucault, "What Is an Author?" in Rabinow, ed., *The Foucault Reader*, 103–13.

11. An example of the latter is Mao Tse-tung, *Basic Tactics*, translated and with an introduction by Stuart R. Schram (New York: Frederick A. Praeger, 1966). It is now accepted that Mao did not write this military manual.

12. For a particularly bad example of not taking Chinese Marxists' commitment to Marxism seriously, see Werner Meissner, *Philosophy and Politics in China: The Controversy over Dialectical Materialism in the 1930s* (London: Hurst and Co., 1990). For an extended critique of Meissner's position, see Nick Knight, *Marxist Philosophy in China: From Qu Qiubai to Mao Zedong, 1923–1945* (Dordrecht: Springer, 2005), 86–90.

13. See, for example, Terrill, *Mao: A Biography*, chapter 6; and David E. Apter and Tony Saich, *Revolutionary Discourse in Mao's Republic* (Cambridge, Mass.: Harvard University Press, 1994), 110–15.

14. There are some notable exceptions. Arif Dirlik, in particular, has brought a sophisticated understanding of Marxism to the study of Marxism in China. See Arif Dirlik, "The Predicament of Marxist Revolutionary Consciousness: Mao Zedong, Antonio Gramsci and the Reformulation of Marxist Revolutionary Theory," *Modern China* 9, no. 2 (April 1983): 182–211; Arif Dirlik, *Revolution and History: Origins of Marxist Historiography in China, 1919–1937* (Berkeley: University of California Press, 1978); and Arif Dirlik, *The Origins of Chinese Communism* (New York: Oxford University Press, 1989). See also Philip Corrigan, Harvie Ramsay, and Derek Sayer, *For Mao: Essays in Historical Materialism* (Atlantic Highlands, New Jersey: Humanities Press, 1979); and the various contributors to Arif Dirlik, Paul Healy, and Nick Knight, eds., *Critical Perspectives on Mao Zedong's Thought* (Atlantic Highlands, New Jersey: Humanities Press, 1997).

15. Knight, *Marxist Philosophy in China*; Nick Knight, "The Laws of Dialectical Materialism in Mao Zedong's Thought—The Question of 'Orthodoxy'," in *Critical Perspectives on Mao Zedong's Thought*, eds. Dirlik, Healy, and Knight, 84–116;

Nick Knight, "Soviet Philosophy and Mao Zedong's 'Sinification of Marxism'," *Journal of Contemporary Asia* 20, no. 1 (1990): 89–109; Nick Knight, ed., *Mao Zedong on Dialectical Materialism: Writings on Philosophy, 1937* (Armonk, New York: M. E. Sharpe, 1990); and Nick Knight, "Lun Mao Zedong yunyong 'fouding zhi fouding' guilü de 'zhengtongxing'" [The 'orthodoxy' of Mao Zedong's handling of the law of the 'negation of the negation'], in *Mao Zedong de zhihui* [The Wisdom of Mao Zedong], ed. Zhang Jingru (Dalian: Dalian chubanshe, 1993), 1549–55.

On Questions of Method I: Rethinking Mao and the Mao Texts

2

> History *does* nothing, it *"possesses* no *immense wealth,"* it *"wages no battles."* It *is* man, real, living man who does all that, who possesses and fights; "history" is not, as it were, a person apart, using man as a means to achieve its own aims; history is nothing but the activity of man pursuing his aims.[1]

IF, AS KARL MARX AND FRIEDRICH ENGELS ASSERT in *The Holy Family,* history should not be conceived as possessing some existence autonomous from the activity of "real, living man," it follows that judgments on the role of historical individuals such as Mao Zedong are made, not by History, but by other "real, living" individuals. This in turn suggests the impossibility of a definitive and universally accepted judgment on Mao and his thought. Historical judgments derive from historians, who are "real, living" individuals whose perspectives are influenced by a host of factors—temporal perspective, political bias, ethical considerations, cultural and intellectual background—that ensure they are no more immune from these sociological, axiological, and temporal influences than the layperson. All histories are therefore interpretations and never definitive reconstructions or judgments. As E. H. Carr has succinctly put it, "History means interpretation."[2] In the thirty years since Mao's death, the climate of opinion on his political career and thought has changed dramatically in both China and the West. The judgment handed down by the "Resolution" of the Sixth Plenum of the 11th Central Committee of the Chinese Communist Party (CCP) in June 1981 sharply criticized Mao's last two decades, rejecting many of his policies and ideas as totally inappropriate to the "realities" of China's level of social and economic development.[3] The "Resolution" attempted to balance this negative appraisal of Mao's later years by a positive assessment of his contribution to the Chinese Revolution up to 1949 and socialist construction of the early 1950s. In short, the Resolution purported to be a definitive evaluation of Mao's place in and contribution to modern Chinese history, and its authoritative tenor undoubtedly exerted a considerable influence on popular and scholarly perceptions of Mao in China, and it continues to do so, for the judgment of the Resolution has never been repudiated or even modified. Moreover, ideological judgments and political developments in post-Mao China have, without doubt, influenced Western scholarly views on Mao, and this reinforces the suggestion that Mao scholars in the West are subject to the same sort of influences to which scholars in other fields are subject. Our views are inevitably and inextricably formed by temporal and political considerations, whether we are conscious of them or not, and, indeed, Mao scholars have frequently shown themselves to be less than conscious that their judgments are not immune from factors that prevent a genuinely empirical reconstruction of Mao and his thought. The judgments we make are no more definitive than the 1981 Resolution, which may be authoritative in a political sense but which certainly does not represent the final and uncontested word on this controversial subject.

If attempts to evaluate Mao Zedong's thought and political career can never be definitive and are subject to the influence of numerous extraneous influences, it suggests the need for a keener awareness and franker admission of the assumptions that underpin and inspire interpretation. As this chapter will demonstrate, the theoretical and axiological assumptions of interpreters of Mao—the questions they have posed or not posed, and the methodological techniques they have deployed—have varied widely and exerted a considerable influence on the conclusions they have reached. The search for the true, the essential, Mao is a chimera, yet it is one frequently invoked to bolster the verisimilitude of judgments on Mao. Since its inception in the early 1950s, the scholarly study of Mao has exhibited, with some few exceptions, a singular disinclination to seriously address the theoretical problems that confront analysis and interpretation of Mao and his thought. The literature on Mao contains numerous unexplored or insufficiently explored assumptions, and it is these we must first investigate and critique before turning to our own exploration of Mao's thought. In this chapter, I argue that this paucity of explicit theoretical reflection and debate is in large part a function of an empiricist epistemology whose influence has been pervasive amongst Mao scholars. I examine the assumptions of empiricism and suggest that its logical inconsistencies render problematic many of the claims to factual authority made in relation to Mao and his thought. I illustrate the critique of empiricism by investigating a range of problems inherent in the study of Mao. These include the problem of "reading" the Mao texts, the periodization of Mao's life and thought, and the identification of the sources of his thought. What emerges from this critique of the field is evidence of an unwillingness to accept that the theoretical approach adopted will determine the outcome of interpretation. It is as though the "facts" speak for themselves; the task of the Mao scholar is merely to observe and report on these "facts" in an impartial manner. But this is not possible, and this suggests as necessary a more theoretically self-conscious approach to the study of Mao and a franker admission of the values and assumptions underpinning analysis. What is required too is recognition that conclusions about Mao are never the absolute truth, let alone the judgment of History; they are the products of theory, molded by the assumptions, values, and temporal perspective of the observer.

Empiricism: Explication and Critique

Underpinning all attempts to create knowledge, be it of subatomic particles or Mao's thought, are assumptions about the relationship between thought and the object of thought.[4] The epistemological project, so deeply embedded in the Western intellectual tradition, has involved the attempt to formulate procedures whereby knowledge is created. By "knowledge" is meant propositions about reality that not only exactly describe reality, but which are universally accepted as factually correct. In order to pursue this objective, epistemology has cast the relationship between thought and its object in terms of a distinction and a correspondence between two realms: the first is a realm of thought, distinct and separate from the realm of reality; the second is a realm of objects that are (assumed to be) constituted in a manner appropriate to their representation in thought. Consequently, while there is a distinction between thought and reality, epistemology's purpose is to demonstrate how a correspondence between the two realms can be achieved so that thought constitutes a perfect reflection of its object.

Epistemology has relied on two different methods to achieve this correspondence between thought and reality. The first designates the experience of the human subject as the privileged level against which claims to knowledge are assessed; the second designates reason—concepts and the relations between them—as the medium through which knowledge is created. The former, known as empiricism, will occupy our attention here, for the latter, rationalism, has had little obvious representation in the field of Mao studies.

For empiricism, it is the experience of the subject of cognition that achieves the correspondence between thought and its object and in so doing creates knowledge. As Barry Hindess and Paul Hirst point out, in empiricist epistemologies, knowledge is "thought to be reducible to, or, more generally, susceptible of evaluation in terms of basic statements which designate what is *given* to the experience of human subjects."[5] Sense data and the results of observation are most commonly designated as the evidential basis of knowledge, for these are held to be the form through which experience provides the raw material for the production of knowledge, usually expressed in the form of observation statements. The experience of the human subject is the ultimate court of appeal in determining what constitutes knowledge. Knowledge of the world results from and is tested against the facts of reality via the agency of experience. From this perspective, reality is held to be a neutral and universal realm that can be accessed and known only through the medium of experience.

The designation of experience as the privileged level against which knowledge claims are assessed bears the implication that observation of reality via experience proceeds in a manner unprejudiced by the preconceptions and values of the observer. To concede otherwise would be to undermine the authority of experience as the basis of knowledge, for it would permit the possibility that experience, far from being a neutral medium, is very much shaped by the observer's assumptions about the world. This is precisely the criticism of positivism (an empiricist epistemology grounded on observation) articulated by Karl Popper.[6] Observations of reality cannot be value-neutral or theory-independent, Popper insisted, for without the orienting role of theory (questions, assumptions, preconceptions, even guesswork), the human subject would not know what to observe, let alone how to observe it. Neither "reality" (the "facts") nor experience can tell us these things; theory alone can do so. Max Weber concurred, arguing that the "meaningless infinity of the world process" requires certain criteria of selection that derive not from reality itself but from the culture of the observer. This ensures that "all knowledge of cultural reality . . . is always knowledge from particular points of view." It is a "naïve self-deception" to assume that the social scientist's standpoint "can be derived from the 'facts themselves'."[7] All observations are theory-dependent. Empiricism is thus rendered an illogical and misleading account of the process of knowledge production.

While Popper's critique represented an important corrective to cruder forms of positivism, his critics have in turn argued that the notion of falsification at the heart of the Popperian philosophy of science suffers from exactly the epistemological fallacy he had identified in positivism.[8] For Popper argued that, while a theory may not be confirmed through its testing against the "facts" of reality, it may be falsified by doing so. His epistemology thus reintroduces positivism via the back door, for it assumes that a theoretically neutral appeal can be made to the facts to demonstrate the falsity of a theory. However, the testing of theories, whether to confirm or falsify them, relies on theory-dependent observations. There is no escaping the dilemma, identified so effectively by Popper himself, that observations are inherently theory-dependent, and they are so whether used inductively or deductively, whether to confirm or falsify a theory. Testing of a theory can proceed only via the assumptions of the theory itself, and this involves a circular, self-referential form of reasoning that cannot be accepted as independent non-theoretical confirmation of the theory's empirical correctness.

It is precisely this circularity of argument that led Hindess and Hirst to reject the epistemological project altogether. Epistemology, they argue, cannot demonstrate how correspondence between thought and its object is effected, save by appealing to assumptions deemed privileged and thus rendered immune from the need for independent validation. In empiricist epistemology this involves an appeal to experience as the neutral medium through which knowledge is created. Yet the asserted ability of experience to create knowledge inevitably involves an appeal to experience itself: "I know experience creates knowledge because experience tells me that this is so." As Hindess and Hirst point out, "The circularity and ultimate dogmatism of all epistemological conceptions should be evident since there can be no demonstration that such-and-such forms of discourse are indeed privileged except by means of forms of discourse that are themselves held to be privileged."[9]

An important consequence of the rejection of epistemology is the abandonment of "knowledge-in-general." Rather than a unified realm of science underpinned by an epistemology able to create objective and universally accepted knowledge, there exists a wide variety of theoretical discourses that construct their own theoretical assumptions, incorporating criteria of selection, protocols of evidence, and methodological procedures. What a discourse creates is not "knowledge-in-general," for its assumptions are specific to that discourse and very unlikely to be accepted by different discourses. The conclusions at which a discourse arrives can only be regarded as arguments or calculations, and not "knowledge" in an objectivist sense. On this basis, Hindess and Hirst contend that a critique of the conclusions of a rival discourse is a dogmatic and essentially redundant exercise; for what such a critique involves is the mobilization of theoretical assumptions not accepted as valid by the rival discourse. Such a critique inevitably involves appeals to supposed empirical realities not recognized by the opposing discourse; these are, rather, objects of discourse constructed in and by discourse. There is no universal, neutral, and supra-discursive empirical realm ("reality-in-general") to which appeals may be directed for adjudication between contending discourses. As Hindess and Hirst argue, it is "no longer possible (in the absence of the epistemological conception) to refer to objects existing *outside* of discourse as the measure of the validity of discourse."[10]

It is precisely this illogical empiricist procedure that is so evident in the field of Mao studies and in particular in critiques of Mao's thought. Stuart Schram, for example, appeals in his extensive writings on Mao to "the evidence," "the facts," "obvious facts," and "Mao's writings" as though these constitute a neutral realm that the Mao scholar can know unproblematically via the agency of experience.[11] He appeals to the validity of personal observations[12] and recommends an "objective examination of the facts" as the epistemological basis of Mao studies.[13] There is no recognition that the "facts" Schram selects for observation are constructed within discourse and have no existence independent of discourse; there is no recognition that the "facts" he urges us to observe "objectively" are those he himself considers significant and that others might approach the study of Mao with different questions and assumptions that render his "facts" irrelevant.

As we will observe, this type of epistemological impropriety is only too common in the field of Mao studies, with numerous studies of Mao's thought proceeding under the same naïve empiricist banner. This has had a number of negative consequences for the field. First, the misapprehension that analysis of Mao's thought can and should proceed via an "objective examination of the facts" has rendered superfluous the articulation and exploration of the theoretical premises that have oriented analysis. Of what relevance is theory if the Mao scholar can proceed directly to examination of "the facts," a process that alone can provide an objective account of Mao's thought; of what need is there for a time-consuming consideration of the reasons why a particular approach and not others has been employed? The answer is: Theory is irrelevant; an explicit recitation of the perspectives and assumptions orienting one's analysis is unnecessary. The first consequence of empiricism in Mao studies has thus been a poverty of theory within the field. Second, the failure to recognize and articulate the theoretical premises of a particular reading of Mao's thought has resulted in a tendency to defend dogmatically one's own interpretation and just as dogmatically attack rival interpretations. After all, if the experience of the Mao scholar is the privileged medium that determines knowledge of Mao's thought, on what possible basis can rival interpretations claim validity? As Rip Bulkeley points out in his own critique of Mao's epistemology, empiricism "can say nothing to explain why some people's experiences are to be preferred to those of others."[14] To circumvent this dilemma, Mao scholars have dogmatically reiterated the validity of their own interpretations, and criticized rival interpretations on the basis of (usually implicit) theoretical assumptions not accepted by those opposing viewpoints. The circularity of this approach is evident and so too is its dogmatism: "Your interpretation of Mao's thought is false because it does not conform to my assumptions, whereas mine does; therefore I'm right and you're wrong."

Evident in debates within the field, which have spanned the last half-century, is contention between rival discourses whose unarticulated or largely unarticulated theoretical assumptions do not conform to each other. There has been no possibility of one discourse triumphing over another, for there is no neutral universal realm ("reality-in-general") to which appeals can be made for validation of one perspective and repudiation of another. And yet, on the basis of empiricism, an illogical and self-referential epistemology, such spurious appeals have constantly been made. The resultant standoff is a puzzle to all concerned, with red-faced professors hurling "facts" at each other in an obvious bad humor. Circular reasoning and dogmatic argument, rather than an advance toward the "truth," has characterized this exercise. A refreshing corrective to these epistemologically driven standoffs would be an admission that one's perspective determines analysis; so too would be an articulation of the theoretical assumptions underpinning analysis and a recognition of the limits to critique and counter-critique.

The Mao Texts: The Role of the Reader

One of the most obvious manifestations of empiricism within the field of Mao studies is the appeal to the Mao texts as validation of the objectivity of a particular interpretation, as though the texts constitute a neutral medium whose function is merely communication of the author's meaning to the reader. The reader, the passive recipient of the text's message, has merely to read ("experience") the text for its meaning to be revealed. Louis Althusser identified a number of basic flaws in this conception of reading (in his case, the texts of Marx).[15] The first involves the assumption that a literal reading of the surface message of the text is sufficient to disclose authorial intent. There is, he argued, no recognition that a text represents a complex structure constructed of different levels of meaning; these may be obscured from the vision of the empiricist reader whose attention is focused on the surface of the text. The second is the tendency to reduce complex texts to an "essence." The motivation underpinning this aspect of an empiricist reading is the need to construct objects of knowledge ("facts") accessible to the experience of the reader. The text is assumed to be a unified field whose message, the author's intention, can be extracted in an unproblematic way. Consequently, the text's contradictions and lacunae are glossed over or swept aside. Both of these dimensions of the empiricist reading strategy are, Althusser argued, illogical and unscientific. They fail to recognize the interaction that operates between reader and text; the reader can never be a passive recipient of the text's message. Rather, reading involves an interrogation of the text from the perspective of the reader; the reader is a dynamic agent in extracting meaning from the text. Reading is an operation that necessitates a series of readings in which the reader moves beyond an initial reading of the text to a scrutiny of the text's deeper levels of meaning. Moreover, the search for the text's "essential essence," which can be portrayed as a scientific representation of the meaning of the text, deflects attention from the need to identify contradictions and lacunae that are central to identifying the problematic at work in the text.

Althusser thus rejected an empiricist strategy of reading. A scientific reading of Marx's *Capital* could only be achieved, he argued, if premised on a rationalist epistemology. However, this reading strategy (asserted rather than effectively demonstrated) faltered on a number of significant counts. The first is precisely its reliance on rationalism, which is subject to the inherent problem of circularity of reasoning that afflicts all epistemologies. In the case of rationalism, reason is the privileged level against which knowledge claims are measured; a privileged realm of concepts is thus established as the benchmark by reference to which a particular reading is judged scientific or not. However, as with empiricism's appeal to experience, rationalism's appeal to reason establishes a self-referential ratiocination: there can be no validation of the objectivity of reason save by appeal to reason itself.[16] The second is Althusser's tendency to approach the text as a structure with certain characteristics that, through correct identification, can reveal the problematic in the text and thus its meaning. This approach draws on the structuralist tradition of Claude Levi-Strauss, who represents the text as "an object endowed with precise properties that must be analytically isolated." The text "can be entirely defined on the grounds of such properties . . . it is an object which, once created, had the stiffness—so to speak—of a crystal."[17] Indeed, the notion of the text as a structure tends to undermine Althusser's persuasive recognition of the dynamic role of the reader, for it makes incumbent on the reader an acknowledgment and comprehension of the properties of the text, properties that exist and await discovery. Yet, a reading strategy designed to identify and enumerate the "precise properties" of the text can only be constructed by lapsing into circular, self-referential, and dogmatic epistemological reasoning.

In opposition to empiricist and rationalist-structuralist conceptions of reading stands the view that the meaning taken from a text depends on the discourse of the reader. From this perspective, reading ceases to be a quest for definitive comprehension of authorial intent; it becomes rather a process in which the reader imposes his framework for understanding on the text, and it is this that activates the text and creates meaning. Far from being a passive recipient of the author's message, the reader is the active, dynamic agent in the process of reading. It is consequently possible to conceive a text giving rise to a multitude of meanings, each a function of the reader's framework for understanding. As Umberto Eco argues, "Texts generate, or are capable of generating, multiple (and ultimately infinite) readings and interpretations."[18] The empiricist conception of reading thus constitutes a highly misleading representation of the process whereby meaning is extracted from a text:

> The standard communication model proposed by information theorists (Sender, Message, Addressee—in which the message is decoded on the basis of a Code shared by both the virtual poles of the chain) does not describe the actual functioning of communicative intercourses. The existence of various codes and sub-codes, the variety of sociocultural circumstances in which a message is emitted (where the codes of the addressee can be different from those of the sender), and the rate of initiative displayed by the addressee in making presuppositions and abductions—all result in making a message an empty form to which various possible senses can be attributed.[19]

Eco also suggests that a significant factor contributing to the meaning drawn from a text is the ideological perspective of the reader. Such is the case "even when [the reader] is not aware of this, even when his ideological bias is only a highly simplified system of axiological oppositions." This suggests that "not only the outline of textual ideological structures is governed by the ideological bias of the reader but also that a given ideological background can help one to discover or to ignore textual ideological structures."[20]

The notion that "ideological bias" determines the nature of a reading—what is seen, what is not seen—has obvious application in the context of a methodological critique of the field of Mao studies. From this perspective, the banner of *Verstehen* (objectivity) raised by Mao scholars is no more than a transparent attempt to disguise the ideological basis of analysis and to bolster the verisimilitude of conclusions reached.[21] There is and can be no objective, ideologically neutral reading of the Mao texts. In such a politically charged project as the interpretation of Mao's thought, the call for "an objective examination of the facts" constitutes either obtuseness or willful misconception. Rather than futile and misleading exhortations to objectivity, an admission and elaboration of the discursive assumptions that underpin reading—including ideological perspective—would be a refreshing and positive step. For it is the theoretical framework of the Mao scholar that allows certain questions to be posed and others to be ignored and which selects certain segments of the Mao texts and constructs them as evidence to validate interpretation. Nowhere is this assumption more clearly validated than in the insistence by some Mao scholars that Mao was a peasant revolutionary. Evidence to this effect is collected from the Mao texts, while evidence that conflicts with it is ignored, and the purpose of this particular "reading" is usually to confirm the heterodoxy of Mao's Marxism. As I demonstrate in chapter 4, there is abundant evidence to support a very different interpretation. Why has this evidence been overlooked? The answer is that the "ideological background" of Mao scholars has concealed this evidence, even though it is (to me, at least) apparent on the surface of the Mao texts. But, then, my "ideological background" is different, and my reading of the Mao texts and my explorations in Mao's thought are consequently different.

The Influences on Mao's Thought: The Problem of Genealogy

Roland Lew nicely captures the problem of identifying the intellectual and cultural sources of Mao and his thought: "As the son of peasants, formed first by Chinese and then by Westernizing ideas, a Marxist cadre in a proletarian party, dealing exclusively with the peasantry but doing so in the name of the proletariat, Mao bears within him a complex 'view of the world' that must be the resultant of these varied influences."[22] The possible sources of Mao's thought were evidently diverse, and these came together over time in a bewildering variety of combinations. There thus exists plentiful scope for different understandings of what led Mao to think and act in particular ways. Was Mao a modern embodiment of the Chinese tradition, his early socialization, formal education, and the complexities of contemporary Chinese realities exerting a profound influence on his intellectual development and political practice? Was the Marxism he endorsed, by contrast, a thin veneer overlaying a deep and abiding commitment to China and its cultural and historical tradition? Conversely, was Mao predominantly influenced by Marxism, an ideology of European origins, his thought and actions consequently explainable by reference to the ideals and ways of thinking of this intellectual tradition? Was Mao's thought a synthesis of the Chinese and Marxist traditions, and if so, what was their relative influence?

Mao scholars have, in general, chosen to perceive Mao as a synthesis of the Chinese and Marxist traditions. There has not, however, been consensus over the relative influence of these traditions, and this indicates considerable theoretical diversity in the approaches adopted by those Mao scholars who have adopted a synthetic approach. Let us examine a few of these studies, commencing with the origins of Mao's philosophy. In his analysis of Mao's materialist dialectics, Vsevolod Holubnychy argues that Mao drew inspiration from both the Chinese and Marxist intellectual traditions, and that, while Mao's writings on philosophy have a place in the Marxist tradition, they also have a connection with the classics of Chinese philosophy.[23] Holubnychy attempts to demonstrate this empirically by analyzing the quotations used by Mao, showing that he referred primarily to Confucian and neo-Confucian writings and the works of Stalin and Lenin; the writings of Marx and Engels are the least quoted.[24] Holubnychy also refers to a large number of commentaries, both Chinese and Western, which have noted the connection between Mao's philosophy and traditional Chinese philosophical thought.[25] The origins of Mao's philosophical thought is thus to be sought in both the Chinese and Marxist traditions, especially its Stalinist variant, but with the Chinese tradition predominating.[26]

John Koller agrees that Mao's philosophical thought can only be understood by reference to both the Marxist and Chinese traditions. It is, however, more than a simple combination of the themes found in these two traditions. It is, rather, a "creative synthesis":

> Maoist thought represents a creative novelty that clearly reveals it to be something more than Marxism transplanted to Chinese soil, or traditional

Chinese thought revised by putting it in new Marxist containers. On the other hand, it clearly has its roots in both of these earlier ideologies, and in fact its uniqueness results from a creative synthesis of traditional Chinese thought and Marxist-Leninist ideology.[27]

Koller attempts to validate his argument by exploring some of the core concepts of these seemingly disparate intellectual traditions. Unsurprisingly, he finds evidence that demonstrates an affinity between them that allowed Mao to draw inspiration from both to construct a "creative synthesis." For example, "we can see here [in Mao's philosophy] an indigenous Chinese basis for the Marxist dialectic. The Hegelian thesis-antithesis-synthesis explanation of change underlying Marxism is similar to the *Yin-Yang* concept of *Taoism*."[28]

Other scholars have noted, in contrast, a profound tension between Chinese and Marxist dialectics, the former emphasizing the unity of opposites as a harmonious relationship, the latter stressing struggle and conflict.[29] Such different readings of these two traditions raises again the theoretical problems associated with the attempt to ascertain in any definitive sense the "real" determinants of Mao's thought, for the apparent consensus shared by many Mao scholars that Mao was a product of both the Chinese and Marxist traditions breaks down over the interpretation of these traditions. There is obviously no unanimity over the essential concepts, or the meaning of such concepts, of either tradition. Intellectual traditions as broad and diverse as these are potentially capable of a multiplicity of interpretations.

An interesting response to this dilemma is found in Frederic Wakeman Jr.'s *History and Will: Philosophical Perspectives of Mao Tse-tung's Thought.*[30] Wakeman makes the assumption that Mao was influenced by the Chinese and Western (both Marxist and non-Marxist) intellectual traditions and presents a series of interpretations of the philosophers, both Western and Chinese, who may have influenced the development of Mao's thought. There are, for example, pen sketches of thinkers as disparate as Wang Fuzhi, Kang Youwei, Immanuel Kant, Friedrich Paulsen, T. H. Green, and G. W. F Hegel, to name but a few. The effect is that of a montage from which the reader can draw virtually any combination of intellectual sources as the foundations of Mao's philosophical thought. One Mao scholar has, however, interpreted Wakeman's selection of philosophers as having an ulterior motive, for he included far more idealist philosophers, both Western and Chinese, than philosophers from the materialist tradition (and in particular, Marxism).[31] Andrew Walder argues that Wakeman commenced from the assumption that Mao was a "voluntarist," and therefore an idealist, and that his task was thus to demonstrate Mao's sources of influence among idealist philosophers.[32]

Stuart Schram has also argued that Mao was influenced by both the Chinese and Marxist traditions. However, from his earliest writings on Mao, he has insisted that the Chinese element of Mao's thought and personality was the predominant influence:

> I have suggested that both Chinese and Western components play a significant role in Mao Tse-tung's patterns of thought and behaviour. The question naturally arises: where are the deepest springs of his conduct? . . . Indeed, it could be argued that, if the categories in which he reasons are basically Marxist, Mao Tse-tung's deepest emotional tie is still to the Chinese nation; and if he is bent on transforming China's society and economy in the shortest possible time, in order to turn her into a powerful modern nation, it is above all in order that she may once more assume that rank in the world which he regards as rightfully hers. In this sense, Mao has "sinified" Marxism indeed.[33]

The view articulated here, that Mao's "deepest emotional tie is still to the Chinese nation," has permeated the writings of this prolific and influential Mao scholar, and it has formed the basis of his view that Mao's approach to philosophy, indeed to Marxism and the problem of its "Sinification," was underpinned by his roots in the Chinese cultural and intellectual tradition.[34] How does Schram attempt to justify this assumption? A form of evidence frequently invoked is the style and source of the language Mao employed.[35] The fact that Mao chose to write in a simple and straightforward manner accessible to the Chinese people and to illustrate his essays and talks with prolific references to and quotations from the Chinese classics and proverbial tradition is interpreted as demonstration that Mao's mental horizons, cognitive approach to philosophical and political problems, and communication style and skills, were to a large extent limited by and drew their nourishment from the deep and exotic soil of the Chinese tradition. The danger with this criterion of evidence is that it lends itself to a Eurocentric view in which the "picturesque" character of the Chinese language, with its colorful phrases and pithy aphorisms, leads to confusion on the part of the non-Chinese observer between the outward form of the Chinese text and the substance with which it deals.[36] It also lends itself to the even more disturbing view that because Mao was Chinese, he was constrained, more so than is the Western scholar, by the intellectual blinkers imposed by his cultural, including linguistic, tradition.[37]

Schram's parallel emphasis on the influence of the Chinese political and social context in which Mao's thought developed (of which more subsequently) raises the implication that any mode of thought not immediately in conformity with contemporary Chinese realities required cultural adaptation. This was to be the fate of Marxism at Mao's hands, according to Schram, for Mao's aim was "to transform the very substance of Marxism to adapt it to Chinese conditions."[38] Indeed, one wonders whether Schram's concession that "Western components" did play a "significant role in Mao Tse-tung's patterns of thought and behaviour" is of any real significance. For if Marxism, a "Western" body of thought, had to have its "very substance" transformed to "adapt it to Chinese conditions," then to all intents and purposes one can dispense with the notion of a genuine influence over and above that of the Chinese tradition and contemporary Chinese realities, for modes of thought alien to these influences required processing, a cultural laundering as it were, before their application in the Chinese context. Consequently, Schram's position may be closer than is at first apparent to those scholars who have perceived Mao's thought and political behavior in essentially Chinese terms. The most obvious are those scholars of the "political-culture" school, as exemplified in the writings of Lucien Pye and Richard Solomon.[39] In this approach, the determinants of Mao's thought and actions are to be sought entirely in the "spirit" of the Chinese political culture: its modes of socialization, characteristic relations of dependence and authority, and ambivalent attitudes toward authority and conflict. Not only was Mao a product of this political culture, he was able to intuitively grasp and exploit its ambiguities and contradictions to further his political ends. In Pye's biographical study of Mao, the wider confines of Chinese political culture are reduced to the authority patterns and relationships within the young Mao's own family. Mao, the mature adult and political leader, can thus only be understood by reference to his early socialization and childhood, and especially his relationship with his mother.[40] Only in this way can Mao's ability to control and evoke emotion be properly understood. The problem of understanding Mao is thus one of "political psychology."[41]

At the other end of the spectrum are those scholars who have interpreted Mao from the perspective of Marxism. Michael Dutton and Paul Healy, for example, regard the "problematic" within which Mao's views on knowledge production were generated as deriving from the Marxist, and particularly Stalinist, tradition. The essential concepts that characterized Mao's epistemology thus have their precursors not in the Chinese tradition but in Marxism. The writings of Marx, Lenin, Bogdanov, and Stalin are consequently examined to construct an epistemological tradition against which Mao's notion of knowledge production can be compared.[42] In similar vein, Paul Healy has analyzed Mao's views on social change entirely from the perspective of Marxism, arguing that Mao was a "paragon of Marxist orthodoxy."[43] Richard Levy also argues that Mao was a Marxist, and that treating him as such is "critical to understanding and analysing his political-economic thought."[44] A further example is Andrew Walder's critique of the China field's tendency to caricature the "determinism" of Marx and the "voluntarism" of Mao.[45] In this study, of which more in chapter 3, Walder concentrates on the compatibility of Mao's views on social change with those of Marx and critiques those Mao scholars—particularly Wakeman Jr. and Schram—who perceive Mao as heavily influenced by "voluntarist" and "idealist" themes in Chinese and Western philosophy. Mao's views on social change are to be assessed, rather, by reference to concepts and categories (such as the concept of "totality") evident in the writings of Marx and other Marxists. Other scholars have similarly chosen to situate Mao's philosophy in the context of the Marxist tradition. Steve Chin, for example, rejects the notion that the Chinese intellectual tradition formed the philosophical basis of Mao's thought.[46] In many areas of philosophy, he argues, the Chinese tradition was at variance with the basic premises of dialectical and historical materialism. An example is epistemology. Traditional Chinese scholars were "invariably rooted in idealism and apriorism"; moreover, they did not abide by the principle so dear to Mao's heart of "verifying cognition through practice."[47] In the case of epistemology, as in all other areas, Mao abjured traditional Chinese philosophy, turning rather to Marxism for the inspiration on which his thought would be founded. Chin's conclusion is that "Mao Tsetung's thought, rather than being a heritage of traditional cultural thinking, is essentially a synthesis of Marxist-Leninist content and particular national form." He makes the bold assumption that his conclusion was reached in a "systematical and scientific manner," and he enjoins readers to "adopt a correct approach in their study."[48] However, what constitutes a "scientific" reading of Mao and how a "correct approach" can be differentiated from an incorrect approach, we are not told.

Let us conclude this section by returning to the issue of how the sources of Mao's thought have been and are to be assessed. Why has there been such strong disagreement amongst Mao scholars? We commenced with a quote from Roland Lew that suggests that the very complexity of the influences on Mao is the main factor leading to differing interpretations. Brantly Womack reiterates this position: "The main source of the conflicting interpretations of the foundations of Mao's thought is the complexity of his intellectual environment."[49] We may query, however, whether it was the complexity of Mao's intellectual environment that has been the "main source" of disagreement. Could it not be rather the diversity of theoretical assumptions (including "ideological background") from which Mao scholars have themselves commenced analysis that constitutes the major factor leading to "conflicting interpretations"? Even if there were unanimity that Mao had been influenced by only one intellectual tradition—the Marxist tradition, say—this would not signal the end of debate. There is more than ample scope for disagreement over the nature of Marxism, its various theoretical currents, the significance and meaning of its concepts, even the meaning to attribute to particular words by Marx, and this dissension emerges not from any particular characteristic of the corpus of the Marx texts (for all bodies of texts, as we have seen, are open to multiple interpretations) but from the very different starting points from which scholars have commenced their reading of these texts. It is the conflicting assumptions upon which competing interpretations are grounded that is the root cause of dissension.

In the attempt to reconstruct the sources of Mao's thought, the focus is thus thrown back onto the assumptions mobilized by the Mao scholar. If the scholar commences from the premise that Mao's thought was inextricably interwoven with and formed by traditional patterns of Chinese thought, abundant textual evidence can be found to validate that position. And it is clear that for scholars like Schram, who believe that Mao's "deepest emotional tie [was] to the Chinese nation" with its rich and compelling intellectual heritage, the Mao texts provide a rich source of data which is made factual by the mobilization of these very assumptions. Mao's writings are indeed liberally sprinkled with references to the Chinese classics, to proverbial saws and legends and popular modes of Chinese speech. But of what relevance is this data if the scholar commences from the assumption that Mao was first and foremost a Marxist and that an understanding of his thought can only be gained by analysis of the Marxist concepts and categories embedded in the Mao texts? The answer is, of course, none. References in the text to the Chinese tradition have no status as "facts" from this latter perspective; the theoretical focus of analysis, being different, constructs other, alternative, data as "facts" and employs these to validate the veracity of the assumptions used. Consequently, no amount of textual evidence is able to "prove" the source of Mao's "deepest emotional ties." As Joseph Esherick has rightly pointed out, "the citation of texts does not prove the origins of theory."[50] Walder, too, has argued that "quotes can be readily found to support almost any position."[51] The implications of this position are that, if it is the assumptions of the scholar rather than something inherent in the texts that leads to diverse interpretations of the source of Mao's thought, it behooves the Mao scholar to be rather more scrupulous in admitting and elaborating these than has hitherto been the case.

The explorations of Mao's thought that appear in this book are primarily underpinned by a concern to understand the dimensions of Mao's thought that are significant from a Marxist point of view. While I do not discount the influence of themes in the Chinese tradition (and, indeed, I discuss one such theme in chapter 5), my interest lies rather in exploring the way in which Mao understood the world from the perspective of a self-proclaimed Marxist. In 1937, Mao recounted to Edgar Snow that

> In the winter of 1920 I organized workers politically for the first time, and began to be guided in this by the influence of Marxist theory and the history of the Russian Revolution. During my second visit to Peking I had read much about the events in Russia, and had eagerly sought out what little Communist literature was then available in Chinese. Three books especially deeply carved my mind, and built up in me a faith in Marxism, from which, once I had accepted it as the correct interpretation of history, I did not afterwards waver. These books were the *Communist Manifesto*, translated by Ch'en Wang-tao and the first Marxist book ever published in Chinese; *Class Struggle*, by Kautsky; and a *History of Socialism*, by Kirkup. By the summer of 1920 I had become, in theory and to some extent in action, a Marxist, and from this time on I considered myself a Marxist.[52]

Many scholars have either ignored or discounted Mao's claim to be a Marxist. Of course, there is no reason why we are obliged to accept Mao's own testimony at face value. However, not accepting Mao's commitment to Marxism comes not from any lack of evidence in the texts; it comes, rather, from a theoretical decision on the part of the Mao scholar to either not see or to downplay such evidence. For my part, it is precisely those dimensions of Mao's thought that recognisably derive from Marxism that are of most interest, and it is these that I have excavated from the vast and highly differentiated terrain of the Mao texts. The evidence for this perspective is, as I demonstrate in the following chapters, abundant and fertile with interpretative possibilities, but it possesses the status of "evidence" only because my theoretical gaze has identified and extracted it from its textual setting. Segments of the texts have thus been activated as evidence through their incorporation into a discursive setting different from their original textual context. In admitting this, I am admitting to no more than the practice in which all Mao scholars have engaged but to which most are unable to confess because of their (often unwitting) deployment of an empiricist strategy of reading.

Continuity and Discontinuity: The Problem of Periodization

The problem of periodization—whether to divide the Mao texts and the development of his thought and political career into discrete temporal periods—is a central one for the Mao scholar. It is not, however, a problem singular to the field of Mao studies, and indeed all spheres of historical interpretation must confront the issue of continuity versus discontinuity.[53] Althusser has referred to this problem as "the first question of the theory of history, the question of the breaks."[54]

Mao Zedong's career as a writer spanned more than sixty years. It coincided with one of the most turbulent and bloody chapters in modern history, and it was against this highly variegated backdrop that he wrote a vast number of documents. The ten volumes of Stuart Schram's *Mao's Road to Power* series contain all the known Mao texts from 1912 to 1949, amounting to many thousands of essays, informal talks and formal speeches, poems, military instructions, annotations, interviews, memoranda, telegrams, inscriptions, sayings, and letters. Similarly, Mao's post-Liberation writings, from 1949 to the early 1970s, occupy many large volumes. The lengthy temporal span and textual fragmentation of this enormous literary output, plus the changing historical background against which it was written, confront the Mao scholar with several vexing methodological difficulties. Is it appropriate, when reading and interpreting the Mao texts, to treat them as a unified "work" (*oeuvre*), from which can be derived views purporting to represent the "essential" Mao?[55] Does such an approach excessively underplay the importance of the historical and political context to which Mao was reacting when writing documents? Is it a more valid methodological approach to periodize Mao's career and allow for discontinuities in the development of his thought, or does periodization merely narrow the temporal confines within which an "essential" Mao is sought? The answers to these questions are not self-evident, and the field of Mao studies has given rise to interpretations that draw on all of these approaches. A number of these will be examined in the remainder of this section. Before turning to this task, however, it is important to note that here, as with the other methodological themes examined in this chapter, there is no extended theoretical discussion to be found in the literature of the field. More often than not, reference to this complex issue (where it appears at all) is dispensed with in a paragraph or two in the prefaces to major studies or in a footnote to lengthy articles. It is precisely this "preface syndrome," this tendency to relegate discussion of theoretical issues and assumptions vital to interpretation to a few throwaway lines, which has left the scholarly literature on Mao in such a parlous theoretical state.

Perhaps the most influential exponent of the theoretical tendency to treat the Mao texts as a unified body of discourse from which can be derived the views of the "essential" Mao is John Bryan Starr.[56] While Starr does not entirely ignore areas of Mao's thought that were discontinuous, the thrust of his analysis is concerned with themes that were characterized by continuity, and he draws evidence from Mao texts widely separated in time to support the notion of an "essence" of Mao's thought. He justifies this major theoretical decision as follows:

> The choice of a thematic, rather than a historical, presentation of Mao's political ideas was a carefully considered one, though it involves certain attendant costs. . . . [A] fundamental concept in Mao's theory of knowledge is that there is a necessary, dialectical relationship between revolutionary theory and revolutionary practice. . . . Because of this fundamental principle, there is a certain illegitimacy in treating his theoretical conclusions in isolation from their practical context. A historical presentation of his political ideas—that is, one that took as its basic outline the various phases of his political career—might approximate more closely his own sense of the necessary relationship between theory and practice. On the other hand, the disadvantage in such a format is that of an inevitable redundancy. Because each of the themes that I think important to treat in order to understand Mao's theory of continuing the revolution was relevant to, and was altered by, the events of each of the periods of his career, a historical treatment would necessitate picking up each of a number of strands in each period, carrying it forward a short period of time, and then dropping it once again. What is gained in epistemological fidelity does not compensate for the attendant lack in clarity. . . . The resultant study is thus by no means disembodied from historical contexts, but it does proceed on the assumption that certain of the ideas that emerged from Mao's political practice transcend the limited relevance of the moment of their conception, form an integrated whole, and thus can usefully be studied as such.[57]

It can be seen from this illuminating passage that, while Starr is cognizant of its potential epistemological improprieties (that is, Starr's approach does not accord with Mao's epistemology), he regards the decision to treat the Mao texts as a supratemporal whole as necessitated by the need for thematic clarity as well as by a belief that certain of Mao's central ideas do constitute an "integrated whole." Starr does not explain why we should necessarily be bound by Mao's epistemology, which suffered from many of the defects of empiricism critiqued earlier. At any rate, with something of a bad conscience for departing from this epistemology, Starr proceeds to a largely "essentialist" interpretation of Mao's political thought. The result is one of the most elegant and sophisticated treatments of Mao's thought available, although those scholars undeterred by the illogicalities of empiricism, their own and purportedly Mao's, would undoubtedly consider it insufficiently anchored to the concrete contexts within which Mao's texts were written.

Another major interpretation that treats Mao and the Mao texts as an integrated whole is Raymond Whitehead's *Love and Struggle in Mao's Thought*.[58] While this interesting study fills a significant gap in terms of ethical treatments of Mao's thought, its author demonstrates virtually no concern with the theoretical problems associated with drawing conclusions from the entire corpus of the Mao texts without regard for the texts' differentiated purposes and historical origins. Similarly, K. T. Fann commences his analysis of Mao's revolutionary humanism by analyzing the humanism of the young Marx; in other words, Fann recognizes the impropriety of reducing Marx to an essence. However, having done so, he proceeds without hesitation to an "essentialist" analysis of Mao's humanism.[59]

At the other end of the spectrum are those scholars who assert that Mao's thought can only be understood by examining the Mao texts within the contexts in which they were written. The clearest exponent of this approach is Brantly Womack, who has provided perhaps the most detailed interpretation of Mao's political thought from 1917 to 1935.[60] On the assumption of the centrality of the unity of theory and practice in Mao's thought, Womack rejects the position adopted by Starr (see above), opting instead for the theoretical stance that "the primary task in understanding Mao's thought is grasping its political context."[61] Womack's analysis is thus based on what he describes as an "*in vivo* interpretation." He explains this approach as follows:

> The purpose of the study is to draw upon the practical nature of Mao's writings and their political context in order to produce an interpretation of his early political thought *in vivo*. I attempt to present emerging political concepts with their original referents and to discuss the subjects which Mao depicts as urgent and important in terms of the practical decision points he was facing as a political actor. This approach is particularly well suited for Mao because his theoretical concepts tend to emerge from a course of practical experience rather than an abstract program. Mao's ex-

plicit theorizing was a reflection of his experience, and the gestation of his concepts in practice provided the referents and the connotative significance of his more theoretical statements.[62]

Womack proceeds to argue that "attention to the unity of theory and practice is the basic principle of Mao's political thought. . . . Thus the primary task in understanding Mao's thought is *grasping its political context*."[63]

Womack's "*in vivo*" approach has been strongly endorsed by perhaps the most influential of Western Mao scholars, Stuart Schram: "The methodology which seems to me appropriate is precisely the one advocated by Brantly Womack."[64] The following comments can therefore be directed at both Mao scholars, although it is Womack who has most self-consciously attempted to implement the methodology he has outlined. First, and perhaps most importantly, is the question: How does one "grasp" a political context? Womack provides no answer to this question, although it appears from his attempted reconstructions of the contexts within which Mao's thought supposedly developed that he shares the assumption held by many empiricist historians that it is possible (to use Leopold von Ranke's aphorism) "to show how it really was." However, it is quite impossible, for the reasons alluded to earlier, "to show how it really was." Consequently, to suggest that the primary task in analyzing the Mao texts is to "grasp" their political context does not solve the central theoretical dilemma but merely serves to introduce a host of new problems. Should the context be reconstructed through the perspective of the Mao texts themselves (a tactic frequently employed by Womack)? If so, is there not the danger that the reconstruction will be hostage to the vantage point, values, and motives of Mao himself to the exclusion of other contemporary points of view? And even if alternative contemporary and retrospective views of the "political context" are widely canvassed, the historian has no alternative but to intervene at some point and make a personal determination of where the "truth" lies, and the intervention of the historian immediately introduces the assumptions, values, and temporal perspective—in short, the theoretical framework—of the historian. We can never "know" a historical or political context in any definitive sense, and our reconstructions of the past inevitably owe much to the assumptions and questions that we in the present mobilize to interrogate the documents that supposedly hold the key to an understanding of the contexts within which Mao wrote.

Second, Womack's *in vivo* approach is premised on a belief in the centrality of the unity of theory and practice to Mao's thought. While I would not wish to challenge that judgment, it is in conflict with Womack's injunction that "the primary task in understanding Mao's thought is grasping its political context." Indeed, it is quite clear that Womack regards practice as the dominant aspect of this unity of opposites; theory recedes in importance on the premise that Mao's political views owed more to the "realities" of contemporary political contexts than to the influence of theory. Such an approach may constitute a useful corrective to the view that abstract Marxist concepts or Chinese traditional values represented the exclusive wellsprings of Mao's thought, but an excessive emphasis on practice errs in the opposite direction: It cannot hope to explain major shifts in the development of Mao's thought that appear to have been inspired by theory at a very abstract level. For example, no amount of attention to the "political context" can reveal the reasons underpinning Mao's conversion in 1920 to a Marxist conception of history that indicated class analysis and class struggle as the revolutionary's primary functions. From the early 1920s, Mao's analyses of Chinese society were couched in terminology for the most part recognizable as deriving from such Marxist categories, and this perception of history in class terms originated from a theoretical conversion rather than a revelation born of practice. Similarly, Mao's application of a united front style of politics (the worker-peasant alliance, for example), while building on populist impulses evident in his pre-Marxist writings, was undoubtedly inspired by theoretical formulations prominent in the writings of Lenin and the directives of the Comintern. Mao's approach to political organization and activity (concepts such as party building, soviets, and the mass line) also drew heavily on themes that were strongly embedded in Marxist theory. Consequently, while attention to the "political context" may provide insights into the manner in which Mao employed these perspectives, to ignore or deemphasise the important orienting role of theory would be to lose sight of one very important aspect of the unity of theory and practice. Mao is on record as endorsing Lenin's dictum "Without revolutionary theory there can be no revolutionary movement,"[65] and this suggests that an emphasis on theory in the analysis of Mao's thought is as important, if not more so, than the influence of practice.

Third, there is the question of epistemology. Mao has frequently been interpreted as being an empiricist; his epistemology, mapped out in "On Practice" and elsewhere,[66] appears to sanction an empiricist approach to the acquisition of knowledge, with experience being the original site from which all knowledge derives. Womack defers to this self-perception of Mao's and refers on occasion to Mao's "peasant-oriented populist empiricism."[67] However, while it is important to take note of Mao's own understanding of epistemology (as any other issue), there is no reason at all why we must necessarily accept Mao's assertions as either valid for his own actions or generally; this is particularly the case with the self-styled empiri-cist.[68] As we observed above, empiricism is an illogical approach to knowl-edge production: Observations of reality are always theory-dependent; there is no such thing as a theoretical or value neutral observation of real-ity. In acquiring knowledge, we never commence from reality but from a theoretical predisposition that orients attention to certain phenomena while ignoring others. The empiricist's "facts" are therefore internal to the theoretical framework of the observer and in no sense independent of the-ory.[69] Consequently, to accept too readily Mao's "empiricism" at face value and employ that epistemology as a category by which to evaluate his ac-tions and thought is to fall into the trap of using a logically flawed episte-mology, one that inevitably leads to an undue emphasis on "practice" and the "political context" in the development of Mao's thought. Indeed, this approach tells us more of the epistemological assumptions of those Mao scholars who employ it than it reveals of the process of knowledge pro-duction in Mao's own case.

The "*in vivo*" approach articulated by Womack and endorsed by Schram is thus beset by a host of problems. Moreover, neither author is consistent in his use of it, for both employ periodizations of Mao's thought and make generalizations that transcend the texts (and therefore presumably the spe-cific "political contexts") within those periods.[70] In doing so, they are in the company of the majority of Mao scholars, for the use of a periodiza-tion of one form or another has been widespread; so too has been the ret-icence over theoretical issues raised by the decision to construct and apply a periodization. The use of a periodization relies on a perception of dis-continuity in the development of Mao's thought and political career, and while evidence for this may be drawn from Mao's or other texts, such ev-idence is relevant only because of the scholar's theoretical assumptions. Pe-riods do not exist autonomously in history; historians create them. The theoretical decision to employ a periodization, and the sort of periodiza-tion used, has a significant influence on interpretation. Michel Foucault has nicely captured the problematic nature of the concept of discontinuity in historical studies as follows:

> Discontinuity . . . has now become one of the basic elements of historical analysis . . . it constitutes a deliberate operation on the part of the histo-rian (and not a quality of the material with which he has to deal): for he must, at least as a systematic hypothesis, distinguish the possible levels of analysis, the methods proper to each, and the periodization that best suits them. . . . The notion of discontinuity is a paradoxical one: because it is both an instrument and an object of research; because it divides up the

field of which it is the effect; because it enables the historian to individu-
alize different domains but can be established only by comparing those domains. And because, in the final analysis, perhaps, it is not simply a concept
present in the discourse of the historian, but something that the historian
secretly supposes to be present.[71]

While the decision to employ a periodization is theoretical, so too is
the decision (such as Starr's) to treat the Mao texts as a supra-temporal *oeuvre* whose dominant characteristic is continuity. Both options are inherently
theoretical, and both will generate different "readings" of the Mao texts
and produce substantially different interpretations. These different "readings" should therefore be read in relation to the theoretical assumptions
upon which each is founded.

Let us look at a necessarily small sample of the periodizations deployed
by Mao scholars and, where available, the explicit assumptions on which
these periodizations are founded. In his *The Function of "China" in Marx,
Lenin and Mao*, Donald Lowe divides Mao's development as a Marxist into
five "major periods": The initial Marxist period, from his conversion in
1920 to approximately 1926; the formative Marxist period, beginning with
his emphasis on a peasant-based revolution in 1927 to the consolidation of
his control of the Party in 1935; the mature Maoist period, from 1935 to
the completion of his concept of "New Democracy" in early 1940; the
Civil War period, from 1940 to 1949; and the post-1949 period, following the victory of the revolution.[72] Lowe explains his use of this periodization in a footnote: "All periodizations are arbitrary; none can fit the
past exactly. Mao's public career as well as the Chinese communist movement, with which he has been so closely identified, can be periodized in
other ways. The present scheme intends to emphasize the major phases of
Mao's intellectual development."[73] In his subsequent interpretation, evidence for this periodization is presented; yet, the admission that "all periodizations are arbitrary," a throwaway line in a footnote, is the extent of
theoretical debate provided to justify the decision to periodize. It is as
though the assumption of discontinuity is so well founded, so self-evidently
the correct one, that no further debate is required.

Lowe's periodization is significant insofar as it is the one adopted by
James Chieh Hsiung in his *Ideology and Practice: The Evolution of Chinese
Communism*.[74] Hsiung has, however, added a later period from 1962 to
cover the Cultural Revolution. He explains his preference for this periodization in terms similar to those used by Lowe: "Although necessarily
somewhat arbitrary, the periodization is designed as a matter of conve-

nience to help trace the intellectual growth of Mao as a Chinese Marx-ist."[75] Again, like Lowe, there is no elaboration of the theoretical assump-tions underpinning this decision to periodize; even the reasons why this particular periodization is a "matter of convenience," we are not told. Starr's counter argument, that periodization could lead to a "loss in clarity" and be inconvenient in terms of thematic analysis, could be equally con-vincing. Neither position is, however, embedded in a broad articulation and justification of theoretical assumptions. The practice within the field has been to merely assert theoretical assumptions in passing, if they are ar-ticulated at all.

Another book-length study of the development of Mao's thought is Raymond Wylie's fine study *The Emergence of Maoism*.[76] Wylie concentrates his attention on the period 1935 to 1945, for it was during these years that Mao rose to power and established his interpretation of Marxism as the Party's orthodoxy. Wylie's criteria for this temporal demarcation are there-fore the ideological debates and political developments of intra-Party life. These criteria are not spelled out in advance, although the reader can glimpse them as the study unfolds. As with Hsiung, the factor of conve-nience is raised as a justification: "These ten years conveniently overlap what is known as the 'Yenan Period' in Chinese Communist historiogra-phy."[77] Wylie also subdivides "these ten years" into nine subperiods and traces the themes that occupy him through each of these.

Finally, it is worth noting in passing several lengthy studies that employ quite detailed periodizations without a justification of any sort. One is Ross Terrill's biography of Mao. In this, Terrill divides Mao's life into no less than twenty-one periods and gives them evocative titles such as "Strug-gle" (1927–1935), "A Ripening Peach" (1945–1949), and "The Furies of Utopia" (1965–1969).[78] Another is Clare Hollingworth's *Mao and the Men against Him*, which divides Mao's life into three major periods: rise to power, 1893–1965; cultural revolution, 1966–1971; and the years of de-cline, 1971–1976. Each of these periods is subdivided. The period of the rise to power, for example, is divided into five shorter periods: 1893–1920, 1920–1935, 1935–1949, 1949–1959, and 1959–1965.[79] Both Terrill and Hollingworth are silent on theoretical issues associated with dividing their field of study into discrete periods. It is evident, however, that their peri-odizations play a vital role in their substantive interpretations.

My own response to the problem of continuity versus discontinuity in the development of Mao's thought is premised on a recognition that a pe-riodization derives not from any intrinsic character of the material under investigation but from the theoretical assumptions on which my research is founded—and in particular the questions I wish to pose the Mao texts.[80] I accept that no appeal to empirical data can in itself be accepted as validation of the correctness of one periodization over another or indeed of the decision to periodize in the first place. I accept Foucault's admonition that the validation of a particular periodization depends on an *a priori* assumption of the existence of the periods constructed by that periodization, and that this involves a circular form of reasoning. The concept of discontinuity, so prevalent in historical studies of all kinds, is inherently problematic. But it is not without its uses. In the "explorations" of Mao's thought in subsequent chapters, I frequently employ periodization as a means of organizing the material under consideration and to demonstrate continuity or discontinuity in the development of particular themes. The reader is no more obliged to accept these periodizations than the substantive interpretations that flow from them. In this, as in all other dimensions of reading, the reader is sovereign.

Conclusion

Thinking about Mao requires consideration not only of Mao himself but also of the various ways in which the field of Mao studies has constructed its object. Several characteristics stand out. The first is (an often implicit) endorsement and application of an empiricist epistemology that takes for granted that knowledge of Mao derives through experiencing the "reality" incorporated in texts, whether those by Mao, by others about Mao, or which purport to capture the "political contexts" in which the Mao texts were written. Experience, undiluted by the values and theoretical perspectives of the Mao scholar, is the privileged medium through which the "truth" is achieved. As I have argued, such an assumption is without logical foundation. The second, and related to this acceptance of empiricism, is a disinclination to explore the theoretical and methodological issues that arise in the project to study Mao. The result has been a field characterized by a poverty of theory.

There can and will be no definitive judgment of Mao, of his thought and place in history. Our understanding of Mao can never be marked by unanimity; there will be interpretations and still further interpretations. As we move further in time from the era in which Mao lived, as the political and social context changes, the values and perspectives of the Mao scholar inevitably alter. The search for the "real" Mao is an illusion, but the possibility of keeping alive debate on Mao, one of the most significant historical figures of the twentieth century, is not, and it is in this spirit that the explorations in Mao Zedong's thought recorded in this book are offered to the reader.

Notes

1. Karl Marx and Friedrich Engels, *The Holy Family, or Critique of Critical Criticism* (Moscow: Progress Publishers, 1975, second ed.), 110. Emphasis in original.

2. E. H. Carr, *What Is History?* (Harmondsworth: Penguin Books, 1964), p. 8.

3. *Resolution on CPC History (1949–81)* (Beijing: Foreign Languages Press, 1981).

4. This critique of epistemology draws on Barry Hindess and Paul Hirst, *Mode of Production and Social Formation: An AutoCritique of Pre-Capitalist Modes of Production* (London: Macmillan, 1977); Barry Hindess and Paul Hirst, *Pre-Capitalist Modes of Production* (London: Routledge & Kegan Paul, 1975); and Barry Hindess, *Philosophy and Methodology of the Social Sciences* (Sussex: Harvester, 1977).

5. Hindess and Hirst, *Mode of Production and Social Formation*, 10. Emphasis in original.

6. Karl R. Popper, *The Logic of Scientific Discovery* (London: Hutchinson, 1972), 27–111.

7. Max Weber, *The Methodology of the Social Sciences* (New York: The Free Press, 1949), 80–82.

8. See Peter Halfpenny, *Positivism and Sociology: Explaining Social Life* (London: Allen & Unwin, 1982), 114–17; also A. F. Chalmers, *What Is This Thing Called Science?* (St. Lucia: University of Queensland Press, 1982, second ed.), 60–76; and Hindess, *Philosophy and Methodology of the Social Sciences.*

9. Hindess and Hirst, *Mode of Production and Social Formation,* 13–14.

10. Hindess and Hirst, *Mode of Production and Social Formation*, 19. Emphasis in original.

11. See Stuart R. Schram, "The Marxist," in *Mao Tse-tung in the Scales of History*, ed. Dick Wilson (Cambridge: Cambridge University Press, 1977), 35; Stuart R. Schram, "Mao Studies: Retrospect and Prospect," *China Quarterly* 97 (March 1984): 122, 125; Stuart R. Schram, "Some Reflections on the Pfeffer-Walder 'Revolution' in China Studies," *Modern China* 3, no. 2 (April 1977): 171–72.

12. Stuart R. Schram, *Mao Zedong: A Preliminary Reassessment* (Hong Kong: The Chinese University Press, 1983), 76.

13. Stuart R. Schram, *The Political Thought of Mao Tse-tung* (Harmondsworth: Penguin, 1969, revised ed.), 73.

14. Rip Bulkeley, "On 'On Practice'," *Radical Philosophy* 18 (Autumn 1977), 7.

15. Louis Althusser and Étienne Balibar, *Reading Capital*, translated by Ben Brewster (London: NLB, 1970), 13–34.

16. See Hindess and Hirst, *Mode of Production and Social Formation.*

17. Quoted in Umberto Eco, *The Role of the Reader: Explorations in the Semiotics of Texts* (Bloomington and London: Indiana University Press, 1979), 4.

18. Umberto Eco, *Semiotics and the Philosophy of Language* (Bloomington and London: Indiana University Press, 1979), 4.

19. Eco, *The Role of the Reader*, 5.

20. Eco, *The Role of the Reader*, 22.

21. Schram, *The Political Thought of Mao Tse-tung*, 73; Benjamin Schwartz, "A Personal View of Some Thoughts of Mao Tse-tung," in *Ideology and Politics in Contemporary China*, ed. Chalmers Johnson (Seattle and London: University of Washington Press, 1973), 352–53; and Benjamin Schwartz, "Presidential Address: Area Studies as a Critical Discipline," *Journal of Asian Studies* 40, no. 1 (November 1980): 15–25.

22. Roland Lew, "Maoism and the Chinese Revolution," *Socialist Register* (1975): 135.

23. Vsevolod Holubnychy, "Mao Tse-tung's Materialist Dialectics," *China Quarterly* 19 (1964): 3–37.

24. Holubnychy, "Mao Tse-tung's Materialist Dialectics": 16–17.

25. Holubnychy, "Mao Tse-tung's Materialist Dialectics": 16, and footnotes 17 and 18.

26. For more on Chinese Mao scholars' views on the origins of Mao's philosophical thought, see Nick Knight ed., *The Philosophical Thought of Mao Zedong: Studies from China, 1981–1989* (Armonk, New York: M. E. Sharpe, *Chinese Studies in Philosophy*, 1992), 20–24.

27. John M. Koller, "Philosophical Aspects of Maoist Thought," *Studies in Soviet Thought* 14 (1974): 47.

28. Koller, "Philosophical Aspects of Maoist Thought": 53.

29. Steve S. K. Chin, *The Thought of Mao-Tse-tung: Form and Content*, translated by Alfred H. Y. Lin (Hong Kong: Centre of Asian Studies Papers and Monographs, 1979), 209.

30. Frederic Wakeman Jr., *History and Will: Philosophical Perspectives on Mao Tse-tung's Thought* (Berkeley: University of California Press, 1973).

31. Andrew Walder, "Marxism, Maoism and Social Change," *Modern China* 3, no. 2 (April 1977): 105.

32. For Wakeman Jr.'s response, see "A Response," *Modern China* 3, no. 2 (April 1977): 161–68.

33. Stuart R. Schram, "Chinese and Leninist Components in the Personality of Mao Tse-tung," *Asian Survey* III, no. 6 (1963): 272–73.

34. Schram has commented that "some people regard me as obsessed with the Chinese roots of Mao and his thought." Stuart R. Schram, "Modernization and the Maoist vision," *Bulletin (International House of Japan)* 26 (1979): 15.

35. Schram, *The Political Thought of Mao Tse-tung*, 112–16.

36. Schram, *The Political Thought of Mao Tse-tung*, 113.

37. For elaboration of this perspective, see my critique of the approach adopted by Werner Meissner, *Philosophy and Politics in China: The Controversy over Dialectical Materialism in the 1930s* (London: Hurst and Co., 1990), in Nick Knight, *Marxist*

Philosophy in China: From Qu Qiubai to Mao Zedong, 1923–1945 (Dordrecht: Springer, 2005), 86–90.

38. Schram, *Mao Zedong: A Preliminary Reassessment*, 35.

39. See Lucien W. Pye, *The Spirit of Chinese Politics: A Psychocultural Study of the Authority Crisis in Political Development* (Cambridge, Mass.: M. I. T. Press, 1968); Richard H. Solomon, *Mao's Revolution and the Chinese Political Culture* (Berkeley: University of California Press, 1971); and Richard H. Solomon, "On Activism and Activists: Maoist Conceptions of Motivation and Political Role Linking State to Society," *China Quarterly* 39 (July–September 1969): 76–114.

40. Lucien W. Pye, *Mao Tse-tung: The Man in the Leader* (New York: Basic Books, 1976), 82–83.

41. Pye, *Mao Tse-tung: The Man in the Leader*, 6–7. For a decisive rejection of this "psychoanalytical approach," see Jerome Ch'en, *Mao and the Chinese Revolution* (London: Oxford University Press, 1965), 19–20, footnote 6.

42. Michael Dutton and Paul Healy, "Marxist Theory and Socialist Transition: The Construction of an Epistemological Relation," in *Chinese Marxism in Flux, 1978–84: Essays on Epistemology, Ideology and Political Economy*, ed. Bill Brugger (Armonk, New York: M. E. Sharpe, 1985), 13–66.

43. Paul Healy, "A Paragon of Marxist Orthodoxy: Mao Zedong on the Social Formation and Social Change," in *Critical Perspectives on Mao Zedong's Thought*, eds. Arif Dirlik, Paul Healy and Nick Knight (Atlantic Highlands, New Jersey: Humanities Press, 1997), 117–53.

44. Richard Levy, "Mao, Marx, Political Economy and the Chinese Revolution: Good Questions, Poor Answers," in *Critical Perspectives on Mao Zedong's Thought*, eds. Dirlik, Healy and Knight, 154–83.

45. Andrew G. Walder, "Marxism, Maoism and social change," *Modern China* 3, no. 1 (January 1977): 101–18; and 3, no. 2 (April 1977): 125–59.

46. See Chin, *The Thought of Mao Tse-tung*, esp. 32–41, where Chin takes issue with Holubnychy's emphasis on the influence of traditional Chinese philosophy on Mao's thought.

47. Chin, *The Thought of Mao Tse-tung*, 134–35.

48. Chin, *The Thought of Mao Tse-tung*, viii.

49. Brantly Womack, *The Foundations of Mao Zedong's Thought, 1917–1935* (Honolulu: University of Hawaii Press, 1982), 198.

50. Joseph Esherick, "On the Restoration of Capitalism: Mao and Marxist theory," *Modern China* 5, no. 1 (January 1979): 51.

51. Walder, "Marxism, Maoism and Social Change": 116.

52. Edgar Snow, *Red Star over China* (Harmondsworth: Penguin, 1972), 181.

53. This holds for the field of Marx studies, and in particular the debate over the young versus the mature Marx. See, for example, Louis Althusser, *For Marx* (London: Verso, 1979), 49–86.

54. Althusser and Balibar, *Reading Capital*, 209.

55. For a discussion of the "idea of the work," see Paul Rabinow ed., *The Foucault Reader* (New York: Pantheon Books, 1984), 103–5.

56. John Bryan Starr, *Continuing the Revolution: The Political Thought of Mao* (Princeton: Princeton University Press, 1979). For other works on Mao by Starr, see "Mao Tse-tung and the Sinification of Marxism: Theory, Ideology and Phylactery," *Studies in Comparative Communism* 3, no. 2 (April 1970): 149–57: "Conceptual Foundations of Mao Tse-tung's Theory of Continuous Revolution," *Asian Survey* XI, no. 6 (June 1971): 610–28; "Maoism and Marxist Utopianism," *Problems of Communism* (July–August 1977): 56–62; "On Mao's Self-Image as a Marxist Thinker," *Modern China* 3, no. 4 (October 1977): 435–42; "'Good Mao,' 'Bad Mao': Mao Studies and the Reevaluation of Mao's Political Thought," *Australian Journal of Chinese Affairs* 16 (July 1986): 1–6.

57. Starr, *Continuing the Revolution*, xi–xii.

58. Raymond L. Whitehead, *Love and Struggle in Mao's Thought* (New York: Orbis Books, 1977).

59. K. T. Fann, "Mao's Revolutionary Humanism," *Studies in Soviet Thought* 19, no. 2 (March 1979): 143–54.

60. Womack, *The Foundations of Mao Zedong's Political Thought*. For other works on Mao by Womack, see "Theory and Practice in the Thought of Mao Tse-tung," in *The Logic of 'Maoism': Critiques and Explication*, ed. James Chieh Hsiung (New York: Praeger, 1974), 1–36; "The Historical Shaping of Mao Zedong's Political Thought," in *Contemporary Chinese Philosophy*, ed. F. J. Adelman (The Hague: Martin Nijhoff Publishers, 1982), 27–62; and "Where Mao Went Wrong: Epistemology and Ideology in Mao's Leftist Politics," *Australian Journal of Chinese Affairs* 16 (July 1986): 23–40.

61. Womack, *The Foundations of Mao Zedong's Political Thought*, xii.

62. Womack, *The Foundations of Mao Zedong's Political Thought*, xi.

63. Womack, *The Foundations of Mao Zedong's Political Thought*, xii. Emphasis added.

64. Stuart R. Schram, "Mao Studies: Retrospect and Prospect," *China Quarterly* 97 (March 1984): 109.

65. *Selected Works of Mao Tse-tung* (Peking: FLP, 1967) I, 304, and II, 382.

66. *Selected Works of Mao Tse-tung* I, 295–310; also "Where Do Correct Ideas Come From?" In Mao Tse-tung, *Four Essays on Philosophy* (Peking: FLP, 1966), 134–36.

67. Womack, *The Foundations of Mao Zedong's Political Thought*, 32, 77.

68. See, for example, Han Hak and Erik Van Ree, "Was the Older Mao a Maoist?" *Journal of Contemporary Asia* 14, no. 1 (1984): 85.

69. See Hindess, *Philosophy and Methodology in the Social Sciences*.

70. Womack concentrates on the period 1917–1935 on the assumption that the paradigm for political action articulated fully during the Yan'an period (1935–1947) first emerged and developed in response to the crises and exigencies of the pre-1935 period. Womack is thus establishing the notion of a "young Mao"

who was in certain important respects qualitatively different from the "mature" or "aged" Mao and whose actions and thought (at least to some extent) prefigured the political views and style of his later career. Womack has also subdivided the 1917–1935 period into several subperiods: Mao before Marxism, Mao's Marxist period up to 1927, the early base area period (1927–1931), and the period of the Jiangxi Soviet. In Stuart Schram's "preliminary reassessment," Mao's thought and career are divided into three major periods: the "formative years" of 1917–1937, the "quarter century of achievement" from 1937 to 1962, and the "final phase" from 1962 to 1976; these periods are also subdivided into smaller temporal units. See Womack, *The Foundations of Mao Zedong's Political Thought*, and Schram *Mao Zedong: A Preliminary Reassessment*.

71. Michel Foucault, *The Archaeology of Knowledge* (London: Tavistock, 1972), 8–9.

72. Donald M. Lowe, *The Function of "China" in Marx, Lenin and Mao* (Berkeley and Los Angeles: University of California Press, 1966), 109.

73. Lowe, *The Function of "China" in Marx, Lenin and Mao*, 109.

74. James Chieh Hsiung, *Ideology and Practice: The Evolution of Chinese Communism* (New York: Praeger, 1970).

75. Hsiung, *Ideology and Practice*, 56.

76. Raymond F. Wylie, *The Emergence of Maoism: Mao Tse-tung, Ch'en Po-ta and the Search for Chinese Theory, 1935–45* (Stanford: Stanford University Press, 1980). See also Raymond F. Wylie, "Mao Tse-tung, Ch'en Po-ta and the 'Sinification of Marxism,' 1936–38," *China Quarterly* 79 (September 1979): 447–80.

77. Wylie, *The Emergence of Maoism*, 4.

78. Ross Terrill, *Mao: A Biography* (New York: Touchstone, Simon and Schuster 1993).

79. Clare Hollingworth, *Mao and the Men against Him* (London: Jonathan Cape, 1985).

80. For my initial periodization of Mao's thought, see Nicholas James Knight, *Mao and History: An Interpretive Essay on Some Problems in Mao Zedong's Philosophy of History* (University of London: Unpublished PhD thesis, 1983).

On Questions of Method II: The Marxism of Mao Zedong

A PROMINENT THEME IN THE FIELD OF MAO STUDIES has been the lack of conformity between Mao's thought and "orthodox" Marxism. The supposed heterodoxy of Mao's Marxism is demonstrated, it is argued, through his failure to conform to a number of fundamental principles self-evidently at the core of Marxism. The first is economic determinism (see chapter 6). Mao's understanding of the relationship between economic base and political-ideological superstructure was unorthodox, for he supposedly stressed developments and struggles in the superstructure rather than, as "orthodox" Marxism does, the primacy of the economic base in historical change. Mao has consequently been branded a "voluntarist," an "idealist," and "utopian," for his ideas deviated from the presumed "economic determinism" of Marxism. As Lucien Pye argues, Mao "grew up to turn Marxism on its head by glorifying voluntarism and human willpower in the historical process."[1] The second is "orthodox" Marxism's supposed view of the peasantry as an essentially conservative class with little if any revolutionary potential; it is the industrial proletariat that will not only lead a modernizing socialist revolution but constitute its main force as well (see chapter 4). By not sharing Marxism's poor opinion of the peasantry, Mao "diverged sharply from orthodoxy, and from the essential logic of Marxism."[2] His reliance on the peasantry in the formulation of his revolutionary strategy and his attribution to the peasants of a leadership role in revolution was a "heresy in act."[3] The third is Marxism's understanding of philosophy. Mao's understanding of, and degree of fidelity to, the philosophy of "orthodox" Marxism was in certain respects quite unorthodox.[4] As Stuart Schram has argued, Mao's handling of the philosophical laws of Marxism raises "serious problems about the conformity of his thinking *as a whole* to the basic logic of Marxism and of Leninism."[5]

Underpinning such judgments of the orthodoxy or otherwise of Mao's Marxism are different and usually quite incompatible interpretations of "orthodox" Marxism. The problem here is that many Mao scholars have either not articulated their understanding of Marxist "orthodoxy" or provided it little detail. How "orthodoxy" emerged, its central concepts and the relationships between them, and the way in which "orthodoxy" is to be distinguished from heterodoxy are issues which Mao scholars by and large have refused to address at a theoretical level. The nature of "orthodoxy," so important as a touchstone against which evaluations of Mao's Marxism are made, is blandly assumed.[6] The result is a field of study marked by a low theoretical level. A further result is an unwillingness to accept the possibility of theoretical coherence in Mao's thought,[7] for the goal of analysis has almost invariably been to evaluate the distance separating Mao's thought from "orthodoxy," and this continuing emphasis on heterodoxy has greatly diminished the possibility of systematic analysis of Marxist concepts in Mao's thought. The search for difference, while not necessarily invalid in itself, is questionable in the absence of any countervailing willingness to seek out similarities between the concepts and concerns of the Marxist tradition and those evident in Mao's thought. But both projects demand a benchmark for evaluation, and that benchmark is an articulated conception of "orthodoxy." This in turn requires a far more sophisticated understanding of Marxism than has hitherto been demonstrated by most Mao scholars.[8]

My contention is, therefore, that the concept of "orthodoxy" occupies a significant, perhaps central, position in the study of Mao's thought. But how are we to understand this concept, and how should it be deployed in the analysis of Mao's thought? There are obviously different possible responses to this question. The most evident (if not clearly articulated) response from Mao scholars is that there is a single Marxist orthodoxy based on the classic texts of Karl Marx and Friedrich Engels, one that can be gleaned through a largely unproblematic empiricist reading. The most striking feature of this conception of "orthodoxy" is its static character. If Marxism is accepted as a developing tradition encompassing a number of hostile theoretical and political currents, the proposition that there exists one fixed and unchanging "orthodoxy" becomes highly implausible; indeed, it is historically untenable. If, therefore, the concept of orthodoxy is to have any utility in the study of Mao's thought, it must be accepted that the criteria that define orthodoxy are themselves historical and as such subject to change. In the course of this chapter, I argue that orthodoxy is a theoretical construction, and like all theory, subject to the erosion of time, the corrosive effects of the unstable world of politics and power, and the shifting currents of intellectual fashion: today's orthodoxy may well be tomorrow's heterodoxy. Judgments regarding the orthodoxy of Mao's thought therefore need to establish which orthodoxy is being employed for purposes of comparison; and if comparisons are to be meaningful, a theoretical reconstruction of the orthodoxy in question is necessary.

Is There an "Orthodox" Marxism?

The renaissance of Marxist theory in Europe in the 1960s and 1970s was occasioned by a rejection by many neo-Marxists of the orthodox form of Marxism enforced by Joseph Stalin.[9] There resulted numerous theoretical excursions whose purpose was to bypass this orthodoxy and return to Marx. The form of Marxism that had become dominant during the Stalinist era was perceived as a caricature of Marx's thought, and the theoretical integrity of Marxism could only be restored through a return to Marx. For some theorists on the Left, epistemological arguments grounded in either rationalism or empiricism reinforced the suggestion that the "real" intention of Marx could be gleaned from a reading of the Marx texts unhindered by the dead hand of orthodoxy, of dogma.[10] Louis Althusser, one of the most influential scholars of this Marxist renaissance, expressed the imperative need for a return to Marx as follows:

> It is essential to read *Capital* to the letter. To read the text itself, complete, all four volumes, line by line, to return ten times to the first chapters. . . . And it is necessary to read *Capital* not only in its French translation . . . but in the German original, at least for the fundamental theoretical chapters and all the passages where Marx's key concepts come to the surface.[11]

While Althusser acknowledged that his own reading of Marx was no "innocent reading," he nevertheless grounded his "guilty reading" on a rationalist epistemology that sought the truth through an accurate portrayal of the problematic at work in the Marx texts, he did this by identifying the silences and lapses on the surface of the text, and the contradictions residing at its deeper levels.[12] Other theorists on the Left (such as Barry Hindess and Paul Hirst) distanced themselves from Althusser by rejecting the realm of epistemology altogether. In so doing, they challenged the possibility that one "true" (and therefore scientific) reading of Marx was possible; different readers would generate different understandings of the Marx texts.[13] A multiplicity of interpretations of Marx and Marxism was thus not only possible but inevitable (see chapter 2).

In this theoretical and political climate, it became difficult to conceive of an orthodox Marxism that could insist, with any widespread degree of acceptance, on the validity of its unified and all-embracing worldview and which could deny any possible legitimacy to rival interpretations. The possibility of a multiplicity of readings of Marx and a concomitant rejection of dogma do not, however, logically preclude the possibility of a version of Marxism achieving widespread acceptance, not only through claims to fidelity to Marx's intentions but also through political enforcement and ideological persuasion. Historically, this is clearly what occurred under Stalin, particularly during the heyday of the Third International. In the context of the international communist movement of the late 1920s and 1930s, Leninist parties of the Third International were subject to the discipline imposed by Stalin through his control of the Communist Party of the Soviet Union. For members of Leninist parties, *partiinost* (party spirit) mandated acceptance of party discipline; it also engendered an organizational climate, a culture of obedience, within which acceptance of Party-endorsed orthodoxy was facilitated.[14] Within this context, a form of Marxism endorsed by Stalin was disseminated and propagated as "orthodox" and very widely accepted as the only valid interpretation of Marxism. Virtually all communist parties consequently accepted that there was one Marxism against which claims to orthodoxy could be tested. Rightly or wrongly, there was an "orthodox" Marxism. To deny the possibility of an "orthodox" Marxism is thus to ignore not only the very unequal power relationships that existed within the international communist movement but also the psychological need on the part of individual communists to believe in the truth of Marxism as defined by their respective communist parties. Yet this is precisely what has been ignored by those theorists on the Left who, in their understandable rush to repudiate Stalin and Stalinist Marxism, insisted (rightly) on the possibility of a multiplicity of readings of Marx and (wrongly) on the rejection of the notion of an "orthodox" Marxism. To abandon the concept of "orthodoxy" makes it difficult, if not impossible, to comprehend and evaluate how and why a particular form of Marxism could take root in countries such as China and how and why individuals, from party leaders and theorists to rank-and-file members, could accept, often without question, a Marxism that had originated from beyond their national boundaries.

The rejection of "orthodox Marxism" is stated most bluntly by Paul Hirst. In his critique of Edward Thompson's *The Poverty of Theory*, he makes the following provocative statement: "There is no such thing as 'orthodox Marxism.' All 'orthodoxies'—Karl Kautsky's, Georg Lukács's, Stalin's—are particular theoretical constructions culled out of the possibilities within the complex whole of Marx and Engels' discourse."[15] The assertion that all "orthodoxies" are "particular theoretical constructions" is an appropriate and logical extension of Hirst's earlier abandonment of epistemology; it is based on a valid recognition of the complex and variegated nature of Marxist discourse and the multiplicity of readings that Marxism has engendered. An implication of Hirst's position is that deployment of "orthodoxy" to evaluate a particular Marxist discourse must be accompanied by a "theoretical construction" of that "orthodoxy." "Orthodoxy" is not, and can never be, a given; like all bodies of discourse, it involves interpretation.

However, much less convincing is Hirst's bald suggestion that "there is no such thing as 'orthodox Marxism'." While Hirst may not have accepted, in the late 1970s, the possibility of an "orthodox" Marxism, very many Marxists (including Marxists in China) have indeed premised their beliefs and actions on appeals to "orthodoxy." They continue to do so, for it is "orthodoxy" alone that can guarantee that policies and strategies are correct and ideology coherent.[16] What is lacking in Hirst's rejection of "orthodox Marxism" is recognition of the political and psychological significance of claims to "orthodoxy." "Orthodoxy" requires acceptance, and to achieve this it must be capable of enforcing adherence to its basic tenets through a combination of political force, social pressure, and ideological persuasion. Consequently, orthodoxy can be perceived as a paradigm in the sense employed by Sheldin Wolin and Thomas Kuhn.[17] For Wolin and Kuhn, a paradigm is more than a theoretical construct, no matter how vociferous its claims to scientific status; it is anchored in the real world, generated by social and political interests, with acceptance of its claims to truth enforced through the threat or employment of sanctions wielded by powerful institutions. A paradigm cannot rely solely on the assertion that it represents the truth, although its adherents usually accept that this is so, their belief reinforced through all available agencies of persuasion. The achievement of hegemonic control is thus the goal of the paradigm, and to the extent to which willing acceptance of the paradigm's claims is achieved, the use of force to compel adherence can be minimized.[18] The apparent absence of force to compel adherence is indicative of the widespread internalization of the claims and values of the paradigm amongst its adherents. Nevertheless, the ultimate sanction remains the power of enforcement, through the use of palpable political and social sanctions when these are deemed necessary.

The concept of "orthodoxy" is thus extremely useful in understanding why particular bodies of ideas achieve dominance. A second and related reason for retaining the notion of an "orthodox" Marxism is that demonstrations of proficiency in the tenets of orthodoxy have served to legitimate power or claims to it.[19] To suggest this is not to make any judgment as to whether power-holders or power-seekers who express themselves in the language of orthodoxy do or do not believe in that orthodoxy; it is only necessary to recognize that their claims to orthodoxy may serve to enhance their legitimacy in the eyes of Party members and followers. The relationship between the concepts of Chinese Marxism and those of "orthodox" Marxism has thus been an issue of considerable political as well as theoretical, significance in China. In Chinese politics, much has hung on the ability to demonstrate the consistency of one's ideas with "orthodoxy," although the construction of "orthodoxy" has varied considerably to suit the claims of those in power. An understanding of the orthodoxy appealed to may therefore facilitate comprehension of the thought of a political leader such as Mao Zedong.

A final reason for retaining the notion of "orthodoxy" is that the attempt to trace and evaluate the genealogy of concepts within the Marxist tradition is facilitated by a recognition that certain concepts within it have, for reasons referred to above, achieved dominance. Whether such concepts represent a "true" interpretation of Marx's thought is not the point. Acknowledgment of the dominance of a particular theoretical current in Marxism allows a point of reference, one that permits comparison and evaluation of certain concepts prominent within the otherwise unmanageably large mass of concepts found in the vast corpus of texts of the Marxist tradition. Evaluation of convergence with or divergence from this dominant theoretical current need not necessarily constitute an act of approval or otherwise, but it does constitute a viable method for unravelling the conceptual relationships that exist in the diverse, complex, and evolving body of Marxist thought. For example, certain themes within Chinese Marxism continue to this day to demonstrate strong conceptual links with "orthodox" Soviet Marxism of the 1930s.[20] The prior history of that orthodoxy, its acceptance as orthodox by Chinese Marxist leaders and intellectuals, and its subsequent elaboration and dissemination in China are issues of considerable significance for understanding the history and development of the ideology of the Chinese Communist Party, of which Mao's thought is such a significant part. Without retaining a conception of "orthodox" Marxism, the project to evaluate the origins and development of Mao's thought is thus made far more difficult, if not impossible.

These arguments for the retention of the concept of "orthodoxy" need to be made, not only in response to neo-Marxists such as Hirst but also in response to those Mao scholars who have doggedly harped on the heterodoxy of Mao's thought. It would seem logical to suggest that identification of heterodoxy requires a conception of the nature of its opposite: orthodoxy. However, the influential Mao scholar Stuart Schram suggests, in an essay on Mao's Marxism, that we can do without it: "There is the implication that if Mao's stance on a given question at a given time is characterized as incompatible with Marxist orthodoxy, this amounts to saying that his thinking was wrong and his policy misguided. As a general proposition, this has never been my view, but since the term 'orthodoxy' appears to have created on occasion the impression that it was, the term had best been abandoned."[21] The irony of this disarming but disingenuous statement is that Schram proceeds, in the very same essay, to make major judgments about the relationship between Mao's thought and "the basic logic of Marxism, and of Leninism."[22] Schram's "abandonment" of the concept of "orthodoxy" is patently an empty rhetorical device, one that has had little if any impact on his subsequent substantive analyses of Mao's Marxism that are replete with judgments (some of a quite moralistic and negative nature) about the compatibility or otherwise of Mao's thought with Marxism.[23] The concept of "orthodoxy" cannot be dispensed with in such a cavalier manner; it has a significant role to play in analysis of Mao's thought. That this in fact has been the case in the field of Mao studies can readily be discerned through analysis of a number of its debates, in which the concept of "orthodoxy" has, time and again, been mobilized to make judgments, whether positive or negative, about the nature of Mao's Marxism. What becomes only too evident from examination of these debates is that Mao scholars have commenced analysis from very different perspectives on what constitutes "orthodox" Marxism, with each appealing to evidence not accepted by rival positions; consequently, no resolution of these debates has been possible. Nevertheless, while the outcome of such debates was and could be no more than a recitation of different positions on Mao's Marxism, the debates are in themselves interesting and instructive, if for no other reason than that rival perspectives on Marxism, often left unarticulated in interpretations of Mao's thought, have been forced into visibility. This is no bad thing, for the issues thrown up by these debates have framed the discourse on Mao and his thought over the last half-century and more. To a brief analysis of these debates we now turn.

Was Mao a Marxist, and If So, What Sort?

In a speech in Moscow in 1957, Mao suggested that "there are Marxists of all degrees, those who are 100 per cent, 90, 80, 70, 60 or 50 per cent Marxist, and some who are only 10 or 20 per cent Marxist."[24] Some two years later, Mao threw doubt on the possibility that he could be regarded as a "100 per cent Marxist" by conceding that he had "not mastered all the domains of Marxist learning."[25] Such statements highlight the difficulties confronted by the Mao scholar in the attempt to determine the extent and nature of Mao's Marxism. An added difficulty is that few of the contributors to the vociferous debates on Mao's Marxism appear aware that an appeal to the writings of Marx or other Marxists cannot empirically or theoretically privilege a particular interpretation of Mao's Marxism. Despite their very different readings of Marx and Marxism, scholars of Mao's thought have doggedly pursued their own interpretations of Mao's Marxism on the grounds that only one "correct" interpretation is possible; all others are therefore incorrect.

The first major controversy over Mao's Marxism occurred in the "Legend of 'Maoism'" debate between Karl Wittfogel and Benjamin Schwartz.[26] In this heated exchange, Wittfogel attacked Schwartz's suggestion that because of the dissimilarity of Chinese and European social and historical conditions Mao had formulated a brand of Marxism that was "heretical" when compared with orthodox Marxism. For Schwartz, "Maoism" could be viewed as a body of thought—political and military strategies, organizational principles, and economic programs—quite distinct from mainstream Marxism. The emergence of "Maoism" was a reflection of the general tendency of Marxism to "disintegrate" or "decompose" as it was applied in social contexts very different from those considered by Marx himself. Wittfogel took strong exception to this interpretation, for its implications were that world communism was not a monolithic movement and that Chinese communism was not largely a copy of Soviet communism. Wittfogel's thesis was that no such thing as "Maoism" existed; rather, the Marxism of Chinese communists was to all intents and purposes the Marxism of their Soviet patrons.

How do these two scholars justify their radically different interpretations of Mao's Marxism? Not surprisingly, we find that each appeals to a very different reading of the texts of Mao and the Marxist tradition to justify his own position. Wittfogel accuses the "Maoists," as he calls them (Schwartz, Conrad Brandt, John K. Fairbank), of "an inadequate understanding of the doctrinal and political Marxist-Leninist background, a deficiency that results in an inadequate selection of texts . . . and an inadequate interpretation of events."[27] Consequently, in order to counter the suggestion that Mao's reliance on the peasantry as the "main force" of the Chinese Revolution represented a "heresy in act," Wittfogel returns to the writings of Marx, Engels, and Lenin and the directives of the Comintern to demonstrate that Mao's strategy was "not unorthodox."[28] Not surprisingly, Wittfogel is able to retrieve from this vast and highly variegated body of literature sufficient quotations to make what appears to be a plausible case: that the orthodox Marxist tradition was conscious of the importance of incorporating the peasantry into the revolutionary process and that this constituted the basis from which Mao drew legitimacy for his strategy of reliance on the peasants, guerrilla warfare based in the countryside, and the establishment of rural soviets (for more on Mao's views on the peasantry, see chapter 4). Wittfogel then turns to Mao's writings, concentrating in particular on the "Report on an investigation of the peasant movement in Hunan" of 1927, to demonstrate Mao's affinity with "orthodox" Marxism.

In responding to this critique, Schwartz takes recourse in part to the same tactic as Wittfogel: He returns to the writings of the Marxist tradition to demonstrate that Wittfogel's interpretation of those writings is incorrect and draws attention to quotations and texts that contradict Wittfogel's thesis. However, Schwartz moves beyond this approach and attacks Wittfogel's reliance on Mao's "Hunan Report." Wittfogel has been overly selective, we are told, in his concentration on this document, and even here, he has misrepresented the thrust of Mao's intentions; he has erred in not widening his analysis to understand how Mao's strategy developed in response to the crises of 1927 and beyond. The "Hunan Report" does "not contain the whole of the Maoist strategy since parts of the strategy represent a response to a situation which did not exist at the time."[29] There is thus disagreement over the significance of this particular text for the interpretation of the orthodoxy of Mao's Marxism.

Underpinning this debate is a significant difference of assumptions regarding the nature of Marxism. Wittfogel accepts that orthodox Marxism did not attribute to the industrial proletariat an exclusive role in the process of revolution, and that even in the context of nineteenth-century Europe, regarded the peasantry as having a significant contribution to make. While Schwartz insists that he never denied that Marx and Engels allowed the peasants a role in history,[30] his interpretation of "Maoism" and Mao's "heresy in act" does rely on an interpretation of Marxism that highlights its presumed emphasis on the historical role of the proletariat and the social and economic conditions of capitalist industrialization as precursors to modernizing revolutions, a perspective that logically precludes the possibility of a modernizing socialist revolution in a rural and largely feudal context.

The important point to emerge from this debate is that both scholars "read" the texts of the Marxist tradition and those by Mao seeking quite different sorts of evidence in order to establish the correctness of their interpretations; each appeals to different texts and quotations to reinforce his own position. The questions arises: Which of these interpretations is the "correct" one? How is the reader to make judgments as to the validity of one reading of Mao's Marxism over another? If one discounts the possibility of appealing to a corpus of neutral "facts" embodied in the texts as the ultimate arbiter of competing interpretations (see chapter 2), the answer must be that there is no "correct" interpretation; there are no uncontested criteria for evaluating the validity of a particular reading of the texts. The decision to prefer Wittfogel's position to Schwartz's or vice versa, or to reject both, is premised on the theoretical and ideological perspective of the reader of the debate rather than the empirical "correctness" or precision of argument of either scholar. Just as Wittfogel and Schwartz of necessity mobilized certain assumptions to "read" the texts of Marx and Mao, so too must the reader of their debate. The contest between Wittfogel and Schwartz was thus doomed to culminate in intellectual stalemate, neither scholar convinced of the validity of the opposing position, regardless of the "evidence" the other produced, with their readers deciding on the basis of their own assumptions.

The same impasse resulted from the even more heated debate that occurred in the pages of the journal *Modern China* in 1976–1977 over the orthodoxy of Mao's views on social change. The debate opened with a salvo fired across the bows of the "China field" (represented by Schwartz, Schram, and Maurice Meisner) by Richard Pfeffer, who accused the field of a gross misinterpretation of Mao's views on social change and his relation to orthodox Marxism. He argued that in order "to achieve a deeper understanding of the thought of Mao Zedong . . . we must struggle to understand Marx's work and transcend the reigning conceptions in our field."[31] Pfeffer proceeded to attack Schwartz's "arbitrary categorization of 'the crucial elements' of the Marxist-Leninist tradition,"[32] for this created a false premise that led to the conclusion that Mao was not an orthodox Marxist. Schram too had erred in emphasizing the influence of the Chinese tradition on Mao and in arguing that Mao's resultant "voluntarism" represented a violation of "the logic of Leninism and Marxism."[33] Meisner is likewise berated for his emphasis on Mao's "utopianism."[34] In transcending these "reigning conceptions in our field," Pfeffer's "main proposition . . . is that understanding the thought of Mao Zedong in theory and practice requires seeing it as a revolutionary development strategy evolved from within the Marxist-Leninist tradition to achieve Marx's communist goals in China."[35] He reinforces his argument that Maoism represented a flexible development of Marxism-Leninism by asserting that Marx would have pursued much the same initiatives as Mao had he faced the same challenges and problems and refers to quotations from the Marxist classics and the writings of contemporary Chinese theorists to demonstrate that "there are striking similarities between Marx and Mao."[36]

Andrew Walder builds on Pfeffer's critique of the "China field" by spelling out in considerable detail its erroneous line and by presenting a heavily documented analysis of Marx to demonstrate the intellectual affinity between Marx and Mao.[37] The "China field" erred, Walder suggests, in utilizing an economic "determinist" interpretation of Marx against which to counterpose and illuminate the "voluntarism" of Mao, in so doing exaggerating the intellectual distance that separated Mao from Marx. Yet the field's interpretation of the "determinism" of Marx is founded, he charges, on very meager scholarship that failed to seriously analyze Marx's own writings. As Walder points out "This relative paucity of at least observable research into Marx's own writings has in no way prevented these writers from assessing Mao's relationship to Marx and the Marxist tradition";[38] it has led to a caricature of Marx's theory of social change that makes accusations of "voluntarism" on Mao's part all the more credible. This caricature has two separate though related themes. In the first, Marx's economic determinism is exaggerated

> by misinterpreting his perception of the causal relationship between economic base and ideological superstructure. As a result, a vulgar and overly determinist view unfolds in which the economic base is invariably attributed with causal primacy, and the superstructure represented as a lifeless reflection of its economic base, possessing no autonomy or capacity for historical initiative. This interpretation, drawn from an overly orthodox or "vulgar" reading of Marx, misrepresents the relationship between base and superstructure in Marx's thought. Marx did not perceive the base and superstructure as discrete categories; rather, he possessed an "organic" conception of society in which base and superstructure described certain aspects of a densely interrelated, dynamic structure.[39]

While Walder concedes a degree of causal dominance to the economic base within the social "totality,"[40] he emphasizes the dialectical interaction (or "inneraction") of the relationship between economic base and superstructure. Consequently, he presents the superstructure as a complex of institutions and practices whose operation is essential for the operation of the economic base; the law and the various instrumentalities of the state thus possess a tangible potential for historical effectivity. Moreover, he argues that the relations of production, the ensemble of class structures and practices, may not be perceived as a discrete conceptual category whose locus is invariably within the economic base; class relations overlap the presumed boundary between base and superstructure, facilitating their dialectical causal relationship.

Walder proceeds to demonstrate that this perception of society as a "totality," in which exists a largely reciprocal relationship between economic base and superstructure, was also the view shared by Mao. Mao's emphasis on the superstructure at certain historical conjunctures cannot, therefore, be taken as a departure from the "essential logic" of Marxism (Schram's phrase),[41] nor does it betoken an "extreme voluntarism" (again Schram's phrase) on Mao's part.[42]

Walder argues that in the second of the themes of the caricatured Marx employed by the China field Marx's theory of the stages of historical progression is interpreted as a mechanical five-stage schema (primitive communism—slave society—feudalism—capitalism—socialism) in which the achievement of socialism must necessarily be preceded by the large-scale development of the productive forces unleashed by industrial capitalism. Those Asian revolutionaries, including Mao, who sought the revolutionary seizure of power and establishment of socialism in largely pre-industrial and pre-capitalist societies were thus guilty of historical impatience for refusing to await the emergence of the "objective" conditions for radical social change. Mao's deviation from Marxism was thus compounded: Not only did he place undue emphasis on the role of the superstructure in historical change, he declined to obey the implied injunction to passivity within "orthodox" Marxism. Walder, as one would expect, queries the propriety of regarding the notion of the five-stage historical schema as Marxist orthodoxy: "Just as the development of capitalism, even in parts of Western Europe, was in no way unilinear or predetermined, neither were the fates of non-European countries predetermined in Marx's writings."[43] If the conception of five predetermined historical stages represents a false reading of Marx's theory of history, it thus becomes invalid to brand Mao "unorthodox" and a "voluntarist" on that basis. Rather, "the key to understanding Mao's relationship to Marx is to examine how Mao employs [the] often-misconceived Marxian method of analysis."[44] On this premise, Walder, like Pfeffer, perceives a far greater theoretical and ideological affinity between Marx and Mao than have the practitioners of the "China field."

How does Walder attempt to validate his position; what theoretical approach is observable in his analysis? One can discern in Walder's reading of Marx the influence of themes present in the writings of European neo-Marxists of the 1960s and 1970s. The tendency to perceive society as a social totality in which causality is not the unqualified privilege of any particular level draws inspiration from the attempt by neo-Marxists to address the conceptual and political difficulties inherent in the conventional base/superstructure schema in which the base invariably exercises causal dominance in its relationship with the superstructure.[45] And this tendency in turn has its roots in the writings of earlier European Marxists, such as Antonio Gramsci, Lukács, and Herman Gorter, who were disinclined to allow overwhelming causal dominance to the economic base in the historical process and who regarded ideology as playing a very significant role in the capacity of the working class to wage an effective revolutionary struggle.[46] To this extent, Walder was counterposing a relatively new reading of Marxism to that of the "China field." But on what basis does Walder claim that this reading of Marx is more valid than that of his opponents? His response is ambiguous. On the one hand, Walder recognizes that quotations from the Marx texts do not in themselves constitute proof of a particular reading;[47] on the other, he does not overtly concede that his own interpretation, for all its careful documentation and precision of argument, represents only one other reading of Marx, one that reflects his own assumptions and premises. The ambiguity of Walder's position is captured in the following statement:

> As the treatment of Marxism in the "China field" illustrates, quotes can be readily found to support almost any position about what Marx was supposed to have said. It is vital, instead, to weave these passages into *an alternative interpretation* of Marx's method of analysis, specifying how he uses his definitions and concepts in his dialectical method of analysis.[48]

The hint provided here, that Walder's reading of Marx is merely "an alternative interpretation" rather than *the* empirically correct interpretation, appears as an adumbration within his otherwise impressive analysis. The overwhelming impression Walder provides is that his purpose is to counterpose his own (correct) reading to that of the (false) reading of the "China field." Yet nowhere does Walder reveal the epistemological basis for his own strategy of reading or for suggesting that his substantive reading has greater empirical validity than that of the "China field." This represents a significant and unfortunate lacuna in Walder's approach, for in failing to address these issues, he lays himself open to the same charges of circularity of reasoning and dogmatism as can be levelled at his opponents. Why should we prefer Walder's reading of Marx and Mao to that of Schram, Schwartz, Wakeman Jr., and Meisner? In the final analysis, the question remains unanswered, and Walder's valiant attempt to infuse a more "flexible" interpretation of Marx into the "China field" appears as just "an alternative interpretation" (as indeed all readings are).

While Walder's analysis is characterized by this theoretical lacuna, even more so are the responses of those he criticizes. Schram's response adopts an injured tone.[49] Rather than formally reiterating his own reading of Marx and Mao and repudiating the possibility that Walder and Pfeffer can prove him wrong through the presentation of "an alternative interpretation," Schram's defense is based on the counter-charge that his critics have not only misread and misrepresented his own interpretation of Marx and Mao but have themselves misread the texts of Marx and Mao. In a sense, Schram is forced to build his defenses thus, as his writings (as we have seen, see chapter 2) provide plentiful evidence of an empiricist approach to reading. If Schram were to concede that "knowledge" of Mao's Marxism derived from sources other than an "objective examination of the facts," he would be obliged to concede that, like Walder's reading of Mao and Marx, his own reading is no more than "an interpretation," one that can lay claim to no privileged status, no inherent validity. Rather, despite the occasional and somewhat misleading caveats in his writings,[50] Schram clings to the view so widespread in the field of Mao studies that a "true" reading is possible, that the Mao texts, subjected to the "informed gaze" of the Mao scholar, can reveal the true intent of their author. That this is not the case is confirmed by the degree and intensity of disagreement within the field, as evidenced by the *Modern China* debate. The Mao texts do not speak for themselves; they are activated anew by each fresh reading, activated in ways that produce different emphases, different and at times sharply conflicting interpretations. And the reasons why one interpretation (such as Schram's) becomes dominant within a field are due not to any presumed empirical validity of that interpretation but to a welter of other factors: the author's productivity, level of institutional support, intellectual movements within the historical and social sciences, and the nature of social and political change in the societies within which interpretations compete.[51] These factors and others have more impact on the extent to which an interpretation becomes dominant than any intrinsic quality of the interpretation itself. But this the empiricist reader may not concede.

Other respondents to the "Pfeffer-Walder revolution in China Studies" also fail to recognize that the debate is being fought out by rival discourses, and that no resolution is thereby possible. Wakeman, for example, suggests that returning to the original German edition could test Walder's interpretation of certain key words in the Marx texts.[52] But would doing so necessarily prove Walder correct or incorrect? Of course not. The German text, as any other, requires interpretation; language and its use are inherently theoretical, and the meaning to attribute to words, concepts, or passages derives from the discourse of the reader rather than from meanings that supposedly adhere to them. Similarly, Meisner, while objecting that he has been falsely charged with judging Mao "a 'heretic' or an 'infidel' who violated timeless truths and orthodoxies,"[53] asserts on the very next page: "It would be difficult to imagine a more fundamental revision of Marxist theory than [Mao's] proposition 'the more backward the economy, the easier . . . the transition . . . to socialism'."[54] Putting aside the contradiction in Meisner's defense, here again is an appeal to a quote from Mao as though it can independently arbitrate the difference between Pfeffer and Walder on the one side and Meisner on the other and adjudicate Meisner's interpretation to be correct. Even John Gurley, whose concluding comments on the *Modern China* debate are largely sympathetic to the position articulated by Pfeffer and Walder, prefaces his summary of the symposium papers with his own reading of Marx, against which to evaluate the various differences of opinion.[55] There is no recognition or discussion of the theoretical factors that generate different readings of a body of texts, an intellectual tradition, or a social or political "reality."

The point at issue here is not the substantive interpretations presented by either of these two debates (although I will return to their concerns in the chapters that follow), but the lack of theoretical debate on the implications of the issues of epistemology and reading for the interpretation of Mao's thought. The contributors to the debates have relied on a largely empiricist position that assumes the possibility of deriving *the* correct interpretation from reading. This theoretical naïveté has contributed to these evident instances of dogmatism in the scholarly study of Mao's thought; scholars adopting very different readings of Marx and Marxism have berated rival interpretations of Mao's Marxism without pausing to consider the theoretical propriety or utility of this exercise. These instances of critique and counter-critique achieve little more than to reveal that the scholars involved are in disagreement; appeals to mutually exclusive assumptions and different empirical realities do not constitute the basis for fruitful debate, but do for a clash of opposed discourses. Moreover, radical critics of the "reigning conceptions in our field" have, by and large, shared the empiricist assumption that a literal reading of the texts is sufficient, that the mere contraposition of rival quotations will demonstrate the validity of one interpretation over another, that the "facts" constitute a neutral realm awaiting the gaze of the disinterested observer, and that recognition and elaboration of theoretical assumptions is not necessary or desirable. Such naïve empiricist assumptions have contributed to the poverty of theory that has characterized the study of Mao's thought.

Conclusion

The evaluation of Mao's Marxism is an inherently problematic exercise, one that involves the mobilization of a range of theoretical assumptions. These include decisions about the content and development of Marxism, the problem of formulating a benchmark by which to evaluate the "orthodoxy" of Mao's Marxism, the relationship between the Mao scholar and the Mao texts in the process of reading, the significance of the political context in which the Mao texts were written and how this context might be reconstructed, and the role of the context in which the Mao texts are interpreted. These decisions are not self evident; neither are the questions to be posed when interrogating the texts.

It is for these reasons that the interpretations of Mao's thought that appear in the following chapters are framed as "explorations," which do not presume to lead to any absolute truth but to conjectures that will, for the time being at least, bear consideration. The conclusions I reach through these explorations are certainly not tentative, for I have a strong sense of the appropriateness of my understanding of Mao's thought, based as it is on a serious and protracted engagement with the Mao texts; nevertheless, they do not claim to represent the final word on the issues raised. For I am only too aware that others may not share my assumptions—about the provenance of Mao's thought and his understanding of and level of commitment to Marxism—and thus find my conclusions unconvincing, regardless of the industry with which I have amassed quotations and references to support my interpretations. And if this is the case, my response is a philosophical acceptance that this is the nature of the beast, that research in the humanities and social sciences proceeds not through any incremental approach to the truth but through debate, through the cut and thrust of ideas. It is in this spirit that the following "explorations" are offered and will hopefully be accepted.

In the next chapter, I turn to one of the most important debates in the history of the study of Mao's thought, that concerning his understanding of the role of the peasantry and working class in the Chinese Revolution. Was Mao a peasant revolutionary, as many have suggested? And in relying on the peasantry did he depart from the "essential logic of Marxism"? To a detailed response to these questions we now turn.

Notes

1. Lucien W. Pye, *Mao Tse-tung: The Man in the Leader* (New York: Basic Books, 1976), 117. See also Stuart R. Schram, *The Thought of Mao Tse-tung* (Cambridge: Cambridge University Press, 1989), 5, 17, 54–55, 67, 96, 113, 168, 200; Maurice Meisner, *Marxism, Maoism and Utopianism* (Madison: University of Wisconsin Press, 1982); Maurice Meisner, *Mao's China and After: A History of the People's Republic* (New York: The Free Press, 1977, 1986); Benjamin I. Schwartz, *Chinese Communism and the Rise of Mao* (New York: Harper Torchbooks, 1951).

2. Stuart R. Schram, "Mao Zedong and the Role of Various Classes in the Chinese Revolution, 1923–1927," in *The Polity and Economy of China: The Late Professor Yuji Muramatsu Commemoration Volume* (Tokyo: Tokyo Keizai Shinposha, 1975), 235.

3. Benjamin I. Schwartz, "The Legend of the 'Legend of "Maoism"'," *China Quarterly* 2 (April–June 1960): 35–42.

4. See Schram, *The Thought of Mao Tse-tung*, 138–40; Stuart R. Schram, "The Marxist," in *Mao Tse-tung in the Scales of History*, ed. Dick Wilson (Cambridge: Cambridge University Press, 1977), 64; Stuart R. Schram, "Mao Tse-tung as Marxist Dialectician," *China Quarterly* 29 (January–March, 1967): 155–65; and John Bryan Starr, *Continuing the Revolution: The Political Thought of Mao* (Princeton: Princeton University Press, 1979), 20–29.

5. Schram, "The Marxist," 64. Emphasis added.

6. For exceptions, see Paul Healy, "Reading the Mao Texts: The Question of Epistemology," *Journal of Contemporary Asia* 20, no. 3 (1990): 330–58; Arif Dirlik, "The Predicament of Marxist Revolutionary Consciousness: Mao Zedong, Antonio Gramsci and the Reformulation of Marxist Revolutionary Theory," *Modern China* 9, no. 2 (April 1983): 182–211; and Arif Dirlik, "Mao Zedong and Chinese Marxism," in *Companion Encyclopedia of Asian Philosophy*, eds. Indira Mahalingam and Brian Carr (London: Routledge, 1997); and Nicholas James Knight, *Mao and History: An Interpretive Essay on some Problems in Mao Zedong's Philosophy of History* (University of London: Unpublished PhD thesis, 1983), chapter 1.

7. Lucien Pye has suggested that "Mao clearly belongs to the school that believes that consistency is the hobgoblin of the small mind." *Mao Tse-tung: The Man in the Leader*, 44.

8. There are exceptions. An example is Walder's fine, rather rationalist, interpretation of social causation in Marxism. Andrew G. Walder, "Marxism, Maoism and Social Change," *Modern China* 3, no. 1 (January 1977): 101–18; and 3, no. 2 (April 1977): 125–59.

9. There were, of course, Marxists before this time who challenged the orthodoxy of the day. Karl Korsch and Georg Lukács were attacked for "theoretical revisionism" by Zinoviev, and their work later criticised by Deborin. See Karl Korsch, *Marxism and Philosophy* (London: NLB, 1970), 14–15; also Georg Lukács, *History and Class Consciousness: Studies in Marxist Dialectics* (London: Merlin Press, 1971).

10. See Alex Callinicos, *Is There a Future for Marxism?* (London: Macmillan, 1982), esp. chapter 3; also Andrew Collier, "In Defence of Epistemology," in *Issues in Marxist Philosophy: Volume III — Epistemology, Science, Ideology*, John Mepham and David-Hillel Ruben, eds. (Brighton: Harvester, 1979), 55–106.

11. Louis Althusser and Étienne Balibar, *Reading Capital* (London: NLB, 1970), 13–14. Examples of this sort of approach are to be found in the introductions, by Ernest Mandel, Martin Nicolaus, David Fernbach, and Lucio Colletti, to the Penguin editions of Marx's writings published in the 1970s.

12. Althusser and Balibar, *Reading Capital*, 14–15.

13. See especially Barry Hindess and Paul Hirst, *Mode of Production and Social Formation: An Autocritique of Pre-Capitalist Modes of Production* (London: Macmillan, 1977); Barry Hindess, *Philosophy and Methodology of the Social Sciences* (Sussex: Harvester, 1977); Anthony Cutler, Barry Hindess, Paul Hirst, and Athar Hussain, *Marx's "Capital" and Capitalism Today* (London: Routledge and Kegan Paul, 1977), vol. I. For the implications of this rejection of epistemology for the process of reading, see Umberto Eco, *The Role of the Reader: Explorations in the Semiotics of Texts* (Bloomington and London: University of Indiana Press, 1979); and Umberto Eco, *Semiotics and the Philosophy of Language* (Bloomington and London: University of Indiana Press, 1979).

14. George Lichtheim argues that the "psychological roots of this urge towards systematisation [of the Marxist philosophy of dialectical materialism] are obvious; so is the *partiinost* character . . . of the resultant 'materialist dialectic'." George Lichtheim, *Marxism: An Historical and Critical Study* (London: Routledge and Kegan Paul, 1961), 253. See also David Joravsky, *Soviet Marxism and Natural Science, 1917–1932* (New York: Columbia University Press, 1961), chapter 2.

15. Paul Hirst, "The Necessity of Theory," *Economy and Society* 8, no. 4 (November 1979): 420.

16. For analysis of contemporary Chinese Marxism's appeal to "orthodox" Marxism, see Nick Knight, "Contemporary Chinese Marxism and the Marxist Tradition: Globalisation, Socialism and the Search for Ideological Coherence," *Asian Studies Review* 30, no. 1 (March 2006): 19–39.

17. Sheldin S. Wolin, "Paradigms and Political Theories," in *Politics and Experience*, eds. P. King and B. C. Parekh (Cambridge: Cambridge University Press, 1968), 125–52; Thomas Kuhn, *The Structure of Scientific Revolutions* (Chicago and London: University of Chicago Press, 1970, second ed.). For an attempt to apply the ideas of Wolin and Kuhn to the China field, see Robert Marks, "The State of the China Field: Or, the China Field and the State," *Modern China* 11, no. 4 (1985): 461–509.

18. For a discussion of Gramsci's conception of hegemony, see Joseph Femia, *Gramsci's Political Thought: Hegemony, Consciousness and the Revolutionary Process* (Oxford: Clarendon Press, 1987).

19. There is no need to belabor this point in the context of Mao and China studies, as there has been an unfortunate tendency to regard Mao's Marxist utterances as having no other motivation than the reinforcement of his own power. See Robert North, *Moscow and Chinese Communists* (Stanford: Stanford University Press, 1953, 1963); Richard C. Thornton, *China: The Struggle for Power, 1917–1972* (Bloomington and London: Indiana University Press, 1973); and Arthur A. Cohen, *The Communism of Mao Tse-tung* (Chicago: Chicago University Press, 1964).

20. See Nick Knight, *Marxist Philosophy in China: From Qu Qiubai to Mao Zedong, 1923–1945* (Dordrecht: Springer, 2005).

21. Schram, "The Marxist," 36.

22. Schram, "The Marxist," 64; see also 52–54, where Schram compares "Mao's vision of history with that of Marx."

23. See for example Schram, *Mao Zedong: A Preliminary Reassessment*; also Schram, *The Thought of Mao Tse-tung*. For an extended critique of this latter volume, see Nick Knight, "Mao Zedong's Thought and Chinese Marxism: Recent Documents and Interpretations," *Bulletin of Concerned Asian Scholars* 25, no. 2 (April–June 1993): 54–63.

24. Mao Zedong, "A Dialectical Approach to Inner-Party Unity," *Selected Works of Mao Tsetung* (Beijing: Foreign Languages Press, 1977) V, 515.

25. Mao Zedong, "Speech at the Enlarged Session of the Military Affairs Committee and the External Affairs Conference," in *Mao Tse-tung Unrehearsed: Talks and Letters, 1956–1971*, ed. Stuart Schram (Penguin, Harmondsworth, 1974), 154.

26. Karl A. Wittfogel, "The Legend of 'Maoism'," *China Quarterly* 1 (January–March 1960), Part 1: 72–86, and *China Quarterly* 2 (April–June 1960), Part 2: 16–34; and Schwartz, "The Legend of the 'Legend of "Maoism"'." For Schwartz's other writings on this theme, see *Chinese Communism and the Rise of Mao*, and *Communism and China: Ideology in Flux* (New York: Atheneum, 1970).

27. Wittfogel, "The Legend of 'Maoism'," Part 1: 75.

28. Wittfogel, "The Legend of 'Maoism'," Part 2: 26.

29. Schwartz, "The Legend of the 'Legend of "Maoism"'", 40.

30. Schwartz, "The Legend of the 'Legend of "Maoism"'", 37.

31. Richard M. Pfeffer, "Mao and Marx in the Marxist-Leninist Tradition: A critique of 'The China Field' and a Contribution to a Preliminary Reappraisal," *Modern China* 3, no. 4 (October 1976): 421–60.

32. Pfeffer, "Mao and Marx in the Marxist-Leninist Tradition," 425.

33. Pfeffer, "Mao and Marx in the Marxist-Leninist Tradition," 427.

34. Pfeffer, "Mao and Marx in the Marxist-Leninist Tradition," 433. Pfeffer does, however, acknowledge that Meisner accepts "Maoism" as "a development of Marxism–Leninism."

35. Pfeffer, "Mao and Marx in the Marxist-Leninist Tradition," 439.

36. Pfeffer, "Mao and Marx in the Marxist-Leninist Tradition," 450.

37. Walder, "Marxism, Maoism and Social Change."

38. Walder, "Marxism, Maoism and Social Change," 102.

39. Walder, "Marxism, Maoism and Social Change," 126–27.

40. Andrew G. Walder, "A Response," *Modern China* 3, no. 4 (October 1977): 387–89.

41. Stuart Schram, "Mao Zedong and the Role of the Various Classes in the Chinese Revolution, 1923–1927," 235.

42. Schram, *The Political Thought of Mao Tse-tung* (Harmondsworth: Penguin, 1969), 135.

43. Walder, "Marxism, Maoism and Social Change," 141.

44. Walder, "Marxism, Maoism and Social Change," 144.

45. See, particularly, Hindess and Hirst, *Mode of Production and Social Formation: An Autocritique of Pre-Capitalist Modes of Production*; Althusser and Balibar, *Reading Capital*; and Louis Althusser, *For Marx* (London: Verso, 1979), 87–128.

46. Antonio Gramsci, *Selections from Prison Notebooks*, edited and translated by Quinton Hoare and Geoffrey Nowell Smith (London: Lawrence and Wishart, 1971); Georg Lukács, *History and Class Consciousness: Studies in Marxist Dialectics*. On Gorter's Marxism and its influence in China, see Nick Knight, "Herman Gorter and the Origins of Marxism in China," *China Information* XIX, no. 3 (November 2005): 381–412.

47. Walder, "Marxism, Maoism and Social Change," 116.

48. Walder, "Marxism, Maoism and Social Change," 116. Emphasis added. See also p. 139 where Walder acknowledges that "it is a fundamentally fruitless undertaking to search for a single Marxist position toward the revolutionary potential of the peasantry, the probability of the development of capitalism in undeveloped areas, or of the 'timing' of revolutions."

49. Stuart Schram, "Some Reflections on the Pfeffer-Walder 'Revolution' in China Studies," *Modern China* 3, no. 2 (1977): 169–84.

50. See, for example, Schram, "The Marxist," 35–36.

51. See Marks, "The State of the China Field: Or, the China Field and the State."

52. Frederic Wakeman Jr., "A Response," *Modern China* 3, no. 2 (April 1977): 161–62.

53. Maurice Meisner, "Mao and Marx in the Scholastic Tradition," *Modern China* 3, no. 4 (October 1977): 401.

54. Meisner, "Mao and Marx in the Scholastic Tradition," 402.

55. John G. Gurley, "The Symposium Papers: Discussion and Comment," *Modern China* 3, no. 4 (October 1977): 443–63.

Working Class and Peasantry in Mao Zedong's Thought, 1923–1945

4

More has been written, perhaps, about the emergence of Mao's preoccupation with the peasantry than about any other single topic in the history of the Chinese Communist movement.[1]

IN HIS *PLAN DE AYALA*, the Mexican revolutionary Emiliano Zapata argued for the repossession of the "fields, timber and water" that landlords had usurped from the Mexican peasants.[2] He called for the restitution of the property rights of the peasants, "despoiled by the bad faith of our oppressors," and a redistribution of land so that the "Mexicans' lack of prosperity and well-being may improve in all and for all." The *Plan*, as brief and unadorned a document as it is, represented a dramatic and powerful clarion call to revolution in the context of the turmoil afflicting Mexico's society, and its articles were, as Zapata's biographer demonstrates, scrupulously observed in the subsequent prosecution of the revolution.[3] The vision portrayed in the *Plan* is essentially an agrarian vision; it dreams of the reestablishment of a fair and just society that had respected the traditional rights, particularly rights to land, of Mexico's peasants. What is absent is any notion of a society different from what it had been, or what it supposedly had been. Nowhere in the *Plan* is there a suggestion that the revolution's objective was to fundamentally alter the traditional character of Mexican society, still less to transform it through industrialization and modernization; there is no suggestion that Mexico's class character should be profoundly altered, and indeed, the notion of revolution as a medium of class struggle is strikingly absent. Zapata's vision of the good society was deeply rooted in traditional Mexican society, and limited by its essentially agrarian character.

Zapata represents, in quintessential terms, the qualities and limitations of the agrarian or peasant revolutionary: strongly motivated by a sense of justice for his peasant followers, yet atavistic in his solutions for their problems; he yearns for a world that is past and projects this onto the future, believing that through revolutionary action the future can be brought into alignment with this imagined past. In this respect, Zapata offers a useful point of comparison to other revolutionaries who have responded to agrarian resentment and unrest. Some, such as the Russian *narodniks* of the nineteenth century, shared with Zapata an undiluted affection for the peasants and perceived in their conditions of existence, and particularly in their relationship to the land, a virtue untainted by the influence of the city and the corrupting spread of capitalism, modern work, and manners. Others are cast in a different mold. They identify with the peasants' grievances and perceive in their anger a source of revolutionary strength; they may also retain some admiration for the qualities of the peasants as a class and their rural conditions of existence. However, their perception of the peasantry is infused with a pragmatic estimation of its limitations, in particular a recognition of the peasants' inability to imagine a world beyond their parochial agrarian horizons.

Where in this range of perceptions of the peasants and their revolutionary potential did Mao Zedong stand? Was Mao a peasant revolutionary, one with a romantic attachment to the peasants and their virtues? Was he, rather, a pragmatic Marxist who discerned the utility of the peasants to the Chinese Revolution but recognized that they required leadership from outside their ranks for a modernizing revolution to succeed? That Mao relied heavily on China's peasants in the formation of his revolutionary strategy and the prosecution of the Chinese Revolution is not in contention. What is contentious is the suggestion that Mao was predominantly if not exclusively a peasant revolutionary, his professed belief in Marxism not extending to respect for the leadership qualities and revolutionary potential of the industrial proletariat. One influential representative of this school of thought, Maurice Meisner, vigorously and repeatedly asserted the view that Mao believed "the sources of revolutionary creativity and social progress resided in the countryside, and the peasantry was the true revolutionary class." Mao was full of "admiration for the innate 'wisdom' of the peasantry" and professed "ardent faith in the revolutionary creativity of the rural masses." Mao's revolutionary hopes were founded on "a faith in the creative energies of the peasantry," and he held "the revolutionary capacities of the urban proletariat" in very low esteem; indeed, his disinterest in the urban working class as a revolutionary class was "virtually total." His thought was characterized by "powerful anti-urban biases," a distaste for the corrupting influence of the cities, and a strongly held belief in the "relative purity" of the countryside.[4] There were thus, according to Meisner, deeply entrenched anti-modern and utopian socialist impulses underpinning Mao's concept of revolution, born of his affinity with and admiration for China's peasants. In similar vein, Isaac Deutscher argued that in justifying his withdrawal from the cities in 1927 Mao "recognized more and more explicitly the peasantry as the sole *active* force of the revolution, until, to all intents and purposes, he turned his back upon the urban working class."[5] Benjamin Schwartz concludes likewise that "Mao turned his back on the industrial proletariat in the face of all theoretical considerations in order to take full advantage of the elemental forces which he found in the villages."[6]

The description of Mao turning his back on the industrial working class is instructive, for it suggests that he *willingly* forsook the struggle in the cities, was contemptuous of the revolutionary potential of the industrial working class, and perceived in the revolutionary potential of the peasantry the only hope for success in the Chinese Revolution. In doing so, Mao supposedly revealed a singular and conscious disregard for the theoretical strictures of Marxism and was quite prepared to commit what Schwartz has termed a "heresy in act" through his reliance on the peasantry in the formation of his revolutionary strategy. In the words of Stuart Schram, perhaps the most influential exponent of the heterodox character of Mao's Marxism, "Mao diverged sharply from orthodoxy, and from the essential logic of Marxism, not only by the sheer importance he accorded to the countryside, but by attributing to the peasants both the capacity to organize themselves, and a clear consciousness of their historical role."[7] Schram argues that Mao became convinced "that the peasantry was capable of being, not merely the leading force, but virtually the sole force, in the revolutionary process." Mao thus supposedly came to believe that "the fate of the Chinese revolution ultimately depended on what happened in the countryside." This conviction was accompanied by an "indifference to the workers and to the cities far beyond anything Lenin's disciples, sitting in Moscow, would have considered admissible."[8]

It is not just scholarly opinion that has categorized Mao as a "peasant revolutionary." His political opponents too have used Mao's supposed neglect or rejection of the working class during the Chinese Revolution to attack him for his failures as a Marxist. The Soviet leader Nikita Khrushchev, for example, recalls Mao's "deviation from true Marxism" as follows:

Mao Tse-tung has always relied on the peasants and not on the working class. That's why he didn't take Shanghai [in 1949]. He didn't want to take responsibility for the welfare of the workers. Stalin properly criticised Mao for this deviation from true Marxism. But the fact remains that Mao, relying on the peasants and ignoring the working class, achieved victory. Not that the victory was some sort of miracle but was certainly a new twist to Marxist philosophy since it was achieved without the proletariat. In short, Mao Tse-tung is a petty-bourgeois whose interests are alien, and have been alien all along, to those of the working class.[9]

Similarly, the memoirs of Otto Braun, the Comintern agent attached to the Chinese Communist Party during the 1930s, are replete with attacks on Mao, in particular for his supposed emphasis on the revolutionary significance and role of the peasantry and his neglect of the working class.[10]

However, some historians of the Chinese Revolution and Mao's role in it are not convinced. Philip Huang, for example, rejects the suggestion that Mao was a peasant revolutionary with a romantic perception of the peasantry. "Mao was no romantic. In affirming the rural revolution, in breaking with Chen Du-xiu's picture of 'the peasants' as 'petty bourgeois,' Mao did not assert the romantic opposite: that all peasants were somehow simple and good, that urban civilisation was somehow intrinsically corruptive, that a return to the rustic was equal to a return to the good."[11] Rather, while Mao did recognize the enormous potential for mass peasant action, he also recognized significant variations among the peasantry, in terms of their class conditions of existence, their willingness to support the revolution and their general ideological outlook. As Huang points out, Mao recognized that petty bourgeois ideology did characterize the thinking of some peasants; the peasantry was not unreservedly supportive of the revolution. Mao's generally positive view of the peasantry was consequently qualified by a pragmatic estimation of distinctions—socioeconomic, political, and ideological—within the peasantry and the limitations to revolutionary action that these distinctions imposed on some segments of the peasantry. Other scholars have similarly rejected the view that Mao's reliance on the peasantry in his revolutionary strategy grew out of a romantic attachment to the peasantry rather than from force of historical circumstances, namely the brutal suppression of the Chinese Communist Party (CCP) and labor movement in urban areas in 1927.[12] As Tony Saich points out, Mao and the CCP never ceased to stress working class leadership over the peasantry after 1927, and "as soon as conditions permitted, the party again reasserted the primacy of urban work over that in the countryside."[13] From this perspective, Mao's approach to the peasantry was closer to Marxist orthodoxy than has normally been credited. As Justus Van der Kroef suggests, "Mao's principal views on the peasantry are wholly derived from Marx and Lenin, as is apparent also from his attempt to identify the peasantry with the Marxist-Leninist class antithesis."[14] Similarly, Trevor Sudama argues that "on the whole one can conclude that . . . in identifying the peasantry and its potential for a positive role in the revolution . . . Mao is operating within the Marxist-Leninist paradigm."[15]

Who then is right? Was Mao a peasant revolutionary? And if so, what sort? What characteristics did he attribute to the peasants, and how did he define their role in the formation of his revolutionary strategy, particularly in relation to other classes in the Chinese Revolution? These questions, as we have seen, are not new, but their centrality to an understanding of Mao's political thought and the character of the Chinese Revolution makes them of abiding concern. Moreover, a spur to reassessment of Mao's views on the peasants and their role in revolution is the greatly increased accessibility to documents by Mao from the 1920s to the 1940s, the crucial period during which his views on revolution took shape. Does this enlarged corpus of documents allow new insights into this vexed issue? The purpose of this chapter is to revisit the issue of Mao and the peasants, to interrogate the documents (old and new) and seek evidence in Mao's own testimony that will allow adjudication of the conflicting interpretations canvassed above. It will do so by examining Mao's views on the peasantry, and particularly its relations with the working class, during four phases in the development of his revolutionary strategy. These phases are:

1. Reunion with the peasants, 1923–1927;
2. Revolution in the countryside, 1927–1930;
3. Working class power and state formation, 1931–1934; and
4. Resistance and reform, 1937–1945.

While there are, as one would expect, differing emphases between (and sometimes within) these four phases, there is an underlying theme that affirms that Mao was not a peasant revolutionary *pur sang*, after the pattern of Zapata, but one who, while deeply respecting the peasants' revolutionary potential and prepared to exploit it, retained a hard-headed appreciation that their contribution to China's revolution was limited by their historically conditioned inability to perceive China's future as one of industrialization, modernity and socialism. It was primarily for this reason that the peasants required the leadership of the working class; it was this class's experience of modern industry and capitalism, its consequent organizational ability, and its separation from the parochialism of the agrarian circle that made it capable of leading China forward into a new, modern, era. While Mao did, as Schram suggests, attribute to the peasants a capacity to organize themselves, that capacity was, Mao believed, limited. The peasants required leadership, of the working class and of the Communist Party, whose ideology designated the working class the "universal class" whose historic mission was to lead other oppressed classes in the revolutionary struggle and to establish a society in which all class distinctions would ultimately be eliminated. Thus, while the Chinese Revolution was destined to be fought largely in China's countryside where the overwhelming bulk of the population was inevitably peasant, Mao remained convinced that the working class was the leading class of the Chinese Revolution, and he strove, despite the historical circumstances which separated him and his movement from the cities in which the working class primarily resided, to strengthen wherever possible the working class component of the revolutionary movement, and particularly its leadership positions and role.

The issue here, then, is Mao's perception of class leadership of the Chinese Revolution. It is not whether, in fact, the working class did or did not lead the revolution. I am interested, rather, in what Mao *himself* thought of the characteristics and qualities of the working class and the peasantry and the relationship between these two classes. To pursue this theme, I examine in detail Mao's writings from 1923–1945, identifying and analyzing references to the working class, the peasantry, and the issue of class leadership of the Chinese Revolution. This reading of the Mao texts suggests that the scholarly and political conclusions (and condemnations) referred to above—that Mao had abandoned a central plank of Marxist orthodoxy through demonstrating "his readiness to turn his back on the industrial proletariat in the face of all theoretical considerations"—is quite misleading.

Reunion with the Peasants, 1923–1927

In his detailed study (of 1975) of the Mao texts then available from the early 1920s, Day noted that Mao's "reunion with the peasantry" began sometime between 1923 and 1925.[16] It is now evident that Mao's awareness of the "pauperisation of the peasants"[17] and their consequent significance to the Chinese Revolution commenced in 1923, although it is doubtful that the peasants ever entirely disappeared from Mao's consciousness, even during his so-called "workers' period" (1921–1923) during which his primary activity was that of labor organizer.[18] At the CCP's Third Congress (June 1923), Mao moved the "Resolution on the Peasant Question," in which he noted that "the life of the peasants has been made increasingly difficult" as a result of the continual wars between the warlords and the increasing economic exploitation of the peasants by "local ruffians and bad gentry." Consequently, "a spirit of rebellion had naturally arisen among the peasants. The widespread peasant antirent and antitax riots are clear evidence of this." The "Resolution" called on the Party "to gather together small peasants, sharecroppers, and farm laborers to resist the imperialists who control China, to overthrow the warlords and corrupt officials, and to resist the local ruffians and bad gentry, so as to protect the interests of the peasants and to promote the national revolutionary movement."[19] According to Zhang Guotao's (not always reliable) recollections, Mao argued, in the debates at the Third Congress, that "in any revolution the peasant problem was the most important problem," and he urged the CCP to emphasize and mobilize the peasants.[20]

This positive assessment is typical of Mao's subsequent attitude to the peasants in the formation of his revolutionary strategy. What is also typical, although seemingly unnoticed by Mao scholars, is a less positive comment which appears in an article by Mao entitled "Hunan under the Provincial Constitution," written a few weeks after the Party's Third Congress: "The thinking of the small peasants has changed little. Their political demands are simply for honest officials and a good emperor."[21] Here, at the outset of Mao's "reunion with the peasants," emerge two conflicting themes that are characteristic of his attitude to the peasantry across the entire period from the 1920s to the 1940s: on the one hand, a recognition of and admiration for the revolutionary potential of the peasantry and an insistence that the CCP had to exploit this potential for the revolution to succeed; on the other, a recognition of the limitations that tradition imposed on the thinking of the peasants and which prevented their conceiving a political and economic future different from the supposed virtues of a bygone era. The resolution of this tension in Mao's thinking on the peasantry was achieved through a persistent assertion of the need for working class leadership of the peasants in both the revolution and the formation of a post-revolutionary state; for it was the working class and not the peasantry whose experience of modern forms of production and consequent organizational acumen imparted it a world outlook of modernity and socialism that the peasants' historically limited outlook made impossible. Mao's positive references to the peasantry's role in revolution are consequently very often balanced by an insistence on the importance of working class leadership, of both the peasants and the revolution as a whole. They are also often accompanied by a none-too-sanguine recitation of the ideological, political, and organizational failings of the peasantry and the problems these failings posed for the successful prosecution of the revolution.

These apparently conflicting themes are evident in several of Mao's most important documents of 1925 to 1927 that refer to the peasantry and the working class and which reveal his thinking about the power configuration of class forces in the Chinese Revolution. In "Analysis of all classes in Chinese society" (December 1925), Mao revealed his awareness of the distinctions existing within the peasantry and identified the peasant problem as "in the main" the problem of the semi-owner peasants (*zigengnong*), half-share croppers (*banyinong*), and poor peasants. Each of these three strata of the "semi-proletariat" was, because of difficult economic conditions and tenuous or nonexistent ownership of land, more revolutionary than landowning peasants; and of these three, the poor peasants were "extremely receptive to revolutionary propaganda."[22] An important dimension of Mao's analysis of the classes and strata in China's countryside thus hinged on the issue of ownership of land, for this was an important determinant of how the peasantry's various strata responded to the revolution. The poor peasants were consequently the most revolutionary (or potentially the most revolutionary) of the classes and strata in China's countryside; they were "the most wretched among the peasants" and would thus "struggle bravely" for the revolution.

In November 1925, Mao had written that "I believe in Communism and advocate the social revolution of the proletariat."[23] He returned to this theme in "Analysis of all classes in Chinese society," praising the revolutionary capacities of the Chinese working class, despite their diminutive numbers:

> Because China is economically backward, there are not many industrial workers (the industrial proletariat). These 2 million industrial workers are primarily in five industries—railways, mining, maritime transport, textiles, and shipbuilding—but the majority are in enterprises owned by foreign capitalists. Therefore, though not very numerous, the industrial proletariat has become the leading force (*zhuli*) in the revolutionary movement. We can see the important position of the industrial proletariat in the national revolution from the strength it has displayed in the strikes in the last four years, such as seamen's strikes, the railway strikes, the strikes in the Kailuan and Jiaozuo coal mines, as well as the general strikes in Shanghai and Hong Kong after the May 30th Incident. The first reason why the industrial proletariat hold this position is their concentration. No other section of the people is so "organized and concentrated" as they are. The second reason is their low economic status. They have been deprived of tools, have noth-

ing left but their two hands, have no hope of ever becoming rich and, moreover, are subjected to the most ruthless treatment by the imperialists, the warlords, and the comprador class. This is why they are particularly good fighters.[24]

Are these the words of a peasant revolutionary? Apparently so, according to Maurice Meisner, who interprets this passage in the following quixotic manner: "If the 4 million members of the potentially reactionary 'middle bourgeoisie' were expendable, so also, *implicitly*, were the members of the urban proletariat, who when all is said and done constituted only a tiny percentage of the 395 million."[25] Meisner here directly contradicts Mao's own words in order to downplay the importance of the working class in his perception of the class forces in the Chinese Revolution, and does so on the basis of the diminutive numerical size of the working class, something Mao had himself explicitly acknowledged. However, it is clear from this document and many others from the 1920s to the 1940s that Mao perceived the issue of class leadership of the revolution not as a function of size but of the working class's conscious recognition of the need for change generated by its exploitation within the emerging class relations of capitalism. This economic experience of the working class led it to be "organized and concentrated" and "particularly good fighters."

Mao returned to the importance of the peasantry to the Chinese Revolution in January 1926 in the "Resolution concerning the peasant movement" presented to the Second Congress of the Guomindang: "China's national revolution is, to put it plainly, a peasant revolution. If we wish to consolidate the foundations of the national revolution, we must, once again, first liberate the peasants."[26] He returned to this theme even more strongly in September 1926 in a controversial article entitled "The national revolution and the peasant movement." Mao commences with the blunt assertion: "The peasant movement is the central problem of the national revolution." Because of the extensive character of China's backward semicolonial economy, the feudal class in the countryside constituted the foundation of the ruling class, and to rid China of its divided and oppressive warlords it was absolutely essential to first rid China of the landlord class. The "rampant savagery" of the landlords toward the peasants was even more severe than that of the comprador class toward the workers, precisely because the comprador class was concentrated in China's large coastal cities, whereas the landlord class was to be found in every county and village throughout the length and breadth of rural China. Moreover, should the peasants attempt to organize themselves, they immediately ran into the brutal oppression of the landlords. For this reason, the situation of the peasants was graver than that of the workers in the cities and their exploitation and oppression even more intense. The political struggle in the two arenas had consequently reached different stages. As Mao pointed out:

> It [the book which Mao was introducing] also helps us to understand the basic nature of the peasant movement in China and makes us realize that the peasant movement in China is a movement of class struggle that combines political and economic struggle. Its peculiarities are manifested especially in the political aspect. In this respect, it is somewhat different in nature from the workers' movement in the cities. At present, the political objectives of the urban working class are merely to seek complete freedom of assembly and of association; this class does not yet seek to destroy immediately the political position of the bourgeoisie. As for the peasants in the countryside, on the other hand, as soon as they rise up, they run into the political power of those local bullies, bad gentry, and landlords who have been crushing the peasants for several thousand years.[27]

The peasant movement thus occupied a central position in the national revolution, and without its successful prosecution, the national revolution could not succeed. Nevertheless, despite the fact that the oppression of the peasants was more widespread and intense than that of the working class and despite the fact that the peasants were numerically vastly superior to the working class, the working class remained, as Mao points out here, "the leader of all revolutionary classes":

> Hence, although we are all aware that the workers, students, and middle and small merchants in the cities should rise and strike fiercely at the comprador class and directly resist imperialism, and although *we know that the progressive working class in particular is the leader of all the revolutionary classes*, yet if the peasants do not rise and fight in the villages to overthrow the privileges of the feudal-patriarchal landlord class, the power of the warlords and of imperialism can never be hurled down root and branch.[28]

According to Schram, Mao was so carried away by enthusiasm for the revolutionary forces unleashed in the countryside that in this document "he turned the axiom of working-class leadership explicitly on its head."[29] While it is true that Mao here went as far as he was ever to go in the direction of elevating the significance of the rural as opposed to the urban struggle, it is certainly not the case that he had turned his long-held belief in the necessity of working class leadership "on its head." His reference to the working class being the "leader of all the revolutionary classes" is far from a "ritual reference," as Schram claims.[30] Were it to be so, one would not expect to find it continually repeated in the Mao documents from the 1920s to the 1940s. Yet, it is there, not only as an expression of Mao's deep conviction that China's revolution, while built in large part on the anger and resentment of the peasants, had to be led by a class whose organizational skills and historical vision could lead the revolution beyond its current stage, during which the resolution of the "peasant problem" loomed as the most urgent task.

Mao's insistence that the peasant movement was vital to the victory of the revolution is expressed with great force and conviction in one of his most famous texts, the "Report on the peasant movement in Hunan," written in February 1927 (although published between March and early April). Much has been made of this document, to either refute or promote the view that Mao had abandoned Marxist orthodoxy by "turning his back" on the working class and the struggle in the cities through his focus on the peasantry and the struggle in China's countryside.[31] While this "Report" should not by any means be discounted and is rightly celebrated as a passionate expression of Mao's views on the peasant movement, it is important to situate it within the broader context of documents written by Mao at or about the same time. This allows a "smoothing out," as it were, of Mao's immediate concerns to permit an appreciation of the deeper and longer-term impulses that anchored his thinking and which allowed him to situate the concerns of a particular moment or stage of the revolution within the revolution's larger temporal frame. This cautionary note is reinforced if we examine two documents from November 1926, that is, at a time when Mao evidently perceived the peasants as the "main force" of the Chinese Revolution.[32] The first, a document entitled "The peasants of Hunan," provides a good deal of statistical and organizational data about the activities and strengths of the peasant associations in the various counties of Hunan. It is a pragmatic working document; Mao was clearly concerned to discover the actual, empirical nature of the peasantry and its level of organization and resistance in particular locations.[33] Under the subheading "Desire for good government," Mao makes the following interesting and familiar observation:

> The political and economic demands of the peasants can still be said to remain quite immature. The peasants have as yet no feeling for such slogans as popular elections of the county magistrate, and even when it comes to village level political demands, they have been quite passive. There has never been a shadow of the "confiscation of land" and "organisation of a workers and peasants government" as spread in the rumours created by the reactionaries.[34]

In another somewhat similar document of November 1926, Mao reports on the suffering and resistance of the peasants in a number of counties in Jiangsu and Zhejiang. Mao reports that in Cixi county a peasant revolt, triggered by famine, high rents, and taxes, was put down, despite the "intrepid" nature of the peasants and their frequent recourse to armed combat. "The reason that this uprising failed," Mao concludes, "was that the popular masses were totally unorganized and had no leadership. Thus it became a primitive revolt and ended in failure."[35]

These two references—one to the immaturity and passivity of the peasants, the other to their disorganization and lack of leadership—should be kept in mind when reading the "Report on the peasant movement in Hunan." For in this document, Mao's focus is well and truly on the countryside, and well and truly on the rising tide of revolution spearheaded by the poor peasants; his objective is to talk up the peasant movement in the face of resistance from within the leadership ranks of his own Party, not to allude to the failings of the peasants (of which he was, as we have seen, acutely aware). The tone of the document is almost euphoric, for Mao could clearly sense the enormous power of the peasant movement then being unleashed in Hunan.[36] For a revolutionary, it was an entrancing prospect, and Mao gives it its full due:

> The present upsurge of the peasant movement is a colossal event. In a very short time, several hundred million peasants in China's central, southern, and northern provinces will rise like a fierce wind or tempest, a force so swift and violent that no power, however great, will be able to suppress it. They will break through all the trammels that bind them and rush forward along the road to liberation. They will, in the end, send all the imperialists, warlords, corrupt officials, local bullies, and bad gentry to their graves.[37]

Mao points once again to the importance of the poor peasants to this revolutionary upsurge. They were the "most revolutionary group" amongst the peasants, and the "vanguard in overthrowing the feudal forces." Their leadership of the peasant associations was "extremely necessary. Without the poor peasants there would be no revolution. To deny their role is to deny the revolution."[38] Mao also clearly felt that, up to that particular stage of the democratic revolution, the poor peasants had achieved more than those living in the cities: "To give credit where credit is due, if we allot ten points to the accomplishments of the democratic revolution, then the achievements of the city dwellers (*shimin*) and the military (*junshi*) rate only three points, while the remaining seven points should go the achievements of the peasants in their rural revolution."[39] This should not, however, be read as a manifestation of a supposed anti-urban bias in Mao's thought but as a strategic assessment of the differing pace and intensity of the revolution in the urban and rural areas. He remained convinced, as we will see, that a successful outcome of the struggle in the cities was essential to the ultimate victory of the revolution.

Apart from this comment, Mao does not elsewhere in this document mention the cities or refer to the leading role of the working class. However, he does so in another document in May 1927, and here the issue of working class leadership of the Chinese Revolution is left in no doubt. In a short speech to welcome delegates to the Pacific Labor Conference, Mao stated:

> The Chinese peasant movement is the main force in the revolutionary process. They should especially go hand in hand with the working class of the whole world and rely deeply on the influence and guidance of the workers' movement. This demonstrates that the workers have quite naturally become the leaders of the peasants.[40]

As we will see, it was not merely the formal occasion that prompted Mao to utter this Marxist orthodoxy. It was characteristic of his long-held belief in the necessity for working class leadership of the peasant movement, a belief that became more pronounced in the years in the wilderness during which he developed and implemented his strategy for revolution in the countryside.

Revolution in the Countryside, 1927–1930

On the eve of his forced retreat into the countryside after the collapse of the United Front in mid 1927, Mao's perception of the class forces of the Chinese Revolution was clearly premised on the view that the peasant problem constituted the revolution's core problem and that the peasants, particularly the poor peasants, represented its "main force." He believed that the revolution was developing more rapidly in the countryside than in the cities, and that the CCP had to recognize and exploit the enormous opportunity represented by the rapid and widespread upsurge in revolutionary activity amongst the peasants. He admired the peasants' capacity for revolutionary struggle and accepted that their demands were an appropriate response to the "layer upon layer of crushing exploitation" under which they lived and labored.[41] However, his view of the peasants was not one of unalloyed admiration. He recognized their faults and limits; their thinking and demands tended towards atavism, and their organizational abilities could not match those of the working class, which had been exposed to the enforced disciplines and imposed rigors of industrial capitalism. Mao saw that the consciousness of the working class, generated by the mechanisms of exploitation and oppression inherent within capitalism, encompassed the need for radical social change in the direction of socialism, industrialization, and modernity. It was for these reasons that Mao felt that, on the one hand, there existed the possibility of alliance between the workers and peasants (particularly the poor peasants) and on the other, that this alliance had to be contracted under the leadership of the working class. Nowhere in the Mao documents of the period 1923–1927 is there any suggestion that the peasants would lead the revolution or that the revolution's ultimate goals coincided with the immediate demands of the peasants.

These sentiments are echoed, if anything even more strongly, in the documents of the 1927–1930 period, during which Mao had supposedly "turned his back" on the working class and the struggle in the cities. It is evident that Mao never voluntarily accepted his separation from the cities and from the bulk of the Chinese working class, and he frequently bemoaned the low level of working class representation in the institutions—the Party, military, mass organizations—that he was attempting to integrate into a coherent and effective revolutionary force. Mao did not choose the largely rural context within which his revolutionary strategy developed; it was thrust upon him by force of circumstance. He had previously accepted that the major theatre of the Chinese Revolution was the countryside, but it would be directed from the cities and by the working class and the Party that claimed to speak on its behalf. However, following the Horse Day Massacre of 21 May 1927 and the subsequent repression that signalled the imminent collapse of the CCP's United Front with the Left Guomindang, Mao accepted the inevitable: It was necessary for the Party to establish its own independent armed force, based on the strength of the peasants and the peasant associations, and for this force to "go up to the mountains."[42] To remain in the cities and to attempt to establish an armed force there was to invite the sort of massacres and reprisals that the Communists and their sympathizers had already experienced. For the moment, the cities and large towns had to be abandoned as sites of mass struggle; undercover operations might persist there, but the focus of mass struggle would, for the foreseeable future, shift to a rural theatre of operations. It is highly unlikely that Mao would have chosen to "go up to the mountains" and separate himself from the urban areas in which the revolution's leading class resided if he had had any other choice. Indeed, he recalled in 1939 that "I used to live in Hankou, and you [the Guomindang] insisted on fighting, *so I had no choice but to go up to the Jinggangshan.* If you go in for fighting the Communists again at this point and start to attack us once more, we will go up the mountains immediately. Yet I think it better that everyone live in the cities."[43] Mao did not "turn his back" on the working class; circumstances dictated reliance on the peasantry, but not abandonment of the principle or the actuality where possible of working class leadership. At the very moment Mao was setting out to put his strategy of rural revolution into operation, he helped frame a document that reiterated the view that "the development of this process [the agrarian revolution] requires a democratic political power of the workers, peasants, and petty bourgeoisie *led by the proletariat* and an armed force of the workers and peasants."[44] This was to remain Mao's view, despite his heavy reliance on the peasants.

Between 1927 and 1930, Mao developed a distinctive revolutionary strategy as he became familiar with the challenges and opportunities presented by armed struggle in an agrarian context in which the overwhelming mass of the population was peasants. In particular, the form of guerrilla warfare perfected by Mao relied heavily on the support provided to his armed forces by the local peasants. It was they who provided sustenance and intelligence, and it was they who enlisted to fight for the confiscation and redistribution of land and for the cancellation of debts to landlords and the lowering of their crippling burden of rent and taxes. Mao's willingness to exploit the anger and resentment of the peasants in this foray into armed struggle and the establishment of rural soviets was no opportunistic exercise, one that cast round for any support at a time when friends and allies were scarce. Rather, Mao genuinely perceived the peasants and their problems as the core of the Chinese Revolution at that stage. He identified with their anger at their "crushing exploitation," and was genuinely committed, at this stage of the revolution, to meeting their demands. It was in his longer term vision of the revolution that he departed from the desires of the peasants, for he was opposed to the view that a return to the imagined virtues of a by-gone era of private ownership of small peasant landholdings overseen by a traditional political caste of "honest officials and a good emperor," was in China's long-term interest.

Mao's faith in the peasants and his focus on the revolution in the countryside thus neither blinded him to the peasants' failings nor deflected him from commitment to a modernizing revolution which would move beyond the peasants' historically limited demands. This point can be underscored by examining Mao's comments of the late 1920s on the characteristics of the peasantry as a class, for it is very clear that he perceived many of the organizational and ideological problems afflicting the CCP and its military wing as deriving from the very large number of peasants recruited, of necessity, into those organizations. He repeatedly commented on these in extremely negative terms when diagnosing "serious organizational errors."[45] A good example appears in the "Draft Resolution of the Second Congress of *Xian* Party Organizations in the Hunan-Jiangxi Border Area" (October 1928).[46] Mao complained in this document that "In the past, the Party in every *xian* [county] had strongly marked characteristics of a peasant party, and showed a tendency to evolve toward non-proletarian leadership. . . . In the past the Party paid little attention to the work in the urban areas, and to the workers' movement."[47] He returned to this point with considerable force later in the same document: "Workers are the vanguard of all the toiling masses, they are the leaders of all the toiling masses. In the past we paid no attention to the workers' movement, let alone leadership by the workers. As a result, the tendency toward a peasant party emerged. This is a very serious crisis for the Party."[48] His strategy for overcoming this "serious crisis" was contained in the following series of recommendations:

- Do your utmost to promote as many worker comrades as possible to leading organs. Executive committees and standing committees at every level should have more than half worker and peasant comrades participating. . . .
- In the course of transforming the Party, we must adopt a completely proletarian point of view. . . .
- At the same time, special attention should be paid to branch work in the urban areas, and excellent worker comrades should also be promoted to become branch Party secretaries and committee members in the rural areas, so as to increase the leadership capacity of the workers and be strictly on guard against the tendency toward a peasant party. . . .
- Party headquarters and soviets at every level should make great efforts to promote workers, so that they will be able to assume leadership positions and lead the struggle. . . .
- At present, basic training work should strive to eliminate the opportunist, feudal, and petty bourgeois thought of the ordinary comrades, and establish among them the revolutionary outlook on life of the proletariat.[49]

Mao believed that only by pursuing organizational strategies such as these "can we prevent the Party from taking a non-proletarian road. . . . Only thus can we enhance the leadership capacity of the proletariat."[50]

His concern over the over-representation of the peasants within the Party and military and the "erroneous tendencies" this caused was restated with considerable force in November 1928:

> The problem of the leading role of proletarian consciousness in the Party is extremely important. It can almost be said that the Party organization in all the *xian* of the border area is entirely a peasant party. If they do not receive leadership from the urban proletariat, they are bound to develop erroneous tendencies. Besides correcting previous mistakes and paying active attention to the workers' movement in the *xian* seats and in other large towns in the countryside, it is also extremely necessary to increase worker representation in the soviets. [51]

Moreover, in December 1929, in one of his strongest statements on correcting "erroneous and nonproletarian ideological tendencies in the Party,"[52] Mao detailed the various defects caused by the large numbers of peasants in the Party and military: "Ultrademocracy" was linked to "small peasant production";[53] "absolute egalitarianism" was a "mere illusion of peasants and small proprietors";[54] and "the source of individualism lies in influences ranging from small peasant thinking to bourgeois thinking within the Party."[55] As Mao pointed out:

> Various kinds of nonproletarian consciousness are very strongly present in the Party of the Fourth Army and are an extremely great hindrance to the application of the Party's correct line. . . . The overall source of the various incorrect tendencies in the Party of the Fourth Army lies, of course, in the fact that its basic units are composed largely of peasants and other elements of petty bourgeois origin.[56]

In October 1930, Mao again complained that the "proletarian base [of the Communist Party] is extremely weak."[57]

The solution to these organizational and ideological problems within the Party and military was clear to Mao: working class leadership. In October 1928, he stated that "this revolution [the bourgeois-democratic revolution] can be carried through only under the leadership of the proletariat."[58] He was to return to the centrality of the working class to China's revolution in November of that year: "[A]t present, China is definitely still at the stage of bourgeois-democratic revolution. . . . Only in the process of such a democratic revolution can a genuine foundation for workers' political power be formed, so as to advance to the socialist revolution."[59] And in December 1928 he was to repeat that "The leader of this [bourgeois-democratic] revolution is the proletariat."[60]

In March 1929 Mao concluded "A letter to our brother soldiers throughout the country" in the following hortatory vein: "Let us raise the bright Red banner and loudly shout, 'Comrades! Come quickly and build our working people's Republic. The working class must be masters of the world, only then will humankind enter into the Great Harmony (*datong*)'."[61] Similarly, in April 1929, in an important letter to the Central Committee, Mao made the following significant assessment of the relationship between the revolutionary struggle in the urban and rural areas and of the relative significance of the working class and peasantry:

> Proletarian leadership is the sole key to the victory of the revolution. Building up the Party's proletarian basis and establishing Party branches in industrial enterprises in key areas are the greatest organizational tasks at present. But, at the same time, the development of the struggle in the countryside, the establishment of soviets in small areas, and the creation and expansion of the Red Army are prerequisites for aiding the struggle in the cities and hastening the revolutionary upsurge. The greatest mistake would therefore be to abandon the struggle in the cities and sink into rural guerilla-ism. But in our opinion, it is also a mistake—if any of our Party members hold such views—to fear the development of the power of the peasants lest it outstrip the workers' leadership and become detrimental to the revolution. For the revolution in semicolonial China will fail only if the peasant struggle is deprived of the leadership of the workers; it will never suffer just because the peasant struggle develops in such a way as to become more powerful than the workers.[62]

It is clear from this passage that while Mao emphasized the importance of the peasant struggle, he emphasized even more the importance of working class leadership of that struggle; as he pointed out, the revolution would only fail "if the peasants are deprived of the leadership of the workers." This passage is also significant as we can discern in it the sort of balance between the urban and rural struggle that Mao felt desirable and would have pursued more actively had he not, of necessity, been obliged to carry out a revolutionary struggle so heavily focussed on the rural dimension of that struggle. For Mao, there was, at that stage of the Chinese Revolution, an organic connection between the urban and rural struggle, a connection that had been weakened through the repressive measures of the Guomindang and its allies, but one which had to be maintained and strengthened lest the peasant struggle degenerate into "rural guerilla-ism."

In the same document, Mao referred to a tactic he had used of organizing underground workers' unions in places occupied by the Red Army.[63] This was in line with his viewpoint that the workers' struggle in the cities and towns had to be strengthened so that the proletariat would be in a position to lead the peasant struggle:

> During this year, we must lay the foundations for the struggle of the proletariat in Shanghai, Wuxi, Ningpo, Hangzhou, Fuzhou, Xiamen, and other places, so that they can lead the peasant struggles in Zhejiang, Jiangxi, and Fujian. The Jiangxi Provincial Committee must be soundly established, and efforts must be made to build a basis among the workers in Nanchang, Jiujiang, Ji'an, and on the Nanchang-Jiujiang Railroad.[64]

The workers' movement had to be strengthened and expanded because the number of workers in the army and Party units under Mao's control was too small, although not negligible. In June 1929, in a Report to the Central Committee, Mao revealed that, in the First, Second, and Third Columns of the Fourth Red Army, and for those military units directly subordinated to the Party in the army, the total number of Party members was 1,329. Of these, 311 were workers, 626 peasants, 106 merchants, 192 students, and 95 others.[65] In a letter to Lin Biao in June 1929, Mao used these figures to make the following instructive comment:

> We are historical materialists. To get at the truth regarding any matter whatsoever, we have to investigate it both from the perspective of history and from the perspective of circumstances. . . . We should never forget the origins and composition of the Red Army. According to the statistics for May . . . the ratio of workers to nonworkers is 23 percent to 77 percent. When we discuss the thinking of an individual, we should not forget his class origin, his educational background, and his work history. This is the attitude toward research of a Communist. Manifestly, there exists in the Party of the Fourth Army an incorrect ideology based on the peasants, the vagrants, and the petty bourgeoisie. This ideology is harmful to the solidarity of the Party and the future of the revolution. It runs the risk of deviating from the proletarian revolutionary standpoint.[66]

Mao reiterated the importance of proletarian leadership of the Red Army and peasants' soviets in another letter to Lin Biao in January 1930,[67] and in a document of October 1930, he commented that "The

Communist Party must establish the leadership of proletarian consciousness . . . and cannot become bogged down in poor peasant ideology."[68]

It is also significant that Mao came to believe that in the years since
1927, insufficient attention had been given to investigation of conditions
in the cities. In "Oppose Bookism" of May 1930, he concluded that "our
previous investigations have also had another very great defect: We have
concentrated on the villages and not paid attention to the cities . . . we
must understand the villages, but we must also understand the cities; otherwise we will be unable to adapt to the demands of revolutionary struggle."[69] A similar theme emerges in a document of October 1930, in which
he called for increased attention to work in the cities: "Today the proletarian uprising has become the principal and indispensable force in seizing the
major cities. . . . Now we should correct the pessimism and neglect of the
work in cities and overcome all difficulties in setting up the work in
cities."[70] He called for strengthening of the trade union movement and its
participation in armed uprisings and strikes.[71]

There is thus ample evidence in the Mao documents of 1927–1930 to
demonstrate that Mao had not "turned his back" on the working class, and
neither was his thinking motivated by "powerful anti-urban biases." If anything, the reverse holds. During the crucial years of Mao's formulation of
a strategy for revolution based in the countryside, he remained convinced
of the importance of working class leadership of the peasants and of the
significance of the struggle in the cities for the victory of the revolution.
In the years that followed, often referred to as the period of the Jiangxi Soviet, he was provided the opportunity to create the institutions of an embryonic socialist state that would translate into practice this belief in the
necessity of working class leadership.

Working Class Power and
State Formation, 1931–1934

Mao's revolutionary strategy is often interpreted in quite a limited fashion.
Not only is there an overly narrow focus on Mao's emphasis on the peasantry but there is little if any consideration of his contribution to the
process of state formation. The latter was an integral dimension of his approach to revolution, for Mao was very conscious of the fact that the
seizure of state power was only a preliminary stage in the long-term process
of the revolutionary transformation of society. What this required was the
creation and management of institutions appropriate to this task, and the
nature of these institutions and, importantly, who wielded power within

them, were critical to the successful achievement of the long-term goals of the revolution. An examination of this dimension of Mao's thought is therefore essential in evaluating the role of the working class and peasantry in his revolutionary strategy.

We have already observed that while Mao respected the peasantry's capacity for revolution and designated this class as the "main force" of the revolution, he was not prepared to cede to it leadership of the revolution. That role was reserved for the working class. During the years in which he was preoccupied with the government of the Jiangxi Soviet, under Communist control from 1931–1934, he was to build this configuration of class forces into the institutions of the new state of which he was titular head.[72] And Mao made his conviction of the need for working class leadership of this new state absolutely clear in August 1933: "For the first time in Chinese history, the workers and peasants are in control of their own state, the workers and peasants have become the ruling class, and the working class is the leading force."[73]

How did Mao institutionalize this view of the relative class power of the peasantry and the working class in the institutions of the Jiangxi Soviet? It is clear that Mao continued to regard the peasants and the resolution of their problems, particularly the issue of land redistribution, as a core policy consideration of the government of the Jiangxi Soviet. He also continued to value the work of the peasant associations (sometimes translated as peasant leagues), and attempted to put in place policies and practices that would facilitate their effective operation. However, Mao also made it abundantly clear, across a range of institutional and policy measures, that the poor peasants, while the most reliable ally of the working class, would not be the preeminent class in control of the institutions of state; that role was reserved for the working class. Ilpyong Kim is consequently quite wrong to suggest that "Mao's concept [of the Jiangxi Soviet] consistently emphasized the equality of the peasantry with the industrial workers in the development and operation of The new political system."[74] The evidence points in quite a different direction: the strengths of the working class and the failings of the peasantry made any such equality impossible; so too did their very different historical roles.

Before turning to an examination of Mao's views on working class representation in and leadership of the state during the Jiangxi Soviet, a word needs to be said about the context within which Mao operated and the nature of the texts which bear his name. From 1931–1934, Mao's position within the leadership of the Chinese Communist Party was weak. Indeed, one scholar has referred to these as Mao's years "in opposition."[75] Mao had found himself, in the years from 1927 during which his revolutionary strategy developed, to be frequently at odds with the Party Centre over issues such as his reliance on the peasantry, his views on guerilla war, and the establishment and operation of rural soviets. Following the Fourth Plenum of the Sixth Central Committee of January 1931, a new leadership came to power in the Party, one dominated by the so-called Returned Students Faction (also called the "Twenty-Eight Bolsheviks") under the control of Wang Ming. This had trained in the Soviet Union and was unsympathetic to Mao's line and to himself personally. This Plenum set about reorganizing the Party's leadership organs in a way that diminished Mao's power and influence. It established a Central Bureau of the Soviet Areas and a subordinate Military Commission, and the membership of these organizations was determined by the Party Centre in Shanghai.[76] Nevertheless, Mao continued to exercise considerable power during most of 1931 in his positions as Acting Secretary of the Central Bureau and as Director of the General Political Department (which came under the Military Commission). However, at the First Party Congress of the Central Soviet Area, held in Ruijin in early November 1931, Mao's policies, particularly on guerilla war, were roundly criticized, and he was removed as Acting Secretary of the Central Bureau. As Stephen Averill points out, "between autumn 1931 and autumn 1932 he was gradually stripped of his most influential formal positions in both Party and Red Army organizations."[77] He retained, however, a number of significant governmental positions. In particular, he was elected Chairman of the Soviet Government's Central Executive Committee, and Chairman of the Council of People's Commissars.

As a result of the First Party Congress of the Central Soviet Area, Mao's power within the Party was thus seriously diminished, although his responsibilities for the establishment and administration of the new Central Soviet Government were expanded.[78] Indeed, as one scholar has concluded, "Mao obtained a strong position in the newly created state apparatus."[79] Moreover, while Mao and the Party leadership were in dispute about the general thrust of Party and military policy, they were not in disagreement over the strategy to pursue in establishing and running the Soviet government. As Ilpyong Kim concludes, "The evidence suggests that the Soviet-trained Party leaders who were in control of the central Party operations and Mao Tse-tung, who led the Central Soviet Government, were in essential agreement on basic organizational approaches and cooperated in the process of implementing them."[80]

These two points—Mao's expanded responsibilities for governmental administration and the "essential agreement" between Mao and his opponents within the Party leadership over basic organizational approaches—bear materially on the discussion which follows. Some of the documents that will be introduced as evidence to establish Mao's insistence on establishing working class dominance of new state institutions appear over his name as Chairman of the Central Soviet Republic. They also appear over the names of his Vice-Chairmen Xiang Ying and Zhang Guotao. The former was closely aligned with the Returned Students Faction in the Party leadership, and Zhang Guotao was identified with the right wing of the Party which similarly had little sympathy with Mao's position. The documents are therefore not always Mao's alone. However, scholarly opinion supports the contention that Mao had not merely appended his name to the documents under duress. He was in fundamental agreement, even with those with whom he was in contention over broader Party and military policies, over the strategy to adopt in the formation of the Jiangxi Soviet's "embryonic state."[81] Moreover, Mao committed himself to this strategy with enthusiasm. As Averill concludes, "Given the pressures and uncertainties imposed by the encirclement campaigns and the blockade, the political institution-building and economic construction work achieved under Mao's overall administrative supervision was impressive."[82]

A similar possible reservation arises in relation to the influence of the Comintern on the establishment and state-building policies of the Jiangxi Soviet. According to Richard Thornton, "the form and content of the Chinese Soviet regime derived directly from Comintern policies."[83] These policies were part of the Comintern's general determination to "bolshevize" the CCP to repress what it perceived as the unorthodox tendency developing in the Chinese Revolution of (supposedly) excessive reliance on peasant leadership of the revolution in China's countryside. The Comintern's strategy involved the insertion into the Chinese Communist Party of a Soviet-trained leadership cadre, the Returned Students' Faction, which was ideologically in tune with Comintern thinking and likely to observe Comintern discipline. In June 1930, the Comintern insisted on the establishment of a "Central Soviet Government," whose fundamental task was "to ensure that the hegemony of the proletariat is solid and is exercised consistently." The importance of proletarian leadership of the Chinese revolution was again asserted in a Comintern Resolution of August 1931. To ensure that the workers played a role in all of its leading organs, the Party had to recruit "fearlessly, systematically, and as a matter of top priority, the best elements among the workers."[84]

The question arises, in light of the Comintern's powerful influence on the CCP at the time of the creation and development of the Jiangxi Soviet, whether Mao's utterances and policies on working class leadership were merely a tactical deference to the Comintern line and not a genuine expression of his own views. That this is not the case can be demonstrated by examining his views on working class leadership and the peasantry in the years preceding the establishment of the Jiangxi Soviet. As we have seen, from 1927 to 1930, during the very years in which Mao's revolutionary strategy was being forged, he continually stressed the importance of working class leadership of both the Party and the Chinese Revolution. He also identified the large numbers of peasants, recruited from necessity into the Party and Army, as the source of the numerous political, organizational, and ideological problems that afflicted those organizations. Thus, his admiration for the revolutionary potential of the peasants was thus balanced by a realistic assessment of their shortcomings as a class and their urgent need for leadership by the working class and its vanguard party. His words then were certainly not those of a revolutionary who willingly embraced rural revolution and uncritically revered the revolutionary potential of the peasantry. They were, rather, the words of one who finds himself forcibly separated from the cities and the working class and compelled to find a strategy which could exploit the dissatisfaction of the peasantry and channel their revolutionary impulse in the direction of a modernizing revolution. Mao did not, therefore, lose sight of the need for working class leadership of the Chinese Revolution, and his words and policies of the Jiangxi Soviet are consistent with those of the 1927–1930 period. They are also, as we will observe, consistent with his views of the Yan'an period, 1937–1945, a period during which Mao rose to undisputed power within the CCP.

It is this consistency of words and policies over an extended period of time that allows us to proceed with some confidence to an examination of the Mao texts of the Jiangxi Soviet. Our purpose is to unearth from these texts his views on both the working class and peasants, the leadership potential and role of these two classes, and the institutional mechanisms Mao put in place to reinforce working class leadership of the first fledgling communist state in China. It will become evident that, for Mao, the centrality of the working class to a modernizing revolution meant there could be no equality between the peasantry and the working class in terms of leadership and ideological outlook.

Mao's perception of the importance of the working class relative to the peasantry can be perceived in a number of institutional and policy areas. The first of these is his move to entrench working-class power through implementation of a class-based electoral system for the various levels of the hierarchy of soviets that would constitute the fundamental building blocks of the new state. This hierarchy of soviets rested on a foundation of *xiang* soviets, which administered a local area that incorporated several villages and included a population ranging from several hundred to several thousand people.[85] The structure of the *xiang* soviet and its relationship to mass organizations at the grass-roots level varied somewhat between 1931 and 1934. However, it was the Representative Congress that theoretically stood at the pinnacle of *xiang* organization, with a Presidium of five to seven persons chosen by and from among the Representative Congress, which oversaw the implementation of policy between meetings of the Congress.[86] What is significant about the *xiang* Representative Congress, from the perspective of Mao's views on working class leadership, is the manner of its election. In a Directive of January 1932, Mao ordered that the deputies to the *xiang* Representative Congress be elected from different class constituencies and that these constituencies be given different weightings. Every fifty poor and middle peasants and "independent labourers" (*duli laodongzhe*) had the right to elect one deputy, whereas every thirteen workers, coolies, and farm laborers could elect one deputy and, from 1933, were given the right to hold electoral meetings separate from those of the peasants. This deliberate institution of electoral imbalance in favor of workers had a significant effect on the class composition of the *xiang* Representative Congresses. In some *xiang* Congresses, almost half of the deputies were defined as "workers," this in a context in which "workers" (even broadly defined in the manner Mao referred to them[87]) were a small percentage of the population.[88]

This class "gerrymander" was repeated at every level in the hierarchy of soviets. In elections to township soviets, there was one deputy elected for every twenty "workers, coolies, and farm laborers," whereas one deputy was elected for every eighty of the remaining classes. The same electoral ratio applied in city soviets subordinate to the provincial soviet. Here, every one hundred "workers, coolies, and farm laborers" elected one deputy, whereas four hundred urban poor and local peasants could elect one deputy. At the level above the *xiang*, the district (*qu*) soviet, whose deputies were drawn from *xiang* and township soviets, Mao prescribed that "workers, coolies, and farm laborers" make up a total of 20 percent of the deputies. Mao stipulated that "rural and urban soviets as well as congresses at the two levels of district and *xian* must all pay attention to the components from the workers, coolies, farm laborers, and Red Army."[89]

At the next level in the hierarchy of soviets, the *xian* (or county) soviet, the number of "workers, coolies, and farm laborers" was increased to 25 percent, and deputies elected to this level from towns were to be 50 percent "workers, coolies, and farm laborers." The same principle was also applied at the level of provincial soviet congress, which stood immediately below the Soviet Central Government. Elections to the provincial congress allowed one deputy for every five thousand rural residents and one for every two thousand urban residents.[90] This ratio was altered in 1933 to provide even greater representation to urban residents, who now elected one delegate for every fifteen hundred residents, compared to one delegate for every six thousand rural residents. This electoral imbalance, in favor of those living in urban areas (and therefore by implication in favor of the working class), was established at each level, from the *xiang* soviet to the National Soviet Congress. At the latter, there was one deputy for each ten thousand urban electors, and one for each fifty thousand rural electors.[91]

The *Temporary Soviet Election Law* of August 1933 (which appeared over Mao's signature) made quite explicit its intention to entrench the leadership of the working class. There is here no deference to the suggestion that each voter's vote should be equal, or even approximately equal, to the votes of all other voters. As article 3 points out:

> The proletariat is the vanguard of the soviets, leading the peasants in the overthrow of the Guomindang political power of the landlords and the bourgeoisie and establishing the soviet political power of the democratic dictatorship of the workers and peasants. In order to strengthen the leadership of the proletariat within the soviet organs, workers shall enjoy an advantage compared to other residents in the proportion of representatives to the number of residents.[92]

In his Report of the Central Executive Committee and the Council of People's Commissars of the Chinese Soviet Republic to the Second National Soviet Congress (January 1934), Mao summed up the class intentions of the machinery of soviet elections and their achievements over the previous two years as follows:

> They [soviets] should arouse class struggle among the workers, develop the agrarian revolution of the peasants, and heighten the activism of the worker and peasant masses under the principle of a workers' and peasants' alliance led by the working class. . . . Concerning the balance of class composition: To guarantee that the proletariat will be the mainstay of leadership within the soviet regime, we applied the method under which thirteen workers and their dependents elected one representative, and fifty peasants or poor people elected one representative, and the same composition is used to organize conferences of deputies at the city and township level. At all levels of deputies' congresses and executive committees from the district to the central level, an appropriate ratio of workers' and peas-

ants' deputies was established. This has guaranteed the alliance between workers and peasants in the organization of the soviet regime, and ensured that the workers occupy the leading position.[93]

The principal institutions of government, composed of a hierarchy of soviets from the level of the *xiang* to the National Soviet Congress, were not, therefore, intended to represent the population of the Jiangxi Soviet equally. Rather, the electoral process that brought the soviets into being was deliberately structured in a manner intended to favor one particular section of the population: the working class. This was in part to compensate for the diminutive size of the working class; it was in conformity, too, with the electoral practice of the Soviet Union.[94] It was also, however, in conformity with Mao's own insistence that the working class play an active and leading role in the establishment of the new state. Moreover, within the soviets themselves, attention had to be given to ensuring that the members of the working class were elected onto leadership committees. As Mao urged, "At the time of electing executive committee members, special attention should be given to worker activists, and large numbers of such elements should be elected to the executive committee to strengthen the leading force of the proletariat in the soviet."[95] This would serve to consolidate "the soviet political power of the dictatorship of the workers and peasants, and to strengthen the leadership of the proletariat."[96]

Second, Mao moved to entrench working class power by ensuring that where possible members of the working class would lead the mass organizations which channelled information to and from the institutions of the state in the Jiangxi Soviet and which facilitated linkage between state and society. Of particular importance was the Poor Peasant League. Despite its title, the Poor Peasant League was not limited to the class whose name it bore. As Mao pointed out in July 1933, "The poor peasant league is not an organization made up purely of a single class, but a mass organization of poor peasants within the jurisdiction of the township soviet."[97] Importantly, leadership of this organization, and by extension, the poor peasants themselves, was not in the hands of the poor peasants, but the working class; and where this had not occurred, Mao stressed, steps had to be taken to ensure that it did. As he pointed out, "Workers in the countryside must join the poor peasant league and form a workers' small group to play an active leading role in the league and unite the broad masses of poor peasants under the leadership of the proletariat, turning the league into the most reliable pillar of the political power of the soviets."[98]

One of the most important functions of the Poor Peasant League during the Jiangxi Soviet was the Land Investigation Movement, although it was only one of several of the Soviet's organizations involved in it. The Land Investigation Movement, as Kim points out, was not merely a strategy in the agrarian revolution that had been unfolding in the Soviet area since 1930. While its objective was certainly to resolve agrarian problems using class analysis and class struggle, its purpose was also to reorganize and reform government structures and mass organizations to facilitate the mobilization of the masses. It was thus an extremely important and broadly based campaign, which had both socioeconomic and organizational objectives.[99] Nevertheless, the Poor Peasant League was crucial for the success of the Land Investigation Movement, and Mao moved to ensure it pursued an appropriate line by strengthening the representation of the working class and labor unions within it. One of the clearest indications of his perception of the limitations of the Poor Peasant League under the leadership of the poor peasants themselves was articulated in July 1933. Here, Mao makes it abundantly clear that working class leadership of this supposedly peasant organization was absolutely essential:

> Only under the leadership of the Communist Party and the soviets can the poor peasant league correctly accomplish all its tasks, and avoid being influenced by the rich peasants or dominated by all sorts of backward peasant consciousness, such as the ideas of absolute egalitarianism and localism. . . . The unions of agricultural workers and craftsmen should try to pass motions at their own congresses about having their membership join the poor peasant league in a body, so as to bring about a constant leading role for the proletariat in the poor peasant league.[100]

Mao was adamant that the Poor Peasant League, crucial to the success of the Land Investigation Movement, would not succeed if left to the leadership of the poor peasants themselves. It was particularly important, he felt, to encourage "farm laborers," who were the "brothers of the urban proletariat in the countryside," to join the Poor Peasant League and form independent small groups of workers within it. These workers' groups "should be an active leader of the organization," and their presence would have the effect, he believed, of uniting poor peasant activists and developing the League generally.[101] He pointed to the example of the township of Shanhe. Here, the Poor Peasant League had not been able to get the Land Investigation Movement started. It was only when the rural labor union and the handicraft workers' union became involved and provided leadership that the Movement got under way. The experience of Shanhe should,

Mao believed, be applied in all rural areas. Consequently, the labor unions leadership should "treat the task of land investigation as one of the important missions of the labor unions."[102] Indeed, the purpose of the involvement of workers in the Poor Peasant League during the Land Investigation Movement was to "establish the leadership of the working class in the countryside."[103] Thus, while the Poor Peasant League remained, as Mao asserted, the "central force" of the Land Investigation Movement, he exhorted the workers in the countryside to join the League "so as to lead the development of the land investigation struggle";[104] for "the labor union is expected to be the leader of the class struggle in the countryside, while the poor peasant league is expected to be the pillar of the struggle."[105]

This formulation—the peasants as the "main" or "central" force, with leadership provided by the working class—is typical of Mao's understanding of the relationship between the peasantry and working class in the Chinese Revolution, and also the roles of each class. Even in a policy area dedicated to change in rural areas, as the Land Investigation Movement appeared to be (particularly the elimination of feudal class relations), Mao was not prepared to leave its leadership to the peasants. Only "a constant leading role for the proletariat in the poor peasant league" could ensure that the League avoid being "dominated by all sorts of backward peasant consciousness."[106]

The importance of the working class to Mao's strategy for state formation in the Jiangxi Soviet is also exemplified by his approach to extending and consolidating the labor unions, which were another mass organization of vital importance to the Party's long-term objectives. The unions were, Mao believed, "pillars in mobilizing the masses," particularly the peasant masses.[107] Mao paid considerable attention to the rights of workers, for not only was this in line with the Party's ideology but it would have the effect of mobilizing workers in support of the Party and its policies. This would "reinforce the leadership of the proletariat."[108] The Party thus had to forcefully implement the Labour Law (promulgated in December 1931 and revised in October 1933).[109] In a lengthy letter of March 1932, Mao exhorted his comrades in the Executive Committee of the Western Fujian Soviet Government to pay particular attention to ensuring the implementation of this Law. The basic provisions of this Law covered entitlements such as the eight-hour working day, wage rises, a minimum wage, improved working conditions, and collective contracts. These were, he felt, "minimum benefits," and their implementation by the Soviet authorities would have the effect of mobilizing "the masses of urban workers." The Soviet Government also had to provide assistance to workers in organizing their trade unions. He sharply criticized those within the government who had neither actively implemented the Labour Law nor investigated the actual conditions of workers, and had merely asserted workers' rights without enforcing these. This negative practice had the effect, Mao believed, of "dampening enthusiasm for the struggle and obscuring class consciousness on the part of the workers."[110] The resolute application of the Labour Law, on the other hand, would "enable the masses of workers to participate actively and speedily in the cause of economic construction, and strengthen their role in the leadership of the peasants."[111]

Data provided by Mao in his lengthy Report to the Second National Soviet Congress of January 1934 suggest that the strategies of actively implementing the Labour Law and encouraging labor unions and the participation of their members in the leadership of other organizations to provide effective class leadership, had borne fruit. Mao commenced by reiterating that "under the soviet régime, workers are the masters. Leading the broad masses of peasants, the workers have shouldered the great responsibility of consolidating and developing the soviet regime."[112] Mao then pointed to the effects of the Labour Law. In the Soviet area, the eight-hour day had "generally" been instituted, and labor inspection units had been established in cities and many villages in order to ensure that employers did not violate the Labour Law. Labor courts had been established to punish employers who transgressed the law, and employment agencies had been established to handle job referrals. The effect of these measures had been that workers' wages had risen in the Soviet areas, in both the cities and rural areas, and their general working conditions (including meals) had improved. It is clear that Mao took considerable pride in these achievements. Because of measures such as the Labour Law, "the lives of workers in the soviet areas have seen tremendous improvement."[113] Moreover, welfare was provided for unemployed workers, with a social insurance system established, with a bureau to oversee its operation.

As a result of the encouragement of the labor unions by the Soviet Government, their membership had greatly expanded. Employing statistics provided by the All-China Federation of Trade Unions, Mao disclosed that labor union membership in the Central Soviet Area and its neighboring soviets stood at 229,000. In the Central Soviet Area itself, less than 5 percent of all workers had not joined the union, and in Xingguo *xian*, which Mao knew intimately from his own detailed investigation of Changgang township,[114] 98 percent of the workers were members of labor unions. Mao perceived the growing strength of the labor unions as confirmation that the Labour Law was improving the lot of workers and thus encouraging their membership. "Because of all this," he concluded, "the workers' lives have greatly improved, the revolutionary activism of the workers has been greatly encouraged, and the workers have played their tremendous role in the revolutionary war and in soviet construction."[115]

The significance of the growing strength of the Labour Unions was also, from Mao's perspective, that Union members were drawn into other government, Party, or mass organizations. For example, some 28 percent of the Labour Union membership (of 70,580) in the Central Soviet Area served in the Red Army and guerilla forces, while another 10 percent worked in the soviets and other revolutionary organizations. This served to increase worker representation in organizations central to the establishment of the Soviet state. This demonstrated, Mao asserted, that "those who say that the workers have gained nothing since the revolution and that the activism of the workers has not been aroused can only be said to be talking nonsense."[116]

Third, Mao attempted, to the extent that he could given his much reduced control over military policy during the years of the Jiangxi Soviet, to entrench working class power by ensuring that leadership of the Red Army and the militias remained, where possible, in the hands of workers. As we have observed, Mao took comfort from the fact that many members of the Labour Unions were also members of the Soviet's military organizations. In a directive of September 1932 on expanding the Red Army, Mao insisted that investigation of class status was important in recruiting for the Red Army. Those who become Red Army soldiers, he declared, "must be the healthiest and most enthusiastic elements among the worker and peasant masses. Only in this way can the Red Army be qualitatively strengthened."[117] However, while Mao welcomed "healthy" and "enthusiastic" peasants into the ranks of the Red Army, it would not be they, ideally at least, who would lead it. This was the prerogative of the working class. To achieve this goal, Mao directed that each military district recruit large numbers of worker cadres "so as to strengthen the leadership of the working class in the Red Guard armies."[118] In his Report to the Second National Soviet Congress of January 1934, Mao reported that his policy had been generally successful: "Worker cadres have increased in number [in the Red Army] and the political commissar system has been universally instituted, so that control of the Red Army is in the hands of reliable commanders."[119] Nevertheless, more remained to be done, and Mao exhorted further consolidation of the Red Army in the hands of workers. As he pointed out, "more people with worker backgrounds should be promoted to positions as military and political commanders at all levels."[120] This was important, as it was necessary to have people with "clear class consciousness and strong leadership ability" within the Army if mistakes were not to be made.[121]

In sum, it is clear that Mao's insistence on working class leadership of the institutions of the Jiangxi Soviet, 1931–1934, was built on a belief in the superior organizational and ideological abilities of the workers. But it was based too on a perception of the failings of the peasantry as a class. He identified many of the organizational problems experienced by the Soviet Government as originating with the peasants. Bureaucratism "infested soviet governments," Mao complained, and he linked it to the "scattered nature of the peasantry, and their lack of proletarian organization and discipline."[122] Mao also recognized that the peasants, themselves deeply immersed in rural feudal class relations and habituated to them, were not necessarily able to mount an effective class analysis. As he pointed out:

> Hidden counterrevolutionaries cannot be recognized at a glance by the peasants. Besides, given the various kinds of deep-rooted feudal relationships in the countryside . . . it will not be an easy task to raise the class consciousness of the peasants to the extent that they all realize that, in the end, it will be essential to eliminate the feudal remnants. To achieve this will definitely require that the Communist Party and the Soviet Government explain it to the peasants very patiently.[123]

This inability of peasants to discern the nature of the rural class structure was a significant problem in the implementation of the Land Investigation Movement. Mao argued that only with the leadership of the Communist Party and the working class could the Poor Peasant League avoid being "dominated by all sorts of backward peasant consciousness, such as the ideas of absolute egalitarianism and localism," which impeded their ability to mount an effective class analysis.[124] The peasants clearly needed leadership, and Mao was in no doubt that the working class had to provide it.

Resistance and Reform, 1937–1945

During the years 1937–1945, often referred to as the Yan'an period after the name of the Communists' wartime capital, Mao's energies were focussed primarily on mapping out a strategy for and leading the Anti-Japanese War of Resistance. A central tenet of this strategy was a reordering of the hierarchy of contradictions that, in Mao's mind, determined the policies the Communists should follow. The intensity and immediacy of the threat posed by the Japanese invasion of the Chinese mainland persuaded Mao that the "principal contradiction" (that is, the contradiction whose resolution was most urgently required at that historical stage)[125] was that between Japanese imperialism and the Chinese nation.[126] National survival, then clearly under threat, was paramount, and other policies, such as the revolutionary transformation of Chinese society in the direction of socialism, had to be moderated in order to attract the widest possible united front of anti-Japanese forces. Landlords and capitalists, as long as committed to patriotic struggle, were to be treated with courtesy and respect and encouraged to become active participants in the struggle to save China from the threat of national extinction. These classes, formerly castigated as "exploiting classes," were no longer the target of class struggle and expropriation. As Mao insisted, "this is not the time to carry out a land revolution." At most, there should be a "partial reduction in rent and interest . . . but the reduction should not be too great."[127] There was thus a switch from the revolutionary rhetoric of the previous fifteen years to a reformist agenda that would appear less threatening to the Communist Party's erstwhile enemies and now possible partners in a coalition of forces opposed to the Japanese invasion.[128]

Given this strategic shift from revolution to national resistance and reform, one might expect to see some moderation of Mao's previously held views on the leadership qualities and roles of the working class and peasantry, allowing an enhanced role to the peasants. After all, the CCP now found itself, even more so than previously, in a rural context very far removed from the cities and large towns in which resided the bulk of China's diminutive working class, thus very reliant on the support of China's peasants. Yet, a close reading of Mao's writings from the period 1937–1945 reveals no such variation in his long-standing assessment of the working class and peasantry in the context of the Chinese Revolution, for Mao remained convinced that this period of resistance and reform constituted no more than a pause, no matter how "protracted," in the revolutionary momentum of Chinese society.[129] Following Japan's defeat, Mao believed, China would recommence its historically ordained progression toward the future, a future characterized by modern industry and socialism. This was, Mao asserted, an "irresistible law," one that described "the inevitable course of history."[130] Mao's thought thus continued to be inspired by a concept of a modern future in which the working class would occupy, economically and politically, the dominant position, and in which other classes, including the peasantry, would recede in significance.

There is abundant evidence that Mao continued to believe in the leadership role of the working class during the 1937–1945 period. Let us commence our examination of this evidence with an excerpt from the longest of his philosophical annotations of 1937:

> As far as the revolutionary leadership [of the Chinese Revolution] is concerned, because of the level of consciousness and the thoroughness of the proletariat, as contrasted with the vacillation of the bourgeoisie, the proletariat occupies the dominant position. This particularly affects the future of the Chinese revolution. . . . In the contradiction between the peasantry and proletariat, the proletariat is dominant. In the contradiction between industrial workers and handicraft workers, industrial workers are dominant.[131]

Despite the rural context within which the Communists were fighting the War of Resistance, Mao referred to the proletariat in April 1939 as "the vanguard in resistance to Japan,"[132] and in July 1939 as "the backbone" of the Anti-Japanese United Front.[133] Mao made this judgment even though he was well aware that in numerical terms the Chinese working class represented but a very small proportion of the Chinese population, and the industrial working class an even smaller proportion of that. Mao estimated in late 1939 that the modern industrial working class numbered only 2.5 to 3 million, and the handicraft workers residing in cities a further 12 million. These diminutive numbers were, however, swollen by the existence of a "great number of rural proletarians."[134] In January 1940, Mao reiterated his estimate that there "are several million industrial workers in China and several tens of millions of handicraft workers and agricultural laborers."[135]

Despite its small size, particularly in relation to the peasantry, the proletariat possessed many "outstanding qualities," Mao asserted. First, it was much more "resolute and thoroughgoing in revolutionary struggle than any other class," and this because it was subjected to the three major forms of oppression: imperialism, feudalism, and the capitalist oppression of the bourgeoisie. It was thus the "most revolutionary" of the classes engaged in the Chinese Revolution. Second, it possessed the revolutionary leadership of the CCP, and it was this leadership that had helped the working class become "the most politically conscious class in Chinese society." Third, because many of the Chinese workers had originally been bankrupt peasants, the working class had "natural ties" to the peasantry, and could therefore readily form a revolutionary alliance with them.[136]

Mao concluded that, despite "certain unavoidable weaknesses," the leadership of the proletariat was essential to the victory of the revolution:

> In spite of certain unavoidable weaknesses, for instance, its smallness (as compared with the peasantry), its youth (as compared with the proletariat

in the capitalist countries), and its low educational level (as compared with the bourgeoisie), the Chinese proletariat is nonetheless the basic motive force of the Chinese revolution. Unless it is participated in and run by the proletariat, the Chinese revolution cannot possibly succeed.[137]

Elsewhere he asserted that "China cannot live without them [the working class], because they are the producers in the industrial sector of the economy. And the revolution cannot succeed without them, because it is the leader of the Chinese revolution and is the most revolutionary class."[138] The Chinese Revolution cannot therefore "do without the leadership of the Chinese proletariat."[139]

Nevertheless, Mao continued to regard extremely positively the contribution made by the peasants to the War of Resistance, and particularly the "poor peasants," deemed by Mao to be "the natural and most reliable ally of the proletariat, and the main contingent of China's revolutionary forces."[140] The "armed struggle in China is, in essence, peasant war," and "the resistance to Japan now going on is essentially peasant resistance." However, heavy reliance on the peasants did not signify ceding the leadership role to them; this would remain firmly in the hands of the working class and its political party, for it is a "peasant war under proletarian leadership."[141] Working class leadership remained essential as the environment within which the War of Resistance was being carried out; "that of the vast countryside" in which the peasants made up a "large proportion of Party membership," gave rise to all sorts of problems, particularly that of "individualism," which ran counter to the need for "proletarian collectivism."[142] Mao thus remained conscious, as he had been since the 1920s, of the failings of the peasantry as a class.

Looking to China's political future, Mao argued that "only under the leadership of the policies of the proletariat" could a democratic republic be completely realized. Increasing evidence of socialism in this republic would be "the growing relative weight of the proletariat and the Communist Party among the political forces of the whole country and the actual or possible recognition of the leadership of the proletariat and the Communist Party by the peasantry, the intellectuals, and the petty bourgeoisie."[143] Moreover, Mao predicted in his important "On Coalition Government" (1945) that the size of China's working class would dramatically increase as "tens of millions of peasants" moved to the cities to work in factories: "In order to build up powerful industries of her own and a large number of modernized big cities, China will have to undergo a process of transforming the rural inhabitants into urban inhabitants." This process—of "turning

China from an agricultural into an industrial country"—would be over-seen by the working class, "which is politically the most awakened and therefore the best qualified for leading the whole revolutionary move-ment."[144]

This view reflects his earlier stated opinion that "in the contradiction between the cities and the countryside, the city is dominant."[145] The im-portance of China's industrial cities meant that the largely rural context of China's resistance to Japan should not lead to an abandonment of resistance in the cities. As he pointed out in 1939,

> stressing the work in the rural base areas does not mean abandoning our work in the cities and in the other vast rural areas which have not become base areas; on the contrary, without the work in the cities and in these other rural areas, our own revolutionary base areas would be isolated and the revolution would suffer defeat. Moreover, the final objective of the revolution is the capture of the cities, the enemy's main bases, and this ob-jective cannot be achieved without necessary and adequate work in the cities.[146]

Similarly, in April 1944, he stated "we must . . . pay attention to work in the big cities . . . and raise the work in the cities to a position of equal importance with that in the base areas."[147] And in June 1944, Mao de-voted an entire Central Party directive to the importance of work in ur-ban areas.[148]

Conclusion

I have argued that from the early 1920s to the mid-1940s Mao continued to regard the industrial proletariat as the leading class of the Chinese Rev-olution and continued to regard the struggle in urban areas as highly sig-nificant. He recognized the serious negative effect that the forced separation from the urban struggle and the industrial proletariat was hav-ing on the capacity of the Communist Party to lead the rural struggle, for he recognized only too clearly the limitations of the peasants as a class and strove where possible to increase the representation of the urban working class in the Party and military, and particularly so in positions of authority, such as branch secretaries. Consequently, while Mao regarded the peas-antry as the main force of the Chinese Revolution and regarded the land question as the core focus of the Party's rural strategy, he never resiled from the view that the peasantry required the leadership of the working class and the Party that spoke in its name.

The significance of this argument is threefold. First, if it is accepted that Mao did indeed retain an unwavering belief in the necessity of working class leadership of China's revolution, including its rural revolution, it puts out of court entirely the suggestion of Schwartz and echoed in the commentaries of many other China scholars that "Mao demonstrated his readiness to turn his back on the industrial proletariat in the face of all theoretical considerations in order to take full advantage of the elemental forces which he found in the village."[149] The same is true of Meisner's suggestion that Mao "distrusted the revolutionary capacities of the urban proletariat" and perceived the peasantry as the "true revolutionary class."[150] The evidence I have presented from Mao's writings suggests that this view, so deeply entrenched in Western commentaries on Mao and his revolutionary strategy, is quite wrong. Mao did not elect to "go up to the mountains," nor did he choose to wage a revolutionary struggle so heavily based on the peasantry. These were not options that Mao willingly chose through some romantic attachment to the peasantry and rural life; indeed, they were not options at all. Mao was compelled, through sheer necessity, to avoid his own destruction and that of the rump of his Party in and around Wuhan in mid-1927, to beat a hasty retreat into the countryside. There is no evidence to suggest that in the absence of this compulsion Mao would have chosen the path he followed from mid-1927. In fact, the evidence for the opposite case is more compelling. As Mao stated, because the Guomindang insisted on fighting, "I had no choice but to go up to the Jinggangshan."[151] It is highly probable that had not Guomindang repression in 1927 made continued revolutionary activity in urban areas all but impossible, Mao would have chosen a path for the Chinese Revolution that more closely integrated its urban and rural dimensions and which allowed more effectively than ended being the case the leadership of the peasant revolution by the working class and the rural areas by the cities.

Mao's heavy reliance on the peasantry after 1927 was thus not something he willingly chose, but something he was compelled to accept given his forcible separation from the struggle in the urban areas. In these seemingly inauspicious surroundings, Mao formulated a strategy for revolution that drew on mass peasant participation and support but which made clear that the peasantry would not lead the revolution. While poor peasants did, as Mao noted on several occasions, possess the capacity for organization and leadership in the context of the rural revolution, their vision was limited and incapable of perceiving the longer-term historical objectives (an industrialized, modern socialist society) for which the revolution in China was being fought. Mao did not accept that the largely rural context in which he found himself would determine the revolution's ultimate objectives, which certainly did not correspond to those of the peasantry as a class. He consequently attempted where possible to promote the leadership of workers within the Party and its mass organizations, to encourage labor unions and to develop the struggle in urban areas, for the sociological and economic characteristics of the modern working class endowed it with organizational and leadership qualities that could be mobilized in pursuit of a revolution that had both modernizing and socialist objectives. It was these leadership qualities and ideology that made the members of the working class, in Mao's words, "particularly good fighters."[152]

Mao's views on the peasantry and its role in revolution cannot, therefore, be isolated from his views on the working class and its role in revolution. There was, in the development of Mao's revolutionary strategy, a necessary relationship between the two classes, and that relationship, contrary to the views of some Mao scholars, was invariably a relationship of subordination of the peasantry to the working class. The peasantry's subordination was not a function of its numerical inferiority, for clearly it represented a very large majority of both China's population and the ranks of China's revolutionary forces; nor was it a function of any hesitancy on its part for revolutionary violence. Rather, it was a function of its incapacity to lead a modernizing revolution and its limited understanding of the revolution's ultimate objectives.

Second, and leading from this point, a recognition of Mao's conviction of the necessity of working class leadership of China's revolution, of both its urban and rural dimensions, necessitates a parallel recognition of the modernizing dimension of Mao's vision for China, a recognition often withheld in commentaries on Mao's political activities and thought. Mao was no material incarnation of the fictitious Chinese peasant rebel Song Jiang; neither was he a rural revolutionary of the order of Mexico's Emiliano Zapata. As we noted at the outset of this chapter, the approach of the peasant revolutionary is characterized not only by reliance on the peasantry but by a pronounced tendency to glorify the peasants and the virtues of rural life. If they refer to urban dwellers at all, it is in pejorative terms, for the cities are held to be the origin of society's ills. They express the goals of revolution in essentially atavistic terms, seeking a restitution of the preexisting rights of the peasants in the face of dispossession of their land and exploitation by an often increasingly rapacious landlord class. The peasant revolutionary's vision is thus one premised on a desire for the restoration of a traditional order, or at least an imagined traditional order, in which fairness and justice are built on a recognition of the legitimate claims of the peasantry. What is absent from the peasant revolutionary's critique of society is any conception of a post-revolutionary society markedly different from this preexisting social order. The classes and class relations of a modern society are absent and so too is the industrialization capable of delivering a modern society.

Mao was, in contrast to peasant revolutionaries like Zapata, a modernizer, one who perceived the historical necessity, indeed inevitability, of an industrial and modern future for China. If Mao had been the romantic rural revolutionary depicted in many commentaries on his life and thought, why did he comment, in June 1930, that the socialization of agriculture could not be achieved without the "assistance and guidance of the workers in the cities?"[153] Why did he speak in 1945 of the need for China "to build up powerful industries of her own and a large number of modernizing big cities," of the need to turn China "from an agricultural into an industrial country," one in which large-scale industries "occupy an absolutely predominant position in [the] national economy?"[154] Why did he move so quickly, once the opportunity arose, to return to the city and to commence the push to industrialize China's economy?

Indeed, Mao's commitment to working class leadership of the peasants in the process of revolution anticipated the approach he would adopt on assuming national power. From early 1949, the CCP under Mao's direction turned its attention from revolutionary struggle based primarily in the countryside and premised on the support of China's peasants to the construction of a modern, industrialized nation-state directed politically and economically from the cities. As Mao commented in March 1949, "From 1927 to the present the centre of gravity of our work has been in the villages—gathering strength in the villages, using the villages in order to surround the cities and then taking the cities. The period for this method of work has now ended. The period of 'from the city to the village' and of the city leading the village has now begun."[155] Nowhere was this shift more apparent than in Mao's determination that the CCP expand its working class membership and reduce the proportion of peasants within its ranks.[156] A halt was called to indiscriminate recruitment of Party members and some "unusable peasant elements" were expelled.[157] Indeed, working class participation and leadership were now stressed across many dimensions of new China's political and economic life. This was in conformity with Mao's vision for China, central to which was modernization, a process to which industry and the working class were central. Mao also believed that the class composition of the Party had to be brought in line with the insistence of Marxism-Leninism that a communist party be the vanguard of the proletariat, led by and primarily for the working class. From this perspective, the very large numbers of peasants in the Party, while a reflection of the need for peasant support during its period of revolutionary struggle in the countryside, were an impediment to the Party's intention to create a socialist society with a modern industrialized economy. For this goal to be achieved, the industrial proletariat would be central not only to new China's economic efforts but to the class composition of its leadership as well.

Mao thus moved in 1949 to implement his long-held vision of a modern and industrialized society, one that placed the working class at center stage; he also moved to institute a revolutionary transformation of the lives and working conditions of China's millions of peasants, a transformation that few if any of his peasant followers might have anticipated or desired in the 1920s and 1930s. Yet the signs were there, as we have seen, for he never concealed his determination that revolution would lead to a modern, industrialized and socialist China, nor that the peasants and their conditions, particularly the property relations that had characterized peasant life in China for so long, would be overthrown to allow the establishment of a socialized form of agriculture. Without this necessary change, the peasants would, as Mao remarked on several occasions in the post-1949 period, "remain peasants," for they retained the peasants' ambivalence (or "dual nature," *liangmianxing*) toward socialism. His view of the peasants thus remained consistent.[158]

Third, recognition of Mao's persistent belief in the necessity of working class leadership of the Chinese Revolution can and should alter widely held conceptions of the Maoist model of revolution. This conception portrays Mao as an essentially agrarian revolutionary, one who willingly immersed himself in the countryside among the peasants, in whose revolutionary potential he held a boundless confidence and optimism, and one content to be separated from the cities with their baleful and corrupting influence. The revolution he led supposedly reflected this predilection for the peasantry and rural life, its ultimate success reinforcing the view that the Maoist model of revolution had to be centered in the countryside and focused on the peasants, endowed as they were with the capacities of organisation and leadership generated by bitter experience of rural oppression and exploitation. This is the popular conception. The evidence from Mao's own writings paints a very different picture. Not only did Mao not choose to "go up to the mountains" but he continually stressed, as we have seen, the importance of working class leadership of China's rural revolution and bewailed the deleterious effects that the over-representation of the peasants in the Party and military was having on those organisations. Mao emphasized the need to bring larger numbers of workers into the Party and military and to appoint them to positions of authority; he likewise stressed the importance of developing the revolutionary struggle in cities and large towns, and of linking the struggles in urban and rural areas.

Mao was thus not content to lead a purely rural revolution, and he strove where possible to alter the sociological composition of the Party and military in favor of the working class and during the period of the Jiangxi Soviet to construct its embryonic state institutions in ways that expressed the power of the working class. While he put great store in the peasants as the "main force" of the Chinese Revolution, he was adamant that it would not be their consciousness which dictated the long-term direction of the revolution, for this could only serve to reinforce economic, political, and cultural impediments to the modernist transformation of China's society. Mao's frequent references from the mid-1920s to the mid-1940s to the necessity of working class leadership of the Chinese Revolution are therefore signposts indicating not only his conception of the future course and strategy of the revolution but the future of China itself. These signposts are more than sufficient to problematize the conventional accounts of Mao's approach to China's revolution and the orthodoxy of that approach. It remains to be seen, however, whether those who have constructed the spurious image of Mao as peasant revolutionary will choose to notice them and rethink this central dimension of Mao's thought.

Notes

1. Stuart R. Schram, "Introduction" to Li Jui, *The Early Revolutionary Activities of Mao Tse-tung* (White Plains, New York: M. E. Sharpe, 1977), xxxvii. See also Stuart Schram, *The Thought of Mao Tse-tung* (Cambridge: Cambridge University Press, 1989), 35.

2. John Womack Jr., *Zapata and the Mexican Revolution* (Harmondsworth: Penguin, 1968), 541–45. See also Eric R. Wolf, *Peasant Wars of the Twentieth Century* (London: Faber and Faber, 1973), 31–32; and John Dunn, *Modern Revolutions: An Introduction to the Analysis of a Political Phenomenon* (Cambridge: Cambridge University Press, 1972), 58–59.

3. Womack Jr., *Zapata and the Mexican Revolution*, 541–45.

4. See Maurice Meisner, *Marxism, Maoism and Utopianism* (Madison: University of Wisconsin Press, 1982), 64, 65, 97, 99, 100, 152, 225. Also Maurice Meisner, *Mao's China and After: A History of the People's Republic* (New York: The Free Press, 1977, 1986), 44–47.

5. Isaac Deutscher, *Ironies of History* (London: Oxford University Press, 1966), 99. Emphasis in original.

6. Benjamin I. Schwartz, *Chinese Communism and the Rise of Mao* (Cambridge: Harvard University, 1951), 76–77.

7. Stuart R. Schram, "Mao Zedong and the Role of the Various Classes in the Chinese Revolution, 1923–1927," in *The Polity and Economy of China: the late Professor Yuji Muramatsu Commemoration Volume* (Tokyo: Tokyo Keizai Shinposha, 1975), 235–36.

8. Stuart R. Schram, *The Political Thought of Mao Tse-tung* (Harmondsworth: Penguin Books, 1969, revised edition), 59–60.

9. Nikita Khrushchev, *Khrushchev Remembers*, with an introduction, commentary, and notes by Edward Crankshaw (London: André Deutsch, 1971), 464–65.

10. Otto Braun, *A Comintern Agent in China, 1932–1939*, translated from the German by Jeanne Moore, with an introduction by Dick Wilson (St. Lucia, Queensland: University of Queensland Press, 1982).

11. Philip C. C. Huang, "Mao Tse-tung and the Middle Peasants, 1925–1928," *Modern China* 1, no. 3 (July 1975): 285.

12. See M. Henri Day, *Máo Zédōng, 1917–1927: Documents* (Stockholm: Skriftserien für Orientaliska Studier, no. 14, 1975), 242–51.

13. See Tony Saich (ed.), with a contribution by Benjamin Yang, *The Rise to Power of the Chinese Communist Power: Documents and Analysis* (Armonk, New York: M. E. Sharpe, 1996), esp. il–l, 281.

14. Justus M. Van der Kroef, "Lenin, Mao and Aidit," *China Quarterly* 10 (April–June 1962): 37.

15. Trevor Sudama, "Analysis of Classes by Mao Tse-tung, 1929–39," *Journal of Contemporary Asia* 8, no. 3 (1978): 361.

16. Day, *Máo Zédōng, 1917–1927: Documents* (Stockholm: Skriftserien für Orientaliska Studier) no. 14, 1975, 42. Schram argues that Mao's "rediscovery [of the peasants] had taken place in the summer and early autumn of 1925." See Stuart R. Schram, "Mao Tse-tung and Secret Societies," *China Quarterly* 27 (July–September 1966), 3. See also Mao's own testimony in Edgar Snow, *Red Star over China* (Harmondsworth: Penguin, 1972), 185–86. Here Mao says: "Formerly I had not fully realized the degree of class struggle among the peasantry, but after the 30 May Incident [1925], and during the great wave of political activity which followed it, the Hunanese peasantry became very militant." Mao is not, however, suggesting that he was prior to 1925 completely unaware of the problems or revolutionary potential of the peasantry; this is clear from his statements of 1923. Rather, the events of 1925 highlighted to Mao the extent of peasant militancy and the opportunities this offered.

17. Day, *Máo Zédōng, 1917–1927: Documents*, 245.

18. "Workers' period" is the title given to this period in Mao's thought by Schram. See Stuart Schram, "Mao Tse-tung's Thought to 1949," in *An Intellectual History of Modern China*, edited by Merle Goldman and Leo Ou-Fan Lee (Cambridge: Cambridge University Press, 2002), 283. For information on Mao's activities during this "workers' period," see Lynda Schaffer, *Mao and the Workers: The Hunan Labor Movement, 1920–1923* (Armonk, New York: M. E. Sharpe, 1982); also Schaffer's "Mao Zedong and the October 1922 Changsha Construction Workers' Strike: Marxism in Preindustrial China," *Modern China* 4, no. 4 (October 1978): 379–418.

19. Stuart R. Schram, ed., and Nancy J. Hodes, associate ed., *Mao's Road to Power: Revolutionary Writings 1912–1949: Volume II, National Revolution and Social Revolution, December 1920–June 1927* (Armonk, New York: M. E. Sharpe, 1994), 164.

20. Schram, ed., *Mao's Road to Power: Volume II*, xxxii. The Chinese text can be found in Zhonggong zhongyang wenxian yanjiu shibian, *Mao Zedong nianpu* [Chronology of Mao Zedong] (Beijing: Renmin chubanshe, Zhongyang wenxian chubanshe, 1993) Vol. 1, 114, note.

21. Schram ed., *Mao's Road to Power, Volume II*, 171.

22. Schram ed., *Mao's Road to Power, Volume II*, 257; Day, *Máo Zédōng, 1917–1927: Documents*, 296–97; Takeuchi Minoru, ed., *Mao Zedong Ji* [Collected Writings of Mao Zedong] (Tokyo: Hokubosha, 1970–72) I, 168–69.

23. Schram ed., *Mao's Road to Power, Volume II*, 237.

24. Schram ed., *Mao's Road to Power, Volume II*, 258–59; Takeuchi, ed., *Mao Zedong Ji* I, 170–71.

25. Meisner, *Marxism, Maoism and Utopia*, 58. Emphasis added.

26. Schram ed., *Mao's Road to Power, Volume II*, 358.

27. Schram ed., *Mao's Road to Power, Volume II*, 391–92.

28. Schram ed., *Mao's Road to Power, Volume II*,. 389. Emphasis added.

29. Schram, *The Thought of Mao Tse-tung*, 39. See also Schram, "Mao Zedong and the Role of the Various Classes in the Chinese Revolution, 1923–1927": 233.

30. Schram, *The Thought of Mao Tse-tung*, 40.

31. See Karl Wittfogel, "The Legend of 'Maoism'," *China Quarterly* 1 (January–March, 1960): 72–86, and no. 2 (April–June, 1960): 16–34; Benjamin Schwartz, "The Legend of the 'Legend of "Maoism"'," *China Quarterly* 2 (April–June 1960): 35–42; Benjamin I. Schwartz, *Chinese Communism and the Rise of Mao*, 73–78; and Arthur A. Cohen, *The Communism of Mao Tse-tung* (Chicago: University of Chicago Press, 1964), 47–50.

32. Schram, ed., *Mao's Road to Power, Volume II,* 509.

33. In this respect, this document mirrors Mao's other rural investigations. See Zhonggong zhongyang wenxian yanjiushi, *Mao Zedong nongcun diaocha wenji* [Collected rural investigations of Mao Zedong] (Beijing: Zhonggong zhongyang wenxian chubanshe, 1982). For a translation of the longest of these rural investigations, see Mao Zedong, *Report from Xunwu,* translated, with an introduction and notes, by Roger R. Thompson (Stanford: Stanford University Press, 1990).

34. Day, *Máo Zédōng, 1917–1927: Documents,* p. 322; Takenchi, ed., *Mao Zedong Ji* I, p. 193.

35. Schram, ed., *Mao's Road to Power, Volume II,* 419.

36. Roy Hoffheinz Jr. has concluded, in rather contradictory terms, that Mao's Hunan "Report" was "an utter fantasy," although not without "certain elements of reality." See his *The Broken Wave: The Chinese Communist Peasant Movement, 1922–1928* (Cambridge, Mass.: Harvard University Press, 1977), 35. The issue here is not so much whether Mao's perception of the peasant movement and its strength was true or not, but the way in which he evaluated the role of the peasants in the revolution and their capacity to operate autonomously from the working class in the prosecution of a modernizing revolution.

37. Schram, ed., *Mao's Road to Power, Volume II,* 430.

38. Schram, ed., *Mao's Road to Power, Volume II,* 439.

39. Schram, ed., *Mao's Road to Power, Volume II,* 433; Takeuchi, ed., *Mao Zedong Ji* I, 211–12.

40. Schram, ed., *Mao's Road to Power, Volume II,* 509.

41. Schram, ed., *Mao's Road to Power, Volume II,* 419.

42. Stuart R. Schram, ed., Nancy J. Hodes, associate ed., *Mao's Road to Power: Revolutionary Writings, 1912–1949: Volume III—From the Jinggangshan to the Establishment of the Jiangxi Soviets, July 1927—December 1930* (Armonk, New York: M. E. Sharpe, 1995), 11; see also 18.

43. Stuart R. Schram, ed., Nancy J. Hodes, associate ed., *Mao's Road to Power: Revolutionary Writings, 1912–1949: Volume VII, New Democracy, 1939–1941* (Armonk, New York: M. E. Sharpe, 2005), 153. Emphasis added.

44. Schram, ed., *Mao's Road to Power, Volume III,* 13. Emphasis added.

45. Schram, ed., *Mao's Road to Power, Volume III,* 71.

46. The title given this Draft Resolution in Mao's *Selected Works* is "Why is it that red political power can exist in China?" For the official version of this document, see *Selected Works of Mao Tse-tung* (Peking: Foreign Languages Press, 1965) I, 63–72.

47. Schram, ed., *Mao's Road to Power, Volume III*, 71–2.

48. Schram, ed., *Mao's Road to Power, Volume III*, 75.

49. Schram, ed., *Mao's Road to Power, Volume III*, 72–78.

50. Schram, ed., *Mao's Road to Power, Volume III*, 73–74.

51. Schram, ed., *Mao's Road to Power, Volume III*, 114.

52. Schram, ed., *Mao's Road to Power, Volume III*, 195.

53. Schram, ed., *Mao's Road to Power, Volume III*, 198.

54. Schram, ed., *Mao's Road to Power, Volume III*, 202.

55. Schram, ed., *Mao's Road to Power, Volume III*, 205.

56. Schram, ed., *Mao's Road to Power, Volume III*, 195.

57. Schram, ed., *Mao's Road to Power, Volume III*, 567.

58. Schram, ed., *Mao's Road to Power, Volume III*, 63.

59. Schram, ed., *Mao's Road to Power, Volume III*, 114.

60. Schram, ed., *Mao's Road to Power, Volume III*, 123.

61. Schram, ed., *Mao's Road to Power, Volume III*, 146. Translation modified. For the original, see Takeuchi Minoru, ed., *Mao Zedong Ji. Bujuan* [Supplement to the Collected Writings of Mao Zedong] (Tokyo: Sōsōsha, 1983–1986), Vol. 3, 21–25. The quoted section is from 24. For further analysis of Mao's use of the Chinese concept *datong* to describe China's future, see chapter 5.

62. Schram, ed., *Mao's Road to Power, Volume III*, 154. See also 241 where Mao repeats this point in his well-known letter to Lin Biao.

63. Schram, ed., *Mao's Road to Power, Volume III*, 156.

64. Schram, ed., *Mao's Road to Power, Volume III*, 158.

65. Schram, ed., *Mao's Road to Power, Volume III*, 171. It will be noted that there is a disparity in Mao's arithmetic here. The numbers add up to 1,330.

66. Schram, ed., *Mao's Road to Power, Volume III*, 187–88.

67. Schram, ed., *Mao's Road to Power, Volume III*, 236.

68. Schram, ed., *Mao's Road to Power, Volume III*, 565.

69. Schram, ed., *Mao's Road to Power, Volume III*, 423.

70. Schram, ed., *Mao's Road to Power, Volume III*, 583–84.

71. Schram, ed., *Mao's Road to Power, Volume III*, 583–84, 587.

72. For general analysis of the Jiangxi Soviet, see Trygve Lötviet, *Chinese Communism, 1931–1934: Experience in Civil Government* (Stockholm: Scandinavian Institute of Asian Studies Monograph Series, 1973); Ilpyong J. Kim, "Mass Mobilization Policies and Techniques Developed in the Period of the Chinese Soviet Republic," in *Chinese Communist Politics in Action*, ed. A. Doak Barnett (Seattle and London: University of Washington Press, 1969), 78–98; Ilpyong J. Kim, *The Politics of Chinese Communism:*

Kiangsi under the Soviets (Berkeley: University of California Press, 1973); W. E. Butler, ed., *The Legal System of the Chinese Soviet Republic, 1931–1934* (Dobbs Ferry NY: Transnational Publishers 1983); Tso-Liang Hsiao, *Power Relations within the Chinese Communist Movement, 1930–1934: A Study of Documents* (Seattle: University of Washington Press, 1961); John E. Rue, *Mao Tse-tung in Opposition, 1927–1935* (Stanford: Stanford University Press, 1966); Warren Kuo, *Analytical History of the Chinese Communist Party* (Taipei: Institute of International Relations, 1968, second edition), Volume 2; Robert C. North, *Moscow and Chinese Communists* (Stanford: Stanford University Press, 1963, second edition), 147–60; and Derek J. Waller, *The Kiangsi Soviet Republic: Mao and the National Congresses of 1931 and 1934* (Berkeley: Center for China Studies, University of California, 1973).

73. Stuart R. Schram, ed., Nancy J. Hodes, associate ed., *Mao's Road to Power: Revolutionary Writings, 1912–1949: Volume IV—The Rise and Fall of the Chinese Soviet Republic* (Armonk, New York: M. E. Sharpe, 1997), 466.

74. Ilpyong J. Kim, *The Politics of Chinese Communism: Kiangsi under the Soviets*, 6.

75. Rue, *Mao Tse-tung in Opposition*.

76. Schram, ed., *Mao's Road to Power, Volume IV*, xxxiii–xxxiv.

77. Schram, ed., *Mao's Road to Power, Volume IV*, xlv.

78. Schram, ed., *Mao's Road to Power, Volume IV*, xlviii–xlix. See also Stuart R. Schram, *Mao Tse-tung* (Harmondsworth: Penguin, 1966), 154–55.

79. Richard C. Thornton, *China, The Struggle for Power, 1917–1972* (Bloomington and London: Indiana University Press, 1973), 56.

80. Kim, "Mass Mobilization Policies and Techniques," 80.

81. The phrase is Thornton's. See *China, the Struggle for Power*, 55.

82. Schram, ed., *Mao's Road to Power, Volume IV*, lxxv.

83. Thornton, *China, the Struggle for Power*, 54.

84. Hélène Carrère d'Encausse and Stuart R. Schram, *Marxism and Asia: An Introduction with Readings* (London: Allen Lane The Penguin Press, 1969), 244–47.

85. Lötviet has argued that the conventional translation of *xiang* as "township" is misleading, as the *xiang* did not necessarily conform to a township or individual village. See his *Chinese Communism, 1931–1934: Experience in Civil Government*, 15n. See also Waller, *The Kiangsi Soviet Republic*, 37–41.

86. Lötviet, *Chinese Communism, 1931–1934: Experience in Civil Government*, chapter 1.

87. In rural areas, "As a rule they [workers] have no land or farm implements at all, though some do own a small portion of their land and farm

implements. They make their living wholly or primarily by selling their labor power. Such persons are workers (including farm laborers). . . . If a family member works in the city, he is a worker." Schram, ed., *Mao's Road to Power, Volume IV*, 548. In his "Investigation of Changang Township" (November 1933), Mao referred to the following occupations as "workers": carpenters, tailors, bricklayers, bamboo products handicraft workers, barbers, and casual laborers. Schram, ed., *Mao's Road to Power, Volume IV*, 619.

88. Lötviet, *Chinese Communism, 1931–1934: Experience in Civil Government*, 27.

89. Schram, ed., *Mao's Road to Power, Volume IV*, 179–80.

90. Information drawn from Lötviet, *Chinese Communism, 1931–1934: Experience in Civil Government*, chapters 1 and 2; Schram, ed., *Mao's Road to Power, Volume IV*, 179–81, 797–98; Takeuchi, ed., *Mao Zedong ji. Bujuan*, vol. 4, 21–23.

91. Schram, ed., *Mao's Road to Power, Volume IV*, 797–98.

92. Schram, ed., *Mao's Road to Power, Volume IV*, 871.

93. Schram, ed., *Mao's Road to Power, Volume IV*, 671–73; Takeuchi, ed., *Mao Zedong Ji* IV, 235–36.

94. Lötviet, *Chinese Communism, 1931–1934: Experience in Civil Government*, 47, note 3.

95. Schram, ed., *Mao's Road to Power, Volume IV*, 476.

96. Schram, ed., *Mao's Road to Power, Volume IV*, 483.

97. Schram, ed., *Mao's Road to Power, Volume IV*, 455.

98. Schram, ed., *Mao's Road to Power, Volume IV*, 455.

99. Kim, *The Politics of Chinese Communism: Kiangsi under the Soviets*, 135–43.

100. Schram, ed., *Mao's Road to Power, Volume IV*, 455.

101. Schram, ed., *Mao's Road to Power, Volume IV*, 396.

102. Schram, ed., *Mao's Road to Power, Volume IV*, 512–13.

103. Schram, ed., *Mao's Road to Power, Volume IV*, 396.

104. Schram, ed., *Mao's Road to Power, Volume IV*, 525.

105. Schram, ed., *Mao's Road to Power, Volume IV*, 438–39. Translation modified.

106. Schram, ed., *Mao's Road to Power, Volume IV*, 455.

107. Schram, ed., *Mao's Road to Power, Volume IV*, 333.

108. Schram, ed., *Mao's Road to Power, Volume IV*, 66.

109. For a translation of the full text of this law, see Schram, ed., *Mao's Road to Power, Volume IV*, 882–96. Waller's conclusion is that this law remained "purely at the level of propaganda" because it could not be implemented in a backward economic area made up largely of peasants, and in

which the only workers were handicraft workers and artisans. However, the data presented by Mao suggests that Waller's conclusion is misleading. See Waller, *The Kiangsi Soviet Republic*, 33.

110. Schram, ed., *Mao's Road to Power, Volume IV*, 188.

111. Schram, ed., *Mao's Road to Power, Volume IV*, 490.

112. Schram, ed., *Mao's Road to Power, Volume IV*, 679.

113. Schram, ed., *Mao's Road to Power, Volume IV*, 680.

114. Schram, ed., *Mao's Road to Power, Volume IV*, 584–622.

115. Schram, ed., *Mao's Road to Power, Volume IV*, 684.

116. Schram, ed., *Mao's Road to Power, Volume IV*, 684.

117. Schram, ed., *Mao's Road to Power, Volume IV*, 269.

118. Schram, ed., *Mao's Road to Power, Volume IV*, 272–73.

119. Schram, ed., *Mao's Road to Power, Volume IV*, 670.

120. Schram, ed., *Mao's Road to Power, Volume IV*, 704.

121. Schram, ed., *Mao's Road to Power, Volume IV*, 111–12.

122. Schram, ed., *Mao's Road to Power, Volume IV*, 333.

123. Schram, ed., *Mao's Road to Power, Volume IV*, 415.

124. Schram, ed., *Mao's Road to Power, Volume IV*, 455.

125. For Mao's discussion of the concept of the "principal contradiction" and its role in prioritizing policies, see Nick Knight, ed., *Mao Zedong on Dialectical Materialism: Writings on Philosophy, 1937* (Armonk, New York: M.E. Sharpe, 1990), pp. 178–87.

126. See for example Stuart R. Schram, ed., Nancy J. Hodes, associate ed., *Mao's Road to Power—Revolutionary Writings, 1912–1949: Volume VII—New Democracy, 1939–1941* (Armonk, New York: M. E. Sharpe, 2005), 731.

127. Schram, ed., *Mao's Road to Power: Volume VII*, 579–80.

128. Schram, ed., *Mao's Road to Power: Volume VII*, 386, 396.

129. Mao informed Edgar Snow: "We are always social revolutionaries; we are never reformists." Schram, ed., *Mao's Road to Power: Volume VII*, 218–19.

130. Schram, ed., *Mao's Road to Power: Volume VII*, 67, 71.

131. Stuart R. Schram, ed., Nancy J. Hodes, associate ed., *Mao's Road to Power—Revolutionary Writings, 1912–1949: Volume VI—The New Stage, August 1937–1938* (Armonk, New York: M. E. Sharpe, 2004), 735–36; see also 648.

132. Schram, ed., *Mao's Road to Power: Volume VII*, 862.

133. Schram, ed., *Mao's Road to Power: Volume VII*, 153.

134. Schram, ed., *Mao's Road to Power: Volume VII*, 299.

135. Schram, ed., *Mao's Road to Power: Volume VII*, 355.

136. Schram, ed., *Mao's Road to Power: Volume VII*, 299–300.

137. Schram, ed., *Mao's Road to Power: Volume VII*, 299–300. See also 284.

138. Schram, ed., *Mao's Road to Power: Volume VII*, 355.

139. Schram, ed., *Mao's Road to Power: Volume VII*, 366.

140. Schram, ed., *Mao's Road to Power: Volume VII*, 299.

141. Schram, ed., *Mao's Road to Power: Volume VII*, 246, 250. See also 355.

142. Schram, ed., *Mao's Road to Power: Volume VII*, 766–67.

143. Schram, ed., *Mao's Road to Power: Volume VII*, 304–5.

144. *Selected Works of Mao Tse-tung* (London: Lawrence and Wishart, 1956), vol. 4, 294–98.

145. Schram, ed., *Mao's Road to Power: Volume VI*, 736.

146. Schram, ed., *Mao's Road to Power: Volume VII*, 291–92. See also *Selected Works of Mao Tse-tung* (Beijing: FLP, 1965), vol. 2, 317.

147. *Selected Works of Mao Tse-tung*, vol. 3, 171.

148. Takeuchi, ed., *Mao Zedong ji, Bujuan*, vol. 7, 185–93. For a translation, see Saich, *The Rise to Power of the Chinese Communist Party: Documents and Analysis* (Armonk, New York: M. E. Sharpe, 1996), 1157–64.

149. Schwartz, *Chinese Communism and the Rise of Mao*, 76–77.

150. Meisner, *Marxism, Maoism and Utopianism*, 99, 138, 225.

151. Schram, ed., *Mao's Road to Power: Volume VII*, 153.

152. Schram, ed., *Mao's Road to Power: Volume II*, 258–59.

153. Schram, ed., *Mao's Road to Power: Volume III*, 447–48.

154. *Selected Works of Mao Tse-tung* (London: Lawrence and Wishart, 1956), vol. 4, 295, 298.

155. "Report to the Second Plenary Session of the Seventh Central Committee of the Communist Party of China" (5 March 1949), in *Selected Works of Mao Tse-tung* IV, 363.

156. *Selected Works of Mao Tse-tung* IV, 364. "On whom should we rely in our struggle in the cities? . . . We must whole-heartedly rely on the working class."

157. Franz Schurmann, *Ideology and Organization in Communist China* (Berkeley: University of California Press, 1971, second edition), 167–69.

158. See *Mao Zedong sixiang wansui* [Long live the thought of Mao Zedong] (n.p.: n.p. 1967), 12, 27; also *Mao Zedong sixiang wansui* [Long live the thought of Mao Zedong] (n.p.: n.p., 1969), 247. Mao also continued to regard China's peasants as a major problem for the achievement of socialism in China: "The serious problem is the education of the peasantry. The peasant economy is scattered, and the socialisation of agriculture, judging by the Soviet Union's experience, will require a long long time and painstaking work." *Selected Works of Mao Tse-tung* IV, 418–19.

Politics and Vision: Historical Time and the Future in Mao Zedong's Thought, 1937–1945

ONE OF THE ISSUES which has most exercised interpreters of Mao Zedong is the problem of the origins of his thought. Three identifiable responses can be discerned. In the first of these, Mao's thought is perceived as a synthesis of traditional Chinese thought and Marxism, the two major intellectual traditions to which he was exposed.[1] In the second, Mao is regarded as a Marxist, and his thought is therefore to be understood by reference to concepts which derive from the Marxist tradition.[2] And in the third, the determinants of Mao's thought are sought in the Chinese historical and philosophical tradition and its political culture through which this tradition is transmitted via the powerful agency of socialization.[3]

Most Mao scholars have adopted the first of these explanations of the origins of Mao's thought, although there remains strong disagreement in such synthetic interpretations as to the relative influence of the Chinese and Marxist traditions. John Koller, for example, sees in Mao's thought something more than a simple combination of themes within these two traditions; it is rather a "creative synthesis":

> Maoist thought represents a creative novelty that clearly reveals it to be something more than Marxism transplanted to Chinese soil, or traditional Chinese thought revised by putting it in new Marxist containers. On the other hand, it clearly has its roots in both these earlier ideologies, and in fact its uniqueness results from a creative synthesis of traditional Chinese thought and Marxist-Leninist ideology.[4]

In contrast, while the influential Mao scholar Stuart Schram concedes that Mao drew inspiration from and was influenced by both Chinese and

Marxist traditions, he makes it abundantly clear that the Chinese element of Mao's thought was predominant in its influence.

> I have suggested that both Chinese and Western components play a signifi-
> cant role in Mao Tse-tung's patterns of thought and behaviour. The question
> naturally arises: where are the deepest springs of his conduct? . . . Indeed, it
> could be argued that, if the categories in which he reasons are basically Marx-
> ist, Mao Tse-tung's deepest emotional tie is still to the Chinese nation; and if
> he is bent on transforming society and economy in the shortest possible time,
> in order to turn her into a powerful modern nation, it is above all in order
> that she may once more assume that rank in the world which he regards as
> rightfully hers. In this sense, Mao has "sinified" Marxism indeed.[5]

The view articulated here, that Mao's "deepest emotional tie is to the Chinese nation," has permeated Stuart Schram's voluminous writings and has constituted the basis for his belief that Mao's thought, including his inter-pretation of Marxism and its "sinification," was underpinned by the Chinese cultural tradition and contemporary Chinese realities. Mao consequently transformed the "very substance" of Marxism, a "Western" body of thought, to "adapt it to Chinese conditions."[6] Because Marxism was a mode of thought alien to Chinese realities and tradition, it required adaptation, a cul-tural laundering as it were, before it could be successfully applied to the Chi-nese context.[7] While Schram does recognize the influence of the Marxist tradition on Mao's thought, the much more powerful influence was "China," and this rendered his "Marxism" heterodox, an exotic offshoot of orthodox European Marxism. Moreover, Schram suggests that Mao's adherence to Marxism weakened over time, and that in the early 1960s his affinity with Buddhist and Daoist dialectics became more pronounced.[8]

The issue of the origins of Mao's thought is thus a contentious one, and even amongst scholars recognizing the influence of both the Chinese and Marxist traditions there is little agreement. As different Mao scholars mobi-lize different theoretical assumptions to read the Mao texts and other sources of evidence, their substantive interpretations inevitably differ (see chapters 2 and 3).[9] For the Mao scholar who commences from the premise that Mao's thought was formed by and inextricably interwoven with traditional pat-terns of Chinese thought, abundant textual evidence can be found in the Mao texts to validate that position. Mao's writings are liberally sprinkled with references to the Chinese classics, proverbs, and popular modes of speech and to contemporary Chinese "realities." By the same token, the Mao texts also contain numerous references to concepts (such as class strug-gle and revolution) clearly deriving from the Marxist tradition. Where Mao scholars place their emphasis, and which "evidence" they extract from the

Mao texts, depends entirely on their presuppositions and particular approach to reading. No definitive reading of the Mao texts is possible.

The analysis which follows does not commence, therefore, from any intention to achieve closure of the debate concerning the origins of Mao Zedong's thought, for this is an unattainable goal. This exploration in Mao Zedong's thought is premised rather on the assumption that a fresh perspective on this foundational issue may be obtained through consideration of the possibility that the origins of Mao's thought varied according to both theme and period. In other words, that it is not possible to generalize about the origins of Mao's thought and that more specific attention to specific themes and their intellectual antecedents is required in the attempt to unravel the problem of Mao's thought and its sources. The theme chosen for analysis in this chapter is Mao's conception of historical time and the future. I analyze the period of the Anti-Japanese War (1937–1945), during which the Communist capital was at Yan'an (and for this reason often called the Yan'an Period). Investigation of this theme during this period is instructive in attempting to unravel the various influences on Mao's thought, from both the Chinese and Marxist traditions. However, it is instructive for a number of other reasons.

First, there is a common misconception that Mao was at his most pragmatic and least utopian during the period of the Anti-Japanese War. The exigencies of the wartime situation, it is suggested, demanded a level-headed recognition of the constraints imposed by objective reality; it was because Mao's thought was so lucidly attuned to these constraints and so little pervaded by utopianism that he was able to lead the Chinese Communist Party (CCP) to eventual victory.[10] The following analysis challenges this view, arguing that there was a very strong utopian dimension to Mao's thought during this period.[11] His thought exhibited the eschatological impulses of an imminent expectation of the final historical era of peace and harmony, characteristically generated by the chaos and violence of large-scale war and political upheaval, and these impulses drew inspiration from and were articulated in terms of utopian themes in both the Chinese and Marxist traditions.

Second, the political strategy of a revolutionary such as Mao depends for its rationality and coherence on a conception of a desired historical future towards which that strategy must be oriented. This historical future exercises a powerful influence on the political actions of the present, for it supplies the criteria by which success of a particular political or military strategy can be evaluated: Does it bring the realization of the future closer? Does it set its realization back? Analysis of Mao's conception of historical time and the future thus contributes to a comprehension of the objectives that inspired his political activity during the crucial years of his rise to power.

Third, the periodization of historical time is a major theoretical problem of great political consequence for Marxism, for no strategy implemented in its name could be deemed appropriate in isolation from the definition and analysis of the contemporary stage which history has reached. Mao's analysis of China during the Yan'an period consequently necessitated a response to the problem of the periodization of historical time within Marxist theory. As we will observe, however, his largely Leninist periodization of contemporary Chinese history and its future was clouded by a periodization drawn from the Chinese tradition. Both the Marxist and Chinese traditions nevertheless contributed to Mao's future-oriented utopian expectation that history would deliver its promise of a communist era of perpetual peace and harmony. However, the rival influences of the Chinese and Marxist traditions during the Yan'an period were to result not in a "creative synthesis," as Koller suggests, but in an uneasy tension between two temporal perspectives whose differences could not readily be reconciled, and Mao was not to satisfactorily reconcile them during the Yan'an period. In the post-1949 period, this tension was to be resolved in favor of Marxism, although, as we will observe in chapter 9, the utopianism of this intellectual tradition was itself to be a declining influence on Mao's thought. By the time the Cultural Revolution erupted in 1966, utopianism of whatever source had largely disappeared from Mao's thought, leaving in its place a bleak vision of the future characterized by unremitting struggle and, eventually, extinction of the human race.

To set this analysis in the context of the countervailing influences on Mao's thought, we commence with a necessarily brief reconstruction of historical time and the future in the Chinese and Marxist intellectual traditions. Where had history come from; where was it going; how would it get there? These were the questions for which Mao sought answers. Rather than gaining a unified view of history and its temporal progression, the rival intellectual traditions at whose confluence he stood provided him conflicting answers. Nevertheless, both traditions stressed the overriding importance of the past to present and future, and this appealed to a revolutionary whose sense of historic continuity was, in the words of one with whom Mao spoke of such issues, to give "depth to his ideas and policies."[12]

Historical Time and the Future in the Chinese Tradition

Historical consciousness necessitates a sensitivity to time, for temporality is the dimension which permits the emergence, development, and decay of humans and the societies to which they belong. Paradoxically, however, the concept of time is itself contingent upon the definition humans give it, for time is not a physical entity immediately perceptible to the senses. Human consciousness of it derives from apparent change and flux and their repetition in the external environment. Moreover, when time is considered historically, its span may well exceed that of a single human generation and may extend beyond millennia. The criteria for comprehending the manner and direction in which time "flows" across vast temporal reaches and for dividing that "flow" into historically discrete periods have thus understandably varied widely.

The traditional Chinese conception of time took as its basis the cycle of natural change through the seasons and the regular motions of the celestial bodies.[13] When applied to human history, the cyclical conception of time appeared reinforced by the Chinese dynastic cycle, passing as it did through periods of growth, maturity, and decay like any other life cycle as one ruling dynasty replaced another in an apparently unending sequence. This cyclical conception of history appeared in various forms in traditional Chinese historical writing. Xun Zi, for example, perceived history as a series of circles passing repeatedly through the same or similar points, while Si-ma Qian perceived patterns of history as being constantly repeated but not necessarily returning to the temporal point of origin.[14] One consequence of such cyclical conceptions of history was the marked tendency in Chinese historiography toward temporal transcendency, the inclination to regard historical lessons as not limited temporally or circumscribed by the particular conditions of the era in which they occurred. Consequently, the "praise and blame" characteristic of Chinese historical writing could seek out and employ salutary examples of proper and improper conduct with no regard for the specific and differentiating characteristics of the period concerned. This tendency toward temporal transcendency is clearly evident in the historical writings of Si-ma Qian,[15] the early medieval Confucianist Xun Yue,[16] Liu Zhiji and Si-ma Guang,[17] as well as the great Qing historian Zhang Xuecheng.[18]

Another very significant consequence of such cyclical conceptions of historical time was a radically diminished perception of cosmic progress. Until the introduction of Buddhism to China, traditional Chinese conceptions of time did not, by and large, incorporate the assumption that the cosmos and humankind's position within it were necessarily heading in any given direction or were improving.[19] This relative lack of any sense of progress was also a function of the Chinese belief in the existence of a legendary golden age of the distant past to which all succeeding dynasties were necessarily inferior;[20] indeed there is a pronounced tendency in Chinese historical writing to regard history as a decline from the moral excellence of this earlier time.[21] Both of these tendencies are in turn related to the comparative absence of utopian thought in Chinese historical writing to which Laurence Thompson has drawn attention.[22] For if, as Nathan Sivin points out, "there was no reason to limit the world's extension into the future,"[23] the formulation of an ideal society as the end product of human history was much less likely to arise than in the Judaic and Christian traditions with their strongly eschatological themes.

However, while it may be true that utopian thought appears to have constituted a relatively minor theme within Chinese historical writing,[24] it is of more than passing interest in the context of analysis of Mao's thought, for during the Yan'an period such utopian themes exerted a considerable influence on his conception of historical time and the future.

Utopian thought probably did, as Timoteus Pokora has argued, constitute an important though largely unrecorded theme in the ideologies inspiring peasant uprisings throughout China's history.[25] Within this theme, the concepts *tai ping* (universal peace), *da tong* (great harmony), and *san shi* (the three ages), which have undoubtedly utopian connotations, have ancient heritage and can be traced back to the famous passage describing *da tong* in the *Li Yun* section of the *Li Ji* (Book of Rites).[26] This passage is relevant to our discussion of Mao's position on historical time and the future during the Yan'an period, and runs as follows:

> When the Great Doctrine prevails, all under heaven will work for the common good. The virtuous will be elected to office, and the able given responsibility. Faithfulness will be in constant practice and harmony will rule. Consequently mankind will not only love their own parents and give care to their own children. All the aged will be provided for, and all the young employed in work. Infants will be fathered; widows and widowers, the fatherless and the unmarried, the disabled and the sick will all be cared for. The men will have their rights and the women their home. No goods will go to waste, nor need they be stocked for private possession. No energy should be retained in one's own body, nor used for personal gain. Self-interest ceases, and thieving and disorders are not known. Therefore the gates of the houses are never closed. This state is called the Great Commonwealth (*da tong*).[27]

Liang Qichao's interpretation of this passage suggests that the realization of a society based on *da tong* is contingent less on the passage of time than on the manifestation and development to the maximum degree of *ren*

or "fellow-feeling" within each individual; such a society was therefore imminently realizable given this condition.[28] However, other influential Chinese interpretations of this passage have generally connected the realization
of such a society with a conception of history in which time flows across
three periods, with very different characteristics and in which a society of
da tong constitutes the final period. In the *Li Ji* itself, history is portrayed as
constituted of three ages: the first a world of "disorder," the second a world
of "small tranquillity" and the third a world of "great unity." A tripartite periodization of history also emerges in adumbrated form in Dong Zhong-
shu's interpretation of Confucianism and in the *Gong Yang* commentary on
the *Qun Qiu* (Spring and Autumn Annals). However, it was a commentary
by He Xiu (129–182 A.D.) on this *Gong Yang* commentary in which the
concept of the "three ages" (*san shi*) is most clearly delineated and the third
age most explicitly equated with the notion of *tai ping* (universal peace).[29]
In He Xiu's conception of historical time, these three ages are characterized by a movement of society from an age of "decay and disorder"
through a period of "approaching peace" to an era of "universal peace."[30]

The concept of the "three ages" was also later to emerge in the historical writing of Wang Fuzhi (1619–1693 A.D.), the Hunanese philosopher
and historian with whose work Mao Zedong was familiar.[31] In Wang's periodization, however, the utopian element is less clearly drawn than in He
Xiu's commentary.[32] Indeed, it was not until the modern era that a systematic utopian exposition of historical time was to appear in the form of
Kang Youwei's *Da Tong Shu*, which sets out in surprising detail a society
founded on the basis of *da tong* as this had been adumbrated in the *Li Ji*.
Pokora argues that as well as being influenced by the Taiping millenarian
doctrine of the mid-nineteenth century, Kang Youwei largely based his
utopian exposition on the *Gong Yang* school, which had integrated the notion of the third age of history with the concept of "universal peace."[33]
Kang's conception of a world premised on *da tong* also drew on Western
evolutionary theories as well as on the more explicit eschatological impulses of Chinese Buddhist philosophy.[34]

Kang's utopianism is of some relevance for our analysis of Mao's conception of historical time and the future, for there is evidence to suggest
that he was during the Yan'an period influenced by certain of the ideas
contained in the *Da Tong Shu*. As we will see, the utopian concepts *da tong*
(great harmony), *san shi* (the three ages), and *tai ping* (universal peace)
emerge as important themes in Mao's perspective on historical time and the
future. We know that during his formative years Mao had been an admirer
of Kang[35] and that he referred to the concept of *da tong* in marginal notes

he made (1917–1918) to Friedrich Paulsen's *A System of Ethics.*[36] Moreover, Kang's *Da Tong Shu* was widely available by the early Yan'an period; its first two sections had been published in the magazine *Buren zazhi* (Compassion) in 1913, and the entire book was published in 1935.[37] The fact that intellectuals close to Mao, especially Chen Boda, were referring to it in the mid 1930s increases the likelihood that Mao was familiar with Kang's book,[38] and he subsequently referred to it in his important speech of 1949 entitled "On the People's Democratic Dictatorship."[39]

The appearance of a tripartite historical periodization in Mao's thought linked to the concept of *da tong* suggests that he did draw during the Yan'an period on the utopian theme in traditional Chinese historical writing to express the eschatological sentiments fueled in him by the contemporary war-induced context of violence and chaos. We will examine how this theme emerged in Mao's writings and also examine the logical problems this periodization of history created when used in conjunction with the other periodization strongly present in his thought at the time, that which drew on the Marxist theory of history.

Historical Time and the Future in the Marxist Tradition

In the Western intellectual tradition, the notion of historical time has frequently and from early times incorporated utopian or eschatological visions of the future. Indeed, the prophets of the Old Testament can be attributed with introducing the dimension of the future into human thought, this being related to an eschatological belief which perceived the future as bringing a more radical participation by God in human affairs.[40] In general, however, Western conceptions of historical time have tended to cluster around two basic viewpoints: that of time moving in cycles and that of a rectilinear flow of time providing for unrepeatability of historic occurrences. The pre-Christian Greek philosophers were by and large exponents of the former view, perceiving history as moving in a cyclical pattern in which society passed continually through a process of degeneration and regeneration. Polybius, for example, maintained that it was possible to perceive a cycle in the types of constitution adopted by different societies, and in the *Croesus,* Herodotus was to assert unequivocally the cyclical nature of the historical process: "If you have understood that you are a man and that you reign over men, be aware that human affairs follow a cycle, the circular movement of which doesn't allow the same people to remain always prosperous."[41]

Another influential exponent of the cyclical theory of history was the Italian philosopher Giambattista Vico (1668–1744 A.D.), who perceived society progressing through a cycle of growth and decay. Vico saw demonstration of his theory in the similarities of the phases through which Western civilization and the antecedent Greco-Roman civilization had passed. Interestingly, Vico's cyclical theory was to have a significant influence on the ideas of Auguste Comte (1798–1857 A.D.), who established a tripartite periodization of history on its basis. In contrast to Chinese conceptions of the three ages, Comte's "law of the three stages" took human intellectual development as the criterion for temporal demarcation rather than the level of chaos or peace.[42] It is also interesting that Comte's is not the only Western theory of historical time which viewed history as passing through three stages. In the twelfth century, the Christian mystic Joachim of Fiore (c. 1130–1201 A.D.) had talked of the three ages as those of the Father, Son, and Holy Spirit.[43] Joachim's philosophy of history was, however, predicated on the flow of time being rectilinear rather than cyclical. This rectilinear conception of historical time, characteristic of much Western religious thought, had found its greatest protagonist in the person of St. Augustine, who explicitly repudiated the cyclical conception of history of the Greek philosophers. For Augustine, the cyclical conception precluded any real novelty of historical occurrence, and yet certain events in human history (particularly the birth of Christ) were, by their very nature, unique and unrepeatable. Consequently, he argued that time must flow in a rectilinear fashion, developing in a straight line from the creation of man, through the fall from grace, to the final judgment at which would occur the ultimate consummation of God's purpose on earth.[44]

Marx's conception of historical time and the future bears some similarity to the Augustinian teleology in that it is firmly rooted in the belief that there is a goal to humankind's passage through time. However, Marx's position cannot readily be characterized as either rectilinear or cyclical. For Marx, historical time derived its direction, periodization, and goal from developments internal to society; the temporal dimension of historical development was necessarily socially contingent. Society progressed through certain historical epochs characterized by different and successively technologically superior modes of production and distinct patterns of social relations. Temporal progression thus involved a periodization founded on both the degree of complexity of the instruments of labor and the nature of social relations and practices.

However, while it is widely accepted that Marx's philosophy of history incorporated the belief that there is a necessary progression of society through different modes of production, it is not universally accepted that he insisted on a fixed order of these stages. Eric Hobsbawm, for example, has argued that "the general theory of historical materialism requires only that there should be a succession of modes of production, though not necessarily any particular modes, and perhaps not in any particular predetermined order."[45] Indeed, a close reading of Marx's writings suggests that he did not perceive in history a fixed and undeviating series of stages, of modes of production, through which all societies must progress.[46] Marx's analysis of Russian society is a case in point, for he did not insist that Russia would necessarily follow the same pattern of historical development as the already industrialized capitalist societies of neighboring Europe. To the contrary, his analysis revealed a dualism within the form of land ownership of the Russian village community (land held in common but farmed separately) that suggested the possibility that the collective element might prevail over private forms of ownership; Russia might thus avoid a capitalist future. "Everything depends," Marx wrote in a letter to Vera Zasulich (1881), "on the historical environment in which it occurs."[47] Similarly, in a letter to the Russian journal *Otechestvenniye Zapiski* (1877), Marx took issue with a critic who had perceived in his analysis of the history of Western Europe a schema for historical development of universal applicability:

> The chapter on primitive accumulation does not pretend to do more than trace the path by which, in Western Europe, the capitalist order of economy emerged from the womb of the feudal order of economy.
>
> But that is too little for my critic. He feels he absolutely must metamorphose my historical sketch of the genesis of capitalism in Western Europe into a historico-philosophical theory of the general path every people is fated to tread, whatever the historical circumstances in which it finds itself, in order that it may ultimately arrive at the form of economy which ensures, together with the greatest expansion of the productive powers of social labour, the most complete development of man. But I beg his pardon. He is both honouring and shaming me too much . . . events strikingly analogous but taking place in different historical surroundings (have) led to totally different results. By studying each of these forms of evolution separately and then comparing them one can easily find the clue to this phenomenon, but one will never arrive there by using as one's master key a general historico-philosophical theory, the supreme virtue of which consists in being superhistorical.[48]

However, despite Marx's denial of authorship of a "general historico-philosophical theory," it remains true that many of his followers perceived in Marxism just such a theory. The Bolsheviks under Lenin, for example, employed a perception of historical development which incorporated a largely unilinear progression of all societies through five fixed stages. Lenin had come to the conclusion very early in his revolutionary career that Russia was not, as some of his Menshevik opponents claimed, an Asiatic mode of production; such an admission would have threatened the possibility that Russia might give rise to a socialist revolution in the near future and would have added credence to the Menshevik counsel that patience and restraint were essential during the lengthy maturation of Russia's productive forces. Lenin therefore insisted that Russia had, during the latter half of the nineteenth century, transformed itself from a largely feudal society into one in which forms of production and class relationship were increasingly capitalist.[49] Russian society, despite its specific characteristics, could be accommodated within the orthodox Marxist schema of historical development. Lenin's rather uncritical espousal of this orthodox five-stage schema emerges in a lecture delivered at Sverdlov University in 1919:

> The development of all human societies for thousands of years, in all countries *without exception,* reveals a general conformity to law, a regularity and consistency in this development; so that at first we had a society without classes—the original patriarchal, primitive society, in which there was no aristocrats; then we had a society based on slavery—a slaveowning society. . . . This form was followed in history by another—feudalism. . . . Further, with the development of trade, the appearance of the world market and the development of money circulation, a new class arose within feudal society—the capitalist class.[50]

The historical development of all societies was thus characterized by progression through fixed stages. This orthodox view was to congeal into dogma with Stalin's assumption of power in the late 1920s, and the five-stage schema was to gain the ultimate imprimatur in his *Dialectical and Historical Materialism,* written in 1938:

> In conformity with the change and development of the productive forces of society in the course of history, men's relations of production, their economic relations also changed and developed.
>   Five *main* types of relations of production are known to history—primitive communal, slave, feudal, capitalist and socialist.[51]

This orthodox Marxist periodization of historical development was by and large the interpretation adopted by Mao Zedong. By the early 1930s,

Chinese protagonists of the concept of the Asiatic mode of production had lost the battle to assert China as a specifically Asiatic form of society and not merely a weakly distinguished variant of European feudalism.[52] Mao had not been one of these protagonists (although there are certainly themes in his historical thought not inconsistent with the concept of an Asiatic mode of production), and the view of historical time and periodization he derived from Marxism was largely orthodox, largely following the Leninist schema.

The conception of the future which Mao drew from the Marxist tradition also tended towards orthodoxy. In this orthodox teleological conception, humankind's temporal progression toward history's goal is accomplished through a dialectical social process in which prevailing patterns of production and social relations are challenged by the emergence of new forces of production and their accompanying class structures; this confrontation, often of a revolutionary character, leads to the eventual supersession of the mode of production by a more advanced form. This view of society progressing through various modes of production in an ascending dialectical and goal-directed manner perceives in the future a final historical stage, built on the highly developed forces of production generated by industrialization, in which the conflict generated by the inherent impulse to historical progression would be extinguished. This negation of the dialectic would result from the disappearance of class antagonism, for this final stage in historical development, the higher phase of communism, would witness the emergence of a society free of class divisions and in which need (rather than work or ownership) would be the criterion governing the distribution of society's now abundant resources. On the basis of this equalitarian principle, conflict would (largely) disappear.

Despite the confidence with which orthodox Marxism anticipated this future, Marx himself was rather reticent about making sweeping futuristic claims. There are, scattered through his writings, sometimes elliptical and enigmatic references to the emergence and characteristics of a future communist society.[53] Such references neither separately nor combined constitute a fully worked-out theory of the future. In Lenin's hands, however, the predictive aspects of Marxism found no such reticence. In *The State and Revolution* (1917), Lenin argued boldly that the inevitable achievement of the higher phase of communism would witness the "withering away" of the state; the state was the political instrument of class oppression, and only with its disappearance along with the disappearance of classes could true freedom be realized. The "withering away" of the state was not only inevitable but a central tenet of Marxism. As Lenin asserted, "Marx deduced from the whole history of socialism and the political struggle that the state was bound to disappear."[54] In this future post-political and advanced industrialized society, there would be no class exploitation and political oppression, and the fundamental class-induced causes of war and conflict would no longer exist.

The inevitable historical future predicted by the orthodox Marxist tradition—of material abundance, equality, freedom from oppression and exploitation, and peace—was a powerful influence on Mao's political thought and behavior, as it was on many of Mao's generation.[55] The historical goals raised by Marxism, founded on a (supposedly) scientific reading of history, provided direction and coherence to political attempts to overthrow and eventually abolish class societies. From this perspective, the past, present, and future are inextricably linked, the future serving to structure the political alternatives of the present.

It is significant that both of the intellectual traditions to influence Mao's thought during the Yan'an period incorporated a vision of a future society of peace and harmony, although the Marxist and Chinese traditions clearly commenced from very different historical perspectives. In the analysis that follows, we will examine the way in which their conceptions of history and the future are articulated by Mao and pay particular attention to the unresolved tensions in his thought created by the tensions between these two historical frameworks. We will also offer some observations on the way in which their visions of the future served to influence the strategies adopted by Mao to achieve the pressing political and military objectives thrown up by an era of war, an era in which his desire for peace and harmony and his confidence in their realization reached eschatological proportions.

"Three Epochs" and "Five Stages": Dual Periodizations in Mao's Thought

There is little philosophical discussion on the nature of time in the Mao texts of the Yan'an period. However, there is, in Mao's "Lecture Notes on Dialectical Materialism" (1937), which he drew largely from Soviet works on philosophy from the early 1930s,[56] a short section on time and space. Here, he incorporates time within the framework of his materialist ontology, arguing that time has an objective existence independent of human consciousness of it:

> Movement is a form of the existence of matter, space and time are also forms of the existence of matter. The movement of matter exists in time and space, and moreover the movement of matter itself is the premise for

these two forms of material existence, time and space. Space and time cannot be separated from matter. . . . Space and time are not independent or nonmaterial things, and are not subjective forms of our consciousness; they are forms of existence of the objective material world. They do not exist objectively outside of matter and matter does not exist outside of them.[57]

Of more interest than this conventional materialist account of the nature of time are the perspectives on historical periodization and the future which emerge during the Yan'an period. For it becomes evident that Mao was using, somewhat surprisingly, not one but two temporal systems by which to evaluate the flow of time and to dissect it into discrete historical periods. In the first, what might be called an adaptation of the *Gong Yang* periodization of history (see previous), Mao invoked a tripartite division of history and used peace (as had He Xiu) as the criterion for establishing boundaries between historical periods. In the second, he employed a periodization which perceived a progression in history from a primitive society of the distant past to a communist society in the future, in short, the five-stage periodization of history which had become Marxist orthodoxy under Lenin and Stalin. This latter periodization was to require some adaptation at Mao's hands to cope with the ambiguities of the capitalist stage in the Chinese context. However, such adaptation was not designed to alter dramatically a periodization which he accepted implicitly as the orthodox Marxist position on historical time. In this periodization (except perhaps for the period which Mao, following Lenin, described as the "bourgeois-democratic revolution"), ownership of the means of production constituted the principal criterion for establishing temporal boundaries.

As one would expect, the simultaneous employment of two forms of periodization, with their rather different criteria, led to difficulties in harmonizing historical periods and temporal divisions. It will become evident, however, that Mao did not himself recognize the contradiction between these two temporal frameworks and that he merely superimposed the orthodox Marxist periodization with its five stages over the Chinese schema with its three epochs. Before turning to a detailed examination of the Mao texts to determine the manner in which he employed these two temporal frameworks, it is worth noting that an alternative historical periodization within the Chinese tradition, namely the dynastic sequence, finds no serious application within Mao's thinking; the criteria by which he apprehended and divided the flow of historical time did not include dynastic changes.

In a section of "Problems of Strategy in China's Revolutionary War" (1936) largely expurgated from the official post-1949 text, Mao distinguished three epochs *(shidai)* in human history:

> The life of humankind is made up of three great epochs—an epoch in which humankind lived in peace, an epoch in which humankind lived at war, and another epoch in which humankind lives in peace. We are at present at the dividing line *(jiaodian)* between the second and third epochs. Humankind's era of wars will be brought to an end by our own efforts, and beyond doubt the war we wage is part of the final battle.[58]

Mao was to repeat this division of human history into three epochs in "On Protracted War" (1938) and also to insist on the imminent realization of the third epoch of "perpetual peace." Once again, most of this passage has been deleted from the official post-1949 text:

> The protracted nature of China's Anti-Japanese War is inseparably connected with the fight for perpetual peace *(yongjiu heping)* in China and the whole world. Never has there been an historical period such as the present in which war is so close to perpetual peace. The life of humanity over the last several hundreds of thousands of years has already passed through two epochs: the epoch of the peaceful life of humanity and the epoch of the warlike life of humanity.[59]

In contrast to He Xiu's conception, Mao's theory of the "three epochs" does not suggest a continued improvement in society as it progressed from the first through to the third epoch. Rather, the transition from the first to the second epoch was, in Mao's imagery, accompanied by a dramatic alteration in the nature of society: peace, formerly the dominant characteristic, gave way to war. This transition did not represent progress; to the contrary, it marked a deterioration in history as humankind abandoned peace and descended into the long and forbidding era of war.

In "On Protracted War," Mao invoked the Marxist framework to explain this degeneration from the first epoch of peace to the second epoch of war. In this document, Mao identified the first epoch of peace with the first stage in the Marxist periodization, namely primitive society. In this first epoch, which had extended over several hundred thousand years, humans had lived in a primitive clan society, which was both classless and communist.[60] The only war waged during this epoch was "against nature" as the level of production was "highly inadequate." Because this society was classless, an all-inclusive "love of humanity" *(renlei zhi ai)* was possible.[61] However, precipitated by the development of the forces of production and the appearance of social divisions, the collapse of this primitive communist society began some 5,000 years ago,[62] and humankind was forced to enter the second epoch of history in which life was characterized by war.[63] Unfortunately, Mao does not expand on those factors at work within primitive society which might have given rise to the development of the productive forces and the consequent appearance of antagonistic social divisions. However, it would appear from his rather cursory description of this transition that he regarded it as being sudden and dramatic in its consequent transformation of a peaceful society to one dominated by war.

While the first epoch of peace was for Mao coterminous with primitive society, the second epoch of war encompassed several stages of the Marxist periodization. In China, the first of these was a slave society, in which a slave-owning class emerged that now enjoyed for the first time in history the leisure to develop abstract forms of philosophical thought.[64] However, because the slave-owning class impeded the development of the forces of production,[65] there was a transition from a slave to a feudal society during the Zhou dynasty (1122–249 B.C.). With this transition, Chinese society "came to a standstill" (*tingdun qilai*).[66] During this feudal period, economics, politics, and culture remained "sluggish" (*chihuan*) or ceased altogether (*tingzhi*).[67] The reason for this sluggish or negligible development was "the extreme poverty and backwardness of the peasants resulting from ruthless landlord exploitation and oppression."[68] This led to numerous peasant uprisings and rebellions, some of which had the effect of toppling dynasties. The dynasties established in their stead did not, however, constitute viable alternatives to the existing socioeconomic system, and feudal rule continued. Nevertheless, while impotent to introduce a historically more progressive mode of production, peasant rebellions were still perceived by Mao as constituting "the real motive force of historical evolution (*jinhua*) in Chinese feudal society."[69] In general, the impression Mao gives of feudal society is of a long period of stagnation in Chinese history during which the impulses for an alternative mode of production did not appear intrinsically due to the absence of new forces and relations of production and new political parties capable of posing a genuine alternative to feudalism.[70] This protracted period of feudal stagnation reinforced Mao's inclination to perceive the history of class society as a long trough in which no substantial development occurred and in which the dominant theme was war.

In the original text of "The Chinese Revolution and the Chinese Communist Party" (1939), there is no indication that feudal stagnation held within it the embryo of an alternative mode of production, namely capi-

talism, destined eventually to supersede it. Rather, the intervention of foreign capitalism in the form of Western imperialism during the Qing dynasty is attributed with initiating the changes that culminated in the
disintegration of the traditional feudal economy and the emergence of
economic and political alternatives to feudalism. Thus, while Mao may not
have overtly endorsed the application of the concept of the Asiatic mode
of production to the Chinese case, and indeed there is no textual evidence
to suggest that he did, the view that Western imperialism was the catalyst
which initiated qualitative change in the Chinese social formation is closer
than Mao may have then realized to such an explanation. As Stuart Schram
has pointed out, Mao was subsequently to reconsider his position on the
lack of intrinsically spontaneous development in China's feudal economy,[71]
and the following sentence was added to the post-1949 version of this document: "As China's feudal society had developed a commodity economy,
and so carried within itself the seeds (*mengya*) of capitalism, China would
of herself have developed slowly into a capitalist society even without the
impact of foreign capitalism."[72] However, during the Yan'an period, Mao
regarded the universalizing force of imperialism as instrumental in the subsequent transformation of Chinese society; this is borne out by the fact that
he dated China's modern era as commencing with the first major incursions of Western imperialism into China in 1840.

In Mao's alternative periodization of history, the tripartite schema
drawn from the Chinese tradition, the entire modern era down to the
Yan'an period was incorporated within the second epoch of war, and
there were obviously numerous historical illustrations which reinforced
Mao's belief that war had been the dominant characteristic of Chinese
society since 1840. In the Marxist periodization, however, the modern
era presented something of a dilemma: China not an industrialized capitalist society presaging a transition to socialism nor was it any longer a
purely feudal society. Where, then, did China fit in the Marxist historical schema, and what implications for the future were indicated by its
temporal positioning within Marxism's five-stage teleological framework?
Mao responded to this dilemma by employing a mode of interpretation
which made allowance for competing and coexisting modes of production in an economically differentiated society such as China.[73] While feudalism still dominated this "semi-feudal, semi-colonial" society, there
existed within the Chinese social formation elements of a number of
other modes of production: compradore-capitalism, domestic capitalism,
even socialism. Mao resolved the problem this economic complexity created by incorporating the entirety of Chinese history since 1840 into the

Leninist category of the "bourgeois-democratic revolution." The basic characteristic of this historical period was the struggle against imperialism and Chinese feudalism.

The criteria Mao employed to identify the period of the "bourgeois-democratic revolution" differ from those employed to demarcate other historical periods in his Marxist periodization. In these other periods, ownership of the means of production was the dominant criterion. However, the confusing differentiation of ownership types in the "bourgeois-democratic revolution" led Mao to use instead the targets struggled against (imperialism and Chinese feudalism) as the key criterion by which to identify and demarcate this particular period. While the factor of ownership was certainly not absent from Mao's analysis, there was nevertheless some loss of consistency in the criteria with which he approached the periodization of Chinese history, this loss of consistency in no small measure a consequence of the increasingly fragmented and unstable character of modern Chinese society.

Mao perceived two distinct stages within the "bourgeois-democratic revolution," with the May Fourth Movement of 1919 the watershed dividing them. Between 1840 and 1919, the revolution had been led by the bourgeoisie, and during this stage of "Old Democracy," as Mao termed it, military struggles (such as the Taiping and Boxer Rebellions and the Revolution of 1911) were accompanied by struggles on the cultural front, especially in education. With the May Fourth Movement, leadership of the "bourgeois-democratic revolution" passed from the bourgeoisie to the proletariat and its vanguard party, the CCP. The transition from the old to the new stage of the "bourgeois-democratic revolution" was a consequence of changes in the domestic and international situation, especially World War I and its ramifications within China and the Russian Revolution of 1917. The forces unleashed by these events (and especially the emergence of the CCP) indicated that a new stage in the revolution had been achieved. As Mao was to point out in "On New Democracy," "revolutions too can be classified into old and new, and what is new in one historical period becomes old in another. The century of China's bourgeois-democratic revolution can be divided into two main stages. . . . Each [stage] has its basic historical characteristics."[74]

With the change of leadership following the May Fourth Movement of 1919, the "bourgeois-democratic revolution" had entered the period of "New Democracy." Mao's own close involvement in the Chinese Revolution had begun at this time, and he had witnessed at close quarters the often dramatic shifts in CCP policy in the years since. Looking back from the vantage point of 1940, Mao divided the period of New Democracy into four distinct stages—1919–1921, 1921–1927, 1927–1936, 1936–1940— each of which was defined by the changing tactics and fortunes of the CCP.[75] Mao's inclination to establish such a detailed periodization of the New Democratic period derived from his sensitivity to the need to formulate policies closely attuned to a rapidly changing political reality; the defining characteristics of a particular historical stage could alter so dramatically that policies previously suitable had to be thoroughly reformulated. A dramatic shift in the political context, such as the events of early 1927 and the attendant rapid shift in Party policy, was sufficient to indicate the end of one historical stage and the emergence of another. The urgent political need to accurately establish the defining characteristics of each particular historical period or stage thus led Mao to resist the tendency to temporal transcendency so evident in traditional Chinese historiography. Each historical period or stage possessed its own "special characteristics,"[76] and it was these which temporally separated one period or stage from another: "The China of today," Mao remarked in 1938, "cannot be compared with China of any other historical period."[77]

It is thus evident that Mao perceived the "flow" of history as being divided into quite discrete epochs, periods, and stages, their specific characteristics capable of close definition, and the divisions between them of careful calibration. He believed that to confuse historical periods could only lead to mistaken political and military strategies. In this sense, Mao's sensitivity to historical periodization was closely aligned with his insistence that Party policy be based on an intimate understanding of the "actual conditions" it confronted at each stage. In this respect, there is in Mao's thought of the Yan'an period a strong vein of pragmatism. There is, moreover, a firm insistence that patience was required in the "protracted" struggle to achieve the goal of victory in the Anti-Japanese War. Indeed, his patience and pragmatism suggest a leader unmoved by utopian speculation and impatient with those entranced by the "vision splendid" of a world of peace, harmony, material abundance, and equality.[78] Yet, parallel to the strongly pragmatic theme in Mao's writings during the Yan'an period runs just such a vision, and it is evident that his political response to the exigencies of the present were strongly future-oriented. Mao's sense of history encompassed a future whose realization depended at least in part on present political struggles based on a judicious reading of the past and present.[79]

The Historical Future: An Era of Perpetual Peace, an Era of Communism

Given Mao's pragmatic inclinations during the Yan'an period, it comes as something of a revelation to discover in his writings numerous references to the future of eschatological dimensions. For Mao, the future was tangible and its realization guaranteed. Indeed, he referred in 1938 to the era of the Anti-Japanese war as the "most progressive period in the history of the Chinese nation," and it was this that indicated the imminent arrival of a future of "perpetual peace."[80] Such optimism is surprising given the unpromising political and military situation at the time. However, his confidence derived inspiration from two intellectual traditions both of which encompassed a utopian vision of the future. The first of these, the utopian theme in the Chinese tradition, suggested to Mao the possibility of an imminent realization of the third epoch of perpetual peace. Mao perceived society as poised on the "dividing line" (*jiaodian*) between the second epoch of war and the third epoch of perpetual peace.[81] This certainty of imminent deliverance from the second epoch of war emerged also in glowing terms in his otherwise rather pragmatic philosophical essay "On Practice" (1937):

> This process, the practice of changing the world, which is determined in accordance with scientific knowledge, has already reached a historic moment in the world and in China, a great moment unprecedented in human history, that is, the moment for completely banishing darkness from the world and from China and for changing the world into a world of light such as never previously existed.[82]

Eschatological thought of this sort characteristically emerges during periods of social upheaval and chaos caused by war, this perceived as the penultimate historical stage prior to the emergence of the millennium. The ultimate stage is portrayed as chaos and upheaval of an even greater intensity and represents the final ordeal, the purifying flame, through which believers must pass before the new era can dawn. This eschatological belief is clearly evident in Mao's writings: "Our war," he promised in 1936, "is the final one, but without doubt it will be the greatest and most brutal."[83] In asserting the certainty of an era of perpetual peace following an intensification of the violence of war, Mao was promising himself and his adherents future compensation for present sufferings, something which would lend impetus to their struggles.

The relationship between this eschatological impulse in Mao's thought and his employment of a periodization incorporating a third epoch of perpetual peace becomes evident when the characteristics of this third epoch are explored. In his scattered references to this future (yet supposedly imminent) golden age, Mao drew heavily on themes within the Chinese utopian tradition to depict its qualities. First and foremost amongst these was a peace that would not be transitory but perpetual. In "On Protracted War" (1938), Mao referred to this era of perpetual peace in terms glowing with eschatological fervor:

> When humankind has arrived at the epoch of perpetual peace, then there will be no more need of war. Neither armies, nor warships, nor military aircraft, nor poison gas will then be needed. At this moment will begin the third epoch in the history of humanity, the epoch of peaceful life during which there will never be war. Throughout all eternity (*yi wan si nian*) our sons and grandsons will never know war again.[84]

Elsewhere in this same document, Mao stressed that this third epoch of peace was virtually at hand: "A new world of perpetual peace and brightness already lies clearly before us."[85] His identification and portrayal of this future era of peace drew on the Chinese millenarian doctrine of *tai ping* (universal peace). This, as we have seen, had been linked by He Xiu with the third epoch in his reinterpretation of the *Gong Yang* commentary, and the intellectual connection between this traditional utopian thought and Mao's eschatology of the three epochs was the concept of a society based on *da tong* (great harmony) popularized by Kang Youwei, who had taken traditional utopian themes and blended them into a detailed vision of a society of perfect harmony and peace. Mao was in fact to describe *da tong* as the general goal of the communist movement. In response to a question by Agnes Smedley in 1937, Mao stated that "Chinese Communists are internationalists; they advocate the world movement for great harmony (*da tong*) . . . only when China is independent and liberated will it be able to participate in the world movement for great harmony."[86]

Perpetual peace and harmony thus represented the principal characteristics of this future third epoch in human history. Mao did not, however, limit the characteristics of the third epoch to these, but the more detailed perspectives he raised were normally predicated on the Marxist premise of a classless communist society. This suggests two important aspects of Mao's view of historical time and the future. First, his conception of the future clearly contained an unresolved confusion between the temporal boundaries of the third epoch of peace and the stages of socialism and communism in the Marxist periodization. By suggesting the imminence of the

third epoch of peace, Mao could not equate it entirely with communist society, and in general he stressed that the achievement of communism lay
well in the future. In "On New Democracy," for example, the attainment of
socialism (not to mention communism) is presented as the "maximum programme" for the CCP, a goal to be achieved only when objective conditions allowed the realization of that program.[87] Yet, Mao's references to the
third epoch of peace are couched in terms which impatiently anticipate its
imminent attainment and which suggest the successful culmination of the
Anti-Japanese War as the temporal boundary separating the second epoch
of war from the third epoch of peace. Indeed, on one occasion he predicted
that war would be eliminated "in the not too distant future,"[88] and on another predicted that the convocation of the United Nations in San Francisco on 25 April 1945 would be the "starting point for this peace."[89]

It is, however, not possible to extricate these two strands of Mao's historical view of the future and merely expose the contradiction, for the two
time-scales were not completely discrete in Mao's thinking, and one tended
to overlay the other, blurring the fine temporal distinctions of which each
separately was potentially capable. And the concatenating factor which
linked these time-scales was class, which derived from Marxism. To class—
its exploitation, oppression, antagonism—could be attributed all of society's
ills. However, the problems associated with this concatenation of historical
periodizations via the agency of class are obvious: Communist society,
whose attributes are predicated on the prior elimination of classes, was not
immediately attainable; the third epoch of peace, many of whose attributes
were also contingent on the prior elimination of classes, was imminent. The
third epoch of peace thus appeared to incorporate at least the socialist as
well as communist phases of the Marxist periodization; this, of course,
could lead to confusion regarding the status and characteristics of socialist
society, for it implies that socialist society itself would be classless, something
not countenanced by orthodox Marxist theory which regards socialism as a
transitional stage between capitalism and communism during which class
and class struggle will decline. It is certainly the case, however, that Mao did
not believe socialist society would be free of classes, and it is safer to regard
this confusion as arising from his employment of two historical periodizations whose temporal boundaries could not be adequately harmonized.

Second, by insisting on the prior elimination of classes as necessary for
the realization of the attributes of both the third epoch of peace and a future communist society, Mao was invoking the same sort of logic employed
by Lenin to predict the inevitable "withering away of the state": Given the
elimination of class divisions, a future communist society or era of perpet-

ual peace would also be rid of the multitude of negative social phenomena, including war, engendered by class.[90] This form of reasoning, an "eliminative utopianism," as Benjamin Schwartz has described it, allowed Mao to assert with absolute confidence the disappearance of all of the deleterious consequences of class society.[91] This becomes evident when we turn to an examination of the specific attributes of the future society Mao envisioned. Mao's approach to "utilitarianism" (*gonglizhuyi*) is a good example. At the Yan'an Forum (1942), Mao referred to utilitarianism as "transcending" (*chao*) all other ideologies, but within class society it operated to the benefit of the dominant economic class; a utilitarianism that benefited all of humanity could only be feasible in a society from which class and class privilege had been eliminated.[92] And in a letter written to Peng Dehuai in May 1943, Mao rejected the possibility of a genuine utilitarianism in class society. In this letter, Mao criticized Peng's "Talk on Democratic Education" (of March 1943) in which Peng had raised the Confucian axiom (*Analects* XV, 23) "*ji suo bu yu, wu shi yu ren*" (what you do not want done to yourself, do not do to others) as a political slogan. Mao did not equivocate in his criticism, for this Confucian form of utilitarianism was quite inappropriate given the continued existence of classes:

> It is inappropriate to put forward the slogan in politics "what you do not want done to yourself, do not do to others"; the present task is to employ war and other political means to overthrow the enemy. The present social base is a commodity economy. Both of these are so-called "what you do not want done to yourself must be done to others." Only after classes have been eliminated can the principle "what you do not want done to yourself, do not do to others" be implemented; then war, political oppression and economic exploitation will be eliminated.[93]

While class divisions remained, utilitarian considerations at both a societal and personal level were therefore necessarily subordinate to class interests. Mao urged the employment of the opposing principle to create a society in which true (that is, classless) utilitarianism would be possible: "the policy of our Party," asserted Mao in 1941, quoting Zhu Xi, "is to 'do unto them as they do unto us,' stick for stick and carrot for carrot."[94]

A related characteristic of the future society also contingent on the elimination of classes was an "all-inclusive love of humanity." At the Yan'an Forum, Mao blamed the division of society into classes for having made this principle inoperable:

> As for the so-called love of humanity, there has been no such all-inclusive (*tongyi*) love since humanity was divided into classes. . . . There will be

genuine love of humanity, and that will be after classes are eliminated all over the world. Classes have split society into many antagonistic groupings; there will be love of all humanity when classes are eliminated and when society is reunited (*fugui yu tongyi*); but not now.[95]

As one would expect of a society in which an all-inclusive love of humanity prevailed, the future communist society in an epoch of perpetual peace would be "the most contented (*meiman*), pleasant and happy (*xingfu*) society for all mankind."[96] On several other occasions, Mao was to refer to "happiness" as a characteristic of such a society.[97] Moreover, communist society would be distinguished from all previous societies by being "rational" (or "equitable," *helide*): "Communism is at once a complete system of proletarian ideology (*sixiang*) and a new social system. It is different from any other ideology or social system, and is the most complete, progressive revolutionary and rational system in human history."[98]

It appears from Mao's references to the future era of peace and communism that his vision was strongly influenced by themes within the Chinese utopian tradition, for this future society would be blessed by peace, harmony, love of humanity, and happiness, and human behavior would be governed by the principle of "reciprocity" (*shu*) from which could derive a truly non-class utilitarianism.[99] The clearest indication of Marxist influence on the utopia envisaged by Mao was its classlessness. As I have suggested, it was the centrality of class and class struggle in Mao's thought that permitted his use of two rather disparate historical periodizations, for ultimately it was the absence or existence of classes which determined whether humankind would live in an era of peace or war. A genuine and perpetual peace would only be possible in a society free from the antagonisms of class hostility. It is no coincidence that Mao regarded the onset of war in human history as dating from the emergence of class divisions within primitive society, nor is it a coincidence that he incorporated the several stages of class society of the Marxist periodization within the second epoch of war. For class was the *bête noire* at whose door could be laid responsibility for all social evils, and war, particularly during the Yan'an period, emerged as the most devastating of these.

The importance of the elimination of class to Mao's perception of the future clearly derived from Marxism. So too did his insistence that China's would be an industrialized and modernized future; no such conception of the future resided in traditional Chinese thought. He was determined that China be transformed from "an agricultural into an industrial country" and believed that large-scale industry would occupy "an absolutely predominant position" in the economy. The China of the future would have both "powerful industries of her own and a large number of modernized big cities," and in order to achieve this would "have to undergo a continuous process of transforming the rural inhabitants into urban inhabitants."[100] This insistence on China's modernized future reinforces the view that he did not regard the future in Rousseauian terms, as a rural idyll untainted by modern industry, although this might be the impression, given the importance of peace and harmony in his conception of the future. However, the strength of his commitment to China's industrialization and modernization precludes such an interpretation, just as it undermines the perception of Mao as a peasant revolutionary (see chapter 4).

It is interesting that absent from the characteristics of Mao's future society is individual liberty. Nowhere in the texts of the Yan'an period is there any reference to the possibility that the era of communism or the third epoch of perpetual peace would witness an enhancement of the freedom of the individual. This silence cannot be explained by reference to a similar silence in the texts of the Marxist tradition, for there is a strong libertarian theme in Marx's writings on the future, and Lenin was preoccupied with freedom from the oppression of the state as an essential characteristic of the higher phase of communism. Mao's silence stems rather from the hostility of Chinese Marxism from its earliest days to liberalism in its Western guise. Mao regarded the liberalism of such formidable Chinese liberals as Liang Qichao and Hu Shi as a misguided ideology, particularly for its incremental nonrevolutionary approach to social change. Moreover, he regarded liberalism's focus on the rights and freedoms of the individual as quite inadequate as a response to the generalized oppression characteristic of class society. Mao's "Combat Liberalism" (1937) demonstrates only too clearly that he associated liberalism with unprincipled compromise, selfishness, egoism, and an unwillingness on the part of the individual to subordinate him- or herself to the needs of the collective. In short, liberalism stemmed from "petty-bourgeoise selfishness, it places personal interests first and the interests of the revolution second."[101]

Mao's vision of the future during the Yan'an period was thus something of a pastiche, a cultural amalgam based on the historical predictions and periodization of Marxism and utopian themes in Chinese thought. While Mao declared his historical optimism derived from the "science" of Marxism, his references to the third epoch of perpetual peace were of obvious Chinese provenance. However, the fervor of his references to an imminently realizable era of perpetual peace was fuelled by the chaotic and violent environment of war which prevailed throughout the Yan'an period, precisely the sort of context in which eschatological visions of a better world characteristically emerge.

That the bellicose context of the Yan'an period was an important factor in Mao's eschatological vision of the future at that time is underscored by the fate of his references to the third epoch of human history, that of perpetual peace, in the post-1949 edited versions of his writings. While the eschatological theme does not entirely disappear from the official version of Mao's *Selected Works,* explicit references to the three-epoch periodization have been deleted, and the possibility of the imminent realizability of perpetual peace removed. There are several possible explanations for this expurgation. First, the concept of the three epochs was considered too obviously of Chinese provenance, and its marriage with the orthodox Marxist periodization (as we have seen) as creating problems in demarcating the boundaries between periods. Moreover, the manner in which Mao employed the three-epoch time-scale could be read as anything but progressive and dialectical, his retrospective ruminations on the primitive communism of history's first era of peace in danger of being interpreted as nostalgia for humankind's lost innocence. The transition to the second era with its antagonistic class divisions and warfare could appear to constitute historical degeneration and the history of the second era of war an extended and violent hiatus between the first and third epochs of peace. The movement of history would thus have entailed the passage through and final ascension from the war-like trough in human history caused by the collapse of the first era of peace. Moreover, the virtues of the third epoch, of perpetual peace would in many respects be those of the first epoch; and this seemingly atavistic projection of an admired past onto a desired future was undoubtedly felt too reminiscent of the traditional Chinese tendency to retrospect on the virtues of the distant past. Second, Mao and his editors clearly felt it necessary to make the realization of a future society of communism and peace more clearly contingent on factors endorsed by the Marxist theory of history. In the official revised version of "On Protracted War," for example, the attainment of perpetual peace is now predicated on the elimination of capitalism.[102] Similarly, the following addition to "Problems of Strategy in China's Revolutionary War" (1936) emphasizes the elimination of states and classes as necessary for the realization of the new era of human history: "When human society advances to the point where classes and states are eliminated, there will be no more wars, counter-revolutionary or revolutionary, unjust or just; that will be the era of perpetual peace for humankind."[103]

Politics and Vision: The Impact of the Future on the Present

The historical optimism and eschatological themes that characterize Mao's Yan'an writings appear somewhat paradoxical in light of the emphasis he placed on gaining the advantage during each battle or stage in the present. These themes, a rather airy utopianism and a down-to-earth pragmatism, exist side by side in this thought.[104] However, Mao did not perceive any contradiction between confidence in the realization of an inevitable historical future and his own determination to undertake the painstaking political effort needed to achieve that historical goal. Mao shared, and had to resolve, this paradox with other true believers of the Marxist tradition, for there is an undoubted antinomy within the orthodox Marxist tradition, akin to the antinomy of free will within the Augustinian philosophy of history, created by the juxtaposition of a historically determined future and exhortations to believers to struggle for its realization.[105] If a particular future is guaranteed by History, why struggle to achieve it?[106]

It is clear that Mao possessed a supreme confidence in the historical goals raised by Marxism; such confidence did not, however, lead to a complacent quietism on his part, and if anything, acted as a spur to his revolutionary activity. How is this coexistence of utopianism and pragmatism to be explained? First, Mao occasionally employed (with due allowance for cultural variation) the "locomotive of history" analogy, often encountered in the Marxist tradition, that likens history to a locomotive, the destination of which is determined by the tracks on which it runs. The most that can be achieved by human effort is the acceleration or retardation of the locomotive along its prescribed course; nothing can be done to prevent the juggernaut eventually reaching its destination. The role of the revolutionary is that of enthusiastic engineer, fuelling the locomotive to increase its progress. In "On Practice," Mao used this analogy to criticize the "diehards" within the revolutionary ranks:

> These people fail to see that the struggle of opposites has already pushed the objective process forward while their knowledge has stopped at the old stage. This is characteristic of all die-hards. Their thinking is divorced from social practice, and they cannot march ahead to lead the chariot of society (*shehui chelun*); they simply trail behind (*zai chezi houmian*), grumbling that it goes too fast and trying to drag it back or put it into reverse.[107]

A similar analogy appears in a speech Mao made in May 1937: "Why do we put forward the three related slogans of 'consolidate peace,' 'fight for democracy,' and 'carry out armed resistance'? The answer is in order to push the wheels of our revolution (*geming chelun*) forward and that circumstances allow us to do so."[108] Similarly, in "On Coalition Government" (1945), Mao argued that the strength of the people of the world was predicated on their increasing consciousness, and unity was an objective factor that "determines the target towards which the cartwheels of world history (*shijie lishi chelun*) are moving, and the path that will be selected to arrive at that target."[109]

Mao's use of a "locomotive of history" style analogy leaves the impression that he perceived judicious political action as capable of accelerating the "objective process" of history along its preordained route. That he did view the course of history from this perspective is apparent from other comments made during the Yan'an period compatible with the "locomotive of history" analogy. For example, in "On Coalition Government," he asserted that "the general trend of history . . . is already clearly decided and will not change."[110] And in the same document, his argument for a coalition government is reinforced by the claim that such a political system is inevitable: "This is the only course China can take, whatever the intention of the Kuomintang or other parties, groups or individuals, whether they like it or not, and whether or not they are conscious of it. This is an historical law, an inexorable trend which no force can reverse."[111] This invocation of a predetermined historical process with inevitable goals appears also in an article of May 1939 written to commemorate the twentieth anniversary of the May Fourth Movement: "If anyone asks why a communist should strive to bring into being first a bourgeois-democratic society and then a socialist society, our answer is: we are following the inevitable course of history."[112] There is thus abundant evidence to suggest that during the Yan'an Period Mao perceived a future communist society within an era of perpetual peace as a necessary stage in the development of history. He was not, however, under any illusion that the progress of history toward its preordained goal would be constant and meet with no setbacks. "History," he averred in 1945, "follows a tortuous (*quzhe*) course."[113] Nowhere was the tortuous course of history more evident than in the pursuit of political objectives through armed struggle, and Mao was to refer to this characteristic of war in his essay "On Protracted War" (1938): "Events have their twists and turns and do not follow a straight line, and war is no exception."[114] Nor did Mao discount the possibility that history might temporarily be thrown into reverse gear. In a speech of 1937, such a reversal was raised as a distinct possibility: "History might reverse its course (*zou huitou lu*) for a while and peace might meet with set backs."[115] However, such setbacks were necessarily temporary, for the pattern of history was set: "A temporary retrogression (*houtui xianxiang*) cannot change the general law of history."[116]

The existence of such textual evidence serves to problematize the frequently encountered assumption that Mao had abandoned the historical determinism of orthodox Marxism. As we have seen, history was for Mao an "objective process" that involved an "inexorable trend" following an "inevitable course." However, the important point is not so much that Mao retained a belief in the teleology and historical determinism of Marxism, which he did (at least during the Yan'an period; see chapter 9), but that this belief could coexist with an emphasis on political action in the present, and that he perceived politics as a means of hastening the realization of inevitable historical goals. There was no contradiction, at least as far as Mao was concerned, between vision and politics, between advocacy of historical determinism and exhortation to political action.

Second, the coexistence within Mao's thought of historical determinism and close attention to the political struggles of the present can also be explained by reference to the function that historical goals performed in providing coherence, rationality, and direction to the formulation of his political and military strategies and tactics. Without historical goals, present activities would unavoidably be random, lacking temporal coordination or long-term purpose, and it is clear that Mao recognized this to be the case. In a speech of 1937, he indicated clearly that historical goals provided direction and coherence to current struggles: "We are fighting for socialism. . . . It is the great future goal to which our present efforts are directed; if we lose sight of the goal, we cease to be communists. But equally we cease to be Communists if we relax our efforts today."[117] The necessity of formulating current tactics in the light of long-term goals is also made clear in the following passage from "Problems of Strategy in China's Revolutionary War" (1936):

> In war as well as politics, planning only one step at a time as one goes is a harmful way of directing matters. After each step, it is necessary to examine the ensuing concrete changes and to modify or develop one's strategic and operational plans accordingly, or otherwise one is liable to make the mistake of rushing ahead regardless of danger. However, it is absolutely essential to have a long-term plan which has been thought out in its general outline and which covers an entire strategic stage or even several strategic stages.[118]

Political and military campaigns were thus dictated not only by the temporally limited exigencies of the present but by the belief that long-range goals could be brought closer to realization by their successful implementation. This connection between present and future is evident in Mao's use of the Leninist distinction between minimum and maximum programs. The minimum program encompasses the tasks of the present historical stage; it elaborates what can be achieved, given the objective constraints of the current situation. Although it falls far short of long-term historical goals (a description of which functions as the maximum program), it is legitimate, for its achievement serves to impel society closer to those goals. In "On New Democracy," Mao employed this distinction to reinforce his argument that China was not objectively ready for socialism and that a minimum program of New Democracy was therefore necessary: "Everybody knows that the Communist Party has an immediate and a future programme, a minimum and a maximum programme, with regard to the social system it advocates. For the present period, New Democracy, and for the future, socialism; these are two parts of an organic whole, guided by one and the same communist ideology."[119] Later in the same document, Mao asserted that "beyond its [communism's] minimum programme, it has a maximum programme, i.e., the programme for the attainment of socialism and communism."[120] Similarly, in "On Coalition Government," Mao used this distinction to rationalize an incremental advance toward communism: "Such is the general or fundamental programme which we advocate for the present stage, the entire stage of the bourgeois-democratic revolution. This is our minimum programme as against our future or maximum programme of socialism and communism."[121]

We have observed that Mao spoke of the "objective process" of history as an "inexorable trend" with "inevitable" goals. Did Mao perceive the political actions initiated by himself and the CCP as an integral component of this "objective process" of history? According to Mao's perception of historical causation, articulated in "On New Democracy," "politics" belonged to society's "basis" (genju), the causally generative area of society, although politics within this basis was subject to the influence of "economics." In fact, Mao referred in this document to "politics" as the "concentrated expression of economics." Developments within the "basis" dictated the direction and ultimate goals of society and its history (for a detailed analysis, see chapter 6).[122] Politics within the "basis" included political organization and action; these were part of the causal mechanism which generated historical progress and influenced its rate of development. As such, Mao did not regard political organization and action as extrinsic elements, detached from the "objective process" of history and functioning as arbitrary external pace-makers; they were integral cogs of the causal mechanism generating society's development. An example is Mao's belief that the political leadership extended by the proletariat and its party to the peasantry was the factor that prevented the degeneration of the Chinese Revolution into a traditional atavistic peasant rebellion.[123] The lack of such political leadership had been a major factor in the long period of stagnation during China's feudal period.[124] For Mao, the emergence in China of an industrial proletariat and establishment of a political party that represented its interests were developments of enormous historical significance within the "basis" of China's society. These developments within the "basis," regardless of the diminutive size of the proletariat, were sufficient to ensure that China's revolution would be modern in character and capable of preparing the ground for the establishment of a socialist society (see chapter 4).

Mao thus perceived "politics" as a vitally important factor in the unfolding of history and the realization of historical goals. However, he did not perceive "politics" as autonomous from other historically generative elements within the "economic" realm of society's "basis" (the forces and relations of production); rather, the effectivity of "politics" to accelerate the historical process was circumscribed by the "economic" realm, just as the further development of the "economic" realm was dependent on developments in the political realm. This mutual interdependence within the "basis" of society indicated the importance of political organization and action, but indicated also the objective limitations interdependence created. Guided by this framework, Mao was prepared to exploit the possibility for political action to its limit but was, during the Yan'an period, very mindful of not rushing ahead of the constraints of the objective situation. It was, nevertheless, on the possibility of exploiting the potential of "politics" to achieve short-term historical goals that Mao premised his confidence in the realization of "inevitable" long-term historical goals. In "On Protracted War," he asserted that the "political" mobilization of human potential united with other necessary social and economic factors constituted the historical premise for the "achievement of a new world of perpetual peace and brightness."[125] Historical factors external to the political realm demonstrated the certainty of such a future, and within the political realm itself, measures taken in accordance with a correct interpretation of the objective situation and historical trends would contribute to the speedier realization of that future. Mao's historical optimism thus reflected a confidence in his own ability to deliver the goods within the political realm, a confidence he doubtless felt justified by the successful outcome of the Anti-Japanese War and the Civil War (1945–1949) that followed.

Conclusion

It is often suggested that Mao was at his most pragmatic during the Anti-Japanese War, and that "utopianism" was a characteristic of his thought and action during other periods of his political career, particularly from the late 1950s. During the Anti-Japanese War, these accounts suggest, Mao addressed himself squarely to the "realities" of the political and military situation and submitted to the limits imposed by objective necessity, and the outcome of this period of lucid pragmatism was victory. While there is a glimmer of veracity in such accounts, they are misleading insofar as they ignore the very significant utopian theme that coexisted with the more pragmatic currents in Mao's thought. The tension between these seemingly contradictory themes is more apparent than real. As we have seen, Mao's pragmatism was provided coherence and direction by his utopianism. The problem of analysis thus becomes one of looking at these apparently contradictory themes in Mao's thought from a dialectical perspective, one which perceives a necessary connection between present and future and between determinism and activism. As Georg Lukács pointed out in his discussion of this problem in Marxist theory, "Fatalism and voluntarism are only mutually contradictory to an undialectical and unhistorical mind. In the dialectical view of history they prove to be necessarily complementary opposites."[126]

A dialectical approach also suggests the possibility of change. I suggested at the outset of this chapter that the debate on the origins of Mao's thought might be usefully extended by allowing that these did not remain constant, that at certain times the Marxist and Chinese traditions contributed significantly, whereas at others one or other became the dominant influence. This suggests that it may be necessary to examine Mao's thought on a theme-by-theme basis, for the mix which made up the intellectual ancestry of his thought may well have varied across themes. In terms of historical time and the future, evidence in the texts supports the view that during the Yan'an Period Mao drew on both the Marxist and Chinese traditions to construct a dual periodization of history. The utopian Chinese conception of the three ages with its future epoch of "perpetual peace" was clearly a significant influence. Similarly, the orthodox Marxist periodization, based largely on a mode of production analysis, also contributed to the utopian impulse in Mao's thought. The tension between these two ultimately irreconcilable temporal frameworks was resolved in the post-1949 period in favor of the Marxist periodization of history, and with the heavy redaction of Mao's writings for the compilation of the official *Selected Works,* the Chinese influence appears only *sotto voce.*

A theme-by-theme analysis thus suggests as necessary a move away from strident and simplistic generalizations regarding the origins of Mao's thought and a more careful elaboration of the genealogy of concepts sought in the Mao texts. Such a reading strategy would allow a more sophisticated, logical, and textually grounded interpretation than has been characteristic of much commentary on the origins of Mao's thought. In chapter 9, this approach is again mobilized to demonstrate the decline of utopianism in Mao's thought during the 1950s and its eventual extinction in the mid 1960s with the onset of the Cultural Revolution. While Mao continued to accept the possibility of a future communist society, he no longer accepted that a future era of perpetual peace could be attained, and this suggests the evaporation of any remaining influence of traditional Chinese utopianism on his thought.

Notes

1. See, for example, Vsevolod Holubnychy, "Mao Tse-tung's Materialist Dialectics," *China Quarterly* 19 (1964): 3–37; and Frederic Wakeman Jr., *History and Will: Philosophical Perspectives on Mao Tse-tung's Thought* (Berkeley: University of California Press, 1973). Representative of this view amongst Chinese Mao scholars is Bi Jianheng, *Mao Zedong yu Zhongguo zhexue chuantong* [Mao Zedong and the Chinese philosophical tradition] (Chengdu: Sichuan renmin chubanshe, 1990); also Chang Ruisen, Zhang Wenru and Ran Changuang, *Mao Zedong zhexue sixiang gailun* [An introduction to the philosophical thought of Mao Zedong] (Beijing: Zhongguo renmin daxue chubanshe, 1985).

2. See, for example, Steve S. K. Chin, *The Thought of Mao Tse-tung: Form and Content,* translated by Alfred H.Y. Lin (Hong Kong: Centre of Asian Studies Papers and Monographs, 1979); Andrew G. Walder, "Marxism, Maoism and Social Change," *Modern China,* vol. 3, no. 1 (January 1977): 101–18; and 3, no. 2 (April 1977): 125–59; Michael Dutton and Paul Healy, "Marxist Theory and Socialist Transition: The Construction of an Epistemological Relation," in *Chinese Marxism in Flux 1978–84: Essays on Epistemology, Ideology and Political Economy,* ed. Bill Brugger (Armonk, New York: M. E. Sharpe, 1985), 13–66; Philip Corrigan, Harvie Ramsay and Derek Sayer, *For Mao: Essays in Historical Materialism* (London: Macmillan, 1979); Adrian Chan, *Chinese Marxism* (London and New York: Continuum, 2003). A Chinese Mao scholar who takes this position is Liu Rong, *Mao*

Zedong zhexue sixiang gaishu [A commentary on Mao Zedong's philosophical thought] (Guangdong: Guangdong renmin chubanshe, 1983).

3. See, for example, Richard H. Solomon, *Mao's Revolution and the Chinese Political Culture* (Berkeley: University of California Press, 1971); Lucien W. Pye, *Mao Tse-tung: The Man in the Leader* (New York: Basic Books, 1976); Lam Lai Sing, *The Role of Ch'i in Mao Tse-tung's Leadership Style* (San Francisco: Mellen Research University Press, 1993). Few Chinese Mao scholars accept this view; the overwhelming majority regard Marxism as an influence on Mao's thought, even if he was also influenced by China's tradition. See, however, Zongli Tang and Bing Zuo, *Maoism and Chinese Culture* (New York: Nova Science, 1996). For analysis of this theme in Mao scholarship in China during the 1980s, see Nick Knight, ed., *The Philosophical Thought of Mao Zedong: Studies from China, 1981–1989* (Armonk, New York: M. E. Sharpe, Chinese Studies in Philosophy, 1992), Introduction.

4. John M. Koller, "Philosophical Aspects of Maoist Thought," *Studies in Soviet Thought* 14 (1974): 47–59.

5. Stuart R. Schram, "Chinese and Leninist Components in the Personality of Mao Tse-tung," *Asian Survey* 111, no. 6 (1963): 259–73. Schram commented that "some people regard me as obsessed with the Chinese roots of Mao and his thought." See his "Modernization and the Maoist Vision," *Bulletin* (*International House of Japan*) 26 (1979): 15.

6. Stuart R. Schram, *Mao Zedong: A Preliminary Reassessment* (Hong Kong: The Chinese University Press, 1983), 35.

7. Stuart R. Schram, *The Political Thought of Mao Tse-tung* (Harmondsworth: Penguin, 1969, revised ed.), 112–16.

8. Stuart Schram, ed., *Mao Tse-tung Unrehearsed: Talks and Letters, 1956–71* (Harmondsworth: Penguin,1974), introduction.

9. For further discussion of the methodological problems involved in reading the Mao texts, see Paul Healy, "Reading the Mao texts: The Question of Epistemology," *Journal of Contemporary Asia* 20, no. 3 (1990), 330–58; see also Paul Healy and Nick Knight, "Mao Zedong's Thought and Critical Scholarship," in *Critical Perspectives on Mao Zedong's Thought*, ed. Arif Dirlik, Paul Healy, and Nick Knight (Atlantic Highlands, New Jersey: Humanities Press, 1997), 3–20.

10. John Bryan Starr, for example, has argued that Mao manifested utopian inclinations during only "two relatively brief periods," his pre-Marxist period (pre-1920) and the period of the Great Leap Forward (1958–1960). "Maoism and Marxist Utopianism," *Problems of Communism* (July–August 1977): 56–62. See also Brantly Womack, *The Foundations of Mao Zedong's Political Thought, 1917–1935* (Honolulu: University of Hawaii Press, 1982), 188–204; Brantly Womack, "Where Mao Went Wrong: Epistemology and Ideology in Mao's Leftist Politics," *The Australian Journal of Chinese Affairs* 16 (July 1986): 23–40; and Stuart R. Schram, *Mao Zedong: A Preliminary Reassessment*. Maurice Meisner has analyzed the utopian element of pre-1949 Chinese Marxism but has, in my view, gone too far in the other direction, emphasizing the utopian element at the expense of recognizing sufficiently the pragmatic currents within Mao's thought and how these coexisted

with utopian tendencies. See his *Marxism, Maoism and Utopianism: Eight Essays* (Madison: University of Wisconsin Press, 1982), and *Mao's China and After: A History of the People's Republic* (New York: The Free Press, 1986, second ed.).

11. I use the term "utopian" here to indicate a belief in a perfect society at some future point in time rather than as it is sometimes employed to indicate a divorce from reality. As our analysis unfolds, it will become evident that a pragmatic approach was for Mao quite compatible with "utopian" inclinations.

12. Mark Gayn, "Mao Tse-tung Reassessed," in *China Readings 3: Communist China*, eds. Franz Schurmann and Orville Schell (Harmondsworth: Penguin, 1967), 104.

13. Nathan Sivin, "Chinese Conceptions of Time," *Earlham Review* 1 (1966): 82.

14. Burton Watson, *Ssu-ma Ch'ien: Grand Historian of China* (New York: Columbia University Press, 1958), 142–43, 153.

15. B. Watson, *Ssu-ma Ch'ien*.

16. Chi-yun Chen, *Hsun Yueh (A.D. 148–209): The Life and Reflections of an Early Medieval Confucianist* (Cambridge: Cambridge University Press, 1975), 135.

17. E. J. Pulleyblank, "Chinese Historical Criticism: Liu Chih-Chi and Ssu-ma Kuang," in *Historians of China and Japan*, eds. W. G. Beasley and E. G. Pulleyblank (London: Oxford University Press, 1961), 134.

18. P. Demieville, "Chang Hsueh-ch'eng and His Historiography," in *Historians of China and Japan*, eds. W. G. Beasley and E. G. Pulleyblank, 167–85.

19. Sivin, "Chinese Conceptions of Time": 84.

20. J. Gray, "History writing in Twentieth Century China: Notes on Its Background and Development," in *Historians of China and Japan*, eds. Beasley and Pulleyblank, 186.

21. Pulleyblank, "Chinese Historical Criticism," 149.

22. Laurence G. Thompson, *Ta Tung Shu: The One-World Philosophy of Kang Yuwei* (London: George Allen & Unwin, 1958), 55.

23. Sivin, "Chinese Conceptions of Time," 84.

24. Gray has described utopian concepts such as the "three ages" in the *Li Ji* as "uninfluential and obscure speculation." Gray, "History Writing," 198.

25. Timoteus Pokora, "Book review of Laurence G. Thompson's *Ta Tung Shu*," *Archiv Orientalni* 29 (1961): 169.

26. Timoteus Pokora, "On the origins of the notions *Tai-ping* and *Ta-t'ung* in Chinese Philosophy," *Archiv Orientalni* 29 (1961): 450.

27. This translation is taken from Liang Ch'i-ch'ao, *History of Chinese Political Thought During the Early Tsin Period* (London: Kegan Paul, Trench, Trubner and Co. Ltd., 1930), 44. As L. G. Thompson points out, translations of this passage vary widely; he offers four alternate translations. See his *Ta Tung Shu*, 27. A further translation can be found in Wm. Theodore de Bary, ed., *Sources of Chinese Tradition* (New York and London: Columbia University Press, 1960) I, 176.

28. Liang Ch'i-ch'ao, *History of Chinese Political Thought*, 44.

29. See Pokora, "On the origins," 450; also Wakeman Jr., *History and Will*, 106–7.

30. Fung Yu-lan, *A Short History of Chinese Philosophy* (New York: The Free Press, 1948), 201.

31. Schram, *The Political Thought of Mao Tse-tung*, 24n. See also Howard L. Boorman, "Mao Tse-tung as Historian," *China Quarterly* 28 (October–December 1966): 86.

32. S. Y. Teng, "Wang Fu-chih's Views on History and Historical Writing," *Journal of Asian Studies* 28, no. 1 (November 1968): 111–23, esp. 115.

33. Pokora, "On the Origins," 450.

34. Gray, "History Writing," 198, 202.

35. See Mao's "Letter to Xiangsheng," of June 1915, in Stuart R. Schram, ed., *Mao's Road to Power, Revolutionary Writings 1912–1949: Volume I, The Pre-Marxist Period, 1912–1920* (Armonk, New York: M. E. Sharpe, 1992), 62–63. See also Edgar Snow, *Red Star Over China* (Harmondsworth: Penguin, 1968, 1972), 161; Schram, *Mao Tse-tung* (Harmondsworth: Penguin, 1966), 25, 27; and Wakeman Jr., *History and Will*, 99.

36. Schram ed., *Mao's Road to Power: Volume I*, 237–38.

37. Thompson, *Ta-Tung Shu*, 20, 26–7; see also Liang Ch'i-ch'ao, *Intellectual Trends in the Ch'ing Period* (Cambridge, Mass.: Harvard University Press, 1959), 98.

38. See Chen Boda, "Lun xin Qimeng Yundong" [On the new enlightenment] in *Xian jieduan de Zhongguo sixiang yundong* [The Chinese thought movement in the current stage], ed. Xia Zhengnong (Shanghai: Yiban shudian, 1937), 67, 89.

39. *Selected Works of Mao Tse-tung* (Peking: FLP, 1967) IV, 414; also *Mao Zedong Xuanji* [Selected Works of Mao Zedong] (Beijing: Renmin chubanshe, 1966) IV, 1360; also Takeuchi Minoru, ed., *Mao Zedong Ji* [Collected Writings of Mao Zedong] (Tokyo: Hokubosha,1970–1972) X, 195.

40. See Milan Machovec, *A Marxist Looks at Jesus* (London: Dorton, Longman and Todd, 1976), 59–64.

41. Jacqueline de Romilly, *The Rise and Fall of States According to Greek Authors* (Ann Arbor: University of Michigan Press, 1977), 11. De Romilly provides a contrasting interpretation of Greek views of historical time to the one offered here.

42. Stanislav Andreski ed., *The Essential Comte* (London: Croom Helm, 1974), 19–41.

43. See Karl Lowith, *Meaning in History* (Chicago: University of Chicago Press, 1949), chapter 8.

44. Henry Paolucci ed., *The Political Writings of St. Augustine* (Chicago: Henry Refinery & Co., 1962).

45. See Hobsbawm's introduction to Karl Marx, *Pre-Capitalist Economic Formations* (London: Lawrence and Wishart, 1964), 19–20.

46. For discussion of this issue, see Umberto Melotti, *Marx and the Third World* (London: Macmillan, 1977).

47. Marx, *Pre-Capitalist Economic Formations*, 145.

48. Quoted in Shlomo Avineri, *The Social and Political Thought of Karl Marx* (Cambridge: Cambridge University Press, 1968), 151–52.

49. See V. I. Lenin, *Collected Works* (London: Lawrence & Wishart, 1964), III, 172, 181, 312, 381, 435.

50. Lenin, *Collected Works* XXIX, 475–76. Emphasis added. For a discussion of the tension between the activist and determinist elements in Lenin's thought, see Nick Knight, "Leninism, Stalinism and the Comintern," in *Marxism in Asia*, eds. Colin Mackerras and Nick Knight (London and Sydney: Croom Helm, 1985), 24–61.

51. J. V. Stalin, *Problems of Leninism* (Peking: FLP, 1976), 862. Emphasis in original.

52. Marian Sawer, "The Politics of Historiography: Russian Socialism and the Question of the Asiatic Mode of Production 1906–1931," *Critique* (Winter–Spring 1978–1979): 16–35, esp. 22. See also Stephen P. Dunn, *The Fall and Rise of the Asiatic Mode of Production* (London: Routledge & Kegan Paul, 1982).

53. See Karl Marx, *Capital Volume 1* (Harmondsworth: Penguin, 1976), 619, 667, 739, 929, 990; Karl Marx, *Early Writings* (Harmondsworth: Penguin, 1975), 348; Karl Marx and Friedrich Engels, *The German Ideology* (London: Lawrence and Wishart, 1974), 54–55; and Karl Marx, "Critique of the Gotha Programme," in Karl Marx, *The First International and After* (Harmondsworth: Penguin, 1974), 346–47, 355. For a thoughtful critique of Marx's "vision of a possible future" which acknowledges his pragmatic recognition that a future communist society would not be altogether free of potentially conflictual demands, particularly those related to production, see William Leon McBride, *The Philosophy of Karl Marx* (London: Hutchinson, 1977), chapter 7.

54. V. I. Lenin, *Selected Works in Three Volumes* (Moscow: Progress Publishers, 1975, 1976), vol. 2, 278.

55. For analysis of Qu Qiubai's views on Marxism's perspective on the future, see Nick Knight, *Marxist Philosophy in China: From Qu Qiubai to Mao Zedong, 1923–1945* (Dordrecht: Springer, 2005), chapter 4.

56. See Knight, *Marxist Philosophy in China*, chapters 9 and 10.

57. Takeuchi, ed., *Mao Zedong Ji* VI, 289. For a full translation of the section on time and space, see Nick Knight, ed., *Mao Zedong on Dialectical Materialism: Writings on Philosophy, 1937* (Armonk, New York: M.E. Sharpe, 1990), 110–12.

58. Takeuchi, ed., *Mao Zedong Ji* V, 88; cf. *Selected Works of Mao Tse-tung* I, 182; and *Mao Zedong Xuanji* I, 158.

59. Takeuchi, ed., *Mao Zedong Ji* VI, 93; cf. *Selected Works of Mao Tse-tung* II, 148–49; and *Mao Zedong Xuanji* II, 442–43. See also Schram, *The Political Thought of Mao Tse-tung,* 391–93.

60. Takeuchi, ed., *Mao Zedong Ji* VI, 93; also Schram, *The Political Thought of Mao Tse-tung,* 391. See also Takeuchi, ed., *Mao Zedong Ji* VI, 98; cf. *Selected Works of Mao Tse-tung* II, 306; and *Mao Zedong Xuanji* II, 585.

61. Takeuchi, ed., *Mao Zedong Ji* VIII, 140; *Selected Works of Mao Tse-tung* III, 91; and *Mao Zedong Xuanji* II, 827.

62. Takeuchi, ed., *Mao Zedong Ji* VII, 98; *Selected Works of Mao Tse-tung* II, 306; and *Mao Zedong Xuanji* II, 585. Note that in the official post-1949 version, this figure has been changed to 4,000 years.

63. Takeuchi, ed., *Mao Zedong Ji* VI, 95; also Schram, *The Political Thought of Mao Tse-tung,* 391.

64. Stuart R. Schram, ed., Nancy J. Hodes, associate ed., *Mao's Road to Power: Revolutionary Writings, 1912–1949—Volume VI: The New Stage, August 1937–1938* (Armonk, New York: M. E. Sharpe, 2004), 814.

65. Schram ed., *Mao's Road to Power: Volume VI*, 821.

66. Takeuchi, ed., *Mao Zedong Ji* VII, 100.

67. Takeuchi, ed., *Mao Zedong Ji* VII, 100.

68. Takeuchi, ed., *Mao Zedong Ji* VII, 100; *Selected Works of Mao Tse-tung* II, 308; and *Mao Zedong Xuanji* II, 586.

69. Takeuchi, ed., *Mao Zedong Ji* VII, 102; *Selected Works of Mao Tse-tung* II, 308; and *Mao Zedong Xuanji* II, 588.

70. Takeuchi, ed., *Mao Zedong Ji* VII, 102; *Selected Works of Mao Tse-tung* II, 308; and *Mao Zedong Xuanji* II, 588.

71. Schram, *The Political Thought of Mao Tse-tung*, 114. See also Karl Wittfogel, "The Marxist View of China (Part 2)," *China Quarterly* 12 (1962): 154–69.

72. *Selected Works of Mao Tse-tung* II, 309; and *Mao Zedong Xuanji* II, 589.

73. See, in particular, "On New Democracy," *Selected Works of Mao Tse-tung* II, 339–84; and *Mao Zedong Xuanji* II, 623–70.

74. Takeuchi, ed., *Mao Zedong Ji* VII, 189; *Selected Works of Mao Tse-tung* II, 370; and *Mao Zedong Xuanji* II, 636.

75. Takeuchi, ed., *Mao Zedong Ji* VII, 74–82, 193–98; *Selected Works of Mao Tse-tung* II, 288–95, 373–78; and *Mao Zedong Xuanji* II, 569–76, 659–64.

76. Takeuchi, ed., *Mao Zedong Ji* V, 87; *Selected Works of Mao Tse-tung* I, 181; and *Mao Zedong Xuanji* I, 157.

77. Takeuchi, ed., *Mao Zedong Ji* VI, 65; *Selected Works of Mao Tse-tung* II, 125; and *Mao Zedong Xuanji* II, 419.

78. See, for example, Stuart R. Schram, ed., Nancy J. Hodes, associate ed., *Mao's Road to Power—Revolutionary Writings, 1912–1949: Volume VII—New Democracy, 1939–1941* (Armonk, New York: M. E. Sharpe, 2005), 348.

79. For discussion of the tension between determinism and activism in Mao's thought, see Knight, *Marxist Philosophy in China*, chapter 10.

80. Takeuchi, ed., *Mao Zedong Ji* VI, 167.

81. Takeuchi, ed., *Mao Zedong Ji* V, 88.

82. *Selected Works of Mao Tse-tung* I, 308; and *Mao Zedong Xuanji* II, 272.

83. Takeuchi, ed., *Mao Zedong Ji* V, 88.

84. Schram, *The Political Thought of Mao Tse-tung*, 392–93; Takeuchi, ed., *Mao Zedong Ji* VI, 95; *Selected Works of Mao Tse-tung* II, 148–49; and *Mao Zedong Xuanji* II, 442–43.

85. Takeuchi, ed., *Mao Zedong Ji* VI, 96; *Selected Works of Mao Tse-tung* II, 150; and *Mao Zedong Xuanji* II, 444.

86. Takeuchi, ed., *Mao Zedong Ji* V, 180.

87. Takeuchi, ed., *Mao Zedong Ji* VII, 177; *Selected Works of Mao Tse-tung* II, 361; and *Mao Zedong Xuanji* II, 647.

88. Takeuchi, ed., *Mao Zedong Ji* V, 88; *Selected Works of Mao Tse-tung* I, 182; and *Mao Zedong Xuanji* I, 158.

89. Takeuchi, ed., *Mao Zedong Ji* IX, 186.

90. Lenin, *Selected Works in Three Volumes* Vol. 2, 240–326.

91. Benjamin I. Schwartz, "Thoughts on the Late Mao: Between Total Redemption and Utter Frustration," in *The Secret Speeches of Chairman Mao: From the Hundred Flowers to the Great Leap Forward*, eds. Roderick Macfarquhar, Timothy Cheek, and Eugene Wu (Cambridge, Mass.: Harvard University Press, 1989), 34–35.

92. Takeuchi, ed., *Mao Zedong Ji* VIII, 132–33; *Selected Works of Mao Tse-tung* III, 85; and *Mao Zedong Xuanji* III, 821.

93. Takeuchi, ed., *Mao Zedong Ji* IX, 13–14. I have followed Legge's translation of the Confucian axiom; see James Legge, *The Four Books* (Hong Kong: Wei Tung Book Store, 1973), 138.

94. *Selected Works of Mao Tse-tung* II, 464; and *Mao Zedong Xuanji* II, 740.

95. Takeuchi, ed., *Mao Zedong Ji* VIII, 140; *Selected Works of Mao Tse-tung* III, 91; and *Mao Zedong Xuanji* III, 827–28.

96. Takeuchi, ed., *Mao Zedong Ji* V, 318.

97. Takeuchi, ed., *Mao Zedong Ji* VII, 173; *Selected Works of Mao Tse-tung* II, 358; and *Mao Zedong Xuanji* II, 644. See also Takeuchi, ed., *Mao Zedong Ji* VI, 227, where Mao asserts "Communism is humankind's most happy (*meiman*) social system."

98. Takeuchi, ed., *Mao Zedong Ji* VII, 176; *Selected Works of Mao Tse-tung* II, 360; and *Mao Zedong Xuanji* II, 646–47.

99. The Confucian concept of *shu* or "reciprocity" is the corollary *of ji suo bu yu, wu shi yu ren* utilized by Mao in his polemic which Peng Dehuai referred to earlier. *Analects* XV, 24 runs as follows: "Tsze-Kung asked, saying, 'Is there one word which may serve as a rule of practice for all one's life?' The master said, 'Is not RECIPROCITY such a word? What you do not want done to yourself, do not do to others'." Legge, *The Four Books*, 138.

100. *Selected Works of Mao Tse-tung* (London: Lawrence & Wishart, 1956), vol. 4, 295–98.

101. Takeuchi, ed., *Mao Zedong Ji* V, 257–60; *Selected Works of Mao Tse-tung* II, 31–33; and *Mao Zedong Xuanji* II, 330–32.

102. *Selected Works of Mao Tse-tung* II, 149; and *Mao Zedong Xuanji* II, 443; cf. Takeuchi, ed., *Mao Zedong Ji* VI, 95.

103. *Selected Works of Mao Tse-tung* I, 183; and *Mao Zedong Xuanji* I, 158.

104. In this respect, Mao's thought is not dissimilar from the thinking of many Western political thinkers and figures. As Sheldon Wolin argues, a vision of "the good" serves as a beacon toward which politics in the present orients itself. The future (or visions of it) thus exerts a very significant influence on the present. *Politics and Vision: Continuity and Innovation in Western Political Thought* (Princeton: Princeton University Press, 2004).

105. For a detailed discussion of the dilemma of determinism in Chinese Marxism, see Knight, *Marxist Philosophy in China*.

106. Karl Popper refers, in *The Open Society and its Enemies,* to the "wide gulf between Marx's activism and his historicism." Taking this as his theme, Charles

Wei-Hsun Fu has argued that this gulf is "uniquely bridged in Mao's Thought." See "Confucianism, Marxism-Leninism and Mao: A Critical Study," *Journal of Chinese Philosophy* 1 (1974): 339–71.

107. *Selected Works of Mao Tse-tung* I, 307; and *Mao Zedong Xuanji* I, 271.

108. Takeuchi, ed., *Mao Zedong Ji* V, 208; *Selected Works of Mao Tse-tung* I, 286; and *Mao Zedong Xuanji* I, 250.

109. Takeuchi, ed., *Mao Zedong Ji* IX, 187.

110. Takeuchi, ed., *Mao Zedong Ji* IX, 186; *Selected Works of Mao Tse-tung* III, 207; and *Mao Zedong Xuanji* III, 932.

111. Takeuchi, ed., *Mao Zedong Ji* IX, 236; *Selected Works of Mao Tse-tung* III, 242; and *Mao Zedong Xuanji* III, 970.

112. Takeuchi, ed., *Mao Zedong Ji* VI, 322; *Selected Works of Mao Tse-tung* II, 238; and *Mao Zedong Xuanji* II, 523.

113. Takeuchi Minoru, ed., *Mao Zedong Ji* IX, 192; *Selected Works of Mao Tse-tung* III, 210; and *Mao Zedong Xuanji* III, 935.

114. Takeuchi, ed., *Mao Zedong Ji* VI, 136; *Selected Works of Mao Tse-tung* II, 210; and *Mao Zedong Xuanji* II, 935.

115. Takeuchi, ed., *Mao Zedong Ji* V, 208; *Selected Works of Mao Tse-tung* I, 286; and *Mao Zedong Xuanji* I, 250.

116. Takeuchi, ed., *Mao Zedong Ji* V, 212; *Selected Works of Mao Tse-tung* I, 289; and *Mao Zedong Xuanji* I, 253.

117. Takeuchi, ed., *Mao Zedong Ji* V, 213; *Selected Works of Mao Tse-tung* I, 290; and *Mao Zedong Xuanji* I, 254.

118. Takeuchi, ed., *Mao Zedong Ji* V, 148; *Selected Works of Mao Tse-tung* I, 233; and *Mao Zedong Xuanji* I, 205.

119. Takeuchi, ed., *Mao Zedong Ji* VII, 177; *Selected Works of Mao Tse-tung* II, 361; and *Mao Zedong Xuanji* II, 647.

120. Takeuchi, ed., *Mao Zedong Ji* VII, 179; *Selected Works of Mao Tse-tung* II, 362–63; and *Mao Zedong Xuanji* II, 649.

121. Takeuchi, ed., *Mao Zedong Ji* IX, 222; *Selected Works of Mao Tse-tung* III, 232; and *Mao Zedong Xuanji* III, 959.

122. Mao made the following instructive comment: "The old politics and economics of the Chinese nation form the basis (*genju*) of its old culture, just as its new politics and economics will form the basis of its new culture." Takeuchi, ed., *Mao Zedong Ji* VII, 150; *Selected Works of Mao Tse-tung* II, 341; and *Mao Zedong Xuanji* II, 625.

123. Takeuchi, ed., *Mao Zedong Ji* VII, 114; *Selected Works of Mao Tse-tung* II, 317; and *Mao Zedong Xuanji* II, 598.

124. Takeuchi, ed., *Mao Zedong Ji* VII, 102; *Selected Works of Mao Tse-tung* II, 309; and *Mao Zedong Xuanji* II, 588.

125. Takeuchi, ed., *Mao Zedong Ji* VI, 96; *Selected Works of Mao Tse-tung* II, 150; and *Mao Zedong Xuanji* II, 444.

126. Georg Lukács, *History and Class Consciousness* (London: Merlin Press, 1971), 4.

Perspectives on Marxism and Social Change in Mao Zedong's Thought: A Study of Three Documents, 1937–1940

6

ENTRAL THEORETICAL PROBLEM of the Marxist theory of history has been the extent to which the economic realm influences politics and ideology, and whether politics and ideology can exert any influence on the economic realm. Within one influential strand of the Marxist tradition—that sometimes referred to as mechanistic or even "vulgar" Marxism—the solution to this problem has been cast in terms of economic determination of politics and ideology. That is, the economic base of society has been represented as the realm invariably exercizing causal dominance, with politics and ideology perceived as a superstructure that merely reflects changes within the economic base.[1] From this perspective, ideologies and political institutions and practices are of peripheral interest since they are unable to independently initiate historical change. The negative theoretical and practical implications of this mechanistic Marxist position are manifold, and, for a Marxist like Mao Zedong immersed in revolutionary struggle, the inherent problems of a reductionist reading of the superstructure could be particularly acute. Not only did Mao have to evaluate the strength of the state against which he would pit his revolutionary forces and the consciousness of groups and classes within Chinese society, he also had to determine the level of political influence exercised by other political parties and anticipate their tactics. An accurate assessment of the role and effectivity of superstructural elements thus constituted an urgent practical task, one that necessitated a theoretical response to the problems of economism and reductionism at the heart of the mechanistic version of Marxism that frequently posed as orthodoxy.

Mao scholars have frequently asserted that Mao either broke with or deviated sharply from orthodox Marxism through his emphasis on the superstructure and by attributing to human consciousness a significant capacity to influence the economic realm. Mao was thus guilty of voluntarism, idealism, and utopianism, and was consequently a most unorthodox Marxist. This line of interpretation, articulated most clearly in the writings of Stuart Schram,[2] Benjamin Schwartz,[3] Maurice Meisner,[4] and Frederic Wakeman Jr.,[5] became a dominant theme in the field of Mao studies, despite the best efforts of a number of radical scholars to challenge it during the 1970s (see chapter 3). In what is known as the *Modern China* debate (named after the journal in which it occurred), Richard Pfeffer[6] and Andrew Walder[7] drew on both classical Marxist and neo-Marxist traditions to argue that the theoretical distance between Mao and Marx was much less pronounced than had been suggested by the "China field" and that Mao could legitimately be situated on the theoretical terrain of Marxism. However, events in China since Mao's death have if anything reinforced the conventional account of Mao's unorthodox reading of the Marxist "base-superstructure metaphor," and the bold attempt by Pfeffer and Walder to introduce a critical and more flexible note into Western Mao studies has evaporated under the glare of economic pragmatism and rationalism that have dominated in both China and the West during the 1980s and 1990s.[8]

Yet the need for a critical exploration of Mao's thought and his understanding of Marxism has not evaporated.[9] One important reason for rethinking the way in which Mao appropriated and employed core themes within Marxist theory is that numerous hitherto unknown texts by Mao were published in China during the 1980s and 1990s.[10] Many documents previously available only in Chinese have been made available in English over the last two decades.[11] Some of these suggest the need to reevaluate interpretations of Mao's thought that have acquired the status of conventional wisdom. Moreover, keeping alive the debate on Mao's views on Marxism and social change can serve to deepen our own understanding of these significant issues. The issues were significant for Mao, and they remain so for us: What influence do economics, politics, and ideology exert in the process of social change; are there different phases of social change, revolutionary and nonrevolutionary, during which the causes of social change alter; how might a theoretical perspective on social change influence a political party or the state's approach to the formulation of policy? As the leader of a revolutionary party, Mao had no option but to reflect on these and related questions and to develop strategies and tactics in light of the theoretical conclusions at which he arrived.

The following analysis of the problem of social change in Mao's thought takes as its point of departure three texts of the early Yan'an period, at a time when Mao was deeply engaged in the attempt to master Marxist theory and philosophy and to apply the results of this study to the problems of the Chinese Revolution. These texts are "On Contradiction" (1937),[12] "On One-Party Dictatorship" (1938),[13] and "On New Democracy" (1940).[14] In each of these documents, Mao addresses the problem of social change and its causes but does so in a rather different manner. What unites these seemingly disparate perspectives is a continued belief in the ultimately determining role of economics, although as we will observe, Mao was attempting to discover an appropriate role for politics, ideology, and culture within an orthodox Marxist theory of social change. The base-superstructure metaphor employed in "On Contradiction" clearly retained the notion of economic determination, although in a rather more flexible and dialectical form than a mechanistic form of Marxism would allow: The elements of the superstructure—politics, ideology, and culture—are attributed with a capacity to influence the economic base in particular historical situations. Yet, when pressed to explain the origins and behavior of political parties, he was to fall back, in "On One-Party Dictatorship," on a rather unreflective materialism that applied a rigid class analysis to the political realm. By the time he wrote "On New Democracy," however, Mao was developing a more complex and flexible perspective on causation and social change, one that, while retaining the ultimately determining role of economics, attributed to the political realm a heightened level of agency. It is clear that the historical role of politics had become a major theoretical and practical problem, one that required a development of Mao's earlier view that politics possessed the same somewhat limited historical influence as culture and ideology.

What is evident from these documents—individually and collectively—is that Mao was grappling with the theoretical tensions and possibilities within the Marxist theory of social change and was seeking a perspective that would allow him to capture the dynamic interaction between the different social realms of the Chinese context. Once discovered, this perspective could function not only as the basis of Mao's vision of China's future but also the strategies and tactics needed to push social change in that direction.

"On Contradiction": Base and Superstructure

While the pre-1949 version of "On Contradiction" is significantly different from the revised official version to be found in Mao's *Selected Works,* two passages dealing with the problem of causation and social change are largely the same in both versions of this document. In these passages, Mao employs the concepts and categories of orthodox Marxism, but he does so in a way that indicates an attempt to distance himself from a mechanistic Marxism that attributed politics and culture with no capacity to influence social change; as a result, a more complex position emerges. The passages here reproduced are from the pre-1949 document; the sections in italics are those that have been excised from the official post-1949 text:

> *I regard all principal and non-principal positions of the aspects of a contradiction as involved in this mutual change.*
>
> Some people think that this is not true of certain contradictions. For instance, in the contradiction between the productive forces and the relations of production, the productive forces are the principal aspect; in the contradiction between theory and practice, practice is the principal aspect; in the contradiction between the economic base and the superstructure, the economic base is the principal aspect; and there is no change in their respective positions. *It should be realized that* **under normal conditions,** *and viewed from a materialist point of view, they really are unchanging and absolute things; however, there are* **historically many particular situations** *in which they do change.* The productive forces, practice and the economic base generally play the principal and decisive role; whoever denies this is not a materialist. But it must also be admitted that *sometimes* such aspects as the relations of production, theory and the superstructure in turn manifest themselves in the principal and decisive role. When it is impossible for the productive forces to develop without a change in the relations of production, then the change in the relations of production plays the principal and decisive role. . . . When the superstructure (politics, culture, etc.) obstructs the development of the economic base, political and cultural changes become principal and decisive. Are we going against materialism when we say this? No. The reason is that we recognize that in the general development of history the material determines the mental. We also—and indeed must—recognize the reaction of mental on material things. This does not go against materialism; on the contrary, it avoids mechanical materialism and firmly upholds dialectical materialism.[15]

Elsewhere in "On Contradiction," Mao again refers to the problem of causation and social change:

> When Marx and Engels applied the law of *the unity of* contradictions to the study of the socio-historical process, they discovered *the basic cause of social development to be* the contradiction between the productive forces and the relations of production, *the contradiction of class struggle,* and the resultant *(you*

zhexie maodun suo chanshengde) contradiction between the economic base and its superstructure (politics, ideology).[16]

The following observations can be made on the basis of this explanation of the Marxist theory of social change. First, Mao identifies several realms of society as having a potential to initiate or influence social change: the forces of production, relations of production, class struggle, economic base, and superstructure. The superstructure is constituted of politics, culture, and ideology. Second, Mao argues that the forces of production are, "under normal conditions" (*yiban qingxing*), the determining influence in the relationship between the forces of production and the relations of production; similarly, the economic base is "under normal conditions" the determining influence in the relationship between base and superstructure. This is, of course, no more than a conventional, rather mechanistic, Marxist perspective on social change. What is significant here is that Mao goes beyond this conventional formulation and attributes both the relations of production and superstructure with a potential to influence social change. They cannot, Mao insists, be perceived merely as passive reflections of the forces of production or economic base respectively; indeed, in "historically particular situations" they can become "principal and decisive."

However, Mao's attribution of a "principal and decisive role" to the superstructure and relations of production is carefully qualified. Mao makes it quite clear that "under normal conditions" (not specified by Mao but presumably a nonrevolutionary situation in which society is relatively stable and change is gradual), the superstructure and relations of production are *not* "principal and decisive," and that, in order to comprehend the nature and operation of a society during such conditions one must examine the economic base and within it, the forces of production, for it is these that "generally play the principal and decisive role." Moreover, the superstructure and relations of production can assume a "principal and decisive role" only during those historical moments when they impede the further development of the economic base and forces of production respectively. At such moments, the superstructure and relations of production take on a dual and contradictory function: obstruction and facilitation of change. This capacity for both obstructing and facilitating change derives not from the relations of production and superstructure themselves but from developments within the opposite and normally principal aspect (the forces of production or economic base) of the contradiction of which they are an aspect. For example, the capacity for change within the superstructure emerges as a result of developments within the economic base; "under normal conditions," these economic developments flow through to the superstructure, and the economic base dictates the outcome of the relationship between it and the superstructure. However, Mao recognized that the superstructure has a differentiated function; it is also capable of obstructing the development of the economic base. This gives the superstructure enhanced causal significance in those "historically particular situations" in which developments within the economic base are outpacing change within the superstructure.

The increased causal effectivity attributed to the superstructure by Mao does not indicate, as some commentators have suggested, a theoretical shift to an invariably superstructural reading of social change.[17] Rather, he believed the superstructure can only become "principal and decisive" in obstructing and then facilitating impulses for change generated within the economic base. The superstructure could only become "principal and decisive" in "historically particular situations," and even here, it was factors external to the superstructure that gave it an increased capacity to determine the rate and, to a lesser extent, the manner of the resolution of the contradictions generated by forces for change within the economic base. Mao's assertion that the contradiction between economic base and superstructure results from the major contradictions within the economic realm of society reinforces this interpretation of the perspective on social change to be found in "On Contradiction."[18] In this document, Mao did not show a willingness to accept that the superstructure could autonomously create the historical context within which it operated; the economic base remained the ultimate determinant of historical and social change. Nevertheless, it is evident that Mao was seeking a theoretical formula for social change in which the superstructure could have a role other than that of passive reflection of the economic base. By conferring on the superstructure a capacity to influence the development of society through obstruction and facilitation of change occurring within the economic base, he was signaling a readiness to perceive in historical causation a dialectical process in which influence was, if not equally reciprocal between base and superstructure, at least not the sole prerogative of the economic base.

This attempt to establish a degree of flexibility within the Marxist theory of social change was a reflection of Mao's concern to have at his disposal a theory capable of comprehending "historically particular situations." Twentieth-century China was, Mao believed, just such a historically particular situation; to understand China, a theory was therefore required that not only incorporated universal laws of historical development but facilitated analysis and comprehension of its particularities. The complexities of the Chinese historical situation—the complex mix of

modes of production within its social formation and the interaction between them, the rapidity of social change, the significant impact of foreign forces on China's economics and politics—militated against an
uncritical use of a theory of social change in which the economic realm
of society was invariably attributed to causal dominance. While the economic base remained the ultimately determining factor, a sensitivity to the
level of historical influence exerted by the superstructure was required,
even to the extent of recognizing that it could sometimes play a decisive
role. As Mao asserted, recognition of a dialectical interaction between
economic base and superstructure, founded on acceptance of ultimate
economic determination, was not in contradiction with the materialism
of Marxism; rather, "it avoids mechanical materialism and firmly upholds
dialectical materialism."[19]

The suggestion that the position articulated in "On Contradiction" retained the notion of ultimate economic determination is strengthened by
his annotations to various Soviet texts on philosophy he was studying at the
time he wrote this important philosophical essay. In a marginal comment
on the theory of social change in Marx's *Capital*, discussed in *A Course on
Dialectical Materialism* (which Mao read between November 1936 and April
1937), Mao wrote: "In the contradiction between the social character of
production and the private character of ownership can be seen the contradiction between the forces and relations of production, and this is the fundamental contradiction. From this fundamental contradiction emerge all
other contradictions, because this fundamental contradiction determines
the development of capitalism."[20] In another annotation to this text, Mao
noted that "in the contradiction between economic base and superstructure, the economic base is dominant."[21] Moreover, in his annotations to *Dialectical Materialism and Historical Materialism*, Mao wrote "material
production is the foundation of the variegated life of humanity,"[22] and that
"it is matter that determines spirit, and not spirit that determines matter."[23]
Further examples of this sort are to be found in Mao's philosophical annotations that suggest that his perspective on social change was not unorthodox, particularly as measured by the criteria of contemporary Soviet
Marxism.[24] This reinforces the view that the discussion of causation and
social change that appears in "On Contradiction" did not have as its purpose the rejection of the notion of ultimate economic determination in
the Marxist theory of social change. Nevertheless, it is clear too that Mao
believed that belief in ultimate economic determination was compatible
with a recognition of the capacity of the superstructure in "historically particular situations" to have an influence on social change. Mao was thus

seeking a flexible rendition of the materialist theory of history that would allow him to address the numerous political, ideological, and cultural challenges that emerged in the course of revolution without jettisoning the materialist premises that made the Marxist theory of social change distinctive.

"On One-Party Dictatorship": Class and Politics

"On One-Party Dictatorship" has, in contrast to the much better known "On Contradiction," been largely ignored by Mao scholars. One reason for this is that this document is the text of an interview given by Mao on 2 February 1938 to the Yan'an correspondent of the *Xin Zhonghua Bao* (*New China News*).[25] It therefore lacks the authorial presence and theoretical authority of the extended philosophical essay "On Contradiction." However, "On One-Party Dictatorship" is a significant text in the attempt to identify and elaborate Mao's theory of social change, for it indicates only too clearly that he retained a perspective firmly founded on the materialism of Marxism. Indeed, the flexible and dialectical materialism of "On Contradiction" is here replaced by a rather more mechanistic and reductionist attempt to explain the emergence and behavior of the political systems of the Soviet Union, Germany, and Italy. Why did each of these political systems, dominated by such mutually antagonistic ideologies, have only a single political party? Mao's response is as follows.

The Soviet Union possessed a one-party system precisely because there existed no "social base" (*shehui jichu*) for any party other than the Communist Party. There was consequently neither the possibility nor necessity for other political parties to exist. Legal proscription was not necessary, because the transformation of the economy into a socialist form meant that the Russian people no longer supported other parties, and they had been discarded.[26] Mao's theoretical justification of a single-party system in the Soviet Union was provided sanction by Stalin's "Report on the Draft Constitution of the U.S.S.R." of 1936, from which Mao quotes with approval. In this "Report" Stalin had asserted:

> A party is a part of a class, its most advanced part. Several parties, and, consequently, freedom for parties, can exist only in a society in which there are antagonistic classes whose interests are mutually hostile and irreconcilable. . . . In the U.S.S.R. there are only two classes, workers and peasants, whose interests—far from being mutually hostile—are, on the contrary, friendly. Hence, there is no ground in the U.S.S.R. for the existence of several parties, and consequently, for freedom for these parties. In the U.S.S.R. there is ground for only one party, the Communist Party.[27]

There was thus, according to Stalin, a growing social cohesion in the Soviet Union founded on the establishment of a socialist economy and the consequent "obliteration" of class differences, and this gave rise to a situation in which only one political party could emerge. Mao accepted and uncritically employed this justification for the Soviet Union's one-party system, a position founded on the view that developments within the political sphere are contingent on developments within the "social base" of society. Mao evidently included class structure and forms of ownership within the concept of the "social base" but not political parties.

When he turned his attention to Hitler's Germany and Mussolini's Italy, the reasons Mao gave for the existence of their (supposedly) one-party systems are based on the same logic. In both societies, the economic base was characterized by class divisions that had given rise to a number of competing political parties. In both states, however, the fascists had attempted to create a one-party system. Through political proscription, the *de jure* status of political parties other than the fascist party had been removed; but their *de facto* existence, which derived from economic divisions within the social base, persisted. This could be demonstrated by reference to anti-fascist activities pursued by these parties both domestically and abroad. Thus, although one-party dictatorships did exist in Germany and Italy, they were not true one-party systems, for other parties continued to exist.[28]

Mao employed exactly the same logic in his rejection of the possibility of a genuine one-party dictatorship in contemporary China (that of the Guomindang [Nationalist Party]).[29] In China, there existed a number of classes that had different economic, political, and ideological interests. In such a variegated social and economic context, there existed no "social base" for a one-party dictatorship. Rather, China's political system possessed a number of different political parties, and these could not unilaterally be "eliminated" through either military or legal means, although the Guomindang government had attempted both. This strategy had been a complete failure, according to Mao. Not only had the other political parties survived, but the strategy had plunged China into ten years of civil war, leaving it weakened in the face of an aggressive Japanese imperialism. The inevitable existence of a number of political parties, resulting from China's differentiated "social base," thus constituted the premise for Mao's call for a national united front of all anti-Japanese political parties.

Mao was therefore attempting to use a materialist explanation of Chinese society and its political realm in order to enhance conviction in a politically inspired argument that the strategy of the Guomindang government could not succeed and indeed was counter-productive to the overriding imperative of combined resistance to Japanese imperialism. Nevertheless, in attributing to the state the capacity to proscribe opposition parties and to create legally, if not in fact, a one-party system, Mao was acknowledging that the state could act forcefully to protect the interests of the dominant economic class and therefore could exert an influence on the process of social change. However, this acknowledgment of the power of the state is founded on an insistence that it is the "social base" that ultimately determines what occurs in other realms of society, particularly in the political realm. Mao's position, articulated in "On One-Party Dictatorship," is thus a materialist one safely situated within the confines of Marxist orthodoxy.

"On New Democracy": Economics, Politics, Culture

What is surprising about "On One-Party Dictatorship" is that, although Mao was concerned to conceptualize the role and influence of superstructural institutions such as the state and political parties, he does not actually use the concept of the "superstructure" to elaborate his case. Nowhere in the document does the term "superstructure" appear. Indeed, this interesting theoretical lacuna mirrors the comparative absence of the concept of "superstructure" in the Mao texts of the early Yan'an period. As we have observed, the concept does appear in "On Contradiction" and several of his philosophical annotations of 1937, but he only very rarely employed it in subsequent documents of the Yan'an period.[30] This lacuna is in stark contrast to the Mao texts of the post-1955 period in which the concept of the superstructure occupies a prominent position; it also warns against hasty and simplistic generalizations about Mao's views on the role of the superstructure in social change, which abound in critiques of Mao's thought and which are almost certainly incorrect, for the Yan'an period at least.

Mao's disinclination to employ the concept of the superstructure after 1937 suggests that he mobilized other conceptual categories when he discussed social change, which he frequently did. These categories emerge in their most complete form in "On New Democracy," without doubt one of the most important theoretical texts of the Yan'an period. While Mao scholars have frequently referred to this document, they have overlooked the evidence in it of a substantial development in Mao's views on the problem of causation in social change. As Roland Lew has argued, "On New Democracy" "needs to be read at several levels" and that it is an "important and paradoxical" document.[31] The following reading of this text explores one level that has remained hidden from the supposedly informed gaze of Mao scholars.

In "On New Democracy," Mao identifies three levels of society—economics, politics, and culture—and explores the relationship among them. As Mao points out:

> Any given culture (as an ideological form) is a reflection of the politics and economics of a given society, and the former in turn has a tremendous influence upon the latter, and politics is the concentrated expression of economics. This is our fundamental view of the relation of culture to politics and of the relation of politics to economics.[32]

This passage is of considerable importance for an understanding of Mao's perspective on social change and in identifying the origins of this perspective. First, the tripartite division of society is itself worthy of note. It suggests that Mao now regarded the differentiation of society into two distinct levels—base and superstructure—as insufficient for a precise understanding of the sequence of causation in the process of social change, and particularly the role of politics within this sequence. In so doing, Mao drew on a theme evident in a volume by the Japanese Marxist Sugiyama Sakae translated into Chinese in the late 1920s and elaborated by the famous Chinese Marxist intellectual Li Da whose works Mao closely studied in the mid to late 1930s. In *Shehui kexue gailun* [*A Survey of Social Science*], Sugiyama had argued, in line with orthodox Marxist theory, that it is the realm of production—the "process of social life"—that "ultimately" determines human thought. However, he introduced into his schema for social change the possibility that all levels of the social totality could have some influence on the process of social change. In order to clarify the relative influence that each level might exert, he separated the superstructure into two realms: Superstructure I is constituted of society's legal and political systems, while Superstructure II is constituted of "consciousness." Superstructure I clearly has more historical influence than Superstructure II, but even the latter possesses the capacity for a reactive influence on Superstructure I and the various economic realms incorporated within "the process of social life." This categorization of the various levels of the social totality and their relative influence in the process of social change was perceived by Li Da, Sugiyama's translator, as an appropriate interpretation of the causal relationship between the economic and noneconomic realms of society, and he incorporated it into his famous text on Marxist philosophy and social theory *Shehuixue dagang* [*Elements of Sociology*] that Mao studied in early 1938.[33]

Second, and following from this point, it is evident that Mao, like Sugiyama and Li Da, perceived the need for a conceptual distinction between politics and culture. It will be remembered that in "On Contradiction" Mao had defined the superstructure as constituted of *both* politics and culture,[34] and as part of a single social category had attributed to them the same causal significance. This equivalence between politics and culture, in terms of influence on the process of social change, disappears in the tripartite formulation of "On New Democracy." Mao now defined politics in a way that gave it a far more prominent role in the causal sequence than was the case with previous formulations. "Politics," Mao asserted, "is the concentrated expression (*jizhong de biaoxian*) of economics." This definition of politics had first been coined by Lenin, who had, however, used it in a context and sense very different from Mao's usage.[35] Mao interpreted Lenin's remarks as a sanction for the construction of a tripartite conceptualization in which politics could assume an enhanced causal significance. Indeed, it is evident from subsequent comments made throughout the Yan'an period that the notion of politics as the concentrated expression of economics persisted as an important interpretive medium. In his "Talks at the Yan'an Forum on Literature and Art" (1942), Mao used it in the following context: "Only through politics can the needs of the class and the masses find expression in concentrated form (*jizhong di biaoxian chulai*). Revolutionary statesmen, the political specialists who know the science or art of revolutionary politics, are simply the leaders of millions upon millions of statesmen—the masses. Their task is to collect the opinions of these mass statesmen, sift and refine them, and return them to the masses who then take them and put them into practice."[36] The connection between the concept of politics as the concentrated expression of economics and the notion of the "mass-line" is clearly drawn here, and in his important document of June 1943 entitled "Some Questions Concerning Methods of Leadership," Mao was again to emphasize the function of politics as being to concentrate (*jizhong chulai*) the "scattered and unsystematic" ideas of "the masses."[37] Politics therefore performed a pivotal role in the process whereby the masses or members of an economic class assumed an increased social cohesion and unity of identification, that is, in the process in which a class develops from being a class-in-itself to being a class-for-itself.[38] Mao's borrowing of Lenin's reference to politics as the concentrated expression of economics was consequently to have considerable theoretical implications, not only for his perception of the causal sequence in social change but also for his distinctive approach to organization and leadership.

Politics could therefore no longer be regarded, as his "On Contradiction" formulation suggests, as largely a reflection of the economic base, and possessing only a limited capacity for influencing the development of society. Rather, politics had been promoted within the causal chain to the extent that culture is now a reflection not just of economics but of economics and politics combined: "Culture is a reflection of the politics *and* economics of a given society."[39] Mao develops the notion of a union of economics and politics as causally responsible for the production of a society's culture as follows: "The old politics and economics of the Chinese nation form the basis (*genju*) of its old culture, just as its new politics and economics will form the basis of its new culture."[40] Here, Mao constructs a new category—the "basis"—from a combination of politics and economics. The "basis" of society represents the causal matrix from which culture emerges, and culture is a reflection of the "basis." Although the concept of a "social basis" (*shehui genju*) had emerged in an earlier text (1937),[41] it is only in "On New Democracy" that the notion of a "basis" comprised of politics and economics (as opposed to the more conventional "economic base" [*jingji jichu*]) becomes a major social category in Mao's thought. Why had Mao felt it necessary to construct such a category, and how did he employ it to arrive at causal explanations about the nature of social change? These questions may best be answered through an explanation of the definition and role of the elements of the "basis" and through analysis of the causal significance attributed to culture by Mao.

The "Basis": Economics and Politics

Mao included in the category of "economics" both the forces of production and the class relations of production. In "On New Democracy," Mao referred to the economic structure (*jingji goucheng*) of society, and this term encompassed wealth-producing factors as well as the class relationships that emerged around them on the basis of ownership. The wealth-producing factors included industrial and commercial enterprises (such as banks and railways), and land.[42] However, ownership and management were also an integral part of economics,[43] and in his discussion of the economics of New Democracy, the regulation of capital is included as a major feature. Economics therefore incorporated structures and relations founded on the criterion of ownership or management of society's productive resources. This is made evident if we turn to chapter 1 of "The Chinese Revolution and the Chinese Communist Party" (1939),[44] in which there is frequent reference to the economic exploitation (*jingji boxue*) suffered by China's peasantry because of the ownership and control of land by the landlord class.[45] This document also makes very clear that the development of capitalism in China was responsible for the emergence of certain characteristic class structures:

> This history of the emergence and development of national capitalism is at the same time the history of the emergence and development of the Chinese bourgeoisie and proletariat. Just as a section of the merchants, landlords and bureaucrats were precursors of the Chinese bourgeoisie, so a section of the peasants and handicraft workers were the precursors of the Chinese proletariat. . . . However, the Chinese proletariat emerged and grew simultaneously not only with the Chinese national bourgeoisie but also with the enterprise directly operated by the imperialists in China.[46]

Mao was also to refer to the economic status (*diwei*) *of* the classes in Chinese society, and to argue that this "entirely determined" their attitude toward the Chinese Revolution.[47]

Having identified the constituent elements of the category of "economics," let us pass on to a discussion of Mao's usage of the concept of "politics." In doing so, it will become evident that he was not inclined to an easy attribution of invariable causal primacy to economics in historical development. The picture that emerges is rather more complex.

For Mao, the category of "politics" incorporated many important features of social life. The first of these was class struggle. It was noted earlier that Mao included under the rubric "economics" the structure of class relations that were characteristic of a particular mode of production. However, Mao perceived the actual struggle *between* classes as political in the broadest sense; class struggle was a manifestation in intensified form of the economically generated hostility between classes, and this hostility was played out in the realm of politics. It is no coincidence that Mao commences his discussion of the politics of New Democracy with an analysis of the role the various classes of Chinese society had played in the Chinese Revolution, and the struggle to establish and defend their economic interests is portrayed as a political struggle.[48] The manifestation at a political level of the economic hostility in class relations was facilitated by several political institutions that emerged to represent particular class interests. Foremost among these was the political party. "The party is," Mao had declared in 1938, "an organization of the most conscious section of a class."[49] Mao consistently asserted a link between the existence and activities of a political party and the material interests of particular class structures. Moreover, he consistently mobilized a class analysis to explain the policies and actions of political parties: "What is even more fundamental for the study of the particular features of the two parties [Communist and Nationalist] is the examination of the class basis (*jieji jichu*) of the two parties and the resultant contradictions which have arisen between each party and other forces at different periods."[50]

Mao consequently invoked the class character (*jiejixing*) of the Guomindang to explain its abrupt change of policy in 1927.[51] Similarly, the Guomindang is portrayed in "On New Democracy" as the political representative of the "big bourgeoisie"[52] and in "On Coalition Government" (1945) as the representative of the "big landlords, bankers and compradores."[53] Mao also insisted that the Chinese Communist Party (CCP) represented class interests, particularly those of the industrial proletariat and peasantry. The CCP's link with the working class was a self-evident one for Mao; without the emergence in China of an industrial proletariat and its exploitation within the context of industrial capitalism, there could have been no communist party (see chapter 4). Moreover, the CCP's representation of peasant interests was a specific feature of Chinese society and the Chinese Revolution,[54] which resulted from the fact that no party had emerged to represent exclusively the economic interests of the peasantry: "As China has no political party exclusively representing the peasants . . . the Chinese Communist Party has become the leader of the peasants . . . being the only party that has formulated and carried out a thoroughgoing land programme."[55] Such examples could be multiplied many times. The important point is that Mao perceived a causal link between political parties and economic class interests; the former emerged from and served to defend the latter.

Another feature of social life Mao included in the realm of "politics" was the state or "state system" (*guoti*).[56] Mao's interpretation of the state ran along conventional Marxist lines, and he viewed it as a political institution of class domination produced by and operating at the behest of the ruling class. In chapter 1 of "The Chinese Revolution and the Chinese Communist Party," analysis of the state during China's feudal period makes the class role of the state abundantly clear: "The feudal landlord state was the organ of power protecting this system of feudal exploitation. . . . The emperor reigned supreme in the feudal state, appointing officials in charge of the armed forces, the law courts, the treasury and state granaries in all parts of the country and relying on the landed gentry as the mainstay of the entire system of feudal rules."[57] Similarly, in "On New Democracy," Mao asserted that the state system is a "question of the status of the various social classes within the state" (*guojia*),[58] and it is evident that his taxonomy of state systems was based on the arrangement of classes, with special emphasis being placed on the ruling class. Mao's rather limited taxonomy of state systems thus included: (1) republics under bourgeois dictatorship; (2) republics under the dictatorship of the proletariat; and (3) republics under the joint dictatorship of several revolutionary classes. These three basic kinds of state system had emerged "according to the class character of their political power."[59]

What is of particular interest in Mao's conception of the state is a distinction between the state system (*guoti*) and the complex of institutions whose function was the actual translation of the economic interests of the ruling class into concrete policies and actions; such institutions included the government, army, legal system, and bureaucracy.[60] This distinction emerges most clearly when Mao turned his attention to the role of government within society: "As for the question of the 'system of government' (*zhengti*) this is a matter of how political power is organized, the form in which one social class or another chooses to arrange its apparatus of political power to oppose its enemies and protect itself. There is no state (*guojia*) which does not have an appropriate apparatus of political power to represent it."[61] Mao proceeds to suggest that the most appropriate system of government for New Democracy would be a democratic centralist system in which people's congresses at all levels from national down to township would be based on universal suffrage. In contrast, the state system would be a "joint dictatorship of all the revolutionary classes." Moreover, not only did Mao indicate a distinction between the system of government and the state system, he raised the possibility that the two might be out of harmony (*buxiang shiying*).[62] This suggests the possibility that Mao did not perceive the translation of the interests of the dominant economic class into institutional or policy forms as entirely automatic. If this is the case, it may well be indicative of Mao's attempt to arrive at a theoretical formulation that allowed politics a degree of autonomy from economic determination without entirely rupturing the linkage between them. This possibility will be explored subsequently.

In "On Coalition Government" Mao returned to the distinction between state and government, and also discussed the army as an integral part of the complex of institutions that comprised the state: "'The army (*jundui*) belongs to the state' (*guojia*)—that is perfectly true, and there is not an army in the world that does not belong to a state. . . . The only kind of state for China to establish is a new-democratic state and, on that basis, she should establish a new-democratic coalition government; all the armed forces of China must belong to such a government of such a state."[63] Similarly, Mao had referred previously (1938) to the Marxist theory of the state and the role it attributed to the armed forces: "According to the Marxist theory of the state (*guojia xueshuo*), the army is the chief component of state power (*guojia zhengquan*). Whoever wants to seize and retain state power must have a strong army."[64] Mao thus regarded the army as operating under the administration of the government, the government itself being the principal organizational apparatus of the state.

Mao therefore represented the state system in class terms. The state system was, as we have seen, "a question of the status of the various social classes within the state." While the concept of the state system entailed the notion of class rule, it suggested the political, rather than purely economic, aspects of class rule; the state system reflected the relative political arrangement of classes within society. The state, on the other hand, consisted of an identifiable complex of political institutions employed by the ruling class to defend its own economic dominance and to suppress class opponents; of these the government and the army were the most significant.

The significance of this distinction between the state system and the system of government will become evident if we turn to an analysis of the causal role of politics within Mao's conception of the "basis" (*genju*) and in his tripartite conceptualization of society generally. For Mao, politics was the concentrated expression of economics; and he located it within the "basis" of society, the causal matrix of economics and politics that gave rise to society's culture. The constituent elements of politics were institutions such as political parties, the state, government, and army. In what sense could such political institutions be a concentrated expression of economics; what was the causal relationship between them and the forces and relations of production that constituted economics? We have already drawn attention to the fact that Mao perceived politics as allowing the needs and interests of a class and the masses to find expression in concentrated form; indeed, it was only through politics that this could be achieved.[65] On this premise, Mao was to formulate a theory of political leadership that took as its point of departure the notion that political leaders and the political institutions they led could actively concentrate the scattered and unsystematic aspirations and attitudes of the class or classes they represented. Politics could therefore assume a central role in building class consciousness and cohesion and in organizing a class for its own defense; without politics, a class could not successfully prosecute its own interests or alter social and economic conditions unfavorable to it.

While Mao attributed an extremely important role to politics in the process of social change, the appearance of certain economic conditions (such as particular forms of production or class structure) necessarily preceded the emergence of their corresponding politics. Politics was a concentrated expression of economics and could not emerge prior to or exist in complete autonomy from the historically necessary conditions generated by economics. For example, the possibility that a communist party might come into being prior to the appearance of capitalism and the creation of an industrial proletariat would have been dismissed by Mao as a historical impossibility.[66] Once such economic conditions had developed, however, the "politics" that emerged could function to concentrate the political energies and attitudes of the proletariat, and the subsequent development of its economic struggles and the resultant position of that class within the structure of class relations were heavily dependent on the efficacy of its politics.

An explanation of the rate and nature of change of a particular society could therefore not ignore the role of politics. An illustration is Mao's perception of the durability of feudalism in traditional China, during which the peasantry lacked effective political organization, leadership, and programs for change; despite numerous peasant rebellions, economic disaffection had not been translated into meaningful opposition to the feudal system. The politics of feudal society had, by and large, consequently been the politics of the landlord class, which produced a state system ensuring the persistence of feudalism and with it the economic domination of the landlord class.[67] The significant characteristic of traditional Chinese society was, of course, that its mode of production was (for Mao) a largely undifferentiated feudalism. In a social formation with several modes of production, such as China had become after Western intervention, politics became differentiated along class lines, allowing a significant threat to be posed at a political level to the politics of the dominant economic class.[68]

Consequently, while the emergence of politics was for Mao subsequent to economics, the causal relationship between them was a reciprocal one. Moreover, causal dominance, at first the prerogative of economics, passed over to politics as it assumed the role of concentrating the attitudes and energies of its class (or classes) and establishing political institutions for the defense of class interests. However, while causal dominance might pass over to politics, economics necessarily continued to exercise a significant residual influence by restraining the variability of politics and thus the limits to potential change.

"Politics" and the Adjustment of Class Struggle

The important distinction between this position and the position articulated in "On Contradiction" is that besides making culture a function of *both* politics and economics, Mao did not in this later position limit the influence of politics to "historically particular situations." Rather, once created by the requisite economics, the politics of a class could maintain the historical initiative and actively prosecute the struggle to secure the interests of that class and the struggle waged at the level of politics could be decisive. Mao's perception of the limitations and potentiality of "politics" in the historical process can be demonstrated by reference to two issues of concern to him during the Yan'an period: the adjustment of class struggle and the role of government in society. Let us look first at Mao's views on the political adjustment of class struggle.

Mao called for the adjustment of class struggle on several occasions during the period of the Second United Front. Such calls were made at times when the extent of class struggle threatened to jeopardize the four-class bloc viewed as essential by Mao for the successful prosecution of the Anti-Japanese War. In his address to the Sixth Plenum of the Sixth Central Committee (1938), Mao made the following instructive statement:

> The same is true of the relationship between the class struggle and the national struggle. It is an established principle that in the War of Resistance everything must be subordinated to, and must not conflict with, the interests and demands of the national struggle. The interests and demands of the class struggle must be subordinated to, and must not conflict with, the interests and demands of the national struggle. At the same time, however, under the conditions existing in class society, class struggle cannot be eliminated; there is no way that it can be eliminated (*wufa xiaomie*). The theory which fundamentally denies the existence of class struggle is a theory which misrepresents the facts (*waiqu de lilun*). We do not deny the class struggle, we adjust it (*tiaojie*).[69]

Similarly, some seven years later Mao was to assert in "On Coalition Government" that the adjustment of class struggle could constitute the premise on which China's future politico-economic system might function. Once again, however, Mao was concerned to stress that contradictions between China's classes would not just disappear:

> Of course, there are still contradictions among these classes, notably the contradiction between labour and capital, and consequently each has its own demands. It would be hypocritical to deny the existence of these contradictions and differing demands. But throughout the stage of New Democracy, these contradictions, these differing demands, will not grow and transcend the demands which all have in common and should not be allowed to do so; they can be adjusted (*tiaojie*). Given such adjustments, these

classes can together accomplish the political, economic and cultural tasks of the new democratic state.[70]

Mao therefore believed that class struggle could be adjusted and, moreover, that the realm of "politics" possessed the capacity to adjust class struggle. In both passages quoted above, Mao suggests an interest that could transcend class interest; this interest was, of course, the national interest. His appeal to seemingly supra-class conceptions (nation, the people, the masses) should not, however, lead to the assumption that such categories were above and beyond the influence of class division and struggle. On the contrary, Mao regarded class division and struggle as the fundamental characteristic of society and class analysis "the fundamental viewpoint of Marxism."[71] Reference to such global categories as "nation" or "the people" thus assumed intrinsic differentiation along class lines. Mao did not, for example, perceive the "common people" (*laobaixing*) as had Chinese populists such as Feng Yuxiang, who perceived the "common people" as a largely undifferentiated and preferably passive entity upon which reforms and benefits might be bestowed.[72] In contrast, Mao's references to "the people" (*renmin*) made no assumption that this category had no class differentiation. Rather, the Marxist perspective on class formations and class struggle that pervaded Mao's thought led to a perception of "the people" as necessarily an alliance of classes between which there remained class contradictions and muted class struggle. "Politics" could therefore adjust class struggle, but it was beyond the capacity of politics to eliminate class struggle altogether. As Mao had pointed out in "On the New Stage" (1938), "class struggle cannot be eliminated,"[73] and in response to a correspondent's question in 1937, Mao had insisted that "prior to the elimination of the class system, there is no way that class contradictions can be abolished."[74]

Why and how did Mao perceive politics as able to adjust class struggle? First, Mao's call for the adjustment of class struggle was predicated on the specific characteristics of the historical situation that then obtained in China. Of these, the existence of certain classes and the form and extent of struggle between them were central. In orthodox Marxist vein, Mao believed the existence of classes and class struggle to be a fundamental and omnipresent feature of all human societies except the most "primitive." However, the principle of the fundamental character of class and class struggle did not assume to anticipate the form and intensity that these might assume at particular historical moments; there were clearly varied specific instances of the general rule (for more on this logic, see chapter 7).

The nature of class struggle within particular historical contexts could not be deduced from a general axiom regarding the existence of class struggle in human society. Consequently, analysis of any historical context had to be premised on investigation of the particular form in which class struggle became manifest; class struggle did not pursue any necessarily preordained pattern but found concrete form by virtue of the constraints imposed by a developing historical situation. Within the framework of such constraints, the class struggle emerged and proceeded; the historically determined character of a particular class struggle determined its intensity and breadth and most importantly, the flexibility of its operation. Mao's analysis of the Chinese context during the Yan'an period indicated that its class struggle was amenable to political adjustment, this possibility predicated on a shared perception by the various classes that because of the threat posed by Japanese imperialism, their economic interests would be protected through adjustment of the struggle between them.

Therefore, although the concept of the adjustment of class struggle might leave the initial impression that Mao perceived class struggle as readily subject to a political throttle, it must be remembered that his attempts to adjust class struggle were made within a specific historical context in which the potential for such political action had been disclosed through a class analysis. Moreover, as we have seen, his call for the adjustment of class struggle did not presume the possibility of the elimination of the contradictions between the classes; it signified rather a belief in the possibility of increasing or decreasing the intensity of the already existing form of that struggle. During the Yan'an period, class contradiction between landlord and peasant could be modified but not eliminated, likewise the contradiction between labor and capital. In 1937, Mao had indicated the political measures that could be taken to modify the intensity of these contradictions: "Within the programme of the United Front, we advocate giving the people democratic rights politically, and economically an improvement in their livelihood. If the workers and peasants are oppressed, it is inevitable that they will rise up in resistance; only by giving them democratic rights and an improvement in their livelihoods can a start be made in reducing this contradiction."[75] More specifically, Mao urged that "the people" be given an assembly, freedom of speech and association, and universal suffrage; economically, workers should receive better remuneration and improved conditions of labor and the peasantry granted reduced rent and taxes. The land question itself should be the subject of legislative procedures and action.[76] It was political measures such as these, Mao believed, that could bring about an adjustment of class struggle and therefore enhance resistance to Japanese imperialism.

Second, it must be remembered that Mao no longer included politics in the superstructure of society as he had in "On Contradiction." Politics was an integral part of society's "basis" (*genju*), and combined with economics it constituted the causal matrix that produced culture. The notion of a political adjustment of class struggle did not, therefore, denote a purely superstructural intervention in the economic realm of society but rather an historical initiative emanating from within the "basis" and constrained by the configuration of forces—economic and political—within it. Moreover, Mao appears to have perceived class struggle in both political and economic terms. Class formations inherently gave rise to economic tensions and conflict, but the struggle between classes also had a very significant political dimension. This helps explain how Mao could insist, on the one hand, that neither class nor class contradiction could be eliminated through political action alone yet believe in the possibility of political intervention to adjust the intensity of class struggle on the other. There were, therefore, definite limits to the causal significance of "politics." The elimination of class struggle was not one of its prerogatives.

"Politics" and the Role of Government

One of Mao's preoccupations during the Yan'an period was the type of government system (*zhengti*) that China should adopt during the New Democratic stage and in the future, and he penned several lengthy and theoretically important documents on government structure and the historical role of government. Mao perceived government as an aspect of the political realm, and an analysis of his views on the role of government can serve to extend our comprehension of the causal significance of "politics" in his schema for social change.

We have already noted that Mao did not perceive a necessary coherence in class terms between the state system (*guoti*) and the system of government, and he suggested the possibility that the two systems could be out of harmony (*buxiang shiying*). Mao was, it seems, prepared to allow a degree of autonomy to government to take the historical initiative. Actions taken by a government system in which the relative status of the various classes in society was not adequately reflected (that is, out of harmony with the state system)[77] were not readily amenable to a mechanistic class explanation. Rather, the structure and operation of government could exert an influence on the process of social change. Mao was well aware that variations in government administration and policy could occur in contexts in which the class structure had remained relatively constant. For example, in 1942 and again in 1944, Mao called for reform of the Communists' own government administration with the slogan "better troops and simpler administration." In so doing, Mao was recognising that the structure and performance of his government could be an important ingredient for success at that particular juncture of the Anti-Japanese War of Resistance.[78] That Mao took problems of government administration seriously is also evidenced by his lengthy analysis of 1942 entitled "Economic and Financial Problems in the Anti-Japanese War."[79] It is clear from this document that Mao accepted the possibility that the administration of government could be responsible for the success or failure of policies formulated in pursuit of broader class interests: "In our economic and financial set-up," Mao declared, "we must overcome such evils as disunity, assertion of independence and lack of co-ordination, and must establish a working system which is unified and responsive to direction and which permits the full application of our politics and regulations."[80]

Mao also believed that government, as with the political party, had the capacity to concentrate the ideas and opinions of the masses.[81] However, for government to perform this function successfully there had to be a "correct line of organization,"[82] one in which channels of communication between government and the people remained open and allowed rapid and effective transmission of information in both directions. The organizational form of government could thus play an important role in determining the ability of government to match intention in policy formulation with actual policy implementation. Mao made this clear in an interview with James Bertram in 1937 in which he declared that the capacity of government to respond to the exigencies of war depended on its organizational structure. China could choose between one of two systems of government: democratic centralist or absolute centralist. In the original version of this interview, Mao argued that the history of humankind's political activities had demonstrated that democratic centralism was the best organizational form and that in times of war such a system increased political and military effectiveness.[83]

Mao was therefore under no illusion as to the importance of government in the attainment of political and economic objectives and thus as a factor in the process of social change. The primary function of government was to provide a coherent organizational structure for the translation of class interests into enforceable laws and policies (for analysis of Mao's position and policies on this during the Jiangxi Soviet, 1931–1934, see chapter 4). There was not, however, a necessarily complete or automatic correlation between class interests and the structure that government assumed or the policies it pursued. Although the historical autonomy of government was limited by social constraints of which class structure was the most important, the nature of government (its organizational form, political outlook of its administrators, methods of policy implementation) could have a significant influence on a developing historical situation. Government was not a lifeless conduit through which class interests were processed unaffected by the nature of the processing medium itself. Rather, government could assume an active role in concentrating, formalizing, and implementing the attitudes and aspirations of the class(es) it represented.

Here again is evidence of Mao's attribution of causal significance to an element of the political realm of society. It must be reiterated, however, that in the "On New Democracy" formulation, government is portrayed as an integral and active element of the "basis" of society and not a superstructural reflection as had been the case in "On Contradiction." Elements of the political realm were a "concentrated expression of economics" and capable of concentrating the ideas and activities of a class or the masses; "politics" could thus perform a significant role in achieving social change. The success or failure of the politics of an economic class had more than a peripheral bearing on its economic fortunes. Moreover, in terms of historical analysis, the performance of a class at a political level could not automatically be deduced from the economic power of that class within society, although the two were necessarily related. Mao was therefore attempting a formulation in which there was a reciprocal causal relationship between "economics" and "politics," one in which occurrences within the political realm could not be reduced to a mechanistic class explanation. In so doing, Mao created a theoretical perspective that would allow (what he hoped to be) an accurate interpretation of the Chinese revolutionary context, and that would appear to remain acceptably orthodox in Marxist terms. By using a concept such as society's "basis" and by explaining social change by reference to developments within it, the appearance of orthodoxy could be maintained, and by astutely (if not altogether accurately) employing a Leninist definition of "politics" as the "concentrated expression of economics," Mao was able not only to incorporate "politics" within this "basis" but to add legitimacy to his position into the bargain.

The Historical Role of Culture

Having explored the causal relationship within the "basis" of society, let us move to an analysis of the role of "culture" within the tripartite conceptualization employed in "On New Democracy." According to Mao, it is the combination of "economics and politics" as society's "basis" that represents

the causal matrix from which culture emerges: "The old politics and economics of the Chinese nation form the basis of its old culture, just as its
new politics and economics will form the basis of its new culture."[84] Elsewhere in "On New Democracy," Mao asserts that a "given culture is the
ideological reflection (*guannianxingtai de fanying*) of the politics and economics of a given society."[85] However, although culture is a reflection of
the "basis" of society, once formed it can begin to exert a significant influence upon the basis. As Mao points out: "It follows that the form of culture is first determined by the political and economic form, and only then
(*ranhou*) does it influence the given political and economic form."[86] Although culture is originally determined (*jueding*) by the "basis," the emergence of a culture capable of exerting an influence on the basis of society
raises the possibility that causal dominance might pass from the "basis" to
the culture it creates. That Mao did *not* perceive this to be the case can be
demonstrated by an exploration of two themes that figure in "On New
Democracy"—culture as reflection; and the relationship between culture
and the "basis" in a social formation, with different modes of production.

Mao declared culture to be a "reflection" of society's politics and economics. Yet, if culture is a reflection, how could it exert an influence on
the "basis" that had produced it? The concept of reflection suggests an in-
substantial image, one incapable of acting independently. However, there
can be no doubt that Mao believed culture did possess a capacity to influence the process of social change. At the Yan'an Forum of 1942, for example, he argued that revolutionary art and literature could "help the
masses to propel history forward."[87] He also elaborated the relationship between culture and politics and energetically denied the possibility of a culture beyond the influence of class:

> In the world today *all culture,* all literature and art belong to definite classes
> and are geared to definite political lines. There is no such thing as art for
> art's sake, art that stands above classes or art that is detached from or in-
> dependent of politics. . . . Party work in literature and art occupies a def-
> inite and assigned position in Party revolutionary work as a whole and is
> subordinated to the revolutionary tasks set out by the Party in a given rev-
> olutionary period. We do not favour overstressing the importance of lit-
> erature and art, but neither do we favour underestimating their
> importance. Literature and art are subordinate to politics, but in their turn
> exert a great influence on politics. Revolutionary literature and art are
> part of the whole revolutionary cause, they are cogs and wheels in it, and
> though *in comparison with certain other and more important parts they may be
> less significant and less urgent and may occupy a secondary position,* nevertheless,

they are indispensable cogs and wheels in the whole machine . . . when we say that literature and art are subordinate to politics, we mean class politics.[88]

Several interesting points emerge from this passage that have a bearing on this concept of "reflection." First, it is instructive that Mao repeatedly emphasized that culture is subordinate (*congshu*) to politics; moreover, that politics is class politics. The subordination of culture to politics indicates that Mao believed culture to be susceptible to the organizing and directing influence of politics. As Mao declared, "All culture [is] . . . geared to definite political lines." While culture in its inchoate form was engendered by class structure, the formalization and concentration of culture and its deployment for political purposes were a function of the political realm. Politics thus occupied a vital intermediate position between the economics of a class and its systematized culture. And it was only in this systematized form that culture could perform an active historical role in defense or pursuit of class interests. The reflection of culture was not, therefore, a completely automatic process; rather, in Mao's usage, the notion of reflection implied an active intervention by politics in the cultural sphere.

Second, by insisting that "all culture . . . belong[s] to definite classes," Mao was asserting that the limits and variability of a culture are established by the nature of the class from which it had emerged. It would be inconceivable, for example, for the culture of the landlord class to portray the peasantry in a favorable light. In a letter written (1944) to the Yan'an Opera Company after viewing its production of "Bi shang Liang shan" (Compelled to ascend Mount Liang), Mao commented on the unfavorable characterizations of the common people in the culture of feudal China: "History is created by the people, but in the old stage plays (in all old literature and art which was divorced from the people), with the old master and his lady and the young master and miss ruling the stage, the people became the dregs, and thus history was turned upside down. Now you have turned it the right way up again, restored history's appearance (*mianmu*), and opened new and unfamiliar aspects from these old plays, for which I offer well-earned congratulations."[89] Not only is the relationship between class and culture made clear in this letter, but also the possibility of a political intervention to organize culture in the interests of a particular class or classes. Thus, while the concept of reflection commences from an assumption of culture as a product of class, a systematized culture that can effectively serve the interests of its class is a function of the organizing influence of politics.

The role of culture can also be elaborated through analysis of Mao's conception of social change in a social formation within which there are a number of modes of production. Mao did not perceive the "basis" as an undifferentiated category. Not only was it differentiated horizontally (that is, as a result of its division into economic and political realms), it could also be characterized by vertical cleavages that separated the competing modes of production that occurred in a complex economically heterogeneous society. Mao recognized the fragmented nature of China's economy and society; China was "colonial, semi-colonial and semi-feudal," and was untypical of any one mode of production, its "basis" being a differentiated mixture of several coexisting and competing politico-economic formations. If the social category of the "basis" allowed the possibility of different modes of production, it followed that culture, itself a reflection of the basis, could also be differentiated. A semi-feudal and semi-colonial basis would thus give rise to a semi-feudal and semi-colonial culture; the "new culture" advocated by Mao would be a reflection of the new economic and political forces within Chinese society.[90] This notion of cultural differentiation emerges clearly in the following passage from "On New Democracy":

> A national culture with a socialist content will necessarily be the reflection of a socialist politics and economy. There are socialist elements (*yinsu*) in our politics and our economy, and hence these socialist elements are reflected in our national culture; but taking our society as a whole, we do not have a socialist politics and a socialist economy yet, so that there cannot be a wholly socialist national culture.[91]

The emergence of a culture is thus governed by developments within the "basis," including the role of politics in organizing culture. Changes within China's basis had been responsible for the appearance and growth of the new culture: "Without the capitalist economy, without the political forces of these classes, the new ideology or new culture could not have emerged."[92] This newly emergent culture would, however, serve its own "basis" rather than the basis of society generally; similarly, a semi-feudal culture would reinforce the semi-feudal politico-economic formation from which it had emerged.

If a culture emerged to serve its own "basis," what might its relationship be to a basis not its own? For example, how would the new culture influence or react with a semi-feudal basis? Although Mao believed in 1940 that China's feudal, semi-feudal, and semi-colonial politics and economics were still dominant (*tongzhi*), there can be no doubt from the stress he placed on revolutionary culture that he perceived it as performing a significant role in

accelerating the decline of these dominant politico-economic formations.[93] Culture could not independently initiate that process; its generation came from within the "basis" itself. Once set in motion, however,
culture could accelerate the process, and by so doing, "propel history forward."[94] What emerges here is that a newly emergent and historically progressive culture could have "a tremendous influence" most obviously on a
declining section of the social basis that it did not reflect. At the same time,
such a culture would promote the development of the basis from which it
was engendered; "the culture of new democracy is on the one hand a reflection of that social form, while on the other hand it gives impetus to the
continued progress of that social form."[95] Mao therefore perceived culture
as playing a dual role: serving its own basis while assisting in the decline of
any basis in contention with its own.

The origin and role of culture becomes less clear, however, if we turn
our attention to the relationship between competing cultures within a differentiated society. Although Mao believed culture was a reflection of its
"basis," he also referred to the possibility that a newly emergent culture
could develop out of a previously established culture, there being a seeming
continuity in cultural development.[96] In "On the New Stage" (1938), Mao
had warned his comrades against ignoring China's cultural heritage: "Contemporary China has grown out of the China of the past; we are Marxist
in our historical approach (*lishizhuyizhe*) and must not lop off our history.
We should sum up our history from Confucius to Sun Yat-sen and take over
this valuable legacy."[97] Mao was to repeat this warning in "On New Democracy," here again stressing the continuity of cultural development:
"China's . . . present new culture, too, has developed out of her old culture;
therefore we must respect our own history and must not lop it off."[98]

The assertion that one culture could develop out of another seems to
place in question the assumption that a culture can only be a reflection of
its own "basis." The concept of cultural continuity stressed in the two passages quoted above appears to suggest that a newly emergent culture could
be signally influenced not only by its basis but also by already existing cultural forms. How is this paradox to be resolved? First, Mao made it abundantly clear that developments within the basis are antecedent (both
causally and temporally) to developments within the cultural realm; before
a new culture could arise, a new basis must have emerged. This new basis
could not emerge spontaneously and relied for its generation on transformations within the old basis. As Mao pointed out, "China's present new
politics and economics have developed out of her old politics and old
economy."[99] The process of emergence of a new basis was, in the Chinese

experience, of a protracted nature, and Mao obviously perceived the old and the new in a dynamic state of coexistence and competition. Because the new basis had emerged from the old, the new (while qualitatively different) could not but be influenced by the old. The culture that emerged from the new basis would thus bear the imprint of this influence from the old basis, the new basis standing in an intermediate position between the two; in this way, the new culture would receive a number of the same influences as the old culture.

Second, the old culture was itself far from being a homogeneous category, being characterized by differentiation along class lines. The positive manner in which Mao referred to China's cultural heritage suggests that he perceived in it progressive elements at odds with the dominant feudal culture. This indeed was the case: "A splendid old culture was created during a long period of Chinese feudal society. To study the development of this old culture, to reject its feudal dross and assimilate its democratic essence is a necessary condition for developing our new national culture. . . . It is imperative to separate the fine old culture of the people which had a more or less democratic and revolutionary character from all the decadence of the old feudal ruling class."[100] Mao perceived certain forms of the old culture (that of the "common people") as sufficiently progressive to be compatible with the new culture, even though there had been dramatic changes in the basis of society. However, the progressive cultural elements from the old culture could only survive if there were a conscious intervention on the part of the "politics" of the new basis, that is, in the form of political action to salvage, organize, and promote old cultural elements deemed useful for the new basis and the new culture. To a certain extent, therefore, the continuity of culture was a function of political action; the manner in which the old culture could influence the new, and the way in which the new could develop out of the old, was amenable to political direction and organization.

Politics and Ideology

The centrality of "politics" in systematizing the culture of a class was due, in Mao's mind, to the scattered and unsystematic way in which ideology emerged from a class in unmediated form. Mao was sensitive to the wide variation in patterns of thought and attitude that appeared to characterize members of the same class. Although a broadly similar socioeconomic environment might serve to establish a class modality of thought and attitude, the range of unmediated class ideology could be extensive: "So long as classes exist, there will be as many doctrines as there are classes, and even various groups (*jituan*) in the same class may have their different doctrines (*zhuyi*)."[101]

How did Mao explain this variability in class ideology, and can his explanation be considered a materialist one? Exploration of Mao's usage of the concept of "stratum" (*jieceng*) can provide answers to these questions. Mao's preoccupation with discovering the particular characteristics of specific historical contexts led him to the conclusion that "class" may not be a sufficiently precise explanatory concept for the comprehension of the variety of modes of thought and attitude within society. The concept of class required further division, for members of a particular class might not share exactly the same socioeconomic conditions. Variations in conditions of work and life within a class could generate different ideological patterns, which required analysis. The concept of stratum thus became an important one for Mao, for it furnished him with a materialist explanation of ideological variability and afforded a rationale for the necessity of political intervention to provide uniformity and coherence to the ideology of a class.

Mao had shown a propensity to divide class into their constituent strata as early as 1925 with his first serious attempt to apply a class analysis to Chinese society.[102] Similarly, in 1933 Mao demonstrated the same sensitivity to the differentiation existing within classes in his analysis of the classes in China's rural areas.[103] During the Yan'an period, his most comprehensive analysis of China's classes appears in "The Chinese Revolution and the Chinese Communist Party" (1939), in which he widely employs the concept of "strata" to facilitate analysis of intra-class differences. It is possible to gain an appreciation of what constituted a stratum from the examples which appear in this document. The "city poor" (*chengshi pinmin*) were classified as a stratum, and it is interesting to note that Mao further subdivided this stratum into more specific sociological categories: bankrupt craftspeople, peasants in search of work, and coolie laborers who rely on uncertain work. Mao designated this stratum a "semi-proletariat" (*ban wuchanjieji*).[104] Small traders were also a stratum, divided into upper and lower strata, the distinction arising from whether the small trader exploited the labor of others or not.[105] "Vagrants" (*youmin*) are characterized as an "unstable social stratum" and included rural and urban unemployed, robbers, gangsters, beggars, prostitutes, and people engaged in superstitious practices.[106] In another document of 1941, Mao applied the concept of strata to rich peasants, merchants, middle peasants, poor peasants, tenant farmers, craftspeople, and vagrants.[107] Similarly, big landlords, bankers, and the comprador bourgeoisie are referred to in various sources as strata.[108]

The following observations can be made from these examples of Mao's usage of the concept of "stratum." First, Mao clearly believed that the concept of class was not sufficiently precise for the definition and elaboration of the particularities of society's economic relationships; sensitivity to intra-class variability was necessary. The same could hold true for the concept of strata itself, which might require further subdivision into occupational categories or categories of scale (for example, small traders large enough to exploit the labor of others). Second, the strata that constitute a class derive their distinguishing characteristics from economic factors; for example, craftspeople and small tradespersons, while both belonging to the petty bourgeoisie, were distinguished from each other by the conditions of work and economic activity that characterized their separate economic niches. Third, the various strata within a class possessed sufficient characteristics in common to constitute an identifiable class; such shared characteristics derived, according to Mao, from family origin, conditions of life (*shenghuo tiaojian*), and political outlook.[109] Fourth, Mao indicated that the concept of strata could be employed in ascertaining the economic origin of political power and political institutions. For example, he wrote: "The Kuomintang is not a homogeneous political party. Though it is controlled and led by the reactionary clique representing the stratum of the big landlords, bankers and compradores, it must not be entirely identified with this clique."[110] Finally, and perhaps most importantly, Mao explicitly linked strata to the emergence of particular ideological patterns; for example, he identified the stratum of vagrants as the source of "roving-rebel and anarchist ideology in the revolutionary ranks."[111]

Mao therefore perceived in the differentiation of a class into a number of strata a materialist explanation for the varied ideas and attitudes that characterized the culture or ideology of a class. This helps explain Mao's willingness to accept a flexible interpretation of the orthodox Marxist doctrine of the class-determined nature of ideology, for although thought and attitude were a function of the material conditions of existence, members of a particular class could experience a variety of such conditions. This could give rise to scattered and unsystematic ideas at some distance from the modality of the ideology of that class. However, such scattered and unsystematic ideas were subject to the influence of "politics," itself an integral part of the "basis" of society. Politics could, through the systematization, organization, and promotion of the culture and ideology of a class, elicit a movement in thought on the part of individuals within a class and under specific historical conditions, in other classes as well. Mao thus believed that changes in thought and ideology derived from the causal "basis" of society.

As noted earlier, the orthodoxy of Mao's approach to the relationship between class and ideology has been frequently questioned in secondary critiques of his thought. The interpretation offered here is at odds with the suggestion that Mao had (during the Yan'an period at least) cut himself adrift from the orthodox Marxist doctrine that ideology is a function of social and economic conditions.[112] Rather than abandoning that position, Mao had attempted to refine it through incorporating a sensitivity to intra-class divisions and through elaborating a theoretical formulation that perceived "politics" as part of society's "basis" and thus capable of systematizing and promoting class culture and ideology.

Conclusion

Mao's formulation in "On New Democracy" of a tripartite schema for understanding social change incorporated "politics" within society's "basis." This allowed a degree of theoretical and practical flexibility that a mechanistic Marxism would have precluded. By the same token, it is clear that Mao was operating on a theoretical terrain whose boundary and concepts were well established. His rearrangement and refinement of inherited Marxist concepts cannot be interpreted as an abandonment of the essential referents of Marxism; they signify rather an attempt to enhance the relevance of that theory. A form of economism (that is, economics as ultimately the determinant factor in social change) is evident in "On Contradiction," "On One-Party Dictatorship" and "On New Democracy." Even the position adopted in "On New Democracy," without doubt containing the most flexible materialist view, specifies the limits to the capacity of politics to initiate social change. "Politics" had perforce to operate within a social context constructed by major structures and forces engendered by the "economic" realm. Mao recognized that "politics" could not eliminate classes but he did believe that it could play a very significant role in concentrating the ability of a class or classes to engage in class struggle. And it was this that most interested Mao, for his various incursions into theory had a very practical objective: winning the revolution.

It is thus apparent that each of the three texts under consideration in this chapter is underpinned by a materialist view of social change, although in each the causal dominance of economics is explained, and qualified, in rather different ways. The differing emphases in these three Mao texts raise questions regarding the propriety of essentialist interpretations of Mao's position on the superstructure.[113] Mao's disinclination to explicitly employ the concept of the superstructure during the Yan'an period after August

1937 and his employment of a different causal formulation in "On New Democracy" suggest the need for an alternative strategy for reading the Mao texts, one that allows for silences, lapses, and contradictions, and which permits the possibility of theory being developmental (for more on issues of method, see chapters 2 and 3). At the very least, crude stereotypes of Mao as a renegade Marxist who invariably stressed the superstructure in his reading of social change are rendered misleading through a close reading of the Mao texts. And in light of theoretical developments within the European neo-Marxist tradition, in which the "base-superstructure" metaphor has been subjected to critical scrutiny and substantial reformulation,[114] it is possible to perceive in Mao's theoretical formulations of 1937–1940 a limited, yet still significant, attempt to renegotiate certain of the more inflexible attributes of the mechanistic version of Marxism often rather misguidedly perceived as orthodox.

Notes

1. This economistic strand of Marxism can be found in the works of early Marxists such as George Plekhanov. See *The Materialist Conception of History* (New York: International Publishers, 1940). The Marx text normally cited for this reading of Marxism is the "Preface" to *A Contribution to the Critique of Political Economy* (London: Lawrence and Wishart, 1971), 19–23, although this text has given rise to a very wide range of interpretations. For an extended interpretation from an anti-Marxist perspective, see John Plamenatz, *German Marxism and Russian Communism* (London: Longmans, 1961). A contrasting position can be found in Derek Sayer, *The Violence of Abstraction: The Analytic Foundations of Historical Materialism* (Cambridge: Basil Blackwell, 1987).

2. See Stuart R. Schram, *Mao Tse-tung* (Harmondsworth: Penguin, 1966); *The Political Thought of Mao Tse-tung* (Harmondsworth: Penguin, 1969, revised ed.); Schram, *Mao Tse-tung Unrehearsed: Talks and Letters, 1956–71* (Harmondsworth: Penguin, 1974); Schram, "The Marxist," in *Mao Tse-tung in the Scales of History*, ed. Dick Wilson, (Cambridge: Cambridge University Press, 1977), pp. 35–69; Schram, "Some reflections on the Pfeffer-Walder 'Revolution' in China Studies," *Modern China* Vol. 3, no. 2 (1977), 169–84; Schram, *Mao Zedong: A Preliminary Reassessment* (Hong Kong: The Chinese University Press, 1983); and Schram, *The Thought of Mao Tse-tung* (Cambridge: Cambridge University Press, 1989), 5, 17, 54–55, 67, 96, 113, 168, 200.

3. For Schwartz's contribution to Mao studies and his views on the "disintegration" or "decomposition" of Marxism, see Benjamin I. Schwartz, "On the 'Originality' of Mao Tse-tung," *Foreign Affairs* 34, no. 1 (October 1955): 67–76; Schwartz, "China and the West in the 'Thought of Mao Tse-tung'," in *China in Crisis*, ed. Ho Ping-ti and Tsou Tang (Chicago: University of Chicago Press, 1968), vol. 1, book 1, 365–79; Schwartz, *Chinese Communism and the Rise of Mao* (Cambridge: Harvard

University, 1951, 1958); and Schwartz "The Essence of "Marxism Revisited: A Response," *Modern China* 2, no. 4 (1976): 461–72.

4. Maurice Meisner, *Marxism, Maoism and Utopianism: Eight Essays* (Madison, Wisconsin: University of Wisconsin Press, 1982); and Meisner, *Mao's China and After: A History of the People's Republic* (New York: The Free Press, 1977, 1986).

5. Frederic Wakeman Jr., *History and Will: Philosophical Perspectives on Mao Tse-tung's Thought* (Berkeley: University of California Press, 1973).

6. Richard M. Pfeffer, "Mao and Marx in the Marxist–Leninist Tradition: A Critique of 'The China Field' and a Contribution to a Preliminary Reappraisal," *Modern China* 3, no. 4 (October 1976): 421–60; Pfeffer, "Mao and Marx: Understanding, Scholarship, and Ideology—a Response," *Modern China* 3, no. 4 (October 1977): 379–86.

7. Andrew G. Walder, "Marxism, Maoism and Social Change," *Modern China* 3, no. 1 (January 1977): 101–18; and 3, no. 2 (April 1977): 125–59; also Walder, "A response," *Modern China* 3, no. 4 (October 1977): 387–93. However, for Walder's recantation, see his "Actually Existing Maoism," *The Australian Journal of Chinese Affairs* 18 (July 1987): 155–66. In this last exercise, Walder lapses into the empiricist maunderings of the China field he critiqued so effectively in his *Modern China* article.

8. For a further attempt to provide an alternative analysis of Mao's thought and his understanding of Marxism, see Philip Corrigan, Harvie Ramsay, and Derek Sayer, *For Mao: Essays in Historical Materialism* (Atlantic Highlands, New Jersey: Humanities Press, 1979).

9. A major attempt to keep alive the tradition of critical commentary on Mao's thought is Arif Dirlik, Paul Healy and Nick Knight, eds., *Critical Perspectives on Mao Zedong's Thought* (Atlantic Highlands, New Jersey: Humanities Press, 1997). See also Nick Knight, *Marxist Philosophy in China: From Qu Qiubai to Mao Zedong, 1923–1945* (Dordrecht: Springer, 2005).

10. See, for example, Takeuchi Minoru, ed., *Mao Zedong Ji Bujuan* [Supplements to the Collected Writings of Mao Zedong] (Tokyo: Sōsōsha, 1983–1986), 10 volumes. The following collections of Mao's writings were published in China. *Mao Zedong zhexue pizhuji* [The philosophical annotations of Mao Zedong] (Beijing: Zhongyang wenxian chubanshe, 1988); *Mao Zedong shuxin xuanji* [Selected letters of Mao Zedong] (Beijing: Renmin chubanshe, 1983); *Mao Zedong zhuzuo xuandu* [Selected readings from the works of Mao Zedong] (Beijing: Renmin chubanshe, 1986), 2 volumes; *Mao Zedong xinwen gongzuo wenxuan* [Selected writings of Mao Zedong on journalism] (Beijing: Xinhua chubanshe, 1983); *Mao Zedong wenji* [Collected writings of Mao Zedong] (Beijing: Renmin chubanshe, 1993–1999), 8 volumes; *Jianguo yilai Mao Zedong wengao* [Draft documents by Mao Zedong since the establishment of the People's Republic] (Beijing: Zhongyang wenxian chubanshe, 1987–19920), 6 volumes; *Mao Zedong junshi wenji* [Collected military writings of Mao Zedong] (Beijing: Junshi kexue chubanshe, Zhongyang wenxian chubanshe, 1993), 6 volumes.

11. In the United States, there is the ongoing project to translate and publish in English all of Mao's pre-1949 writings, the *Mao's Road to Power* series, edited by

Stuart Schram, which will eventually result in ten very substantial volumes. Two volumes of Mao's post-1949 writings published in English are Michael Y. M. Kau and John K. Leung, eds., *The Writings of Mao Zedong, 1949–1976 (September 1949–December 1955)* (Armonk, New York: M.E. Sharpe, 1986); and Michael Y.M. Kau and John K. Leung, eds., *The Writings of Mao Zedong, 1949–1976 (January 1956–December 1957)* (Armonk, New York: M. E. Sharpe, 1992).

12. For the official version of "On Contradiction," see *Selected Works of Mao Tse-tung* (Peking: Foreign Languages Press, 1965) I, 310–47; also *Mao Zedong Xuanji* [Selected Works of Mao Zedong] (Beijing: Renmin chubanshe, 1966) I, 274–312. The Chinese text of the pre-Liberation version of this essay is to be found in Takeuchi, ed., *Mao Zedong Ji Bujuan* V, 240–78. For analysis of the differences between the original and official versions of this essay, see Nick Knight, "Mao Zedong's *On Contradiction* and *On Practice:* Pre-Liberation Texts," *China Quarterly* 84 (December 1980): 641–68; also Nick Knight, "Mao Zedong's *On Contradiction:* An Annotated Translation of the Pre-Liberation Text," *Griffith Asian Papers No. 3* (Nathan: School of Modern Asian Studies, Griffith University, 1981), esp. 3–11. For a detailed analysis of Mao's writings on philosophy from 1937, see Nick Knight, ed., *Mao Zedong on Dialectical Materialism:Writings on Philosophy, 1937* (Armonk, New York: M. E. Sharpe, 1990).

13. "Yu Yan'an xin Zhonghuabao jizhe tanhua (Lun yidang zhuanzheng) [A talk with a reporter from *New China News* in Yan'an], in Takeuchi Minoru, ed., *Mao Zedong Ji* [The collected writings of Mao Zedong] (Tokyo: Hokubosha, 1970–72) V, 305–21. For a translation of the document, see Nick Knight, ed., *Philosophy and Politics in Mao Texts of the Yan'an Period* (Armonk, New York: M. E. Sharpe, *Chinese Studies in Philosophy*, Winter 1987–1988), 83–104.

14. The official version of "On New Democracy" is in *Selected Works of Mao Tse-tung* II, 339–84, and *Mao Zedong Xuanji* II, 623–70. The original version is in Takeuchi, ed., *Mao Zedong Ji* VII, 147–208.

15. Knight, ed., *Mao Zedong on Dialectical Materialism*, 185–86; cf. *Selected Works of Mao Tse-tung* I, 335–36; *Mao Zedong Xuanji* I, 330–31. Emphasis added.

16. Knight, ed., *Mao Zedong on Dialectical Materialism*, 177; cf. *Selected Works of Mao Tse-tung* I, 328; *Mao Zedong Xuanji* I, 292.

17. See notes 2 to 5, above. See also Arthur Cohen, *The Communism of Mao Tse-tung* (Chicago and London: University of Chicago Press, 1964); also Tsou Tang, "Mao Tse-tung Thought, the Last Struggle for Succession and the Post-Mao Era," *China Quarterly* 71 (September 1979): 498–527, esp. 498–504.

18. Knight, ed., *Mao Zedong on Dialectical Materialism*, 177; cf. *Selected Works of Mao Tse-tung* I, 328; *Mao Zedong Xuanji* I, 292.

19. Knight, ed., *Mao Zedong on Dialectical Materialism*, 86; cf. *Selected Works of Mao Tse-tung* I, 336; *Mao Zedong Xuanji* I, 331.

20. *Mao Zedong zhexue pizhuji*, 67.

21. *Mao Zedong zhexue pizhuji*, 87–90.

22. *Mao Zedong zhexue pizhuji*, 145–56.

23. *Mao Zedong zhexue pizhuji*, 296.

24. For elaboration of this point, see Knight, *Marxist Philosophy in China*, chapters 5, 9 and 10.

25. "Yu Yan'an xin Zhonghuabao jizhe tanhua (Lun yidang zhuansheng)," Takeuchi, ed., *Mao Zedong Ji* V, 305–21.

26. Mao was to remain consistent on this point throughout the Yan'an period. In "On Coalition Government" (1945), he reiterated that the "Russian system has been shaped by Russian history . . . the people support the Bolshevik Party alone, having discarded all the anti-socialist parties." Here, as in "On One-Party Dictatorship," Mao accepted that the "social base" dictated the existence and nature of political institutions. *Selected Works of Mao Tse-tung* III, 235; Takeuchi, ed., *Mao Zedong Ji* IX, 226.

27. J. V. Stalin, *Problems of Leninism* (Peking: Foreign Languages Press, 1976), 803.

28. "Yu Yan'an xin Zhonghuabao jizhe tanhua (Lun yidang zhuanzheng)," Takeuchi, ed., *Mao Zedong Ji* V, 309–10.

29. "Yu Yan'an xin Zhonghuabao jizhe tanhua (Lun yidang zhuanzheng)," Takeuchi, ed., *Mao Zedong Ji* V, 311–20.

30. See for example the quote from Stalin in the first chapter of "The Chinese Revolution and the Chinese Communist Party," a chapter not written by Mao but included in his *Selected Works*. See *Selected Works of Mao Tse-tung* II, 312; *Mao Zedong Xuanji* II, 592; Takeuchi, ed., *Mao Zedong Ji* VII, 107.

31. Roland Lew, "Maoism and the Chinese Revolution," *The Socialist Register* (1975): 115–59.

32. Takeuchi, ed., *Mao Zedong Ji* VII, 149; *Selected Works of Mao Tse-tung* II, 340; *Mao Zedong Xuanji* II, 624, 330–31. In the original text, Mao does not refer to economics as the base (*jichu*).

33. For details of Sugiyama Sakae's interpretation of Marxism and its influence on Li Da, and Li Da's influence on Mao, see Nick Knight, *Li Da and Marxist Philosophy in China* (Boulder, Colorado: Westview Press, 1996), 124–28, and chapter 6. For Mao's annotations to Li Da's *Shehuixue dagang*, see *Mao Zedong zhexue pizhuji*, 205–84.

34. Knight, ed., *Mao Zedong on Dialectical Materialism*, 177, 185–86; cf. *Selected Works of Mao Tse-tung* I, 328, 335–36; *Mao Zedong Xuanji* I, 292, 330–31.

35. Lenin had employed the definition in a series of articles attacking Leon Trotsky and Nikolay Bukharin for their economic policies for the trade unions, suggesting that his own political approach was the appropriate policy: "It is strange that we should have to return to such elementary questions, but we are forced to do so by Trotsky and Bukharin. They have both reproached me for 'switching' the issue, or for taking a 'political' approach, while theirs is an 'economic' one. . . . This is a glaring theoretical error. I said again in my speech that politics is the concentrated expression of economics, because I had earlier heard my 'political' approach rebuked in a manner which is inconsistent and inadmissible for a Marxist. Politics must take precedence over economics. To argue otherwise is to forget the ABC of Marxism. . . . What the political approach means, in other words, is that the wrong attitude to

the trade unions will ruin the Soviet power and topple the dictatorship of the proletariat." V. I. Lenin, "Once again on the Trade Unions, the current situation and the mistakes of Trotsky and Bukharin," in V. I. Lenin, *Collected Works* (Moscow: FLPH, 1963) XXXII, 83. It is clear from the official version of "On New Democracy" that Mao was aware of Lenin's definition of politics as "the concentrated expression of economics," but there is no citation in the original text. Cf. *Selected Works of Mao Tse-tung* II, 340, 382; and Takeuchi, ed., *Mao Zedong Ji* VII, 149.

36. *Selected Works of Mao Tse-tung* III, 86–87; *Mao Zedong Xuanji* III, 823; Takeuchi, ed., *Mao Zedong Ji* VIII, 135.

37. *Selected Works of Mao Tse-tung* III, 119; *Mao Zedong Xuanji* III, 854; Takeuchi, ed., *Mao Zedong Ji* IX, 27–28.

38. For Marx's description of this process, see *The Poverty of Philosophy* (Moscow: Progress Publishers, 1955), 150.

39. *Selected Works of Mao Tse-tung* II, 340; *Mao Zedong Xuanji* II, 624; Takeuchi, ed., *Mao Zedong Ji* VII, 149. Emphasis added.

40. *Selected Works of Mao Tse-tung* II, 341; *Mao Zedong Xuanji* II, 625; Takeuchi, ed., *Mao Zedong Ji* VII, 150.

41. Takeuchi, ed., *Mao Zedong Ji* VI, 268.

42. *Selected Works of Mao Tse-tung* II, 353; *Mao Zedong Xuanji* II, 639; Takeuchi, ed., *Mao Zedong Ji* VI, 167.

43. This is made clear in *Selected Works of Mao Tse-tung* II, 353; *Mao Zedong Xuanji* II, 639; Takeuchi, ed., *Mao Zedong Ji* VII, 167.

44. Accepted here as reflecting Mao's views, although not written by Mao himself. See *Selected Works of Mao Tse-tung* II, 305.

45. *Selected Works of Mao Tse-tung* II, 308; *Mao Zedong Xuanji* II, 588; Takeuchi, ed., *Mao Zedong Ji* VII, 102.

46. *Selected Works of Mao Tse-tung* II, 310; *Mao Zedong Xuanji* II, 590; Takeuchi, ed., *Mao Zedong Ji* VII, 104–5.

47. *Selected Works of Mao Tse-tung* II, 319; *Mao Zedong Xuanji* II, 601; Takeuchi, ed., *Mao Zedong Ji* VII, 117–18.

48. *Selected Works of Mao Tse-tung* II, 348–52; *Mao Zedong Xuanji* II, 633–38; Takeuchi, ed., *Mao Zedong Ji* VII, 160–66.

49. Takeuchi, ed., *Mao Zedong Ji* V, 305.

50. *Selected Works of Mao Tse-tung* I, 327; *Mao Zedong Xuanji* I, 291.

51. *Selected Works of Mao Tse-tung* I, 339; *Mao Zedong Xuanji* I, 303.

52. *Selected Works of Mao Tse-tung* II, 349; *Mao Zedong Xuanji* II, 634; Takeuchi, ed., *Mao Zedong Ji* VII, 162.

53. *Selected Works of Mao Tse-tung* III, 248; *Mao Zedong Xuanji* III, 976; Takeuchi, ed., *Mao Zedong Ji* IX, 245.

54. *Selected Works of Mao Tse-tung* II, 287; *Mao Zedong Xuanji* II, 568; Takeuchi, ed., *Mao Zedong Ji* VII, 72.

55. *Selected Works of Mao Tse-tung* III, 248; *Mao Zedong Xuanji* III, 976; Takeuchi, ed., *Mao Zedong Ji* IX, 245.

56. *Selected Works of Mao Tse-tung* II, 351; *Mao Zedong Xuanji* II, 637; Takeuchi, ed., *Mao Zedong Ji* VII, 165.

57. *Selected Works of Mao Tse-tung* II, 307; *Mao Zedong Xuanji* II, 587; Takeuchi, ed., *Mao Zedong Ji* VII, 101.

58. *Selected Works of Mao Tse-tung* II, 351; *Mao Zedong Xuanji* II, 637; Takeuchi, ed., *Mao Zedong Ji* VII, 165.

59. *Selected Works of Mao Tse-tung* II, 350; *Mao Zedong Xuanji* II, 636; Takeuchi, ed., *Mao Zedong Ji* VII, 163–64.

60. *Selected Works of Mao Tse-tung* II, 307; *Mao Zedong Xuanji* II, 587; Takeuchi, ed., *Mao Zedong Ji* VII, 101.

61. *Selected Works of Mao Tse-tung* II, 352; *Mao Zedong Xuanji* II, 638; Takeuchi, ed., *Mao Zedong Ji* VII, 165.

62. *Selected Works of Mao Tse-tung* II, 352; *Mao Zedong Xuanji* II, 638; Takeuchi, ed., *Mao Zedong Ji* VII, 165.

63. *Selected Works of Mao Tse-tung* III, 246; *Mao Zedong Xuanji* III, 974; Takeuchi, ed., *Mao Zedong Ji* IX, 241.

64. *Selected Works of Mao Tse-tung* II, 225; *Mao Zedong Xuanji* II, 512.

65. *Selected Works of Mao Tse-tung* III, 86–87; *Mao Zedong Xuanji* III, 823; Takeuchi, ed., *Mao Zedong Ji* VIII, 135.

66. On this point, Mao remained consistent. In 1964 Mao was asked by a visitor from Zanzibar whether "the time is ripe for the establishment of a communist party in Africa." Mao's immediate response was: "The question of establishing a communist party must rest on whether there are any industrial workers." Joint Publication Research Service, *Miscellany of Mao Tse-tung Thought (1949–1968)* (Arlington, Virginia: February 1974), part 2, 367.

67. *Selected Works of Mao Tse-tung* II, 308; *Mao Zedong Xuanji* II, 588; Takeuchi, ed., *Mao Zedong Ji* VII, 102.

68. *Selected Works of Mao Tse-tung* II, 341; *Mao Zedong Xuanji* II, 625; Takeuchi, ed., *Mao Zedong Ji* VII, 150.

69. Takeuchi, ed., *Mao Zedong Ji* VI, 248; cf. *Selected Works of Mao Tse-tung* II, 200; *Mao Zedong Xuanji* II, 491.

70. *Selected Works of Mao Tse-tung* III, 230; *Mao Zedong Xuanji* III, 957; Takeuchi, ed., *Mao Zedong Ji* IX, 219.

71. *Selected Works of Mao Tse-tung* III, 11; *Mao Zedong Xuanji* III, 747; Takeuchi, ed., *Mao Zedong Ji* VI, 289.

72. See James E. Sheridan, *Chinese Warlord: The Career of Feng Yü-hsiang* (Stanford: Stanford University Press, 1966), esp. chapter 12. For a discussion of the "populist" element in Mao's thought, see James R. Townsend, "Chinese Populism and the Legacy of Mao Tse-tung," *Asian Survey* 17, no. 11 (November 1977): 1003–15.

73. Takeuchi, ed., *Mao Zedong Ji* VI, 248; *Selected Works of Mao Tse-tung* II, 200; *Mao Zedong Xuanji* II, 491.

74. Takeuchi, ed., *Mao Zedong Ji* V, 225.

75. Takeuchi, ed., *Mao Zedong Ji* V, 225.

76. Takeuchi, ed., *Mao Zedong Ji* V, 225.

77. *Selected Works of Mao Tse-tung* II, 352; *Mao Zedong Xuanji* II, 638; Takeuchi, ed., *Mao Zedong Ji* VII, 165.

78. *Selected Works of Mao Tse-tung* III, 116, 177; *Mao Zedong Xuanji* III, 851, 905.

79. Takeuchi, ed., *Mao Zedong Ji* VIII, 183–354. A truncated version appears in *Selected Works of Mao Tse-tung* III, 111–16; *Mao Zedong Xuanji* III, 845–51. A full translation appears in Andrew Watson, ed., *Mao Zedong and the Political Economy of the Border Region* (Cambridge: Cambridge University Press, 1980).

80. *Selected Works of Mao Tse-tung* III, 115; *Mao Zedong Xuanji* III, 850–51.

81. *Selected Works of Mao Tse-tung* III, 87; *Mao Zedong Xuanji* III, 823; Takeuchi, ed., *Mao Zedong Ji* VIII, 135.

82. *Selected Works of Mao Tse-tung* (London: Lawrence and Wishart, 1956), vol. 4, 205.

83. Takeuchi, ed., *Mao Zedong Ji* V, 299.

84. *Selected Works of Mao Tse-tung* II, 341; *Mao Zedong Xuanji* II, 625; Takeuchi, ed., *Mao Zedong Ji* VII, 150.

85. *Selected Works of Mao Tse-tung* II, 369; *Mao Zedong Xuanji* II, 625; Takeuchi, ed., *Mao Zedong Ji* VII, 150.

86. *Selected Works of Mao Tse-tung* II, 340; *Mao Zedong Xuanji* II, 624; Takeuchi, ed., *Mao Zedong Ji* VII, 149.

87. *Selected Works of Mao Tse-tung* III, 82; *Mao Zedong Xuanji* III, 818; Takeuchi, ed., *Mao Zedong Ji* VIII, 128. For a translation of the original text of these talks, see Bonnie S. McDougall, *"Talks at the Yan'an Conference on Literature and Art": A Translation of the 1943 Text with Commentary* (Ann Arbor: Michigan Papers in China Studies, no. 39, 1980).

88. *Selected Works of Mao Tse-tung* III, 86; *Mao Zedong Xuanji* III, 822; Takeuchi, ed., *Mao Zedong Ji* VIII, 134. Emphasis added.

89. Takeuchi, ed., *Mao Zedong Ji* IX, 95.

90. *Selected Works of Mao Tse-tung* II, 370; *Mao Zedong Xuanji* II, 655–56; Takeuchi, ed., *Mao Zedong Ji* VII, 188.

91. *Selected Works of Mao Tse-tung* II, 379; *Mao Zedong Xuanji* II, 665; Takeuchi, ed., *Mao Zedong Ji* VII, 200.

92. *Selected Works of Mao Tse-tung* II, 370; *Mao Zedong Xuanji* II, 855–56; Takeuchi, ed., *Mao Zedong Ji* VII, 188.

93. *Selected Works of Mao Tse-tung* II, 341; *Mao Zedong Xuanji* II, 625; Takeuchi, ed., *Mao Zedong Ji* VII, 150.

94. *Selected Works of Mao Tse-tung* III, 82; *Mao Zedong Xuanji* III, 818; Takeuchi, ed., *Mao Zedong Ji* VIII, 128.

95. Takeuchi, ed., *Mao Zedong Ji* IX, 134.

96. *Selected Works of Mao Tse-tung* II, 381; *Mao Zedong Xuanji* II, 667; Takeuchi, ed., *Mao Zedong Ji* VII, 202.

97. *Selected Works of Mao Tse-tung* II, 209; *Mao Zedong Xuanji* II, 499; Takeuchi, ed., *Mao Zedong Ji* VI, 260–61.

98. *Selected Works of Mao Tse-tung* II, 381; *Mao Zedong Xuanji* II, 667; Takeuchi, ed., *Mao Zedong Ji* VII, 202.

99. *Selected Works of Mao Tse-tung* II, 381; *Mao Zedong Xuanji* II, 667; Takeuchi, ed., *Mao Zedong Ji* VII, 202.

100. *Selected Works of Mao Tse-tung* II, 381; *Mao Zedong Xuanji* II, 667; Takeuchi, ed., *Mao Zedong Ji* VII, 202.

101. *Selected Works of Mao Tse-tung* II, 363–64; *Mao Zedong Xuanji* II, 648; Takeuchi, ed., *Mao Zedong Ji* VII, 178.

102. *Selected Works of Mao Tse-tung* I, 13–14; *Mao Zedong Xuanji* I, 3–11; Takeuchi, ed., *Mao Zedong Ji* I, 161–74.

103. *Selected Works of Mao Tse-tung* I, 137–39; *Mao Zedong Xuanji* I, 113–15.

104. Takeuchi, ed., *Mao Zedong Ji* VII, 122.

105. Takeuchi, ed., *Mao Zedong Ji* VII, 124.

106. *Selected Works of Mao Tse-tung* II, 325–26; *Mao Zedong Xuanji* II, 609; Takeuchi, ed., *Mao Zedong Ji* VII, 207.

107. Takeuchi, ed., *Mao Zedong Ji* VIII, 18.

108. *Selected Works of Mao Tse-tung* III, 221; *Mao Zedong Xuanji* III, 948; Takeuchi, ed., *Mao Zedong Ji* IX, 207.

109. *Selected Works of Mao Tse-tung* II, 322; *Mao Zedong Xuanji* II, p. 604; Takeuchi, ed., *Mao Zedong Ji* VII, 121.

110. *Selected Works of Mao Tse-tung* III, 221; *Mao Zedong Xuanji* III, 948; Takeuchi, ed., *Mao Zedong Ji* IX, 207.

111. *Selected Works of Mao Tse-tung* II, 325–26; *Mao Zedong Xuanji* II, 609; Takeuchi, ed., *Mao Zedong Ji* VII, 127.

112. Paul Healy has, on the basis of a very careful textual analysis of Mao's writings, persuasively argued that Mao's views on social change remained orthodox after 1955 as well. "A Paragon of Marxist Orthodoxy: Mao Zedong on the Social Formation and Social Change," in *Critical Perspectives on Mao Zedong's Thought*, ed. Arif Dirlik, Paul Healy, and Nick Knight (Atlantic Highlands, New Jersey: Humanities Press, 1997), 117–53.

113. A good example of an interpretation that stresses continuities in Mao's thought and regards Mao texts of whatever vintage, from 1917 to 1976, as a single corpus of documents from which can be extracted a single essential "Mao," is John Bryan Starr, *Continuing the Revolution: The Political Thought of Mao* (Princeton: Princeton University Press, 1979), esp. xi–xii.

114. See, for example, Louis Althusser, *For Marx* (London: Verso, 1979); also Louis Althusser and Étienne Balibar, *Reading Capital* (London: New Left Books, 1970); also Tom Bottomore, ed., *Modern Interpretations of Marx* (Oxford: Basil Blackwell, 1981).

Mao Zedong and the "Sinification of Marxism"

7

THE "RESOLUTION" ADOPTED by the Sixth Plenum of the Eleventh Central Committee of the Chinese Communist Party (CCP) in June 1981 constituted a major reevaluation of Mao Zedong's contribution to Chinese Marxism, and his role in the Chinese Revolution and period of socialist construction. Mao's "theory of continued revolution under the dictatorship of the proletariat," which had underpinned and rationalized the Cultural Revolution of the late 1960s and early 1970s, was denounced as "entirely erroneous."[1] Similarly, the "Resolution" charged that, during the decade from 1956 to 1966, Mao was guilty of serious "theoretical and practical mistakes concerning class struggle in a socialist society."[2] Such negative judgments are, however, balanced in the "Resolution" by a strong affirmation of the positive role played by Mao during the pre-1949 period, and his leadership, policies, and theoretical innovations are represented as central to the eventual victory of the Chinese Revolution:

> In the 22 years from 1927 to 1949, Comrade Mao Zedong and other Party leaders managed to overcome innumerable difficulties and gradually worked out an overall strategy and specific policies and directed their implementation, so that the revolution was able to switch from staggering defeats to great victory. Our Party and people would have had to grope in the dark much longer had it not been for Comrade Mao Zedong, who, more than once rescued the Chinese revolution from grave danger, and for the Central Committee of the Party which was headed by him and which charted the firm, correct political course for the whole Party, the whole people and the people's army.[3]

It is evident that, in the years following his death, China's post-Mao leaders attempted to stake their claim to ideological legitimacy on their adherence to the form of Marxism that Mao developed and utilized during the revolutionary period, and during the 1980s, numerous articles appeared in the Chinese media and theoretical journals extolling various aspects of Mao's contribution to Marxist theory during the Yan'an period.[4] One aspect of Mao's Marxism singled out for praise was its insistence on the "integration" of the universal truths of Marxism with the realities of Chinese society and the Chinese Revolution. The "Resolution" of the Sixth Plenum in fact perceived the origin of Mao Zedong Thought in this "integration":

> Our Party had creatively applied the basic tenets of Marxism-Leninism and integrated them with the concrete practice of the Chinese revolution. In this way, the great system of Mao Zedong Thought came into being and the correct path to victory for the Chinese revolution was charted. This is a major contribution to Marxism-Leninism.[5]

This acclamation of Mao's contribution to the integration of Marxist theory with Chinese realities during the 1930s and 1940s has persisted in the CCP's ideology in the years since the 1981 "Resolution," and indeed, subsequent generations of China's leaders have been keen to represent their understanding of Marxism in terms first pioneered by Mao, for Mao had supposedly pioneered a methodology by which Marxism's seemingly abstract formulations could be applied to Chinese society to reveal its particular characteristics, thus allowing the formulation of appropriate policies. The development of policy in the post-Mao era could, therefore, similarly be based on a supposedly objective understanding of China's reality informed by Marxism's universal historical laws. The continued political and ideological significance for the CCP of this ideological formula—integrating the universal theory of Marxism with the "concrete practice" of the Chinese Revolution and the "realities" of Chinese society—thus makes it appropriate to explore the distinctive manner in which Mao understood it. In the late 1930s, Mao described this formula as the "Sinification of Marxism," an innovation described by Stuart Schram as Mao's "greatest theoretical and practical achievement."[6]

It is the purpose of this chapter to analyze the *form* of Mao's "Sinification of Marxism." In other words, the chapter will attempt to reconstruct the logic that permitted Mao to harmonize his insistence on the universality of Marxism as a theory of history with his simultaneous emphasis on China's particular characteristics. Western critiques of Mao's "Sinification of Marxism" have clustered around two lines of interpretation. The first suggests that the "Sinification of Marxism" was essentially a function of Mao's Sinocentrism and entailed the elevation of the Chinese tradition and contemporary Chinese realities at the expense of Marxism's universal truths; it involved a "nationalistic emphasis on *Chinese* experience."[7] The second argues that the "Sinification of Marxism" was an ideological ploy used by Mao to enhance his own position in the power struggle with the Moscow-oriented Returned Students' Faction within the CCP that favored a more orthodox reading of Marxism than did Mao.[8] In contrast, the following analysis suggests that Mao's "Sinification of Marxism" was an attempt to discover a formula by which the universal theory of Marxism could be applied in a particular national context *without abandoning the universality of that theory*. To understand the logic Mao used to harmonize these two seemingly conflicting imperatives—adherance to a universal theory and close attention to China's particular characteristics—requires a reconstruction of his views on science and the scientific method. How are universal laws of nature and society derived? How are such laws to be applied once they have achieved the status of universality? Do all societies obey a single universal law, and what of societies that do not appear to do so? How is a constantly changing reality to be understood? It is questions such as these that Mao grappled with as he sought to comprehend the realities of Chinese society and the dynamics of the Chinese Revolution while drawing inspiration from Marxism's univeral theory of history.[9]

Mao and Science: The Universal and Particular

Mao's view of science was based firmly on a belief that the inductive method represented the only reliable means of gaining access to the truth of the objective world. Following classic inductive logic, Mao believed that investigation of reality commenced from numerous observations of specific instances, and only then could the observer draw conclusions (in the form of natural laws) from the available evidence. Mao consistently rejected the deductive approach, perceiving it as contrary to the Marxist scientific method:

> In discussing a problem, we should start from reality and not from definitions. . . . We are Marxists, and Marxism teaches us that in our approach to a problem we should start from objective facts, not from abstract definitions, and that we should derive our guiding principles, policies and measures from an analysis of these facts.[10]

Mao's conception of the inductive method is captured in his frequent use of the four-character phrase "seeking truth from facts" (*shishi qiu shi*), a slogan that would be mobilized after his death to justify a dramatic turn away from his policies on socialism and toward the embrace of capitalism, an ideological about-face that reveals only too clearly the empiricist vacuity of such an epistemological position (of which more later; see also chapter 2). Mao defined the components of this phrase as follows: "'Facts' are all the things that exist objectively, 'truth' means the internal relations of objective things, namely their regularities (*guilüxing*), and 'to seek' means to study."[11] To "seek truth from facts" represented for Mao "the scientific approach,"[12] and in order to pursue this approach one had to "appropriate the material in detail and subject it to scientific analysis and synthesis."[13]

Mao made it clear that natural laws are the end result of numerous observations of the real world. As he pointed out in his "Lecture Notes on Dialectical Materialism," the task of Marxist philosophy "when studying is not to arrive, through thought within the brain, at the relationship which exists between various phenomena, but to arrive at that relationship *through investigation of the phenomena themselves*."[14] The founders of Marxism had, Mao believed, "pointed out the necessity of a philosophy which grew out of analysis founded on real life and real relations."[15] He deemed it possible for "exceedingly extensive laws and formulations" that incorporated the conclusions of the various natural and social sciences to be derived from the observations of concrete facts;[16] the "sense perceptions and impressions" humans gain in the course of practice constituted the foundation of all objective knowledge.[17] Mao was, however, reticent about the number of observations needed prior to the formulation of natural laws, although he did suggest that "a sudden change" would take place in the brain of the observer when the point was reached at which concepts emerged from the observation of the facts under investigation.[18] The necessary number of observations would, it appears, be determined by the nature of the phenomenon under investigation. A sufficient number of observations had been made when obvious trends appeared to the observer, and these emerged in the form of concepts in the brain of the observer that captured the essence, the distinguishing characteristics, of the phenomenon. There are, however, no clear guidelines in Mao's Yan'an writings on the actual process of law derivation. Nevertheless, by examining the manner in which Mao employed the term "law" (*guilü*), we can make some general comments on the status of natural "law" in his thought and use this as the premise from which to reconstruct his views on the "Sinification of Marxism."

In the philosophy of science as this has developed in the Western intellectual tradition, the concept of a scientific "law" has come to denote a universally valid description of the characteristics and behavior of a
phenomenon. In the inductive paradigm, this description is founded on a
value-neutral observation of numerous particular instances of the category
under investigation. The assumption is made that, because all observed instances have behaved in a certain manner (that is, indicated a regular and pre-
dictable pattern of behavior), all instances in that category will behave in a
like manner. The important point is that the formulation of a law is based
on presumption of exact replication of all instances (whether observed or
unobserved) within a category. The law thus has universal validity.

This is supposedly how an inductive scientific methodology operates.
Many philosophers of science have pointed to its logical fallacies, including the impossibility of an observation of reality being completely innocent of the values and preconceptions of the observer and the impossibility
of framing a law that claims to cover unobserved instances of the phenomenon described by that law. Neither of these objections to inductivism
is explicitly acknowledged or addressed by Mao, but his approach to science and the formulation of natural laws does indicate an awareness that
inductivism contains problems that require some modification of its
methodology. This can be seen in Mao's approach to the derivation of laws
(of nature, society, history, war, for example), which did depart in important detail from inductivism. According to Mao, although laws of universal status did exist, it was also possible to derive laws that did not have
universal status and that were applicable only to particular instances within
a general category. That it was possible, in Mao's view, to formulate "laws"
of limited (rather than universal) validity is made evident if we examine his
analysis of the phenomenon of war. In a document of 1936 entitled
"Problems of strategy in China's revolutionary war," Mao makes the following instructive comment:

> The different laws for directing wars are determined by the different cir-
> cumstances of those wars—differences in their time, place and nature
> (*xingzhi*). As regards the time factor, both war and its laws develop; each
> historical stage has its special characteristics, and hence the laws in each his-
> torical stage have their special characteristics and cannot be mechanically
> applied in another stage. As for the nature of war, since revolutionary war
> and counter-revolutionary war both have their special characteristics, the
> laws governing them also have their own characteristics, and those apply-
> ing to one cannot be mechanically transferred to the other. As for the fac-
> tor of place, since each country or nation, especially a large country or

nation, has its own characteristics, the laws of war for each country or nation also have their own characteristics, and here, too, those applying to
one cannot be mechanically transferred to the other. In studying the laws
for directing wars that occur at different historical stages, that differ in nature and that are waged in different places and by different nations, we must
fix our attention on the characteristics and development of each, and must
oppose a mechanical approach to the problem of war.[19]

It is evident from this interesting passage that Mao rejected the notion
that there can only be laws of war in general. On the contrary, it is possible and desirable to seek out "laws" describing the regularities of specific
theaters of war. This is because the laws of war develop, altering as the nature and context of war alter. Laws arising from events in one geographi-
cal area may not be relevant in another place or for that matter in the same
location at a different time. The laws of war may also vary according to the
"nature" of war, whether it is revolutionary or counter-revolutionary. Indeed, a "law" may be derived from a particular war which, because of the
unique admixture of time, place, and "nature," may be inapplicable in any
other situation. A "law" thus becomes a description of the regularities exhibited by a particular instance of a general category (for example, a particular battle or campaign) rather than of the category itself (in this case,
war in general). A "law" of this sort has validity only for the instance in
question and because of the (perhaps) unrepeatable nature of that particular instance can have no pretension to a general validity for other instances
of war within the category of war as a whole.

It could be argued that, for Mao, the particular instance became (for
purposes of law derivation) a category in itself and thus legitimately capable of generating a covering "law." However, such an argument involves two
problems. First, it suggests the possibility of an infinite regression in which
a phenomenon (such as war) is capable of continued subdivision to provide
increasingly more particular laws having increasingly less general validity.
Second, there is the problem of repeatability. The inductive procedure, to
which Mao subscribed, demands that a scientific law must describe the
characteristics of a phenomenon that will be exactly repeated in each and
every manifestation of that phenomenon whether in the past, present, or
future. A law thus has a predictive capacity premised on the certainty of the
repeatability of the behavior of the category described by that law. It seems,
however, that Mao was not overly concerned with repeatability, and he was
to accord the status of "law" to descriptions of seemingly unrepeatable particular instances; from this perspective, the concept of a scientific law as pos-

sessing a high degree of predictability for all instances within the same category appears to lose force. Mao's handling of the concept of "law" suggests that it may only possess a relative and temporary validity, its applicability over and above the particular circumscribed by the improbability of an exact replication of the particular characteristics of the instance from which the law was derived. Mao, indeed, referred to the historical relativity of the "laws" that he employed: "All the laws for directing war develop as history develops and as war develops; nothing is changeless."[20] In Mao's hands, a "law" of a particular instance does not automatically have universal validity; it provides, however, a description of the characteristics of that instance useful in understanding it and from which specific policy responses could be developed. The very specificity of such a "law" is conducive to an appreciation of the exact regularities (guilüxing) of that particular instance and may be of some use in providing practical lessons for the understanding of other instances within the category to which it belongs; no assumption can be made, however, that an immediate extrapolation or prediction can be made on the basis of such a particular "law." As Mao asserted, "the laws of war for each country or nation . . . have their own characteristics."[21]

From Mao's references to particular "laws," it appears that the notion of extrapolation and prediction did not play a prominent role. He believed strongly that it was necessary to avoid a mechanical application of a "law," the general applicability of which may be limited by the uniqueness of the particular instance from which it derived (for example, within the category of revolution, the differences between the Chinese and Russian revolutions had to be recognized). Mao was interested in particular "laws" for their utility, largely for the purpose of formulating political and military strategy. Knowledge of the regularities evident in one instance (that is, its "law") could aid in the interpretation of the regularities of a related instance, but such knowledge, if mechanically applied, could conceal its regularities and lead to mistaken tactics. As Mao was to point out, "the laws of war in each historical stage have their special characteristics and cannot be mechanically applied in another stage."

Are we to assume, then, that for Mao there could be no transcendence of the particular to allow the formulation of laws having a more general and ultimately a universal validity? Although there is without doubt a Heraclitean element in Mao's thought ("nothing is changeless"),[22] it is quite evident that he did believe in the existence of universal laws which, while built upon (but at the same time transcending) the particular, provided a framework for the interpretation and explanation of nature, history, and society. There can be no doubt that Mao perceived the universal laws of

Marxism-Leninism in this light. Mao perceived the derivation of such universal laws as proceeding (in accord with inductive logic) from the particular to the general. He believed that if one is to arrive at objective truth, the connection between the particular and the general had to be maintained: "In the nature of things, the particular and the general are inseparably linked; once separated they depart from objective truth."[23] Mao perceived the "laws" governing the particular as constituting the building blocks from which "laws" of wider generality were constructed, each level of this inductive pyramid resting and relying on an immediately lower level of generality until the entire edifice rested on "laws" describing regularities at the level of the particular instance. Although "all genuine knowledge originates in direct experience," Mao accepted that experience accumulated and recorded by ancestors and contemporaries (that is, indirect experience) could be coupled with one's own direct experience to provide the data for the construction of this pyramid of "laws."[24] Laws previously formulated, provided they were "scientifically abstracted" from the direct experience of others, could be employed to complete a scientific view of reality. Thus, by Mao's criteria, it was valid to accept a universal theory such as Marxism as representing a scientific reflection of objective reality if it had been constructed with regard to the norms of inductive procedure, building from the particular to the universal and utilizing the distilled wisdom of "scientifically abstracted" indirect experience. Mao did not perceive, therefore, any contradiction between utilizing an inductive methodology under an overarching worldview, for he accepted implicitly that this worldview (Marxist dialectical and historical materialism) had been constructed in accordance with the idiosyncratic inductivism he espoused. Indeed, he claimed that, having learned to look "at questions in an objective and many-sided way," he and his comrades could claim to be "scientific Marxists."[25]

There are obviously serious logical difficulties with Mao's position. The construction of an inductive pyramid to permit the formulation of universal laws is threatened by his insistence that "laws" of the particular instance may not be capable of replication. The absence of the criterion of repeatability in framing "laws" of low generality calls into question the possibility of utilizing such "laws" as the raw material from which universal laws are constructed. Mao's insistence on building from the particular to the general thus rested on an unresolved contradiction in his methodological approach. The important point remains, however, that Mao believed it possible to formulate both universal laws and particular "laws," however tenuous the logical connection between them. It will become evident that this distinction between universal laws and particular "laws" was central to the way in which Mao approached the problem of sinifying Marxism, taking a universal theory of history and providing it with a national form without detracting from its universal status.

The Form of Mao's "Sinification of Marxism"

One of the distinguishing features of Mao's approach to the interpretation of phenomena was his insistence on grasping the regularities that characterize the particular instance, and his concomitant distrust of applying universal laws in an undiscriminating manner that ignored the distinguishing regularities of other particular instances. This sensitivity to the importance of grasping the specific manifestation of universal laws led Mao to perceive in Marxism a methodology capable of facilitating his quest for comprehension of the particular. In keeping with this position, Mao was not overly preoccupied with the historically specific content of Marx's analysis of the onset and dynamics of European industrial capitalism, although he was certainly persuaded by the philosophy of history that Marx drew from this analysis. Marx's views on the origins of history, the driving force of historical change, the stages in history, and the goal toward which history was ineluctably moving—all of these provided the broad framework from within which Mao regarded history. However, as he made clear on many occasions, this perspective on the broad sweep of history did not and could not provide the specific details of individual phases of history and particular sites of struggle. These had to be revealed through close analysis of the relevant empirical realities. Thus, while Mao drew inspiration from the universal laws of the Marxist philosophy of history, he perceived these only as guidelines for detailed investigation to reveal the regularities, the particular "laws," of the phenomenon under consideration. He was thus impatient with those of his comrades who could recite the laws and principles of orthodox Marxism and were familiar with the historically specific content of the Marxist classics, but who were unable to apply the methodology of Marxism to gain a deep understanding of the historical evolution of Chinese society and the dynamics of the Chinese Revolution. His hostility to the uncritical use of the content of the Marxist classics is reflected in a document of 1941 entitled "Resolution of the Central Committee of the Chinese Communist Party on the Yan'an Cadre School." Here, Mao insisted that cadres learn to extract from Marxism that which would be useful in prosecuting the Chinese Revolution and not become preoccupied with laws and principles that may have been relevant to class struggle and revolution in a European or Russian context but which had little relevance in the Chinese context. Above all, cadres had to learn to separate the content of the Marxist classics from their "essence," and for Mao this meant discovering and then applying the methodology at the heart of Marxist theory:

> At present the fundamental weakness of the Yan'an Cadre School lies in the lack of contact between theory and practice, between what is studied and what is applied, and there exists the serious fault of subjectivism and dogmatism. This fault manifests itself in letting students study a plethora [*dadui*; literally, "large heaps"] of *abstract* Marxist-Leninist principles, and not paying attention (or hardly paying attention) to understanding their essence and how to apply them in the concrete Chinese situation. In order to correct this defect, it must be stressed that the purpose of the study of Marxist-Leninist theory is to enable the student to correctly apply it in the resolution of the practical problems of the Chinese Revolution, and not the ill digested cramming and recitation of principles found in books. Firstly, we must let students distinguish the words and sentences of Marxism-Leninism from its essence; secondly, we must let the students comprehend this essence . . . ; thirdly, the students must study and gain mastery over applying this essence in China's concrete environment; all formalistic, hollow study is to be abandoned. In order to achieve this purpose, besides teaching Marxist–Leninist theories, education in Chinese history and conditions, and Party history and policy, must be increased.[26]

It is obvious from this quote that Mao's confidence in Marxism had nothing to do with the *content* of Marx's analyses. Such content was necessarily specific to a particular mode of production (capitalism in Western Europe) at a particular historical moment (the mid-nineteenth century). The characteristics of that particular historical conjuncture described by Marx—its economic history, class structure, and the nature of its class struggle—represented the historically specific content of Marx's analysis, something that had to be differentiated from the laws of history he formulated.

It is significant that Mao regarded the principles and laws of Marxism-Leninism as "abstract" and not necessarily of immediate utility in the Chinese context. Mao regarded such abstract principles and laws of Marxism-Leninism as constituted of assertions of the universalized status of certain phenomena. Although he implicitly accepted the validity of Marxism's universal laws, he did not accept that they could specify the manner in which the phenomena they described manifest themselves in particular historical contexts. The universal law of class struggle is a good example. Class struggle is a universally existing social phenomenon; it is a significant characteristic of all societies (except the most primitive). However, the Marxist law that asserts the universality of class struggle had nothing to say, in Mao's view, about the way in which class struggle would occur within a particular historical context. Thus, this universal law (while deriving initially from observations of numerous particular instances of class struggle) remained "abstract" in the absence of its application to determine the form class struggle might take in a further particular instance. It is in this sense that Mao could accept the laws of Marxism as being universally valid while at the same time being "abstract." It is also in this sense that the inductivist and empiricist element in Mao's thought could coexist (somewhat uneasily) with a confidence in certain overarching universal laws and principles.

Mao's conflict with the "dogmatists" within the CCP must be seen primarily as a profound disagreement over this interpretation of Marxism and how it should be employed. In contradistinction to Mao, the "dogmatists" believed that the content of Marx's study of the dynamics of Western European capitalism and its resultant class structure and struggle did have relevance in the context of the Chinese Revolution, despite the dissimilarity of conditions. The principles derived from and describing the historically specific content of Marx's analysis were not, however, perceived by the "dogmatists" as having only localized applicability and were regarded as representing the universal truths of Marxism. Mao insisted, in contrast, that in utilizing Marx's writings on European capitalism it was necessary to abstract a more generalized law from the historical content in order to allow the application of that law elsewhere. He regarded the process of deriving such universally applicable laws as the scientific procedure that permitted the construction of the ultimate level in the inductionist pyramid. By this procedure, Marx's "laws" describing the particular instance of class struggle in nineteenth-century Europe could be separated from the law that described the category of class struggle in universal terms: Class struggle exists in all societies (save the most primitive). Marx's generalizations about the class structure and struggle in Europe were consequently equivalent, for Mao, to particular "laws." By abstracting the universal principle from such particular "laws," it was possible to derive laws at the highest level of generality, laws that possessed universal validity and that were unconstrained by any historically or culturally specific content. Therefore, the universal law that asserted the ubiquity of class struggle in all societies could direct attention to the centrality of that phenomenon within society, but it could not indicate how class structure and class struggle would manifest itself in any particular society at any point in time. The disclosure of the nature of class struggle within a specific historical context could result only from empirical analysis to reveal the regularities of class struggle in that context, the conclusions of which could then be framed as a particular "law."

In his "Sinification" speech of October 1938 entitled "On the New Stage," Mao insisted that Marxism was "universally applicable."[27] It is clear, however, that Mao refused to entertain the notion that the particular "laws" arising from Marx's analysis of European capitalism possessed universal status, for their relevance was limited by the specific nature of the historical context from which they had arisen. To isolate the universal character of Marxism, what was required was a process of abstraction (divorcing principle from content) whereby "laws" of limited historical relevance could generate universal laws divorced from specific historical limitations. The universal laws resulting from this process were necessarily "abstract," for they were devoid of any content that restricted their universal validity. However, Mao believed that the production of universal laws represented only one element of the theoretical system of Marxism. The production of universal laws was not an end in itself, for such laws had to be utilized at the level of the particular instance to guide investigation of the phenomena they described at an abstract level. In this way, a universal law could aid in the elucidation of the particular, and only by the union of the two could the universal law cease to be an abstraction. Without application to determine specific manifestations of a universal law, it necessarily remained "abstract"; the connection between universal and particular was ruptured. However, Marxism could not be abstract in this sense, for it was defined in Mao's mind as the unity of the the universal and particular, the universal applied and given specific form at the level of the particular. The universal laws of Marxism did not represent the totality of Marxism but rather one element of a complete theoretical system that comprised universal (or "abstract") laws utilized to disclose "laws" at the level of the particular instance; Marxism would remain incomplete without the union of the universal and particular in this manner. Consequently, when Mao asserted in "On the New Stage" that "there is no abstract Marxism, only concrete Marxism,"[28] he was indicating that Marxism as a complete theoretical system was defined by the application of its universal laws in specific historical circumstances rather than that there were no abstractions in Marxism at all. The function of "abstract" Marxism was to provide universally applicable laws that would facilitate the elucidation of the regularities of particular historical instances. Without these abstractions (its universal laws), an aimless empiricism would be the result, but without the application of these abstractions to specific historical situations, Marxism would represent a sterile system of thought unanchored to dynamic historical realities. Mao's insistence on the application of the universal laws of Marxism to reveal the particular characteristics of the Chinese context was therefore predicated on a distinctive view of Marxism as a complete theoretical system rather than on a capricious desire to subordinate Marxism in favor of China's empirical realities, as some commentators have suggested. Mao perceived his view of the Marxist theoretical system as logically tenable because of its emphasis on applying the universal principles of Marxism to reveal the realities of the Chinese Revolution and Chinese society.

Thus, for Mao, Marxism's utility did not end with the provision of universally applicable laws. He also perceived in Marxism a methodology whereby such laws could be applied to concrete historical situations; in other words, the process of application itself was an integral feature of Marxism as a total theoretical system. As Mao was to point out in "On the New Stage," it was necessary to study "the viewpoint (*lichang*) and methodology with which they [Marx and Lenin] observed and solved problems."[29] This methodology encompassed several essential features, including a consciousness of history, the analysis of a historical situation in its entirety, and class analysis. These methodological dimensions of Marxism provided the key that could disclose the way in which the universal manifested itself within specific historical instances. Mao could therefore only conceive of Marxism as a complete theoretical system in its application. Consequently, Marxism in the Chinese context consisted of Marxism's universal laws applied through detailed investigation to disclose the regularities (or particular "laws") that characterized Chinese society and the Chinese Revolution. Once disclosed, these particular "laws" became an integral part of Marxism within that historically defined situation. It is in this sense that Mao could call for the "Sinification of Marxism," for Marxism could only become complete in the historical context of China through its "Sinification":

> There is no such thing as abstract Marxism, but only concrete Marxism. What we call concrete Marxism is Marxism that has taken on a national form, that is, Marxism applied to the concrete struggle in the concrete conditions prevailing in China, and not Marxism abstractly used. If a Chinese Communist, who is part of the great Chinese people . . . talks of Marxism apart from Chinese particularities (*tedian*), this Marxism is merely an empty abstraction. Consequently, the Sinification of Marxism—that is to say, making certain that in all its manifestations it is imbued with Chinese particularities (*texing*), using it according to those particularities (*tedian*)—becomes a problem that must be understood and solved by the whole Party without delay.[30]

Inherent in Mao's "Sinification of Marxism" is the notion that Marxism as a complete theoretical system (rather than just a series of universal laws) is definable only within a concrete historical context, and this because there is in Marxism a necessary union between the universal and the particular "laws" to which the universal laws draw attention. Thus, although the "Sinification of Marxism" is, as Raymond Wylie claims, a "culturally charged term," it does not claim an exclusively Chinese cultural privilege over Marxism.[31] Within a different cultural or historical context, Marxism's universal laws would need to be conjoined with the particular "laws" characteristic of that specific context, and because its particular "laws" would be different from those of the Chinese context, that particular Marxism would differ accordingly. Both forms of Marxism would nevertheless share a common stock of universal laws. Mao was to repeat, in "On New Democracy" (1940), this necessity for a union between the universal truths of Marxism and the particular characteristics of the Chinese context:

> In applying Marxism to China, Chinese Communists must fully and properly integrate the universal truth of Marxism with the concrete practice of the Chinese revolution, or in other words, the universal truth of Marxism *must be combined with* specific national characteristics and acquire a definite national form if it is to be useful, and in no circumstances can it be applied subjectively as a mere formula.[32]

Here again, the emphasis was on Marxism as finding completion (and through this completion, utility) by its integration with the particular "laws" of an historically and culturally specific context. This view of Marxism led logically to an insistence on the need for close attention to the particular characteristics of Chinese society and history. Mao was to return to this point again and again in subsequent writings of the Yan'an period, and he made no attempt to conceal his impatience with those Chinese Marxists who were preoccupied with foreign history and revolutionary models to the neglect of Chinese history and conditions. He perceived this preoccupation as a manifestation of an incorrect interpretation of Marxism, one that regarded the content and historically particular "laws" of a largely European form of Marxism as automatically relevant to the Chinese context. In "Reform our study" (1941), Mao identified three conditions having a deleterious effect within the CCP: The study of current conditions was being neglected, as were the study of history and the application of Marxism-Leninism. For Mao, these failings were a result of an incorrect interpretation of Marxism, and his critique of them was inspired by a view of Marxism that insisted on the integration of Marxism's universal laws with the particular "laws" that described the regularities characteristic of China as a specific historical instance; that integration was only possible through detailed investigation and close knowledge of China's history and current conditions. Mao believed that Marxists laboring under a dogmatic misinterpretation of Marxism were guilty of "subjectivism," an epithet intended to indicate divorce from reality and a preoccupation with theory for its own sake:

> With this attitude, a person does not make a systematic and thorough study of the environment, but works by sheer subjective enthusiasm and has a blurred picture of the face of China today. With this attitude, he mutilates (*geduan*) history, knows only Greece but not China, and is completely in the dark about the China of yesterday and the day before yesterday. With this attitude, a person studies the theories of Marx, Engels, Lenin and Stalin in the abstract and without any aim, not inquiring what connection they may have to the Chinese Revolution. He goes to Marx, Engels, Lenin and Stalin not to seek the standpoints and methods with which to study the theoretical and tactical problems but to study theory purely for theory's sake.[33]

During the *Zhengfeng* (Rectification) movement of 1942–1944 there was a heavy emphasis on eradicating this "subjectivism." The *Zhengfeng* documents reveal a preoccupation with disclosing the distinguishing characteristics (the particular "laws") of the Chinese Revolution and Chinese society and the need to formulate policies in line with those characteristics. *Zhengfeng* must consequently be seen, in large part, as a move to gain Party-wide acceptance of the "Sinification of Marxism" (as Mao perceived it), a formulation that had found acceptance amongst an important segment of Party leaders and intellectuals since 1938 but had not found wide audience or comprehension amongst rank-and-file cadres.[34]

In "On the New Stage," Mao had asserted that Marxism had to be regarded as a guide to action. He returned to this theme frequently in the *Zhengfeng* documents, and it represented the major theme of his keynote speech originally entitled "Reform in learning, the Party and literature" (1942):

> Our comrades must understand that we do not study Marxism-Leninism because it is pleasing to the eye, or because it has some mystical value . . . Marxism-Leninism has no beauty, nor has it any mystical value. It is only extremely useful . . . Marx, Lenin, and Stalin have repeatedly said, "Our doctrine is not dogma; it is a guide to action." . . . Theory and practice can be combined only if men of the Chinese Communist Party take the standpoints, concepts, and methods of Marxism-Leninism, apply them to

China, and create a theory from conscientious research on the realities of the Chinese Revolution and Chinese history.[35]

It is clear that Mao regarded a sinified Marxism as a union between Marxism's universal laws and the particular "laws" that described the characterizing regularities of the Chinese context. How did he perceive this theoretical system as a "guide to action"? It must be stressed that Mao did not regard it as incorporating the formulae for automatic and necessarily correct policy responses to the various political, economic, and military contingencies that might arise in the course of revolution. The function of a sinified Marxism was to facilitate as accurate an interpretation of the Chinese context as possible. With this information, the CCP's leaders would be in a position to formulate strategies and tactics commensurate with the objective possibilities and limitations of the concrete situation. Such strategies and tactics could only be regarded as appropriate in their conception rather than as necessarily correct. Having a clear and hopefully accurate picture of the historical situation would act as a guide to action by ruling out inappropriate policy responses and presenting certain strategies and tactics as preferable or even obvious. Here again, the influence of the inductive method is revealed in Mao's method of formulating policies: Under no circumstances could one arbitrarily formulate strategies or tactics *a priori,* but only via a careful analysis of the characteristics of a historically specific situation. One had always to work "upwards" from the facts rather than attempting to impose a predetermined blueprint for action on reality. Mao made this clear in "Reform our study": "Marx, Engels, Lenin and Stalin have taught us that we should proceed from objective realities and that we should derive laws from them to serve as a basis for our actions."[36]

It is in this context that Mao's theory of practice finds relevance.[37] A sinified Marxism could only serve as a guide to action by presenting an accurate assessment of a historical situation. It was up to the political leader or cadre, utilizing direct and indirect experience and taking full cognizance of the regularities (particular "laws") of the situation, to draw the necessary inferences and formulate an appropriate policy response. The only method of ascertaining whether a seemingly appropriate policy was correct was by implementing it and evaluating the results. If there was an equivalence between intention and outcome, then the policy and the interpretation upon which it was based were indeed correct; a disparity between intention and outcome indicated either faulty analysis of the situation or formulation of a seemingly appropriate but incorrect response. In the latter case, adjustment of analysis of the objective situation or reformulation of policy, or both, was called for. And only by engaging with reality, by "seeking truth from facts" and "closely combining theory with practice," could the requisite knowledge be acquired to close any gap between the intention and outcome of policy.[38]

Mao thus believed that Marxism was a complex theoretical system that could only find complete definition within a historically specific setting. Mao's "Sinification of Marxism" was not, therefore, a question of subordinating Marxism to Chinese reality, history, or culture, nor was it merely a tactical move in the power struggle with the Returned Students' Faction. It was, rather, a function of his belief that the universal laws of Marxism did not in themselves represent the complete theoretical system of Marxism. For Marxism to become complete in the Chinese context, its universal laws had to be united ("integrated") with the particular "laws" that described China's identifying characteristics. Mao believed that this union of the universal and the particular allowed the completion of the Marxist system and created a genuinely Chinese Marxism that nevertheless did not detract from the universal status of Marxism as a theory of history.

Notes

1. "On Questions of Party History: Resolution on Certain Questions in the History of our Party since the Founding of the People's Republic of China," *Beijing Review* XXIV, no. 27 (6 July 1981): 20–21.

2. "On Questions of Party History," 20.

3. "On Questions of Party History," 13.

4. For a sample of such articles translated into English, see Nick Knight, ed., *The Philosophical Thought of Mao Zedong: Studies from China, 1981–1989* (Armonk, New York: M. E. Sharpe, *Chinese Studies in Philosophy*, 1992); see also Nick Knight, "Mao Studies in China: A Review of *Research on Mao Zedong Thought*," *CCP Research Newsletter* 2 (Spring 1989): 13–16.

5. "On Questions of Party History," 12.

6. Stuart Schram, *Mao Tse-tung* (Harmondsworth: Penguin, 1966), 68.

7. Mark Selden, *The Yenan Way in Revolutionary China* (Cambridge, Mass.: Harvard University Press, 1971), 191. Emphasis in original. According to Raymond Wylie, Mao was concerned to create "a new variant of Marxism that exhibited a scientific revolutionary content within a Chinese national form." See his *The Emergence of Maoism: Mao Tse-tung, Ch' en Po-ta, and the Search for Chinese Theory 1935–1945* (Stanford: Stanford University Press, 1980), 90. See also Raymond Wylie, "Mao Tse-tung, Ch'en Po-ta and the 'Sinification of Marxism,' 1936–38," *China Quarterly* 79 (September 1979): 447–80. Jack Gray suggests that it involved "modifying [Marxist-Leninist] generalizations to fit the very different circumstances of China." see his *Mao Tse-tung* (Guildford and London: Lutterworth Press,

1973), 41. Stuart Schram has argued that Mao denied altogether the existence of "a universally valid form of Marxism," and that he was preoccupied "with the glory of China." See his *The Political Thought of Mao Tse-tung* (Harmondsworth: Penguin, 1969, revised ed.), 112–16. Frederic Wakeman Jr. argues that Mao "wished to temper the universal theory of Marxism with the specific practice of revolution in China." See his *History and Will: Philosophical Perspectives on Mao Tse-tung's Thought* (Berkeley: University of California Press, 1973), 229. Soviet analysts denounced Mao's sinification of Marxism as a product of his "Great-Han Chauvinism." See, for example, *A Critique of Mao Tse-tung's Theoretical Conceptions* (Moscow: Progress Publishers, 1972), 70–71. See also Maurice Thorez's criticism of Mao's "curious theories." "What would remain," he asked, "of the universal principles of Marxism-Leninism after its 'Chinification' by some, its 'Frenchification' by others, or its 'Russification'?" In Hélène Carrère d'Encausse and Stuart R. Schram, *Marxism in Asia: An Introduction with Readings* (London: Penguin, 1969), 309.

8. Robert C. North argues that Mao was "adapting Russian Communist political theory to meet peculiar Chinese requirements and the convenience of his own climb to power." See his *Moscow and Chinese Communists* (Stanford: Stanford University Press, 1963), 193. Wylie also argues that Mao's sinification of Marxism "emerged and developed in the context of a fierce struggle for supreme power in the CCP between Mao and the Returned Students." See his "Mao Tse-tung, Ch'en Po-ta and the 'sinification of Marxism',": 462. See also Wylie, *The Emergence of Maoism,* 52. Stuart Schram suggests that "Mao's [sinification] speech of October 1938 thus announced, in effect, the terms of the final showdown between himself and the 'Returned Student' faction." See his "The Cultural Revolution in Historical Perspective," in *Authority, Participation and Cultural Change in China*, ed. Stuart Schram (Cambridge: Cambridge University Press, 1973), 17.

9. For analysis of the philosophical dimensions of Mao's thought, including his epistemology, see Nick Knight, *Marxist Philosophy in China: From Qu Qiubai to Mao Zedong, 1923–1945* (Dordrecht: Springer, 2005), chapters 9 and 10.

10. *Selected Works of Mao Tse-tung* (Peking: Foreign Languages Press, 1967) III, 74; *Mao Zedong Xuanji* [Selected Works of Mao Zedong] (Beijing: Renmin chubanshe, 1966) III, 810; Takeuchi Minoru, ed., *Mao Zedong Ji* [Collected Writings of Mao Zedong] (Tokyo: Hokubosha, 1970–1972) VIII, 118. Mao was to repeat his rejection of the deductive method many years later in his critique of the *Soviet Manual of Political Economy*: "Human knowledge always encounters appearances first. Proceeding from there, one searches out principles and laws. The text does the opposite. Its methodology is deductive, not analytical. According to formal logic, 'People all will die. Mr Chang is a person. Therefore Mr Chang will die.' This is a conclusion derived from the premise that all human beings die. This is the deductive method. For every question the text first gives definitions, which it then takes as a major premise and reasons from there, failing to understand that the major premise should be the result of researching a question. Not until one has gone through the concrete research can principles and laws be discovered and

proved." See Mao Tse-tung, *A Critique of Soviet Economics*, tr. Moss Roberts (New York: Monthly Review Press, 1977), 74.

11. *Selected Works of Mao Tse-tung* III, 22; *Mao Zedong Xuanji* III, 759; Takeuchi, ed., *Mao Zedong Ji* VII, 322. Translation modified.

12. *Selected Works of Mao Tse-tung* II, 339; *Mao Zedong Xuanji* II, 623; Takeuchi, ed., *Mao Zedong Ji* VII, 148.

13. *Selected Works of Mao Tse-tung* III, 21; *Mao Zedong Xuanji* II, 757; Takeuchi, ed., *Mao Zedong Ji* VII, 320.

14. Nick Knight, ed., *Mao Zedong on Dialectical Materialism: Writings on Philosophy, 1937* (Armonk, New York: M. E. Sharpe, 1990), 96–97. Emphasis added.

15. Knight, ed., *Mao Zedong on Dialectical Materialism*, 98.

16. Knight, ed., *Mao Zedong on Dialectical Materialism*, 97.

17. Knight, ed., *Mao Zedong on Dialectical Materialism*, 135.

18. Knight, ed., *Mao Zedong on Dialectical Materialism*, 135.

19. *Selected Works of Mao Tse-tung* I, 181–82; *Mao Zedong Xuanji* I, 157; Takeuchi, ed., *Mao Zedong Ji* V, 86.

20. *Selected Works of Mao Tse-tung* I, 182; *Mao Zedong Xuanji* I, 157–58; Takeuchi, ed., *Mao Zedong Ji* V, 87–88.

21. In September 1956, Mao admonished representatives of Latin American Communist Parties not to mechanically apply the experience of the Chinese Revolution in their own countries. The differences in conditions between countries (their "particular laws") meant that any attempt to do so would end in failure. Adapting his "Sinfication of Marxism" formula, Mao advised them that "the universal truth of Marxism-Leninism and the concrete conditions of your own countries—the two must be integrated." *Selected Works of Mao Tsetung* (Peking: Foreign Languages Press, 1965) V, 326.

22. For Mao's acknowledgment of Heraclites as the "father of dialectics," see Knight, *Marxist Philosophy in China*, 190.

23. Takeuchi, ed., *Mao Zedong Ji* VI, 269; see also Schram, *The Political Thought of Mao Tse-tung*, 183.

24. *Selected Works of Mao Tse-tung* I, 300; *Mao Zedong Xuanji* I, 264–65.

25. Stuart R. Schram, ed., Nancy J. Hodes, associate ed., *Mao's Road to Power— Revolutionary Writings, 1912–1949: Volume VI—The New Stage, August 1937–1938* (Armonk, New York: M. E. Sharpe, 2004), 540.

26. Takeuchi, ed., *Mao Zedong Ji* VIII, 43. Emphasis added.

27. *Selected Works of Mao Tse-tung* II, 208; *Mao Zedong Xuanji* II, 498–99; Takeuchi, ed., *Mao Zedong Ji* VI, 259.

28. Takeuchi, ed., *Mao Zedong Ji* VI, 261.

29. *Selected Works of Mao Tse-tung* II, 209; *Mao Zedong Xuanji* II, 498–99; Takeuchi, ed., *Mao Zedong Ji* VI, 259.

30. Schram, *The Political Thought of Mao Tse-tung*, 172. Translation modified. For the original text, see Takeuchi, ed., *Mao Zedong Ji* VI, 261; also *Selected Works of Mao Tse-tung* II, 209; *Mao Zedong Xuanji* II, 499–500.

31. Wylie, *The Emergence of Maoism,* 52.

32. *Selected Works of Mao Tse-tung* II, 380–81; *Mao Zedong Xuanji* II, 667; Takeuchi, ed., *Mao Zedong Ji* VII, 202. Emphasis added.

33. *Selected Works of Mao Tse-tung* III, 21; *Mao Zedong Xuanji* III, 757; Takeuchi, ed., *Mao Zedong Ji* VII, 320.

34. For examples of the discussions by CCP intellectuals in favor of the "Sinification of Marxism," see Knight, *Marxist Philosophy in China,* chapters 7 and 11.

35. *Selected Works of Mao Tse-tung* III, 43; *Mao Zedong Xuanji* III, 778; Takeuchi, ed., *Mao Zedong Ji* VIII, 75.

36. *Selected Works of Mao Tse-tung* III, 21; *Mao Zedong Xuanji* III, 757; Takeuchi, ed., *Mao Zedong Ji* VII, 320.

37. For a translation of the original text of "On Practice," see Knight, ed., *Mao Zedong on Dialectical Materialism,* 132–53. For commentary on Mao's theory of practice, see Knight, *Marxist Philosophy in China,* chapter 10.

38. Stuart R. Schram, ed., Nancy J. Hodes, associate ed., Lyman P. Van Slyke, guest associate ed., *Mao's Road to Power—Revolutionary Writings, 1912–1949: Volume VII—New Democracy, 1939–1941* (Armonk, New York: M. E. Sharpe, 2005), 783–84.

Mao Zedong on the Chinese Road to Socialism, 1949–1969

8

FOR MANY WESTERN INTERPRETERS OF CHINESE MARXISM, the Yan'an period (1936–1947) constituted the high point of Mao Zedong's career as a Marxist intellectual.[1] It was during this period that Mao penned some of his most important theoretical works. It was during this period too that he grappled with the problem of producing a Sinified Marxism that, in theory at least, retained the universal dimension of Marxism while integrating it with the particular characteristics and needs of the Chinese Revolution, a process one scholar has described as Mao's "greatest theoretical and practical achievement."[2] Moreover, the authoritative post-Mao Chinese view of Mao's contribution to the Chinese Revolution during the Yan'an period, including his contribution to the development of the "guiding ideology" of the Chinese Communist Party (CCP), is overwhelmingly positive. As the 1981 "Resolution" on Party history asserts, "Our Party and people would have had to grope in the dark much longer had it not been for Comrade Mao Zedong, who more than once rescued the Chinese revolution from grave danger."[3]

Assessments of Mao's ideas and policies during the 1950s and 1960s are, however, much less positive, and in some cases extremely negative. Stuart Schram, writing from the perspective of the Cultural Revolution, argued:

> If, throughout most of his career, Mao's ideas were on the whole well attuned to China's needs, the drama of the years since 1958 [the start of the Great Leap Forward] has been the increasingly flagrant divorce between the belief in human omnipotence born of his guerilla experience and the objective difficulties of economic development. Mao's belief that political

zeal can advantageously replace technological competence has involved him in a conflict not only with reality, but with a majority of the Central Committee of the Chinese Communist Party.[4]

The CCP's 1981 "Resolution" agrees with this assessment, arguing that from 1958 "Mao Zedong and many leading comrades . . . had become smug about their successes, were impatient for quick results and overestimated the role of man's subjective will and efforts." Moreover, these failings led in due time to the Cultural Revolution, which was "responsible for the most severe setback and the heaviest losses suffered by the Party, the state and the people since the founding of the People's Republic" in 1949.[5]

While negative judgments of this sort are commonplace, much less evident is appreciation of the fact that in attempting to formulate a strategy for the socialist transition in China involving the industrialization and modernization of China's society and economy, Mao was navigating in largely uncharted waters, for he was seeking a developmental strategy very different from the Soviet model on which China had relied during the early 1950s.[6] Mao had by the mid-1950s come to regard the experiences of socialist transition in the Soviet Union as largely unsuited to Chinese conditions, for China was a poor country with little industry and a huge rural sector that relied on primitive agricultural techniques. By 1949, China's industrial development was still very limited, and at a much lower level than Russia's prior to its 1917 revolution; the new Soviet state had a more extensive industrial base and greater access to the capital required to underwrite its program of rapid industrialization than did China in 1949. Mao's growing disenchantment with the Soviet model, with its emphasis on centralized state control of the economy and expensive large-scale heavy industrial projects, prompted him to seek an alternative strategy for development in harmony with the particular characteristics and needs of China's society and economy.[7] Indeed, Mao's Chinese road to socialism broke new ground in suggesting a strategy for development that appeared to avoid the disadvantages of the Soviet model, particularly its lack of relevance to Chinese conditions. While now largely dismissed as a failure,[8] the Chinese road to socialism was, from the 1950s to the 1980s, regarded by many in both the developed and developing worlds as a possible alternative to the authoritarianism of Soviet state socialism on the one hand and the inequities of Western capitalism on the other.[9] Moreover, as some commentators have argued, China's rapid economic growth since 1978 would not have been possible without the economic foundation laid during Mao's tenure as China's leader. The economic results of Mao's Chinese road to socialism, this perspective argues, were thus not as negative as mainstream Western commentary and authoritative post-Mao Chinese statements suggest.[10]

Evaluating the consequences of the Chinese road to socialism is not, however, the purpose of this chapter. It is, rather, to explore those ideas and concepts that inspired Mao's alternative developmental strategy for China's socialist transition. Certain themes evident in Mao's pre-1949 thought—the ubiquity of contradictions, aspects of the Marxist theory of historical change—emerged with renewed vigor in the 1950s and 1960s but were frequently reconceptualized to account for the changed conditions in which China found itself; other themes, such as his view of the future, went through dramatic change (see below and chapter 9). Another concept that had not been stressed in Mao's thought earlier, the theory of "permanent revolution," emerged at the time of the Great Leap Forward to rationalize its impatient economic and political objectives. The coalescence of these themes in Mao's thought led to a particular view of socialist transition and the policies needed for its successful prosecution, which departed in considerable detail from the Soviet model that had influenced his thinking in the early 1950s. However, when talking of a "Chinese road to socialism" one must be cautious in ascribing to Mao a carefully preconsidered and fully coherent perspective on socialist transition, for his views during the 1950s and 1960s frequently emerged in response to unfolding events in the international arena and domestic context. Nowhere is this more in evidence than in his response in the mid 1950s to rapidly changing circumstances within the international communist world, with their implications for the direction of China's domestic political and economic development. Nevertheless, while Mao's perspective was in part reactive and in part an application of preexisting themes in his thought, one can espy in the mix of concepts and ideas that came together under the rubric of the "Chinese road to socialism" a broad strategy for socialist transition that departed in significant detail from its Soviet counterpart. It therefore commands attention if one is to understand the evolution of the socialist dimension of Mao's thought and the trajectory of China's political history during the 1950s and 1960s.

Mao's Response to the Events of 1955–1956

It is clear that the mid 1950s represented something of a watershed in the development of Mao's thinking on problems of socialist transition. What were the factors that led to this watershed? The first was the successful outcome of the campaign to cooperativize China's agriculture and the (apparently) positive response of China's peasants to this campaign. The speed with which the campaign's objectives were being achieved represented, Mao thought, a "fundamental change," one that suggested the possibility of accelerating the tempo of China's progress toward socialism and communism. The success of agricultural cooperativization suggested to Mao that the CCP's program for change had now been demonstrated to be excessively cautious, and he referred scornfully to the "rightist conservatism" of those whose thinking was unable to keep "pace with the development of the objective situation."[11] He believed that the positive response of China's peasantry to the call for the cooperativization of agriculture stood in marked contrast to the Soviet experience in which the peasants had had to be coerced, often with great violence, into joining cooperatives. Mao realized that the success of agricultural cooperativization could function as the premise for a new approach to socialist transition, one that combined a different strategy to that used by the Soviet Union with a more rapid pace of development; it would also allow him the political maneuverability needed to prosecute this alternative economic strategy in the face of conservative opposition within the CCP.

The second factor was the deStalinization speech made by the Soviet leader Nikita Khrushchev at the XXth Congress of the Communist Party of the Soviet Union (CPSU) in February 1956. In his so-called "Secret Speech," Khrushchev launched a bitter attack on Joseph Stalin and his methods of leadership. Stalin had "acted not through persuasion, explanation, and patient cooperation with people," Khrushchev declared, "but by imposing his concepts and demanding absolute submission to his opinion."[12] He was guilty of flouting internal Party regulations, serious abuses of "socialist legality," and acting in an arbitrary and willful manner that led to serious damage to the Party and the national interests of the Soviet Union. In his "Report" to the XXth Congress, Khrushchev also attacked core aspects of the Marxism that Stalin had established as orthodoxy for the international communist movement. In particular, Khrushchev backpedalled on the mechanical Stalinist view of historical development, a view that dictated a fixed and undeviating path to socialism that all nations must follow. He argued that although a transition to socialism was still inevitable, each nation would make that transition in a manner dictated by its own particular circumstances and need not neccesarily follow a revolutionary path. His position therefore emphasized not uniformity but the diversity of forms which the transition to socialism might take:

With the fundamental changes that have taken place on the world scene, new prospects have also opened up for countries and nations to make the transition to socialism. . . . It is very probable that forms of transition to socialism will become more and more varied. And it is not necessarily true that pursuit of these forms involves civil war in all cases.[13]

There can be no doubt that Khrushchev and other Soviet leaders took an "extremely nonchalant attitude towards the possible repercussions of their own ideological pronouncements."[14] For in criticizing Stalin and conceding that there could be varying roads to socialism, and not just that followed by the Soviet Union, Khrushchev was implicitly calling into question the ideological supremacy of the Soviet Union within the international communist movement. This weakening of the ideological leadership of the Soviet Union was a significant factor in Mao's decision to move away from a policy of "leaning to one side," a policy of reliance on the Soviet Union in foreign affairs, emulation of its model for economic development, and deference to it on ideological issues.[15] However, while Mao may have seized the opportunity created by Khrushchev's pronouncements at the XXth Congress to formulate a road to socialism specifically tailored to Chinese conditions, he perceived more clearly than did Khrushchev the ramifications of his maladroit handling of the Stalin issue. In 1958, Mao recalled his ambivalent reaction to the revelations of the XXth Congress: "When Stalin was criticized in 1956, we were on the one hand happy, but on the other hand apprehensive. It was completely necessary to remove the lid, to break down blind faith, to release the pressure, and to emancipate thought. But we did not agree with demolishing him at one blow."[16]

Contradictions in Socialist Society

The weakening of Soviet authority within the international communist world occasioned by Khrushchev's attack on Stalin prompted Mao to formulate more clearly the theoretical premise for his belief that contradictions would remain an important characteristic of socialist society. Stalin had asserted in 1936 that the achievement of socialism in the Soviet Union had witnessed the "obliteration" of contradictions amongst its people.[17] Mao could not agree with such an analysis. In "On Contradiction" (1937), Mao had objected to Stalin's thesis of the "obliteration" of contradictions in a socialist society. "Even under the social conditions existing in the Soviet Union," Mao had declared, "there is a difference between workers and peasants and this difference is a contradiction, although unlike the contradiction between labour and capital, it will not become intensified into antagonism or assume the form of class struggle." Mao's divergence from Stalin's position was made quite explicit when he declared: "The question is one of different kinds of contradiction, not of the presence or absence of contradiction. Contradiction is universal and absolute, it is present in the process of development of all things and permeates every process from beginning to end."[18]

Motivated by the changed conditions initiated by Khrushchev's "Secret Speech," Mao turned to an analysis of the contradictions characterizing Chinese society, and did so to establish a theoretical framework within which the development of policy for China's socialist transition could proceed. In "On the Ten Great Relationships" (April 1956), he argued that correct analysis and handling of contradictions could prevent mistakes in the formulation and implementation of policy, the implication being that it had been Stalin's failure to accept the existence of contradictions within Soviet society that had led to such serious negative consequences.[19] Mao proceeded to detail several contradictions within the Chinese economy, and in each instance proposed solutions to those contradictions by means of a paradox. In solving the contradictory relationship between heavy industry on the one hand and light industry and agriculture on the other, it was necessary to increase investment in light industry and agriculture in order to develop heavy industry. This in itself constituted a significant departure from Soviet practice which had consistently and one-sidedly stressed the role of heavy industry at the expense of light industry and agriculture. In similar vein, Mao challenged those who wanted greater industrial development in China's hinterland to concentrate on making use of and further develop industry in coastal regions. For those who wanted an expansion of China's military capability, the correct method was to decrease the level of military expenditure and increase investment in economic construction. On the relationship among the state, the units of production, and the individual producers, Mao argued that an increase in rewards to individual producers and greater autonomy for local units of production would benefit the industrialization of the entire country. Similarly, on the question of the relationship between the center and the regions, Mao started from the premise of putting the interests of the whole state first; this, paradoxically, necessitated giving greater autonomy and initiative to the regions. Increased decentralization, as Mao had discovered during the Yan'an period, allowed the implementation of centrally determined policy in a manner appropriate to local conditions; this same principle applied whether fighting a revolution or constructing a socialist society.

Mao then turned his attention to the other contradictions characterizing Chinese society. Of these, the relationship between China and other countries is perhaps the most significant, for here Mao stressed that China had to learn from the good points of other countries, not just the Soviet Union. In the revised official version of "On the Ten Great Relationships," his criticism of over-reliance on the Soviet Union is made even more explicit.[20] China henceforth had to "learn all that is genuinely good in the political, economic, scientific and technological fields and in literature and art. But we must learn with an analytical and critical eye, not blindly, and we mustn't copy everything indiscriminately and transplant mechanically."[21] Above all, China should not adopt an arrogant attitude that might prevent a genuine appreciation of its weaknesses and must display a willingness to learn from the strong points of other nations. Nevertheless, China's weakness paradoxically constituted a strength. Using a metaphor he was to invoke frequently during the 1950s and early 1960s,[22] Mao referred to China as being "poor and blank." Yet these conditions—of economic and cultural poverty—indicated a subjective advantage, "poorness" being the starting point on the road to development and "blankness" signifying a receptivity to cultural change. As Mao pointed out, "Those who are poor want change; only they want to have a revolution, want to burst their bonds, and seek to become strong. A blank sheet of paper is good for writing on."[23] China's backwardness and poverty thus provided her population with an urgent desire for development.

In the light of the political context in which this speech was written, how should "On the Ten Great Relationships" be interpreted? First, by enumerating and analyzing the major contradictions within the Chinese society and economy, Mao was laying the theoretical foundation for a transition to socialism geared to China's specific characteristics. China would no longer slavishly follow a foreign model but would draw on its own experiences and conditions and critically absorb the strong points of other nations, whether socialist or not. Second, Mao hoped by such analysis to prevent the abuses of power which had resulted from Stalin's incorrect analysis of the "obliteration" of contradictions within the Soviet Union and his subsequent presumption that there would be unanimity on all policy questions. As contradictions would, Mao believed, remain a persistent and significant feature of socialist society, unanimity imposed by dictatorial methods would lead to negative consequences. Third, Mao's paradoxical solutions to the contradictions within China's economy suggest an attempt to persuade China's economic planners that their goals would still be realized through the change in economic direction that he envisaged: that a departure from the Soviet emphasis on heavy industry would have the effect of improving heavy industry's performance, and that some relaxation of central control of the economy would benefit the entire nation.

Mao thus believed that socialist society continued to be characterized by contradictions and that their existence was a positive factor for it was contradictions—their ceaseless emergence, development, and resolution—that pushed society forward. Without contradictions, change and development would not be possible, and without change and development, socialism and communism would be impossible goals. If contradictions existed, they had to be recognized, brought out into the open, and resolved; ignoring or repressing contradictions could lead to those contradictions developing into antagonisms which could damage the socialist cause. This is the central theme of Mao's important speech of February 27, 1957, "On the Correct Handling of Contradictions Among the People."[24] Building on a distinction he had made in "On Contradiction" between antagonism and contradiction, Mao argued that it was possible to differentiate between two different categories of contradiction, antagonistic and nonantagonistic.[25] Contradictions vary in type according to whether they exist among "the people" (*renmin*) or between the enemy and the people; the former are nonantagonistic, the latter are antagonistic. Nonantagonistic contradictions could be handled and resolved by peaceful means, whereas antagonistic contradictions could only be resolved by recourse to violence and force. While contradictions among the people were nonantagonistic, they had to be handled correctly or there was a danger they could be transformed into an antagonistic form. The uprisings in Hungary in 1956 indicated that this danger always faced a socialist government. Mao thus conceded that even in socialist society contradictions existed between the government and the people. These included the contradictions "among the interests of the State, the interests of the collective and the interests of the individual; between democracy and centralism; between leadership and led; and the contradiction arising from the bureaucratic style of work of certain government workers in their relations with the masses."[26] Such contradictions were, however, "among the people" and as such nonantagonistic. Efforts had to be made, nevertheless, to correctly handle such contradictions to avoid their transformation into an antagonistic form.

In order to avoid contradictions developing to the point of antagonism, Mao deemed it necessary to allow a more open atmosphere in which differing opinions could emerge and contend. This would have the effect of bringing contradictions out into the open so they could be evaluated and resolved without damage being done to the cause of socialist construction.

This, in part, was the reasoning behind Mao's decision to allow an "open-door" rectification of the CCP, in which non-Party persons would be allowed to raise criticisms of the Party. The slogan "Let a hundred flowers bloom, let a hundred schools of thought contend" had been first suggested in 1956, but it was not until May of 1957 that the "Hundred Flowers" campaign got underway that allowed this "blooming and contending." Because socialism had been basically consolidated in China, Mao expected that this campaign would be conducted in an atmosphere of "gentle breezes and mild rain."[27] What transpired was an unexpected and intense outpouring of criticism of the Party by non-Party intellectuals. Moreover, this criticism was accompanied by student unrest, and it was this that prompted Mao to change course. In the first week of June, the campaign was transformed into an anti-rightist campaign, the target of which were those who had accepted Mao's invitation to voice their opinions and criticisms. One result of the "Hundred Flowers" campaign was that it confirmed Mao's belief that contradictions were still very much in evidence in Chinese society, although in the event it turned out that some of these contradictions were of an antagonistic character requiring the machinery of the state for their forceful resolution.

The importance of the "Hundred Flowers" campaign lies in the fact that Mao did not presume the CCP to be above criticism, despite its vanguard status. To the contrary, it was necessary, he believed, for the Party to undergo periodic rectifications in order to prevent a deterioration of its revolutionary workstyle and neglect of its long-term revolutionary goals. The "Hundred Flowers" campaign is also important because it signalled Mao's willingness to go outside the Party for support if it appeared to be failing in its duty. Both of these themes were to reappear with a vengeance in Mao's thought during the Cultural Revolution when he launched a massive attack on the Party for its failure to maintain a correct revolutionary line. The "Hundred Flowers" campaign was therefore an indication of Mao's willingness to diverge from significant elements of Leninism that stressed the vanguard character of the communist party and its leading role in the revolutionary struggle; a concomitant of this emphasis on the party in Lenin's thought had been his distrust of the sort of mass spontaneity that Mao so frequently encouraged to resolve political problems or to achieve economic goals.[28]

Permanent Revolution

Mao's belief that contradictions would persist in socialist society and beyond was an important premise of his theory of "permanent revolution" (*buduan geming*).[29] This theory suggested that the victory of 1949 had not signalled the end of the Chinese Revolution. Rather, new contradictions (demands, problems, tensions, and tasks) would emerge as China strove to modernize and build a powerful socialist economy and a society unified around the values of socialism.[30] These continually emerging contradictions necessitated a maintenance of revolutionary zeal, for socialist construction had to be perceived as a phase of a revolution that would continue well into the future; it would have many stages, each with its own tasks and objectives. In a speech to the Supreme State Conference in January 1958, Mao declared:

> I stand for the theory of permanent revolution. Do not mistake this for Trotsky's theory of permanent revolution. In making revolution one must strike while the iron is hot—one revolution must follow another, the revolution must continually advance. The Hunanese often say, "Straw sandals have no pattern—they shape themselves in the making." Trotsky believed that the socialist revolution should be launched even before the democratic revolution is complete. We are not like that. For example after the Liberation of 1949 came the Land Reform; as this was completed there followed the mutual aid teams, then the low-level cooperatives, then the high-level cooperatives. After seven years the cooperativization was completed and productive relationships were transformed; then came Rectification. After Rectification was finished, before things had cooled down, then came the Technical Revolution. [31]

Mao was to end this particular speech with a quote from Sun Yat-sen, the father of the Chinese Revolution: "The revolution has not yet been completed. Comrades must still bend every effort."[32] Mao was to repeat this formulation of the concept of "permanent revolution" in an important document, also of January 1958, entitled "Sixty Articles on Work Methods":

> Our revolutions come one after another. Starting from the seizure of power in the whole country in 1949, there followed in quick succession the anti-feudal land reform, the agricultural cooperativization, and the socialist reconstruction of private industries, commerce, and handicrafts. . . . Our revolutions are like battles. After a victory, we must at once put forward a new task. In this way, cadres and the masses will forever be filled with revolutionary fervour, instead of conceit.[33]

It is clear from these references that Mao could foresee no cessation of the revolutionary struggles within China. As soon as one revolutionary task had been completed, another would emerge to occupy the attention and energies of the revolutionaries. This would continue without cessation, and hence the state of revolution would be "permanent." Such a perspective on the revolution had implications for Mao's view of the future and historical time. Does the concept of "permanent revolution" suggest that he saw the revolution continuing even after the attainment of communism? Would contradictions continue to emerge, necessitating revolutionary responses? The logic of Mao's theory of the ubiquity and universality of contradictions led inevitably to a perception of communist society in which contradictions would still exist and in which revolutionary struggles, although not class struggle, would persist: "Will there be revolutions in the future when all the imperialists in the world are overthrown and classes are eliminated? What do you think? In my view, there will still be the need for revolution. The social system will still need to be changed and the term 'revolution' will still be in use."[34] As we will observe in chapter 9, after 1955 the notion of communism as a settled society of perpetual peace and harmony (the Yan'an perception) is replaced in Mao's thought by anticipation of a society in which development would continue, which would still be characterized by struggle and contradiction, and which would have to pass through "many stages and many revolutions" on its relentless progression through time.[35]

The Great Leap Forward

The theory of "permanent revolution" emerged at the beginning of 1958, just as China was about to embark on the Great Leap Forward. For Mao, the Great Leap Forward represented another of the "revolutions" which constituted the permanent revolution. Through this campaign, Mao hoped to propel China from its state of underdevelopment to a state of modernization and industrial development in the space of a few short years. Why did Mao believe the Great Leap Forward could achieve this ambitious goal? After all, conventional Marxist theory argued that it was developments in the forces of production that initiated radical systemic changes in the class relations of production and the superstructure. For example, a transformation of the order of the transition from feudalism to capitalism supposedly relied on the development and widepread expansion of the forces of production—industry, commerce, trade—characteristic of the historically novel mode of production of capitalism. In what sense, then, could Mao as a Marxist envisage a transition to an industrialized socialism premised on a campaign to alter the class and working relations and ideology of the mass of the Chinese people? The answer lies in Mao's rather distinctive understanding and deployment of the categories of the political economy of Marxism,[36] for it was in terms of Marxist theory that he rationalized the approach to dramatic economic advance that he hoped would flow from the Great Leap Forward.[37]

Despite widespread suggestions that he had abandoned the materialist premise of Marxism, Mao believed that the forces of production remained ultimately determinant in the process of historical change and development. A detailed survey of his texts of the 1950s and early 1960s establishes that this is the case.[38] The corollary of this belief was that no substantive development of China's political economy in the direction of industrial socialism could be achieved through political and ideological means in the complete absence of any prior development of the forces of production. But how much development of the forces of production was required before, through political means, a further widespread advance of the productive forces could be achieved? Mao believed that relatively small-scale changes and development within the forces of production, such as the level of industrialization already achieved in the Chinese economy, were sufficient to trigger the process of rapid economic development, if facilitated by an appropriate political and ideological transformation of Chinese society. Radically restructuring China's relations of production and superstructure along socialist lines would create the conditions that would mobilize the enthusiasm of the Chinese people for economic change and improvement and thus generate a "leap forward" of the productive forces. There would be a multiplier effect, as it were, as the potential of the economic gains achieved in the early 1950s, now impeded by inappropriate political and economic institutions and conservative ideology, was unlocked to allow a rapid expansion. Moreover, changes within the relations of production and superstructure could be pursued with relatively little in the way of capital investment, of which China was poorly endowed, involving rather changes in the relationships between people at a productive and ideological level. Mao therefore perceived the changes required for a "leap forward" in China's productive forces in human and ideological rather than in purely technological and economic terms (although he did not altogether ignore the economic foundation on which a rapid economic advance would occur). China might not have the financial resources to pursue the Soviet pattern of development, in which vast amounts of capital squeezed from the agricultural sector were pumped into the creation of an extensive heavy industrial sector. What China did possess was a huge population, receptive to the changes required for a rapid advance toward socialist industrialization. Through a reorganization of the working conditions and relationships of China's millions and a transformation in their ideology, industrial development and hence the preconditions for a transition to communism could be achieved.

In this perspective resides a basic difference between Mao's and Stalin's Marxism. Under Stalin, there prevailed the assumption that a transition to communism required first and foremost the development of Russia's productive forces: the creation of modern economic institutions, extensive industrialization based on heavy industry, sophisticated technological infrastructure, and a mechanized agricultural sector.[39] Through development of the productive forces along these lines, changes would result in other areas of society, particularly the relations of production, that would lead to communism. In the attainment of communism, widespread development of the productive forces would be decisive; communist relations of production and communist ideology would emerge as the economy increasingly exhibited the qualities of a communist economy.

Mao saw the process of development in a rather different light. His emphasis was much more on the human aspects of social and economic development rather than on its purely technological or narrowly economic dimensions. This is illustrated by his succinct criticism of Stalin: "He saw only things, not man."[40] It is also illustrated by his criticism of the *Soviet Manual of Political Economy,* a Soviet text that argued that the full development of the forces of production was essential before a transition to communism could be achieved:

> It is not enough to assert that the development of large industry is the foundation for the socialist transformation of the economy. All revolutionary history shows that the *full development* of new productive forces is not the prerequisite for the transformation of backward production relations. Our revolution began with Marxist-Leninist propaganda, which served to create new public opinion in favour of revolution. After the old production relations had been destroyed new ones were created, and these cleared the way for the development of new social productive forces. With that behind us we were able to set in motion the technological revolution to develop social productive forces on a large scale.[41]

The "full development" of the forces of production was thus not necessary for a transformation in the relations of production; transformations in the relations of production and superstructure could give rise to rapid and large-scale expansion of relatively small-scale developments of the productive forces already achieved. Mao premised his view of the Great Leap Forward on this perspective of historical change. Consequently, through the organization of the People's Communes, relations of production would be altered, and through ideological campaigns, attitudes and values inconsistent with communism would be transformed.

More concretely, Mao perceived the Great Leap Forward as achieving its goals through the deployment of an alternative approach to economic and industrial management. The overreliance of the Soviet model on very large industrial enterprises had to be discarded in favor of a more balanced use of medium and small-scale enterprises. This would have several benefits. First, it would allow a more rational utilization of human resources, enterprises being decentralized and located in areas where there was abundant labor. Second, such a policy would serve to educate a broader range of China's workforce in the technical skills associated with modern industry. Third, through decentralization of industry, the subjective enthusiasm of the Chinese people (so evident to Mao in the success of cooperativization in 1955) could be more readily harnessed. Fourth, the establishment of small and medium sized enterprises was a less capital intensive operation than the establishment of large enterprises. This policy initiative was described as "walking on two legs," for it rejected an excessive reliance on large industrial complexes at the expense of smaller but still economically viable, enterprises.[42]

Mao's alternative economic strategy also emphasized self-reliance, which meant getting along with low or medium levels of technology instead of advanced technology requiring a large capital investment. China just did not have the economic capacity to use advanced technology in all areas of production. It was therefore necessary to employ a strategy that combined low or medium levels of technology with high labor inputs, and through the optimal deployment of the resource that China possessed in abundance (human labor), rapid economic growth could be achieved.

The success of the Great Leap Forward was therefore predicated on Mao's theoretical belief that changes in the relations of production and superstructure, combined with an alternative strategy for economic development, would bring about a rapid advance of the Chinese economy. However, he did not believe that it was possible to maintain a constant high rate of development through such measures. Rather, he believed the development of society and the economy proceeded through a wave-like form of advance: periods of rapid development alternated with periods of consolidation in which gains made during periods of rapid advance would be strengthened and broadened. The Great Leap Forward thus represented a period of rapid advance, which would of necessity be followed by a period of consolidation. At the Chengdu Conference of 1958, Mao referred to this wave-like form of advance as follows:

> Under the general line of going all out and aiming high to achieve greater, faster, better and more economical results, a wave-like form of progress is the unity of opposites, deliberation and haste, the unity of opposites, toil and dreams. If we have only haste and toil, that is one-sided. To be concerned only with the intensity of labour—that won't do, will it? In all of our work, we must use both deliberation and haste. . . . This means also the unity of hard fighting with rest and consolidation.[43]

The failure of the Great Leap Forward in economic terms and its calamitous human consequences suggests that the perspective on political economy that inspired it was deeply flawed.[44] If one assumes that it was Mao's conception of economic development that underpinned the onset and progress of the Great Leap Forward (and there is not agreement on this),[45] at what dimension of his thought should criticism be primarily directed? Mao's belief that the "full development" of the forces of production is not a prerequisite for a major economic advance might well be legitimate, as viewed from a particular Marxist perspective.[46] However, this belief leaves open the question of just how extensive development of the forces of production need be before a politically inspired campaign to achieve rapid economic growth could stand any chance of success. There were no clear answers within Marxist theory to this question; neither did the historical experiences of socialism in the Soviet Union and elsewhere offer any guidance. Mao recognized that the economic transformation and consolidation of the early to mid 1950s, which laid the partial foundations of a modernized and industrialized economy, did not constitute the "full development" of the forces of production. Nevertheless, they were in his mind extensive enough to suggest that a more rapid pace of economic development could be achieved through a campaign to remove social and ideological impediments to economic growth. This estimation, encouraged by the success of agricultural collectivization, predisposed Mao to the view that China could economically bypass and outstrip what he saw as the rather plodding and increasingly unsocialist Soviet model for economic growth and at the same time move China toward a more advanced form of socialism. Mao's response was to make the attempt and see what transpired. In this event, the failure of the Great Leap Forward confirmed that China was not ready for such a bold experiment; it suggests that Mao had indeed overestimated the extent to which China's previous economic success readied the Chinese economy for a politically driven rapid expansion.

Mao's Marxism of the 1950s and 1960s

It is evident from his writings of the 1950s and 1960s that Mao remained convinced that Marxism's universal truths had to be integrated with Chinese realities for Marxism to have any utility in the Chinese context. This was an important premise for the "Chinese road to socialism." As Mao reaffirmed in April 1956, the "study of universal truth must be combined with Chinese reality. Our theory is made up of the universal truth of Marxism-Leninism combined with the concrete reality of China."[47] In "A Talk to Music Workers" (August 1956), Mao returned to the point made in "On the New Stage" (1938), that China, as a particular instance of historical development, manifested the universal laws of history in its own specific way. He likened this variation in the particular manifestation of universal laws to the leaves of a tree: "at first sight they all look much the same, but when you examine them closely, each one is different; to find two absolutely identical leaves is impossible."[48] Similarly, in a speech to the Ninth Plenum of the Eighth Central Committee (1961), Mao was to apply this "tree" analogy directly to Marxism, and once again his purpose was to indicate that Marxism's universal laws did not and could not presume how such laws might assume concrete form in any particular historical context: "Marxism-Leninism is basically one (*genben yiyang*) with different twigs and leaves, like a single tree that has many twigs and leaves. Circumstances vary in different countries. In the past we suffered from having paid attention to universal truths without paying attention to investigation and study."[49]

In asserting the Chinese instance to be a particular manifestation of universally valid historical laws, Mao was once again insisting that Chinese Marxism (despite its success in China) could *not* be assumed to have any necessary relevance in other historical contexts. While Chinese Marxism incorporated experience which Marxists in other countries might find useful, it could not be automatically applied in a foreign context as though it constituted a body of universal truths unconstrained by national particularities. In a discussion with representatives of Latin American Communist Parties in September 1956, Mao emphasized that they should utilize Chinese experience selectively and only where it clearly corresponded to the characteristics of their own countries:

> The experience of the Chinese revolution, that is, building rural base areas, encircling the cities from the countryside and finally seizing the cities, may not be wholly applicable to many of your countries, though it can serve for your reference. I beg to advise you not to transplant Chinese experience mechanically. The experience of any foreign country can serve only for reference and must not be regarded as dogma. The universal truth of

Marxism-Leninism and the concrete conditions of your own countries—
the two must be integrated.[50]

Mao therefore continued to believe that Marxism, as a complete ideological system, was constituted of a body of universal laws plus particular
"laws" specific to each historical situation; these particular "laws" would alter as the context altered. The universal laws of Marxism, however, could
not be changed (see chapter 7).

Mao's differences with the Soviet leader Khrushchev grew out of a
complex matrix of historical factors, one of which was disagreement over
what constituted the universal and unalterable laws of Marxism. At the
XXth Congress of the CPSU, Khrushchev had suggested that the transition from capitalism to socialism could now, because of a change in world
conditions, come about through nonviolent means: Revolution no longer
constituted the indispensable medium through which the transition had to
be achieved. There now existed the possibility of a peaceful transition to
socialism in some capitalist and ex-colonial countries, this peaceful transition coming about through the winning of parliamentary majorities by socialist and communist parties.[51]

Khrushchev's notion of a peaceful transition to socialism via the parliamentary road offended Mao's Marxism in several ways. First, Khrushchev's
reliance on the parliaments of capitalist nations represented an abrogation
of the universal law of Marxism that the capitalist state is a class state whose
function is to protect the economic interests of the ruling class. It also suggested a misunderstanding of the historical significance of the parliament
in capitalist systems: Parliament was not the locus of power, nor did it necessarily comprise the dominant feature of the state apparatus. Mao believed
that should a socialist or communist party eventually secure a majority in
parliament, the rules of the game would be promptly redrawn by the ruling class to ensure a hollow victory for the forces of reform. In a talk to a
delegation from the Japan Socialist Party in 1964, Mao insisted that they
would never achieve power through parliamentary means, and should it
look as though they would, the ruling class would redraw electoral boundaries, alter the constitution, declare their party illegal—whatever it took to
prevent them from taking power. It was therefore useless to talk of using
the state to bring about "structural reform" of the capitalist system, for the
state had at its disposal the armed forces with which to crush any possible
threat to the interests of the ruling class:

> The first aspect of the superstructure, the basic and principal thing, is the
> armed forces. If you want to reform them, how do you go about it? An

Italian [Mao is probably referring here to Togliatti] put forward this theory, and said that the structures must be reformed. Italy has an army and police force of several hundred thousand; what method can be used for their reform? . . . You and I are of one mind on this, we don't believe in structural reformism.[52]

Second, Khrushchev's accent on the peaceful nature of this transition was for Mao a clear departure from the Marxist view that the ruling class in any society would never relinquish power without an intense struggle. "The bourgeoisie," Mao declared, "will never hand over state power of their own accord, but will resort to violence."[53] Consequently, seizure of state power required the violence of revolution; it was inconceivable that a peaceful transferral of power could be achieved. Similarly, Mao regarded as a clear revision of Marxism Khrushchev's belief that the eventual worldwide victory of socialism could come about via "peaceful competition" between the socialist and capitalist camps; there would eventually be an armed confrontation between these two inherently antagonistic blocs.

Mao was therefore constrained to reject the notion of a peaceful transition to socialism via the parliamentary road, for it represented a departure from the universal laws of Marxism. Khrushchev was guilty of "revisionism," for he had tampered with laws which, because of their universal status, could not be altered. Needless to say, the laws of Marxism "revised" by Khrushchev were those designated as universal by Mao himself; that Khrushchev did not perceive such laws as beyond revision was beside the point. For his part, Khrushchev regarded Mao as an unbending "dogmatist" unwilling to alter those dimensions of Marxism that history had demonstrated to be no longer valid; in particular, the development of nuclear weapons made a violent confrontation between capitalism and communism utterly unthinkable.[54] The disagreement was therefore over what constituted the universal laws of Marxism, and it is clear that Mao very definitely perceived himself as having the correct appreciation of these essential truths. With Khrushchev's "revision" of Marxism's univeral laws, it appeared to Mao that he was now the only remaining Communist leader faithfully safeguarding the purity of the Marxist ideological heritage.

Mao's Marxism and the Cultural Revolution

We have already noted that the concept of contradictions comprised a very significant element of Mao's approach to understanding Chinese society. The contradictions could be of two types—antagonistic and nonantagonistic—and it was possible for the latter to develop into the former if not handled correctly. There was, therefore, given the multiclass character of the Chinese "people," a constant potential for nonantagonistic contradictions to become antagonistic and require a violent struggle for their resolution. That Mao perceived such a potential for antagonism is indicated by his response to the failure of the Hundred Flowers campaign; because the contradiction between the CCP and China's intellectuals had not been handled correctly, it had become antagonistic and had resulted in a struggle that necessitated recourse to force. The concept of "permanent revolution," which was constructed on the basis of the theory of contradictions, also suggested a perception of historical development that incorporated a belief in continued upheavals and periods of struggle within society as it advanced toward communism.

Mao's perception of the nature of society and the development of history thus predisposed him to accept the possibility of large-scale struggles during the socialist transition. In addition, several specific aspects of Mao's analysis of Chinese society in the early 1960s led to a conviction that a struggle of revolutionary dimensions was unavoidable if the goals of the Chinese Revolution were not to be vitiated. First, Mao held a distinctive view of the role of the superstructure within society. By "superstructure," Mao meant the political, ideological, and cultural dimensions of society, which were by and large a reflection of the economic base; feudal forms of production and class relations, for example, gave rise to a feudal ideology and distinctively feudal political institutions. Mao came to believe, however, that reflection within the superstructure of developments within the economic base was not necessarily immediate or entirely automatic. By the end of the 1950s, much of the ownership system of the Chinese economy (the principal aspect of the economic base) had been transformed into socialist or semi-socialist forms. In terms of orthodox Marxist theory, one would have expected the superstructure of Chinese society to consequently alter to reflect this fundamental transformation of the economic base. Mao, however, recognized that this process had not been satisfactorily accomplished. By way of explanation, Mao suggested that there tended to be a time lag between developments in the economic base and the consequent transformation of the superstructure.[55] Some sections of the population clung stubbornly to ideas and attitudes of the past; political institutions became bureaucratically conservative and unresponsive to developments within the economy. Through ideological conservatism and institutional inertia, certain areas of the superstructure could thus constitute a logjam that impeded further development of the economic base.

However, there were those whose ideology faithfully reflected developments within the economic base, and their mission was to challenge the conservative ideology of others and to bring about political change. Developments within the economic base were therefore reflected unevenly throughout the superstructure, and it consequently became an arena for struggle; only through a satisfactory resolution of that struggle could the superstructure be brought into line with its economic base. This process of ensuring faithful superstructural reflection of developments within the economic base would continue without cessation as economic advances necessitated renewed assaults on conservative aspects of the superstructure.

Mao thus perceived the superstructure as an important and at times vital arena in the struggle to achieve a socialist society. During the early 1960s, Mao came to the realization that negative ideological and cultural features of China's feudal society stubbornly persisted amongst sections of the population and that this would require an extensive ideological campaign to weaken the hold of the force of habit within Chinese society. Such a campaign would differ from the struggles of the past in which the clash of classes at an economic level had been the dominant form. As Mao pointed out:

> The form of the struggle is different as the era is different. As to the present, the social and economic systems have changed, but the legacy of the old era remains as reactionary ideology in the minds of a relatively large number of people. The ideology of the bourgeoisie and the upper stratum of the petty bourgeoisie will not change at a stroke. Change may take time, and a long period of time at that.[56]

Second, Mao's belief that a struggle of revolutionary dimensions might be needed was also fostered by his perception that a "new bourgeoisie" was emerging in Chinese society. Mao's preoccupation with the emergence of a "new bourgeoisie" developed during the early 1960s. In a speech in January 1962, Mao asserted that "in socialist society new bourgeois elements continue to emerge,"[57] and in "The First Ten Points" (1963), he complained that "in addition to the old bourgeoisie who continue to engage in speculation and profiteering activities, there also emerge in today's society new bourgeois elements who have become rich by speculation."[58] Moreover, Mao declared, rather alarmingly, in a talk to an Algerian Cultural Delegation in April 1964, that there were many such "new bourgeois elements" within the CCP itself.[59]

Mao's belief that a "new bourgeoisie" could emerge within socialist society has significant implications for Marxist theory. For if the ownership system had been basically transformed into a socialist type, how was it possible for such a class to emerge? Mao's response was that the emergence of a "new bourgeoisie" was largely a product of the relations of production and ownership system, and thus could be explained by Marxist theory. China's ownership system, was still not yet completely socialist and was characterized by three different property types: ownership by the state, ownership by the collective, and individual ownership. This differentiation in the ownership system was regarded by Mao as an important factor facilitating the emergence of a "new bourgeoisie." As he pointed out, "If there are three types of ownership there will be contradiction and struggle."[60] However, to fully understand Mao's position on this issue, it is necessary to refer to his views on the "dual nature" of China's peasantry. The peasants were, by virtue of their economic position and class outlook, petit-bourgeois in character.[61] As small producers, they retained an ambivalence (or "dual nature") toward the socialization of property, and this ambivalence would persist until the realization of a system of ownership by the whole people (that is, by the state) in the rural areas. Until that time, the peasants would, Mao remarked drily, "remain peasants."[62] In the communiqué of the Tenth Plenum of September 1962, some of these small producers were attributed with producing a "spontaneous tendency toward capitalism,"[63] and in Mao's speech at the Plenum, he made clear that the persistence of the petit-bourgeoisie (which itself was made possible by continued differentiation in the ownership system)[64] was a significant factor in the production of a "new bourgeoisie":

> We can now affirm that classes do exist in socialist countries and that class struggle undoubtedly exists. Lenin said: After the victory of the revolution, because of the existence of the bourgeoisie internationally, because of the existence of bourgeois remnants internally, because the petit bourgeoisie exists and continually generates a bourgeoisie, therefore the classes which have been overthrown within the country will continue to exist for a long time to come and may even attempt restoration.[65]

Mao's perception of the emergence of a "new bourgeoisie" was, therefore, largely a function of his belief that, while there continued a differentiated ownership system which maintained both the peasantry as a class and its "dual nature," the socioeconomic factors existed for the generation of individuals who gravitated toward a form of economic activity characteristic of an incipient bourgeoisie: profiteering and speculation, the exploitation of hired hands, engaging in usury, and the buying and selling of land.[66]

Mao's views on the emergence of a "new bourgeoisie" were closely allied to his belief that classes and class struggle would continue to exist throughout the socialist transition. The struggle between the classes would be fought out on various fronts, within either the economic base or the superstructure. The ingredients for a revolutionary struggle therefore existed within Chinese society: class formations whose relationships could well become antagonistic and a superstructure, large sections of which were out of step with developments in the economic base. These elements of Mao's thought, plus his views on "permanent revolution," underpinned his belief that it was necessary to continue the revolution under the dictatorship of the proletariat. The theory of "continuing the revolution" (jixu geming) was never developed by Mao but was elaborated by some of his radical supporters (branded the "Gang of Four" after Mao's death) and served as a theoretical justification for the radical policies pursued during the Cultural Revolution. Zhang Chunqiao in particular argued that it was necessary during the socialist transition to restrict "bourgeois right."[67] Without the restriction of "bourgeois right," social inequalities, rather than diminishing, would grow, and without a continuous revolution under the dictatorship of the proletariat, the bourgeoisie would reemerge to negate the goals of the revolution and take China along the road to capitalism. Only through continual suppression of capitalist tendencies and emerging inequalities and the purging of "capitalist roaders" could a capitalist restoration be prevented and socialism achieved, and this state of "continuous revolution" would have to be maintained until the economic base had been transformed into a fully socialist form.[68]

As the 1960s progressed, Mao became increasingly convinced that the contradictions of China's society were becoming antagonistic. In particular, he believed that a significant segment of the Party's leadership was intent on introducing capitalist measures which, if left unchecked, would expand and eventually negate the gains of the revolution and lead China down the path to capitalism. If this were allowed to happen, the revolution would have been fought in vain. This was something Mao was not prepared to countenance, and he began to entertain the possibility of an intense and, if necessary, violent struggle to resolve the antagonistic contradictions that had emerged in the wake of the Great Leap Forward. The Party, in failing to keep to a socialist road, as Mao understood this, would necessarily be the principal object of struggle.

The Cultural Revolution that broke out in 1966 is significant in the context of a discussion of Mao's thought for several reasons. First (and as with the theory and practice of the Hundred Flowers movement), Mao indicated his willingness to depart from a central principle of Leninism by not only launching an attack on the Party but by mobilizing non–Party elements as the spearhead of that attack. For Lenin, a communist party represented the vanguard of the working class, its most advanced and politically conscious section. In the Leninist conception, there is no suggestion that the vanguard party might itself become an agent of retrogressive ideas, policies, and actions that could threaten the attainment of the revolutionary goals of the working class. Mao, however, made no assumption that the Party was above and beyond the struggles within society; contradictions and ideologies of a class nature were inevitably reflected within the Party, and it could thus be inhabited by negative and counter-revolutionary elements. Such elements had to be struggled against, and if their position within the Party was so powerful that they could not be dislodged by an intra–party struggle, then it would be necessary to mobilize progressive forces from the wider community to defeat them. During the years of the Cultural Revolution, Mao led a coalition of nonparty elements (students, youth, the military, sections of the working class) in his attack on those within the Party deemed to have taken "the capitalist road." However, while Mao demonstrated a rather different appreciation of the vanguard status of the communist party than had Lenin, he would not, despite its widespread failings, permit its complete destruction. In February 1967, Maoist radicals proposed a reorganization of China into communes modelled after the Paris Commune. Mao refused to allow such a reorganization, for it was not clear to him what the role of the Party would be in such a federation of communes.[69] Moreover, at the Ninth Party Congress of April 1969, Mao set about rebuilding the Party along orthodox Leninist lines.[70]

Second, Mao argued, in the context of the Cultural Revolution and his polemic with the Soviet Union of the early 1960s, that it was possible for a socialist system to degenerate into a capitalist form, and that this degeneration could occur through a process of "peaceful evolution."[71] The notion of a "peaceful evolution" from a socialist (or basically socialist) society into capitalism suggests that Mao no longer viewed as inevitable the transition of society through socialism to communism. Indeed, Mao's speeches and writings of the Cultural Revolution reveal the extinction of the historical optimism that had characterized his thought during the Yan'an period (see chapter 9). The future is now represented as a series of gargantuan struggles, the outcome of which was not certain: "The victory or defeat of the revolution can be determined only over a long period. If it is badly handled there is always the danger of a capitalist restoration. All members of the party and all the people of our country must not think that after one, two, three or four great cultural revolutions there will be peace and quiet. They must always be on the alert and must never relax their vigilance."[72] The concept of a "peaceful evolution" from socialism to capitalism also sits somewhat uncomfortably with Mao's theory of contradictions, that a "peaceful evolution" could lead to a restoration of capitalism suggests that a major transformation of society could come about through merely incremental changes and without the struggle characterizing the relationship between the opposed aspects of a contradiction. The concept of "peaceful evolution" appears, indeed, to represent something of an improvised formula devised to explain a contingency not readily incorporated within the Marxist framework of history. As we have observed, Mao had refused to entertain the notion that there might be a peaceful transition from capitalism to socialism and had accused Khrushchev of "revisionism" for suggesting such a possibility. Yet here was Mao suggesting a possibility seemingly equally incompatible with the Marxist theory of history.

Third, the documents of the Cultural Revolution raise the question whether Mao continued to believe his contribution to Marxist theory to have been only his discovery and analysis of the particular "laws" of Chinese society. Prior to the Cultural Revolution, Mao had laid no claim to have added to the universal laws of Marxism. He had admonished visiting revolutionaries not to mechanically apply the experiences of the Chinese Revolution to their own countries; even though these had been successful, the specific nature of Chinese society precluded their exact replication in another context. Mao's analysis of the particular "laws" of the Chinese Revolution was not, therefore, of universal status; it could be applied in other countries only with a sensitivity to their specific characteristics. The discourse of the Cultural Revolution leaves the impression, however, that Mao's contribution to Marxism had transcended its specifically Chinese origins, and had assumed universal relevance.[73] There can be no doubt that this claim was an integral feature of China's ongoing polemic with the Soviet Union; by claiming a universal status for Mao Zedong Thought, China was laying claim to a prerogative over Marxism that had, before 1956, been Moscow's. With Khrushchev's "revisionism" and the open split between the two parties, the Marxist apostolic succession had been diverted to those who were now (supposedly) the genuine defenders of Marxism.

Conclusion

The Sixth Plenum of the Eleventh Central Committee of the CCP in June 1981 (some five years after Mao's death) roundly condemned Mao's thought and actions during the Cultural Revolution. Mao had ignored his own injunction "to seek truth from facts," had overemphasized the acuteness of class struggle within socialist society, and had led China into ten years of turmoil and chaos. A similar harsh judgment was made of Mao's attempt to forge a Chinese road to socialism during the late 1950s. He was guilty of overlooking "objective economic laws" and had become "impatient for quick results and overestimated the role of man's subjective will and efforts."[74]

Now, some twenty-five years later, the judgment of the Sixth Plenum remains in place as the Party's authoritative view of Mao's Chinese road to socialism. The Party and its leaders have not resiled from the view that, in virtually all respects, the ideas underpinning Mao's policies of the late 1950s and 1960s were fundamentally mistaken. They have retreated from the socialist initiatives of those decades and opened the economy to the influences of domestic and global capitalism.[75] The apparently modest reforms initiated by the Third Plenum of 1978 have expanded to the point that the China of the first decade of the twenty-first century bears very little resemblance to Mao's China.[76] Mao undoubtedly would have welcomed some of the results of these reforms: the surge in economic development and increased sophistication of the economy, the growth of China's military capacity, and China's very much enhanced influence in regional and international politics. Mao certainly desired the industrialization and modernization of China; as with the Chinese reformers of yesteryear, he sought wealth and power for his nation. However, Mao would have been horrified at the social and political impact of the reforms: massive inequality, widespread corruption, the widening urban-rural divide, and the deepening influence of capitalism in all spheres of Chinese society, including the entry of capitalist entrepreneurs into the ranks of the CCP. He would, with some justification, point to these negative consequences of the reforms as a vindication of his view of the early 1960s that the Party was straying from its revolutionary and anti-capitalist path and that, if allowed to continue, would bring about a restoration of capitalism in China. Indeed, what he feared in the years leading up to the Cultural Revolution has, in large measure, come to pass in the years following his death. Yet, while his diagnosis of the dangers to the socialist project in China appear, with hindsight, to have had some foundation, it is probable that the measures he initiated did nothing more than facilitate the changes he feared most. For in the long run the chaos and violence of the Cultural Revolution and its attendant economic losses created not support for the socialist project but widespread antipathy and indifference and fatigue with constantly recurring political campaigns. It thus created a context in which Mao's successors found little effective resistance to their determination to implement a radical shift in economic policy that signalled, if not the death knell of socialism in China, its very serious debilitation. Nevertheless, it remains the case that a residual socialist ethos still inhabits the Party that Mao helped to create in 1921, and it may be that this will curb the worst excesses of China's radical departure from the Chinese road to socialism.[77] As China searches, under Hu Jintao, for a pattern of development that will lead to a "harmonious society," echoes from the Maoist past thus remain audible, if only faintly.[78]

Notes

1. For sympathetic views on Mao's ideas and policies, see Philip Corrigan, Harvie Ramsay, and Derek Sayer, *For Mao: Essays in Historical Materialism* (Atlantic Highlands, NJ: Humanities Press, 1979); Jack Gray, *Mao Tse-tung* (Guildford and London: Lutterworth Press, 1973); and Adrian Chan, *Chinese Marxism* (London and New York: Continuum, 2003).

2. Stuart R. Schram, *Mao Tse-tung* (Harmondsworth: Penguin, 1966), 68.

3. *Resolution on CPC History (1949–81)* (Beijing: Foreign Languages Press, 1981), 10–11.

4. Stuart Schram, "Mao Tse-tung as Charismatic Leader," *Asian Survey* VII, no. 6 (June 1967): 386.

5. *Resolution on CPC History*, 28, 32.

6. Susanne Ogden has argued that "the Chinese reliance on the Soviet model was so complete [in the early 1950s] that the Chinese copied the Soviets in almost every major area." See her *China's Unresolved Issues: Politics, Development, and Culture* (Englewood Cliffs, N.J.: Prentice Hall, 1989), 38. For a contrary point of view that points to the influence of Mao's Yan'an experience on the early post-revolutionary years of nation-building, see Ronald C. Keith, "The Relevance of Border-Region Experience to Nation-Building in China, 1949–52," *China Quarterly* 78 (1979): 274–95.

7. For analysis of the economic dimensions of Mao's Chinese road to socialism, see Alexander Eckstein, *China's Economic Revolution* (Cambridge: Cambridge University Press, 1977).

8. Andrew G. Walder, "Actually Existing Maoism," *The Australian Journal of Chinese Affairs* 18 (July 1987): 155–66; Edward Friedman, "After Mao: Maoism and Post-Mao China," *Telos* 65 (Fall 1985): 23–46; Chalmers Johnson, "The Failure of Socialism in China," *Issues and Studies* 21, no. 1 (July 1979): 22–33; Steve Reglar, "Mao Zedong as a Marxist Political Economist: A Critique," *Journal of Contemporary Asia* 17, no. 2 (1987): 208–33.

9. See Samir Amin, *The Future of Maoism* (New York: Monthly Review Press, 1983); Charles Bettelheim, *Economic Calculation and Forms of Property*, translated by

John Taylor, introduction by Barry Hindess (London: Routledge and Kegan Paul, 1976); Michel Chossudovsky, *Towards Capitalist Restoration: Chinese Socialism After Mao* (London: Macmillan, 1986); Neil G. Burton and Charles Bettelheim, *China Since Mao* (New York: Monthly Review Press, 1978); Rossana Rossanda, "Mao's Marxism," *Socialist Register* (1971): 53–80; Steve Andors, "Hobbes & Weber vs. Marx & Mao: The Political Economy of Decentralization in China," *Bulletin of Concerned Asian Scholars* 6, no. 3 (1974): 19–34; Stephen Andors, *China's Industrial Revolution: Politics, Planning, and Management, 1949 to the Present* (London: Martin Robertson, 1977); John G. Gurley, *Challengers to Capitalism: Marx, Lenin and Mao* (San Francisco: San Francisco Book Co., 1976), chapter 5.

10. See, for example, Maurice Meisner, *Mao's China and After: A History of the People's Republic* (New York: Free Press, 1986, revised edition); and Maurice Meisner, *The Deng Xiaoping Era: An Inquiry into the Fate of Chinese Socialism, 1978–1994* (New York: Hill and Wang, 1996).

11. See Mao's "Preface" to *Socialist Upsurge in China's Countryside* (Peking: Foreign Languages Press, 1957), 7–10.

12. For the text of the "Secret Speech," see Dan N. Jacobs, ed., *From Marx to Mao and Marchais* (New York and London: Longman, 1979), 160–230; also Nikita Khrushchev, an introduction by Edward Crankshaw to *Khrushchev Remembers* (London: André Deutsch, 1971), 559–618.

13. Hélène Carrère d'Encausse and Stuart R. Schram, *Marxism and Asia: An Introduction with Readings* (London: Penguin, 1969), 283.

14. Benjamin I. Schwartz, *Communism and China: Ideology in Flux* (New York: Atheneum, 1970), 96.

15. For Mao's earlier discussion of the historical necessity for China to "lean to one side," see *Selected Works of Mao Tse-tung* (Peking: Foreign Languages Press, 1967) II, 364.

16. Stuart Schram, ed., *Mao Tse-tung Unrehearsed: Talks and Letters, 1956–71* (Harmondsworth: Penguin, 1974), 101.

17. J. V. Stalin, *Problems of Leninism* (Peking: Foreign Languages Press, 1976), 803.

18. *Selected Works of Mao Tse-tung* I, 318; see also Nick Knight, ed., *Mao Zedong on Dialectical Materialism: Writings on Philosophy, 1937* (Armonk, New York: M. E. Sharpe, 1990), 166–67.

19. The original text of this speech can be found in Schram, ed., *Mao Tse-tung Unrehearsed*, 61–83. The official revised version is in *Selected Works of Mao Tse-tung* (Peking: Foreign Languages Press, 1977) V, 284–307.

20. For analysis of the differences between the original and official versions of this speech, see Stuart R. Schram, "Chairman Hua Edits Mao's Literary Heritage: 'On the Ten Great Relationships'," *China Quarterly* 69 (March 1977): 126–35.

21. *Selected Works of Mao Tse-tung* V, 303.

22. For various references to the "poor and blank" metaphor in Mao's thought, see *Selected Works of Mao Tse-tung* V, 244, 265; Schram, ed., *Mao Tse-tung Unrehearsed*, 92, 231; Joint Publication Research Service, *Miscellany of Mao Tse-tung*

Thought (1949–1968) (Arlington, Virginia: February 1974) I, 122, 147; *Mao Ze-dong Sixiang Wansui* [Long Live Mao Zedong Thought] (n. p.: n. pub., 1969), 485; K. Fan, ed., *Mao Tse-tung and Lin Piao: Post-Revolutionary Writings* (Garden City, New York: Anchor Books, 1972), 261.

23. Schram, ed., *Mao Tse-tung Unrehearsed*, 83.

24. *Selected Works of Mao Tse-tung* V, 384–421. The original version of this speech can be found in Roderick Macfarquhar, Timothy Cheek, and Eugene Wu, eds., *The Secret Speeches of Chairman Mao: From the Hundred Flowers to the Great Leap Forward* (Cambridge, Mass.: Harvard Contemporary China Series No. 6, 1989), 131–90.

25. How orthodox from a Marxist perspective is the concept of "non-antagonistic contradictions?" Shlomo Avineri argues that it is a "bastard" term, "meaningless within Marx's frame of thought." See his *The Social and Political Thought of Karl Marx* (Cambridge: Cambridge University Press, 1968), 175.

26. *Selected Works of Mao Tse-tung* V, 385–86.

27. For Mao's views on the "Hundred Flowers" campaign, see *Selected Works of Mao Tse-tung* V, 366–71, 408–14.

28. See V. I. Lenin, *What Is to be Done?* (Peking: Foreign Languages Press, 1975), 25. For a useful analysis of the importance of the vanguard party to Leninism, see Marcel Liebman, *Leninism under Lenin*, trans. Brian Pearce (London: Jonathan Cape, 1975), 25–61. For analysis of the influence of Leninism on Mao, see Stuart R. Schram, "Chinese and Leninist Components in the Personality of Mao Tse-tung," *Asian Survey* III, no. 6 (1963): 259–73.

29. For Mao's earlier references to "permanent revolution" and his rejection of the Trotskyist interpretation of the concept, see *Selected Works of Mao Tse-tung* I, 290; and *Selected Works of Mao Tse-tung* (London: Lawrence and Wishart, 1956) IV, 176.

30. See Stuart R. Schram, "Mao Tse-tung and the Theory of the Permanent Revolution, 1958–1969," *China Quarterly* 46 (1971): 221–44.

31. Schram, ed., *Mao Tse-tung Unrehearsed*, 94.

32. Schram, ed., *Mao Tse-tung Unrehearsed*, 95.

33. Jerome Ch'en, ed., *Mao Papers: Anthology and Bibliography* (London: Oxford University Press, 1970), 62–63.

34. Ch'en, ed., *Mao Papers*, 65.

35. Mao Tse-tung, *A Critique of Soviet Economics*, translated by Moss Roberts, with an introduction by James Peck (New York and London: Monthly Review Press, 1977), 71.

36. See Reglar, "Mao Zedong as a Marxist Political Economist." Also Richard Levy, "Mao, Marx, Political Economy and the Chinese Revolution: Good Questions, Poor Answers," in *Critical Perspectives on Mao Zedong's Thought*, eds. Arif Dirlik, Paul Healy. and Nick Knight (Atlantic Highlands, NJ: Humanities Press, 1997), 154–83.

37. This is made very clear in Mao's critical commentary on Soviet economics. Mao Tse-tung, *A Critique of Soviet Economics*.

38. See Paul Healy, "A Paragon of Marxist Orthodoxy: Mao Zedong on the Social Formation and Social Change," in *Critical Perspectives on Mao Zedong's*

Thought, eds. Arif Dirlik, Paul Healy, and Nick Knight (Atlantic Highlands, NJ: Humanities Press, 1997), 117–53; also Nicholas James Knight, *Mao and History: An Interpretive Essay on Some Problems in Mao Zedong's Philosophy of History* (London: University of London, unpublished PhD thesis, 1983), chapter 4.

39. See, for example, J. V. Stalin, "The results of the first five-year plan," in J. V. Stalin, *Problems of Leninism*, 578–630.

40. *Mao Zedong sixiang wansui* [Long live Mao Zedong Thought] (Taiwan: n.p., 1967), 156.

41. Mao Tse-tung, *A Critique of Soviet Economics*, 51. Emphasis added.

42. See *Peking Review* 48 (27 November, 1970): 14–17.

43. Schram, ed., *Mao Tse-tung Unrehearsed*, 106.

44. For analysis of the political context that led to the Great Leap Forward, see Frederick C. Teiwes with Warren Sun, *China's Road to Disaster: Mao, Central Politicians, and Provincial Leaders in the Unfolding of the Great Leap Forward, 1955–1959* (Armonk, New York: M. E. Sharpe, 1999).

45. Not all scholars are convinced that Mao and his thought should be held solely responsible for the failure of the Great Leap Forward. There were other factors, particularly the way in which the campaign was implemented by lower-level cadres. See, for example, Levy, "Mao, Marx and Political Economy."

46. See Corrigan, Ramsay, and Sayer, *For Mao: Essays on Historical Materialism*; and Chan, *Chinese Marxism*.

47. Schram, ed., *Mao Tse-tung Unrehearsed*, 82.

48. Schram, ed., *Mao Tse-tung Unrehearsed*, 84.

49. *Mao Zedong sixiang wansui* (1967), 262.

50. *Selected Works of Mao Tse-tung* V, 326.

51. Carrère d'Encausse and Schram, *Marxism and Asia*, 282–87.

52. *Mao Zedong sixiang wansui* (1967), 156.

53. *Selected Works of Mao Tse-tung* V, 495.

54. See Khrushchev, *Khrushchev Remembers*, 469–71.

55. Mao could draw on Marx's authority here. Marx had asserted, somewhat ambivalently, that "[t]he changes in the economic foundation lead *sooner or later* to the transformation of the whole immense superstructure." Karl Marx, *A Contribution to the Critique of Political Economy* (London: Lawrence and Wishart, 1971), 21. Emphasis added.

56. Ch'en, ed., *Mao Papers*, 144–45.

57. Schram, ed., *Mao Tse-tung Unrehearsed*, 168.

58. Richard Baum and Frederick C. Teiwes, *Ssu-ch'ing: The Socialist Education Movement of 1962–66* (Berkeley: Chinese Research Monographs, University of California, 1968), 61.

59. *Mao Zedong sixiang wansui* (1969), 488; see also 424, where Mao declared "the bourgeoisie can reemerge (*xinsheng de*), and this is what happened in the Soviet Union."

60. Mao Tse-tung, *A Critique of Soviet Economics*, 107.

61. *Selected Works of Mao Tse-tung* V, 474.

62. *Mao Zedong sixiang wansui* (1969), 247.

63. Baum and Teiwes, *Ssu-ch'ing*, 60. See also *Selected Works of Mao Tse-tung* V, 260–61.

64. *Peking Review* 25 (21 June 1963), 17.

65. Schram, ed., *Mao Tse-tung Unrehearsed*, 189.

66. Baum and Teiwes, *Ssu-ch'ing*, 61. For an alternative interpretation of Mao's views on the "new bourgeoisie," see Joseph Esherick, "On the 'Restoration of Capitalism': Mao and Marxist Theory," *Modern China* 5, no. 1 (January 1979): 41–78.

67. Chang Chun-chiao, "On Exercising All-Round Dictatorship over the Bourgeoisie," *Peking Review* 14 (4 April 1975): 5–11.

68. For a detailed discussion, see John Bryan Starr, "Conceptual Foundations of Mao Tse-tung's Theory of Continuous Revolution," *Asian Survey* 11, no. 6 (June 1971): 610–28. See also John Bryan Starr, *Continuing the Revolution: The Political Thought of Mao* (Princeton: Princeton University Press, 1979), 300–307.

69. *Mao Zedong sixiang wansui* (1969), 671–72; and Schram, ed., *Mao Tse-tung Unrehearsed,* 278. See also Stuart R. Schram, "The Marxist," in *Mao Tse-tung in the Scales of History*, ed. Dick Wilson (Cambridge: Cambridge University Press, 1977), 47–48.

70. As the Party Constitution adopted by the Ninth Congress stipulates, "The organizational principle of the Party is democratic centralism. . . . The whole party must observe unified discipline: The individual is subordinate to the organization, the minority is subordinate to the majority, the lower level is subordinate to the higher level, and the entire Party is subordinate to the Central Committee." *The Ninth National Congress of the Communist Party of China (Documents)* (Peking: Foreign Languages Press, 1969), 119–20.

71. Baum and Teiwes, *Ssu-Ch'ing*, 119.

72. Ch'en, ed., *Mao Papers*, 139.

73. See particularly the references to Mao Zedong Thought in the "Draft Party Constitution" circulating toward the end of 1968. The text of this Constitution is in *China Quarterly* 37 (January–March 1969): 169–73.

74. *Resolution on CPC History*, 32–46.

75. For analysis of the CCP's recent attempts to integrate globalization into its ideology, see Nick Knight, "Contemporary Chinese Marxism and the Marxist Tradition: Globalisation, Socialism and the Search for Ideological Coherence," *Asian Studies Review* 30, no. 1 (March 2006): 19–39; and Nick Knight, "Imagining Globalisation: The World and Nation in Chinese Communist Party Ideology," *Journal of Contemporary Asia* 33, no. 3 (2003): 318–37.

76. For an early analysis of China's retreat from socialism, see Nick Knight, "From the 2nd Plenum to the 6th NPC: The Retreat Gathers Speed," *The Australian Journal of Chinese Affairs* 12 (July 1984): 177-94.

77. See, for example, Hu Jintao's speech at the 2005 Fortune Global Forum. <http://english.peopledaily.com.cn/200505/17/print20050517_185302.htm> (17 May 2005).

78. The concept of "harmonious society" incorporates a stress on social equality, expansion of employment, and improvement of the social security system. It also emphasises alleviation of the plight of China's poverty-stricken rural dwellers and migrant workers. See "China Strives for Harmonious Society, Central Economic Conference," *People's Daily Online*, 6 December 2004. <http://english.people.com.cn/200412/06/eng2004l2o6_166180.html> (15 March 2006).

From Harmony to Struggle, from Perpetual Peace to Cultural Revolution: Changing Futures in Mao Zedong's Thought **9**

COMING AS IT DID towards the end of Mao Zedong's life, the Cultural Revolution that erupted in 1966 has frequently been represented as the quintessence of the Maoist approach to social and political change.[1] From this perspective, the frenetic and often violent activities of the Red Guards were the logical manifestation of Mao's political ethic, one that assumed the pervasiveness of struggle and contradiction within society, be it a capitalist or socialist society. Implicit in this perception are several assumptions that have contributed to a distorted interpretation of Mao's personal role in the Cultural Revolution and the significance of the Cultural Revolution in Mao's thought and political career. In the first of these, the activities of the Red Guards and the course followed by the Cultural Revolution are seen as premeditated by Mao himself; it was he who was the sole architect and strategist of this prolonged spasm of political and social disorder, for it was he who would be the beneficiary of the power he would wrest from his opponents. However, the picture that emerges from the "unrehearsed" Mao texts of the Cultural Revolution is not that of the omnipotent master dramatist, single-handedly directing the course of events toward a predetermined end. Rather, the picture is of a leader somewhat bemused by the unanticipated consequences of his own actions. For example, on October 24, 1966, Mao commented "One big character poster, the Red Guards, the great exchange of revolutionary experience, and nobody—not even I—expected that all the provinces and cities would be thrown into confusion. The students also made some mistakes, but the mistakes were mainly made by us big shots (*laoye*)."[2] He was to voice a similar sentiment on the following day in a talk to a Central Work Conference: "I myself had not foreseen that as soon as the Beijing University poster was broadcast, the whole country would be thrown into turmoil."[3] Similarly, rather than closely directing the Cultural Revolution, Mao was prepared, at least in its initial phase, to permit it to proceed largely unhindered from interference and direction from the Centre. "In my opinion," he asserted in August 1966, "we should let the chaos go on for a few months. . . . Stop interfering for the time being."[4] Mao's motivation for minimizing direction from the Centre was clearly to allow the antagonistic contradictions in Chinese society to reveal themselves fully, and in the struggle between them, the options for future policy directions would become clearer. A significant example is Mao's response to the developments in Shanghai in early 1967, in which he rejected the proposition that the whole of China should emulate the establishment of a People's Commune in Shanghai.[5] Mao is, therefore, often revealed in the texts of his speeches and talks as responding to, rather than being the initiator of, the dramatic events of the early stages of the Cultural Revolution.[6] While Mao was clearly not a powerless bystander in the emergence and unfolding of the Cultural Revolution, the image of Mao as the omnipotent and prescient demiurge of history is not borne out by his own testimony.

Second, and more important for the central theme of this chapter, there has been a highly problematic tendency in commentaries on both Mao and the Cultural Revolution to represent the Cultural Revolution as the ultimate distillation, the essential essence, of Mao's thought: If we are to understand Mao's thought and his approach to politics, it is with the Cultural Revolution that we must commence, for this was the ultimate political chapter in Mao's life, the defining moment toward which the current of his life and thought logically flowed.[7] The teleological dangers of this perspective are quite evident, for the Mao of the Cultural Revolution is here represented as the prism through which earlier stages in his life and thought are to be viewed, and particular characteristics of these earlier stages that do not appear at face value to contribute to the realization of the Cultural Revolution are discounted or ignored entirely. However, the Mao of the Yan'an Period (1936–1947) or the Mao of the early years of the Chinese Communist Party (1921–1927) were not and should not be seen as merely necessary precursors to the supposedly ultimate and defining period of Mao's life and thought, the Cultural Revolution.

A graphic example of important distinctions between stages in the history of Mao's thought, and one that might well remain concealed if one employs a teleological approach based on the Cultural Revolution as the culminating moment in Mao's thought, is the dramatically altered conception of the future in Mao's thought between the years of the Yan'an period and the years leading up to and immediately following the onset of the Cultural Revolution. As we observed in chapter 5, commentary on Mao's thought has largely ignored the eschatological and utopian themes characteristic of his thought during the Yan'an period, a theme that anticipated the imminent realization of an era of perpetual peace and harmony. These eschatological and utopian themes largely disappear in Mao's thought in the 1950s and do not appear linked in any tangible way with his later conception of the future. Mao's earlier utopianism is thus overlooked as attention is focused on the more dramatic ethic of struggle, contradiction, and conflict that defined Mao's conception of politics and history immediately before and during the Cultural Revolution.

Building on chapter 5, this chapter examines Mao's conception of the future leading up to and during the Cultural Revolution and notes the shift from the optimism of the Yan'an period to the pessimism of the Cultural Revolution, the shift from harmony to struggle, indicated in the Mao texts. I argue that a major factor which led, in the 1950s and early 1960s, to Mao's declining confidence in the future, and the loss of his previous utopian expectation of an imminent realization of an era of perpetual peace and harmony, was his absolute acceptance of a number of major theoretical premises that derived from orthodox Marxism. The first of these was Mao's belief in the *unlimited* capacity for development of the forces of production, which he believed to be the ultimately determining factor in the unfolding of human history. The irony here is that Mao's positive assessment of the potential of humankind to continually develop the forces of production contributed substantially to the decline and eventual evaporation of his earlier optimism. The second was his belief in the universality of contradictions, a principle that no society, even a communist society, could elude. Rather than giving Mao confidence in the future, acceptance of the limitless capacity for development of the forces of production and the contradictions and consequent struggles this inevitably engendered in all other areas of society precluded any possibility that at some point in the future, no matter how far distant, a state of peace and harmony, of equilibrium, could ever be achieved.

This argument is significant, not only because it identifies the future as a factor in explaining Mao's willingness to entertain the possibility of not just one but a series of cultural revolutions, but also because it challenges the idea, so pervasive in both Western and Chinese readings of Mao's thought, that he had abandoned a central plank of orthodox Marxism: the forces of production as the demiurge of history. Similarly, Mao's acceptance that contradictions would inevitably persist into and beyond a future

communist society demonstrates that his conception of the future was infused with a certain logic, a logic that in its origins if not its application
drew heavily on the theoretical and philosophical dimensions of orthodox
Marxism. The argument is significant also as it challenges the conventional
view that the Cultural Revolution was a function of Mao's "utopianism."
As we will observe, Mao's thought leading up to and during the Cultural
Revolution was, rather, characterized by a dramatic decline in "utopianism" and an increasingly pessimistic view of the future.

Pessimism and Revolutionary Struggle: The 1950s and early 1960s

As we observed in chapter 5, during the Yan'an period Mao employed two
periodizations of history. The first was a largely conventional interpretation
of Marxism based on the five-stage periodization that had become orthodoxy under Lenin and Stalin. In this schema, society progressed from the
primitive and classless communist society of antiquity, through various
forms of class society (slave, feudal, capitalist), and following a transitional
socialist phase, to the higher phase of communism, the telos of history, a
phase in which classes and the struggles they engender would disappear.[8]
Consequently, the higher phase of communism is portrayed as something
of a plateau in human history, for the underlying impulse for change and
progress would have exhausted itself and finally wither away.[9] The other
periodization used by Mao drew on the concept of the "three ages" (*san
shi*) from the Chinese tradition.[10] This notion of the three ages speaks of
the "Great Commonwealth" (*da tong*) of the future as a society in which
"self-interest ceases," "disorders are not known," and in which "all under
heaven will work for the common good."[11] The third and last of the three
ages in human history is characterized by "universal peace" (*tai ping*); society would move from an age of "decay and disorder" through a period of
"approaching peace" to an era of "universal peace."[12]

Drawing on both Marxism and utopian themes in the Chinese tradition, Mao's perception of the future was thus astoundingly optimistic
throughout the Yan'an period. Both of these historical traditions perceived
the final phase of history as a stable society whose predominant characteristic would be peace. Furthermore, Mao spoke of this era of peace as em-
inently realizable and of human history as poised on the dividing line
between the era of war and the final era of peace. The third epoch of
peace was thus virtually at hand. For Mao, "a new world of peace and
brightness already lies clearly before us."[13]

Early evidence of a decline in Mao's utopianism can be seen in the revisions in the early 1950s to his pre-1949 writings to prepare them for republication in the official *Selected Works of Mao Tse-tung*. While the eschatological theme was not entirely excised, explicit reference to the "three ages" was removed, and the realization of the future era of peace and harmony was made, in line with Marxist theory, much more clearly contingent on the elimination of capitalism, classes, and states.[14] A utopian future of peace and harmony was thus no longer realizable in the near future, and its possibility is rarely mentioned again.[15] The shift from optimism to pessimism in Mao's thought was therefore not immediate after 1949. Indeed, Mao retained the view that the future of humankind would incorporate a communist era, although he was, apart from a brief and ambivalent spell during the euphoric early stage of the Great Leap Forward, increasingly pessimistic about its early realization. As the 1950s progressed, Mao's public predictions of the realization of communism assumed a ritualistic character,[16] and in his private utterances, a future communist society is increasingly portrayed in tones altogether lacking his earlier unbounded confidence.[17] Pessimism and optimism thus coexisted in Mao's thought, with optimism declining in significance as his vision of the future became increasingly bleak.

Three aspects of Mao's conception of the future that indicate this declining optimism emerge clearly from his writings and speeches of the 1950s and early 1960s. The first is the recognition that socialism, as a transitional phase between capitalism and communism, would be a lengthy process. Indeed, it would, Mao now recognized, last "a very long time."[18] In October 1957, he commented that "it is hard to say for sure right now just how long the transition period will be." However, it would, he added, "go on for many years."[19] Similarly, in the communiqué of the Tenth Plenum (1962), the transition period was imprecisely anticipated as lasting "for scores of years or even longer,"[20] and in another text of the early 1960s, socialism is portrayed as "a relatively long historical stage" in the development of society.[21]

Second, although Mao continued to insist that the eventual realization of communism was inevitable, his conception of the characteristics of this future society was dramatically different from that of the Yan'an period. In the 1950s and early 1960s, communism is portrayed not as a society in which there will be peace and harmony but one in which struggles and even revolutions would persist, these set in motion by the limitless capacity for development of the forces of production and the contradictions they generated. For example, a 1956 text, inspired by Mao and revised by him, asserted that "in a socialist or communist society, technical innovations and changes in the social system will continue to take place. Otherwise the development of society would come to a standstill and society could no longer advance. Humanity is still in its youth. The road it will traverse will be longer by no one knows how many times than the road it has already travelled."[22] Later in that year, Mao emphasized that a future communist society would not be immune from the capacity for development inherent within the forces of production and, indeed, that "revolutions" would continue to occur:

> Will there still be revolutions in the future when all the imperialists in the world are overthrown and classes are eliminated? What do you think? In my view, there will still be the need for revolution. The social system will still need to be changed and the term "revolution" will still be in use. Of course, revolutions then will not be of the same nature as those in the era of class struggle. But there will still be contradictions between the relations of production and the productive forces, between the superstructure and the economic base. When the relations of production become unsuitable, they will have to be overthrown. If the superstructure (ideology and public opinion included) protects the kind of relations of production the people dislike, they will transform it.[23]

Similarly, in his "Sixty Articles on Work Methods" (1958), Mao again asserted that in a future communist society "ideological and political struggles between people will continue to occur, and so will revolutions; they will never cease. . . . However, the nature of struggles and revolutions will be different. They will not be class struggles, but struggles between advanced and backward techniques."[24] In another text, Mao is recorded as predicting that "in the period of communism there will still be uninterrupted development" and "technological revolution and cultural revolution" would also occur; "communism will surely have to pass through many stages and many revolutions."[25]

Third, it is clear that Mao no longer regarded communism as the final stage in the development of human history. There would, Mao believed, be continuous change and numerous stages of development within communist society, and it was this belief that led to the recognition that communism itself must also eventually disappear, to be superseded by some other more advanced form of social and economic organization. Rather than representing a temporal plateau, arrival at which would signal the final exhaustion of the developmental impulses within society, communist society was just another, albeit very important, stage in human history.

Thus, while communism might remain for "thousands and thousands of years," it eventually would come to an end.[26] At the Chengdu Conference (1958), Mao revealed, in an intriguing statement, that his conception of the future was in no way limited to communism and its demise but extended even to the extinction of the solar system:

> The universe, too, undergoes transformation, it is not eternal. Capitalism leads to socialism, socialism leads to communism, and communist society must still be transformed, it will also have a beginning and an end, and it will certainly be divided into stages, or they will give it another name, it cannot remain constant. . . . There is nothing in the world that does not arise, develop and disappear. Monkeys turned into humans, humankind arose; in the end the whole human race will disappear, it may turn into something else, at that time the earth itself will also cease to exist. The earth must certainly be extinguished, the sun too will grow cold. . . . All things must have a beginning and an end.[27]

A similarly prophetic and visionary conception of the future appears in Mao's "Talk on Questions of Philosophy" (August 1964) in which he again predicts the eventual demise of humankind and the emergence of "something more advanced." "Humankind will also finally meet its doom. When the theologians talk about doomsday, they are pessimistic and terrify people. We say the end of humankind is something which will produce something more advanced than humankind. Humankind is still in its infancy."[28]

The Universality of Contradictions and the Limitless Capacity of the Forces of Production

Mao's view of the future during the 1950s and early 1960s was therefore not constrained by any notion of communist society as the final utopia toward which human history was inexorably moving and which, once attained, would signal the cessation of struggles and contradictions characteristic of all previous societies. While communism remained a significant chapter in the future of humankind, it no longer represented a utopia of the sort envisaged during the Yan'an period. Not only had the optimism of the Yan'an period largely evaporated, but gone too was the suggestion that a harmonious and peaceful society represented the telos of history. Contradictions and the struggles between humans that these engendered were the dominant motif of society, and no society—past, present, or future—could escape contradictions, for this was a characteristic of all matter in the universe. Mao's certainty that communism would be riven by contradictions thus rested on an ontological belief that all things and processes, without exception, contained contradictions.

An important manifestation of this ontology in Mao's writings of the 1950s and early 1960s is his many references to the law of the unity of opposites. Mao had written perhaps his most famous essay "On Contradiction" in 1937, in which he had insisted that "contradiction exists universally and in all processes, whether in the simple or complex forms of motion, whether in objective phenomena or ideological phenomena."[29] While there can be no doubt that Mao's worldview had been heavily influenced by this belief at that time,[30] it is also apparent that he only fully accepted the logical implications of the principle of the universality of contradictions in the 1950s, when he came to accept that even a future communist society could not be free of contradictions. In "On the correct handling of contradictions among the people" (February 1957), Mao reaffirmed his earlier view that "Marxist philosophy holds that the law of the unity of opposites is the fundamental law of the universe. This law operates universally, whether in the natural world, in human society, or in human thought."[31] From the atom through class struggle in socialist society to the wider international arena and to the universe beyond, everything was constituted, in Mao's mind, of contradictions, of the unity of opposites.[32] And so it would continue, for without contradictions and the struggle between them, all motion within the universe would cease, and indeed the universe itself could not exist. Any dispensation for communist society from this natural law, one that governed the very nature of matter within the universe, would have been starkly and manifestly illogical. By recognizing that the law of the unity of opposites would persist even into communism, Mao's conception of history and the future thus assumed a certain logicality, if one that was rather bleak and pessimistic in its outlook for humankind, for he believed contradictions that emerged within communist society and the struggle between them would eventually result in its demise and that communism would be replaced by something else. There could be no completion in human history, no final stage; in the fullness of time, humankind would itself disappear, to be replaced by "something more advanced."

But were all contradictions of equal significance in the unfolding of human history, and was there a particular contradiction that would determine the character of the struggles in a future communist society? It is clear from his writings of the 1950s and early 1960s that Mao continued, in line with orthodox Marxism, to regard the forces of production as the most significant causal factor in the change and development of human society.[33]

Mao defined the forces of production, as did Marx, as constituted of three components: "Humans, means of labour . . . and objects of labour constitute the three major elements of the forces of production."[34] On each occasion Mao provided a definition of the forces of production, he included humans as a component,[35] and indeed, insisted that humans were the "most important factor" (shouyao yinsu) of the forces of production.[36] In November 1956, Mao referred to the forces of production as "the most revolutionary factor. When the productive forces have developed there is bound to be a revolution."[37] Moreover, Mao later suggested the inevitability of the forces of production advancing, this creating an imbalance between them and the relations of production and the superstructure. This imbalance constituted the major contradiction, and the resolution of the struggle it engendered impelled society forward: "The productive forces are always advancing, therefore there is always imbalance."[38] Mao believed that there was a limitless capacity for development on the part of the human factor within the forces of production and thus no possibility of a cessation of struggle and change: "In the fields of the struggle for production and scientific experimentation, mankind makes constant progress and nature undergoes constant change; they never remain at the same level. Therefore man has constantly to sum up experiences and go on discovering, inventing, creating and advancing."[39] The ceaseless development within the forces of production was a function of humans having, in Mao's opinion, a limitless potential to develop the skills and instruments, in short, the technology, which would increasingly extend their dominance over nature. "Human knowledge and the capacity to transform nature have no limit . . . what cannot now be done, may be done in the future."[40]

For Mao, the tendency of the forces of production to advance more rapidly than did the relations of production and the superstructure was a function, of the creative role played by humans within the forces of production; and it was consequently this realm that generated the most significant contradictions and struggles within society. For it was humans, intimately involved in the immediate process of production, who perceived the necessity for change of those things that impeded further development of the forces of production. It was therefore through the perceptions of the human qua laborer that the imperative for change was communicated to other realms within society, to the relations of production and the superstructure, and the struggles within these realms, both to achieve and prevent change, were ultimately a consequence of developments within the forces of production. As Mao pointed out in 1956, "The productive forces consist of two factors: One is man and the other tools. Tools are made by men. When tools call for a revolution, they will speak through men, through the labourers, who will destroy the old relations of production and the old social relations."[41] Because the capacity of humans to develop technology that could transform nature had "no limit," the capacity of the forces of production to develop similarly knew no bounds and would not be exhausted by the advent of communism. The basic impulse for change and development, and the mechanism through which this impulse established contradictions and struggle leading to further change, would endure as long as humans strove to extend their mastery over nature; being human, they could do no other. And as a result, as Mao asserted in 1957, there would still be struggle "ten thousand years from now."[42]

The "Utopianism" of the Great Leap Forward

During the 1950s and early 1960s, Mao's conception of the future became increasingly pessimistic, and the utopianism characteristic of the Yan'an period, while not entirely absent, diminished very significantly in his thought. But what of the Great Leap Forward, which is widely regarded in both Western and Chinese commentaries as a manifestation of Mao's "utopianism"? John Bryan Starr, for example, has suggested that "utopianism figured prominently in Mao's writings" between "1958–59, a particularly euphoric period in Mao's career."[43] Similarly, Maurice Meisner speaks of Mao's "utopian visions of communism" at the time of the Great Leap Forward, of his holding a belief in the "imminent advent of communism."[44] Stuart Schram likewise perceived the utopianism of the Great Leap Forward as an expression of Mao's "revolutionary romanticism."[45] Post-Mao Chinese judgments of the Great Leap Forward and Mao's role in it make a similar point.[46] The virtually unanimous judgment has thus been that Mao's thought at the time of the Great Leap Forward was "utopian." But was it? Did Mao believe in the imminent realization of communism at this time, and if so, did he continue to perceive communism as the "ideal and flawless state" and the final phase in human history?[47]

Mao's utopianism at the time of the Great Leap Forward, if such it was, was comprised largely of an impatient and unrealistic expectation of rapid economic growth flowing from the ambitious social and ideological transformations implemented at that time. Indeed, it is clear that Mao anticipated that China's industrial and agricultural development would be so rapid that it would surpass the major capitalist economies in a very short time. For example, in May 1958, he suggested that China would be able to increase its steel production from 11 million to 40 million tons in 5 years and catch up with the steel production of Great Britain and the United States in seven and fifteen years respectively.[48] Similarly, in November he predicted that China's per capita grain production would almost double in three years.[49] As a result of these dramatic increases in production, China could confidently expect to become a "modernized, industrialized, and highly cultured great power" within fifteen years.[50] Such rash predictions are quite characteristic of the impatient tenor of Mao's thinking at this time.

However, when it came to the possibility of an imminent realization of communism, Mao's position was rather more ambivalent. At the Beidaihe Conference of August 1958, Mao tempered the suggestion that the transition to communism could be achieved in "three, four, five, or six years or a little bit more" by asserting that "the first precondition of communism is plenty." The transition to communism therefore required the achievement of the following five preconditions: "(1) extreme abundance of products; (2) an elevation of communist ideology, consciousness, and morality; (3) popularization and elevation of culture and education; (4) disappearance of the three differences and the remainders of bourgeois right; and (5) gradual disappearance of the functions of the state other than in relation to the external world."[51] Consequently, "the present cannot be called communism, the level is too low; one can only talk about elements and sprouts of communism, and one shouldn't lower the high standards of communism."[52] Mao conceded that two of the important preconditions for the transition to communism—the abolition of commodity production and the elimination of bourgeois right—could not be contemplated given current conditions. Indeed, he admitted that commodity production would have to be expanded for the benefit of socialism.[53] It can be seen from the demanding set of preconditions for the achievement of communism, articulated at the Beidaihe Conference and subsequently, that even had the Great Leap Forward succeeded in economic terms (which it did not; quite the reverse),[54] China would not have been ready, in Mao's eyes, for the transition to communism, which had to come, he thought, "step by step."[55]

Not only are there scattered through the Mao texts of the Great Leap Forward less than utopian assertions that the realization of communism was contingent on the achievement of many prior conditions beyond China's present capacity, there is also evidence of Mao's growing pessimism. In a rambling speech to the Second Session of the Eighth Party Congress in May 1958, Mao spoke of the necessity for preparation for the "final disaster."

> I now wish to discuss the gloomy side of things. We must prepare for major disasters. With thousands of *li* of bare earth, great droughts and great

floods are possible. We must also prepare for major wars. What should we do if the war maniacs drop atom bombs? Let them drop the atom bomb! The possibility is there as long as the warmongers exist. We must also prepare for troubles in the Party, for splits. There will be no splits if we handle it well; but this is limited to certain circumstances; one cannot say that splits are impossible. . . . If the Party should split, there would be chaos for a time.[56]

Interestingly, this "gloomy" prognosis—about the possibility of major natural disasters, lack of unity in the Party, and war—occurs alongside Mao's last reference to the possibility of permanent peace.[57] Here, however, reference to it is embedded in a scenario that conceives permanent peace as a possible outcome of a major atomic conflagration in which two-thirds of the world's population would be annihilated and capitalism totally eliminated. It is clear that, while some of his earlier optimism remained, it was now increasingly dominated by pessimism. Mao's temperament was not, as Craig Dietrich asserts, characterized during the Great Leap Forward by an "airy optimism,"[58] but by a complex mixture of pessimism and optimism, a mixture in which pessimism had become dominant. Although the Great Leap Forward did witness a brief rekindling of Mao's faith in the future, it lacked the unalloyed optimism of the Yan'an period. Moreover, as Starr points out, Mao's dalliance with "utopianism" at this time was short lived and quickly abandoned.[59]

The Cultural Revolution: Farewell to Utopia

With the onset of the Cultural Revolution in 1966, Mao's limited and declining optimism of the 1950s and early 1960s was snuffed out. With the last glimmer of his utopianism gone, the future now appeared to Mao as a grim series of struggles, the outcome of which could not be guaranteed but which must be waged to prevent the complete reversal of any gains won in the course of revolution and socialist transition. He raised, on several occasions, the possibility that the Cultural Revolution, then being waged, would not be the final one; there would have to be several more cultural revolutions, and even then there would be no "peace and quiet":

The victory or defeat of the revolution can be determined only over a long period of time. If it is badly handled there is always the danger of a capitalist restoration. All members of the party and all the people of our country must not think that after one, two, three or four great cultural revolutions there will be peace and quiet. They must always be on the alert and must never relax their vigilance.[60]

Similarly, in a talk in May 1967, Mao reiterated that cultural revolutions of the magnitude of the present one would be a recurring feature during the foreseeable future.

> If the world outlook is not transformed, how can the Great Proletarian Cultural Revolution be called a victory? If the world outlook is not transformed, then although there are 2,000 power holders taking the capitalist road in this Great Cultural Revolution, there may be 4,000 next time. The cost of this Great Cultural Revolution has been very great, and even though the question of the struggle between the two classes and the two roads cannot be resolved by one, two, three or four Great Cultural Revolutions, still, this Great Cultural Revolution should consolidate things for a decade at least. In the course of one century, it may be possible to launch such a revolution two or three times at most.[61]

Moreover, in one of his "Instructions" of the Cultural Revolution, Mao cautioned that "the defeated class will continue to struggle. Its members are still about and it still exists. Therefore we cannot speak of the final victory, not for decades. We must not lose vigilance. . . . It is wrong to talk about the final victory of the revolution in our country light-heartedly; it runs counter to Leninism and does not conform to the facts."[62]

From Harmony to Struggle, from Perpetual Peace to Cultural Revolution

There is a dramatic contrast between Mao's conception of the future during the Yan'an period and that during the Cultural Revolution. The shift—from optimism to pessimism, from an imminently realizable future of perpetual peace to a future of recurring cultural revolutions—is quite pronounced. This decline and eventual disappearance of optimism in Mao's thought suggests as faulty the view that the Cultural Revolution was inspired by Mao's utopian expectations of the possibility of accelerating the process of history to rapidly achieve the onset of communism. Rather, the Cultural Revolution was necessary, in Mao's mind, precisely because the transition to communism could only be espied in the very distant future, if at all, and was imperilled by hostile forces that could so easily reverse the revolution's hard-won gains. And even were communism to be realized, in what sense would it differ from the present? Contradictions and struggles, although not of a class nature but still extensive, would continue to occur; and communism itself, again like the societies of past and present, would eventually succumb to the erosive forces of time, to be supplanted by something else. Eventually, humankind would disappear altogether, as the earth ceased to exist and the sun cooled.[63] In the face of this appallingly bleak apocalyptic vision, what possible political strategy could assume any lasting significance?

The Cultural Revolution was thus for Mao a holding action, in the present, to defend what had been achieved, rather than a coherent strategy which linked the imperfect present to a future "ideal and flawless state" of society. The onset of the Cultural Revolution, and his willingness to entertain the possibility of a recurring cycle of such devastating campaigns, thus signalled the demise of utopianism in Mao's thought. No longer driven by a vision of a perfect and finished state of society in the future toward which political action in the present was oriented, Mao's political actions increasingly lost the future-directed rationality and coherence that his pre-1949 strategies had possessed. The consequence of this absence of utopian vision is, as Paul Tillich points out, to become "imprisoned in the present and quickly fall back into the past."[64] Rather than being too utopian at the time of the Cultural Revolution, Mao was, if anything, insufficiently utopian—indeed was not utopian at all, having lost the vision that could effectively guide China out of its "stagnant, sterile present."[65]

It is no coincidence that at the time of the Cultural Revolution, low levels of pragmatism accompanied Mao's lack of utopianism. Pragmatism and utopianism are not in opposition; they are, rather, necessary complements of coherent future-directed political action. Without utopia, a political movement possesses no goal toward which its actions in the present can be oriented; it has no compass with which to guide its present policies and no vision of the good society against which to evaluate its progress.[66] The decline and eventual disappearance of utopianism in Mao's thought thus removed the possibility of his formulating a coherent strategy for political action in the present; hence his inclination, in the last decade of his life, to respond to issues rather than direct them. In contrast, the utopianism of the Yan'an period was accompanied by very high levels of pragmatism. Mao, at that time, recognized with great astuteness the constraints of the present, and he did so while articulating a utopian vision of a world of peace and harmony, one from which exploitation, oppression, and consequent conflict had been eliminated. His political strategies were informed by this utopian vision and their progress evaluated against its criteria; it was utopia that provided coherence to political strategies and allowed pragmatic and reasoned responses that tested the constraints of the present in the quest to move society closer to desired and confidently anticipated goals.

While the decline and eventual demise of utopianism in Mao's post-1949 thought may have resulted in the loss of future-directed coherence in his political strategies, this does not signal that his thought was altogether without logic or coherence, as some commentators have suggested.[67] Indeed, as I have pointed out in this chapter, the demise of utopianism in Mao's thought was related logically if somewhat ironically to his confidence in the limitless capacity of humans to develop the forces of production, to extend their technical mastery over nature. For Mao, the forces of production, of which the consciously producing human was the most significant dimension, were the most revolutionary force for social change. Changes in the forces of production, of even diminutive proportions, inevitably led to contradictions and struggles in the relations of production and superstructure whose resolution would in the fullness of time facilitate further change and development of the forces of production; this cycle would recur without end, for there was no inherent mechanism in humans or their society that could extinguish the fundamental impulse in humans to develop the forces of production. Mao scholars, with some limited exceptions,[68] have overlooked the dominance attributed by Mao to the forces of production in his etiology of social change, choosing to concentrate instead on his apparent emphasis on the relations of production and superstructure, and particularly the latter.[69] But for Mao, it was not these latter realms of the social formation that drove the entire process of historical change. They were very significant, it is true, as sites of struggle, but they were not the demiurge of history; they were not the bedrock on which the historical drama was founded. Only the forces of production, with their limitless capacity for expansion, could perform that central role. This was a fundamental law of history, one that extended to all societies, past, present, and future. Communism could no more escape from this impulse for change and development than could the class societies of the present.

Similarly, the decline and eventual demise of utopianism in Mao's thought was also related, in a logical way, to his acceptance of an ontology in which all things and processes in the universe, without exception, were impelled to generate contradictions between which there was inevitably struggle that lead to movement and change. All motion within the universe, including change and development in human society, was a manifestation of this most fundamental quality of matter. If this was the case, how could a future communist society be exempted from this universal law? Mao's response, logically enough, was that a future communist society would also be characterized by contradictions and the struggles these generated. Looked at from this perspective, is it any wonder that Mao's vision of this future society lost its utopian varnish?

It is worth commenting in passing that the logic underpinning the decline of Mao's utopianism bore a marked affinity with orthodox Marxism. Both in his insistence on the primacy of the forces of production in social change and his ontological belief in the universality of contradictions, Mao's thought was in conformity with a particular version of Marxist orthodoxy.[70] One does not have to belabor this point by insisting that Mao's thought, in its entirety, was orthodox. It is sufficient to demonstrate that in these two fundamental tenets of orthodoxy Mao's thought was not unorthodox. In their determination to highlight Mao's heterodoxy, many Mao scholars have overlooked the orthodox character of these dimensions of Mao's thought and consequently failed to identify his declining optimism and the reasons for it. Mao was supposedly "utopian" for launching campaigns such as the Cultural Revolution. But the reverse is more probably the case: Mao launched the Cultural Revolution because of his lack of utopianism, this prompted by a belief in core elements of Marxist orthodoxy. And one only has to look at Friedrich Engels's *Dialectics of Nature* to perceive that Mao's bleak prophecies of the end of humankind are themselves anticipated in the writings of the founders of Marxism.[71]

At the very least, it is clear that the Cultural Revolution, while in a temporal sense the final chapter of Mao's life, cannot be regarded as the defining moment of his political career or the essential essence of his thought. It is without doubt a very significant moment, but it is not the defining moment, and there should be no suggestion that the preceding chapters in his life and political career were merely necessary precursors to this, the final consummation of the "Maoist ethic"—the Cultural Revolution. The marked decline in optimism in Mao's thought, from the Yan'an period to the Cultural Revolution, was not a function of some teleological process in which the current of Mao's thought advanced ineluctably toward its finished and essential form. The change, from optimism to pessimism, grew rather out of an altered theoretical and ideological perception of the possibility of achieving utopia through human action. During the Yan'an period, Mao's war-inspired eschatology was bolstered by themes in both the Chinese and Marxist traditions that promised an imminent realization of an era of perpetual peace and harmony. During the 1950s and early 1960s, on the other hand, Mao's deep-seated acceptance of the limitless capacity for development of the forces of production coupled with a recognition that no society, even communist, could be free of contradictions, compelled him in a quite logical manner to accept that not only was communism not imminent but that once realized it would manifest the same fundamental laws as those that had governed previous societies.

Looking far into the future, Mao was thus able to discern that communism could not be the final destiny of History, the last port of call, which once reached, would witness the cessation of those contradictions and struggles that had brought it there, for beyond lay something else, and in the fullness of time, oblivion for humankind. The bright promise of History, so readily accepted by the younger Mao, thus evaporated as the older Mao came to accept, at the very core of his being, the transitoriness of all things. The transition from optimism to pessimism was complete. And all that remained was struggle.

Notes

1. See, for example, C. L. Chiou, *Maoism in Action: The Cultural Revolution* (St. Lucia: University of Queensland Press, 1974); Richard Baum with Louise B. Bennett, eds., *China in Ferment: Perspectives on the Cultural Revolution* (Englewood Cliffs, N. J.: Prentice-Hall, 1971); Maurice Meisner, *Mao's China and After: A History of the People's Republic* (New York: The Free Press, 1986), part 5; Joan Robinson, *The Cultural Revolution in China* (Harmondsworth: Penguin, 1969, 1970); Stuart R. Schram, "The Cultural Revolution in Historical Perspective," in *Authority, Participation and Cultural Change in China*, ed. Stuart R. Schram (Cambridge: Cambridge University Press, 1973), 1–108; Robert Jay Lifton, *Revolutionary Immortality: Mao Tse-tung and the Chinese Cultural Revolution* (New York: W. W. Norton and Co., 1976); Jack Gray and Patrick Cavendish, *Chinese Communism in Crisis: Maoism and the Cultural Revolution* (London: Pall Mall Press, 1968); Jean Esmain, *The Cultural Revolution* (London: Andre Deutsch, 1975); Hong Ying Lee, *The Politics of the Chinese Cultural Revolution: A Case Study* (Berkeley: University of California Press, 1978); An Tai Sung, *Mao Tse-tung's Cultural Revolution* (Indianapolis: Pegasus, 1972); Ito Kikazo and Shibata Minoru, "The Dilemma of Mao Tse-tung," *China Quarterly* 35 (July–September, 1968): 58–77; Richard Solomon, *Mao's Revolution and the Chinese Political Culture* (Berkeley: University of California Press, 1971); Tang Tsou, "The Cultural Revolution and the Chinese Political System," *China Quarterly* 38 (April–June, 1969): 63–91; Stanley Karnow, *Mao and China: Inside China's Cultural Revolution* (New York: Viking Penguin, 1984); Wang Xizhe, "Mao Zedong and the Cultural Revolution," in *On Socialist Democracy and the Chinese Legal System: The Li Yizhe Debates*, eds. Anita Chan, Stanley Rosen, and Jonathan Unger (Armonk, New York: M. E. Sharpe, 1985). For a critique of the literature on the Cultural Revolution, see Mobo C. F. Gao, "Maoist Discourse and Critique of the Present Assessments of the Cultural Revolution," *Bulletin of Concerned Asian Scholars* 26, no. 3 (July–September, 1994): 13–32.

2. Stuart R. Schram, ed., *Mao Tse-tung Unrehearsed: Talks and Letters, 1956–1971* (Harmondsworth: Penguin, 1974), 265, also 268; for the Chinese version, see *Mao Zedong Sixiang Wansui* [Long Live Mao Zedong Thought] (n. p.: n. pub., 1969), 654, also 656.

3. Schram, ed., *Mao Tse-tung Unrehearsed*, 271; *Mao Zedong sixiang wansui* (1969), 658.

4. Jerome Ch'en, ed., *Mao Papers: Anthology and Bibliography* (London: Oxford University Press, 1970), 35; for the Chinese version, see *Mao Zedong Sixiang Wansui* [Long Live Mao Zedong Thought] (n. p.: n. pub., 1967), 40.

5. See Joint Publication Research Service, *Miscellany of Mao Tse-tung Thought (1949–1968)* (Arlington, Virginia: February 1974) II, 453–54; *Mao Zedong sixiang wansui* (1969), 670–71.

6. For a similar viewpoint, see Edward Rice, *Mao's Way* (Berkeley: University of California Press, 1972, 1974).

7. See footnote 1; see also Leslie R. Marchant, *To Phoenix Seat: An Introductory Study of Maoism and the Chinese Communist Quest for a Paradise on Earth* (Sydney: Angus and Robertson, 1973); John Bryan Starr, *Continuing the Revolution: The Political Thought of Mao* (Princeton: Princeton University Press, 1979); Raymond L. Whitehead, *Love and Struggle in Mao's Thought* (New York: Orbis Books, 1977); Harrison E. Salisbury, *The New Emperors: Mao and Deng—A Dual Biography* (London: HarperCollins, 1993).

8. Takeuchi Minoru, ed., *Mao Zedong Ji* [Collected Writings of Mao Zedong] (Tokyo: Hokubosha, 1970–1972) VI, 49–145. The revised version appears in *Selected Works of Mao Tse-tung* (Peking: FLP, 1967) II, 113–94; and *Mao Zedong Xuanji* [Selected Works of Mao Zedong] (Beijing: Renmin chubanshe, 1966) II, 407–84. See also "The Chinese Revolution and the Chinese Communist Party," in Takeuchi, ed., *Mao Zedong Ji* VII, 97–139; *Selected Works of Mao Tse-tung* II, 305–34; and *Mao Zedong Xuanji* II, 584–617.

9. For a critique of this dimension of Marxism, see Gustav A. Wetter, *Dialectical Materialism: A Historical and Systematic Study of Philosophy in the Soviet Union* (New York: Praeger, 1958).

10. See Timoteus Pokora, "On the Origins of *T'ai-p'ing* and *Ta-t'ung* in Chinese Philosophy," *Archiv Orientalni* 29 (1961): 448–54.

11. See Liang Ch'i-ch'ao, *History of Chinese Political Thought During the Early Tsin Period* (London: Kegan Paul, Trench, Trubner and Co. Ltd., 1930), 44. See also Laurence G. Thompson, *Ta Tung Shu: The One-World Philosophy of Kang Yu-wei* (London: George Allen and Unwin, 1958), 27.

12. Frederic Wakeman Jr., *History and Will: Philosophical Perspectives on Mao Tse-tung's Thought* (Berkeley: University of California Press, 1973), 106–7; also Fung Yu-lan, *A Short History of Chinese Philosophy* (New York: The Free Press, 1948), 201.

13. Takeuchi, ed., *Mao Zedong Ji* VI, 96.

14. Cf. Takeuchi, ed., *Mao Zedong Ji* VI, 95; *Selected Works of Mao Tse-tung* II, 149; *Mao Zedong Xuanji* II, 443.

15. For a rare reference, see Joint Publication Research Service, *Miscellany of Mao Tse-tung Thought* I, 108–9. Here, however, reference to a future era of peace is set in the context of a discussion of the "gloomy side of things." It altogether lacks the optimism and confidence of Mao's earlier references.

16. See, for example, *Long Live Leninism* (Peking: FLP, 1960), 34–35.

17. See, for example, Schram, ed., *Mao Tse-tung Unrehearsed*, 228.

18. *Selected Works of Mao Tsetung* (Peking: FLP, 1977) V, 475, also 409, 423; *Mao Zedong Xuanji* [Selected Works of Mao Zedong] (Beijing: Renmin chubanshe, 1977) V, 458, also 390, 404.

19. *Selected Works of Mao Tsetung* V, 500; *Mao Zedong Xuanji* V, 482.

20. Richard Baum and Frederick C. Teiwes, *Ssu-ch'ing: The Socialist Education Movement of 1962–66* (Berkeley: Chinese Research Monographs, University of California, 1968), 60.

21. See Point II of "The First Ten Points" in Baum and Teiwes, *Ssu-ch'ing*, 60.

22. "On the Historical Experience of the Dictatorship of the Proletariat," *New China News Agency* 1531 (5 April 1956), supplement 238, 5. It is now evident that Mao read and revised this important 1956 text. See *Jianguo yilai Mao Zedong wengao* [The Mao texts following the establishment of the People's Republic of China] (Beijing: Zhongyang wenxian chubanshe, 1992) 6, 59–67.

23. *Selected Works of Mao Tsetung* V, 338; *Mao Zedong Xuanji* V, 318–19.

24. Ch'en, ed., *Mao Papers*, 65.

25. Mao Tsetung, *A Critique of Soviet Economics*, trans. Moss Roberts (New York and London: Monthly Review Press, 1977), 57–58, 71; *Mao Zedong sixiang wansui* (1969), 339, 350–51.

26. Schram, ed., *Mao Tse-tung Unrehearsed*, 227; *Mao Zedong sixiang wansui* (1969), 559.

27. Schram, ed., *Mao Tse-tung Unrehearsed*, 110; *Mao Zedong sixiang wansui* (1969), 170.

28. Schram, ed., *Mao Tse-tung Unrehearsed*, 228; *Mao Zedong sixiang wansui* (1969), 559.

29. *Selected Works of Mao Tse-tung* I, 317. For a full translation of the original version of "On Contradiction," annotated to demonstrate all variations between the original and official post-1949 versions of the text, see Nick Knight, ed., *Mao Zedong on Dialectical Materialism: Writings on Philosophy, 1937* (Armonk, New York: M. E. Sharpe, 1990), 154–229. For a detailed analysis of Mao's philosophical writings and their roots in the Soviet philosophy of the 1930s, see Nick Knight, *Marxist Philosophy in China: From Qu Qiubai to Mao Zedong, 1923–1945* (Dordrecht: Springer, 2005), chapters 9 and 10.

30. See Nick Knight, "Mao Zedong's *On Contradiction* and *On Practice*: Pre-Liberation Texts," *China Quarterly* 84 (December, 1980): 641–68.

31. *Selected Works of Mao Tse-tung* V, 392; *Mao Zedong Xuanji* V, 372. Translation modified. For a translation of the original version of this text, see Roderick Macfarquhar, Timothy Cheek, and Eugene Wu, eds., *The Secret Speeches of Chairman Mao: From the Hundred Flowers to the Great Leap Forward* (Cambridge, Mass.: Harvard Contemporary China Series No. 6, 1989), 131–90.

32. *Selected Works of Mao Tse-tung* V, 382–83, 392, 516; *Mao Zedong Xuanji* V, 362, 372, 498.

33. For a detailed analysis of this theme in Mao's thought, see Paul Healy, "A Paragon of Marxist Orthodoxy: Mao Zedong on the Social Formation and Social Change," in *Critical Perspectives on Mao Zedong's Thought*, eds. Arif Dirlik, Paul Healy, and Nick Knight (Atlantic Highlands, NJ: Humanities Press, 1997), 117–53.

34. Joint Publication Research Service, *Miscellany of Mao Tse-tung Thought* II, 435; *Mao Zedong sixiang wansui* (1969), 604. Cf. Karl Marx, *Capital Volume 1* (Harmondsworth: Penguin, 1976), 284.

35. See, for example, *Selected Works of Mao Tse-tung* V, 337–38; *Mao Zedong Xuanji* V, 317–19.

36. *Selected Works of Mao Tse-tung* V, 337–38; *Mao Zedong Xuanji* V, 317–19.

37. *Selected Works of Mao Tse-tung* V, 337–38; *Mao Zedong Xuanji* V, 317–19.

38. Mao Tse-tung, *A Critique of Soviet Economics*, 81; *Mao Zedong sixiang wansui* (1969), 359–60.

39. *Peking Review* 26 (23 June 1967), 2.

40. Mao Tse-tung, *A Critique of Soviet Economics*, 137; *Mao Zedong sixiang wansui* (1967), 157.

41. *Selected Works of Mao Tse-tung* V, 338; *Mao Zedong Xuanji* V, 319.

42. Macfarquhar, Cheek and Wu, eds., *The Secret Speeches of Chairman Mao*, 319, 422.

43. John Bryan Starr, "Maoism and Marxist Utopianism," *Problems of Communism* (July–August 1977): 58.

44. Meisner, *Mao's China and After*, 231, 235.

45. Stuart R. Schram, "Mao Tse-tung as a Charismatic Leader," *Asian Survey* VII, no. 6 (1967): 386.

46. See *Resolution on CPC History (1949–81)* (Beijing: FLP, 1981).

47. See Northrop Frye, "Varieties of Literary Utopias," in *Utopias and Utopian Thought*, ed. Frank E. Manuel (Boston: Souvenir Press, 1965, 1966), 31.

48. Joint Publication Research Service, *Miscellany of Mao Tse-tung Thought* I, 123.

49. Joint Publication Research Service, *Miscellany of Mao Tse-tung Thought* I, 134–35. See also Schram, ed., *Mao Tse-tung Unrehearsed*, 105. Here Mao predicted that China's agriculture would be transformed in eight to ten years.

50. Joint Publication Research Service, *Miscellany of Mao Tse-tung Thought* I, 97; see also 158.

51. Macfarquhar, Cheek, and Wu, eds., *The Secret Speeches of Chairman Mao*, 434, 484.

52. Macfarquhar, Cheek, and Wu, eds., *The Secret Speeches of Chairman Mao*, 447.

53. Macfarquhar, Cheek, and Wu, eds., *The Secret Speeches of Chairman Mao*, 458, 465.

54. See Frederick C. Teiwes with Warren Sun, *China's Road to Disaster: Mao, Central Politicians, and Provincial Leaders in the Unfolding of the Great Leap Forward, 1955–1959* (Armonk, New York: M. E. Sharpe, 1999).

55. Macfarquhar, Cheek, and Wu, eds., *The Secret Speeches of Chairman Mao*, 465.

56. Joint Publication Research Service, *Miscellany of Mao Tse-tung Thought* I, 108–9.

57. Joint Publication Research Service, *Miscellany of Mao Tse-tung Thought* I, 109.

58. Craig Dietrich, *People's China: A Brief History* (New York and Oxford: Oxford University Press, 1986), 122.

59. Starr, "Maoism and Marxist Utopianism," 56, 58–59.

60. Ch'en, ed., *Mao Papers*, 139.

61. Joint Publication Research Service, *Miscellany of Mao Tse-tung Thought* II, 459; *Mao Zedong sixiang wansui* (1969), 676–77. See also Schram, ed., *Mao Tse-tung Unrehearsed*, 283.

62. Ch'en, ed., *Mao Papers*, 159.

63. Schram, ed., *Mao Tse-tung Unrehearsed*, 110, 228.

64. Paul Tillich, "Critique and Justification of Utopia," in *Utopias and Utopian Thought*, ed. Frank E. Manuel (Boston: Souvenir Press, 1965), 296–309.

65. Frank E. Manuel, "Introduction," in *Utopias and Utopian Thought*, ed. Manuel, xxi.

66. See Sheldon Wolin, *Politics and Vision: Continuity and Innovation in Western Political Thought* (Princeton: Princeton University Press, 2004).

67. See Benjamin Schwartz, "Thoughts on the Late Mao: Between Total Redemption and Utter Frustration," in *The Secret Speeches of Chairman Mao*, eds. MacFarquhar, Cheek, and Wu, 21; also Lucien W. Pye, *Mao Tse-tung: The Man in the Leader* (New York: Basic Books, 1976), 44; Ross Terrill, *Mao: A Biography* (New York: Touchstone, Simon & Schuster 1993, revised ed.), 451.

68. See Paul Healy, "A Paragon of Marxist Orthodoxy." See also Nicholas James Knight, *Mao and History: An Interpretive Essay on Some Problems in Mao Zedong's Philosophy of History* (London: University of London, Unpublished PhD thesis, 1983), chapter 4.

69. See, for example, Stuart R. Schram, *The Thought of Mao Tse-tung* (Cambridge: Cambridge University Press, 1989), 5, 17, 54–55, 67, 96, 113, 168, 200.

70. For a discussion of the problem of "orthodoxy" within Marxist philosophy and its significance for evaluating Marxism in China, see Knight, *Marxist Philosophy in China*, chapter 2.

71. Friedrich Engels, *Dialectics of Nature* (Moscow: FLPH, 1954), 49–50. Here Engels states: "Millions of years may elapse, hundreds of thousands of generations be born and die, but inexorably the time will come when the declining warmth of the sun will no longer suffice to melt the ice thrusting itself forward from the poles; when the human race, crowding more and more about the equator, will finally no longer find even there enough heat for life; when gradually even the last trace of organic life will vanish; and the earth, an extinct frozen globe like the moon, will circle in deepest darkness and in an ever narrower orbit about the equally extinct sun, and at last fall into it."

Bibliography

Althusser, Louis. *For Marx*. London: Verso, 1969.

Althusser, Louis, and Étienne Balibar. *Reading Capital*, translated by Ben Brewster. London: NLB, 1970.

Amin, Samir. *The Future of Maoism*. New York: Monthly Review Press, 1983.

Andors, Steve. *China's Industrial Revolution: Politics, Planning, and Management, 1949 to the Present*. London: Martin Robertson, 1977.

———. "Hobbes & Weber vs. Marx & Mao: The Political Economy of Decentralization in China." *Bulletin of Concerned Asian Scholars* 6, no. 3 (1974): 19–34.

Andreski, Stanislav, ed. *The Essential Comte*. London: Croom Helm, 1974.

Apter, David E., and Tony Saich. *Revolutionary Discourse in Mao's Republic*. Cambridge, Mass.: Harvard University Press, 1994.

Avineri, Shlomo. *The Social and Political Thought of Karl Marx*. Cambridge: Cambridge University Press, 1968.

Baum, Richard, with Louise B. Bennett, eds., *China in Ferment: Perspectives on the Cultural Revolution*. Englewood Cliffs, N. J.: Prentice-Hall, 1971.

Baum, Richard, and Frederick C. Teiwes. *Ssu-ch'ing: The Socialist Education Movement of 1962–66*. Berkeley: Chinese Research Monographs, University of California, 1968.

Bettelheim, Charles. *Economic Calculation and Forms of Property*, translated by John Taylor, introduction by Barry Hindess. London: Routledge and Kegan Paul, 1976.

Bi Jianheng. *Mao Zedong yu Zhongguo zhexue chuantong* [Mao Zedong and the Chinese philosophical tradition]. Chengdu: Sichuan renmin chubanshe, 1990.

Boorman, Howard L. "Mao Tse-tung as Historian." *China Quarterly* 28 (October–December 1966): 82–105.

Bottomore, Tom, ed. *Modern Interpretations of Marx*. Oxford: Basil Blackwell, 1981.

Braun, Otto. *A Comintern Agent in China, 1932–1939*, translated from the German by Jeanne Moore, with an introduction by Dick Wilson. St. Lucia, Queensland: University of Queensland Press, 1982.

Bulkeley, Rip. "On 'On Practice'," *Radical Philosophy* 18 (Autumn 1977): 3–9, 15.

Burton, Neil G., and Charles Bettelheim, *China Since Mao*. New York: Monthly Review Press, 1978.

Butler, W. E., ed. *The Legal System of the Chinese Soviet Republic, 1931–1934*. Dobbs Ferry NY: Transnational Publishers 1983.

Callinicos, Alex. *Is There a Future for Marxism?* London: Macmillan, 1982.

Carr, E. H. *What is History?* Harmondsworth: Penguin Books, 1964.

Carrère d'Encausse, Hélène, and Stuart R. Schram. *Marxism and Asia: An Introduction with Readings*. London: Allen Lane The Penguin Press, 1969.

Chalmers, A. F. *What Is This Thing Called Science?* St. Lucia: University of Queensland Press, 1982, second ed.

Chan, Adrian. *Chinese Marxism*. London and New York: Continuum, 2003.

Chang Chun-chiao. "On Exercising All-Round Dictatorship over the Bourgeoisie." *Peking Review* 14 (4 April 1975): 5–11.

Chang, Jung, and Jon Halliday. *Mao: The Unknown Story*. London: Jonathan Cape, 2005.

Chang Ruisen, Zhang Wenru, and Ran Changuang. *Mao Zedong zhexue sixiang gailun* [An introduction to the philosophical thought of Mao Zedong]. Beijing: Zhongguo renmin daxue chubanshe, 1985.

Chen Boda. "Lun xin Qimeng Yundong" [On the new enlightenment]. Pp. 67–89 in *Xian jieduan de Zhongguo sixiang yundong* [The Chinese thought movement in the current stage], edited by Xia Zhengnong. Shanghai: Yiban shudian, 1937.

Chen, Chi-yun. *Hsun Yueh (A.D. 148–209): The Life and Reflections of an Early Medieval Confucianist*. Cambridge: Cambridge University Press, 1975.

Ch'en, Jerome. *Mao and the Chinese Revolution*. London: Oxford University Press, 1965.

———, ed. *Mao Papers: Anthology and Bibliography*. London Oxford University Press, 1970.

Chin, Steve S. K. *The Thought of Mao-Tse-tung: Form and Content*. Translated by Alfred H. Y. Lin. Hong Kong: Centre of Asian Studies Papers and Monographs, 1979.

"China Strives for Harmonious Society, Central Economic Conference." *People's Daily Online*, 6 December 2004. english.people.com.cn/200412/06/eng2004 12o6_166180.html (15 March 2006).

Chiou, C. L. *Maoism in Action: The Cultural Revolution*. St. Lucia: University of Queensland Press, 1974.

Chossudovsky, Michel. *Towards Capitalist Restoration: Chinese Socialism After Mao*. London: Macmillan, 1986.

Cohen, Arthur A. *The Communism of Mao Tse-tung*. Chicago: University of Chicago Press, 1964.

Collier, Andrew. "In Defence of Epistemology." Pp. 55–106 in *Issues in Marxist Philosophy: Volume III—Epistemology, Science, Ideology*, edited by John Mepham and David-Hillel Ruben. Brighton: Harvester, 1979.

Corrigan, Philip, Harvie Ramsay, and Derek Sayer. *For Mao: Essays in Historical Materialism*. London: Macmillan, 1979.

A Critique of Mao Tse-tung's Theoretical Conceptions. Moscow: Progress Publishers, 1972.

Cutler, Anthony, Barry Hindess, Paul Hirst, and Athar Hussain. *Marx's "Capital" and Capitalism Today*. London: Routledge and Kegan Paul, 1977. Vol. I.

Day, M. Henri. *Máo Zédōng, 1917–1927: Documents*. Stockholm: Skriftserien für Orientaliska Studier, no. 14, 1975.

De Bary, Wm. Theodore, ed. *Sources of Chinese Tradition*. New York and London: Columbia University Press, 1960.

Demieville, P. "Chang Hsueh-ch'eng and His Historiography." Pp. 167–85 in *Historians of China and Japan*, edited by W. G. Beasley and E. G. Pulleyblank. London: Oxford University Press, 1961.

De Romilly, Jacqueline. *The Rise and Fall of States According to Greek Authors*. Ann Arbor: University of Michigan Press, 1977.

Deutscher, Isaac. *Ironies of History*. London: Oxford University Press, 1966.

Dietrich, Craig. *People's China: A Brief History*. New York and Oxford: Oxford University Press, 1986.

Dirlik, Arif. "Mao Zedong and Chinese Marxism." In *Companion Encyclopedia of Asian Philosophy*, edited by Indira Mahalingam and Brian Carr. London: Routledge, 1997.

———. *The Origins of Chinese Communism*. New York: Oxford University Press, 1989.

———. "The Predicament of Marxist Revolutionary Consciousness: Mao Zedong, Antonio Gramsci and the Reformulation of Marxist Revolutionary Theory." *Modern China* 9, no. 2 (April 1983): 182–211.

———. *Revolution and History: Origins of Marxist Historiography in China, 1919–1937*. Berkeley: University of California Press, 1978.

Dirlik, Arif, Paul Healy, and Nick Knight, eds. *Critical Perspectives on Mao Zedong's Thought*. Atlantic Highlands, New Jersey: Humanities Press, 1997.

"Draft Party Constitution." *China Quarterly* 37 (January–March 1969): 169–73.

Dunn, John. *Modern Revolutions: An Introduction to the Analysis of a Political Phenomenon*. Cambridge: Cambridge University Press, 1972.

Dunn, Stephen P. *The Fall and Rise of the Asiatic Mode of Production*. London: Routledge & Kegan Paul, 1982.

Dutton, Michael. *Streetlife China*. Melbourne: Cambridge University Press, 1998.

Dutton, Michael, and Paul Healy. "Marxist Theory and Socialist Transition: The Construction of an Epistemological Relation." Pp. 13–66 in *Chinese Marxism in Flux, 1978–84: Essays on Epistemology, Ideology and Political Economy*, edited by Bill Brugger. Armonk, New York: M. E. Sharpe, 1985.

Eckstein, Alexander. *China's Economic Revolution*. Cambridge: Cambridge University Press, 1977.

Eco, Umberto. *The Role of the Reader: Explorations in the Semiotics of Texts*. Bloomington and London: University of Indiana Press, 1979.

———. *Semiotics and the Philosophy of Language*. Bloomington and London: University of Indiana Press, 1979.

Engels, Friedrich. *Dialectics of Nature*. Moscow: FLPH, 1954.

Esherick, Joseph. "On the Restoration of Capitalism: Mao and Marxist Theory." *Modern China* 5, no. 1 (January 1979): 41–78.

Esmain, Jean. *The Cultural Revolution*. London: Andre Deutsch, 1975.

Fan Hao. *Mao Zedong he ta de guwen* [Mao Zedong and his adviser]. Beijing: Renmin chubanshe, 1993.

Fan, K., ed. *Mao Tse-tung and Lin Piao: Post-Revolutionary Writings*. Garden City, New York: Anchor Books, 1972.

Fann, K. T. "Mao's Revolutionary Humanism." *Studies in Soviet Thought* 19, no. 2 (March 1979): 143–54.

Femia, Joseph. *Gramsci's Political Thought: Hegemony, Consciousness and the Revolutionary Process*. Oxford: Clarendon Press, 1987.

Foucault, Michel. *The Archaeology of Knowledge*. London: Tavistock, 1972.

———. "What Is an Author?" Pp. 103–13 in *The Foucault Reader*, edited by Paul Rabinow. New York: Pantheon Books, 1984.

Friedman, Edward. "After Mao: Maoism and Post-Mao China." *Telos* 65 (Fall 1985): 23–46.

Frye, Northrop. "Varieties of Literary Utopias." In *Utopias and Utopian Thought*, ed. Frank E. Manuel. Boston: Souvenir Press, 1965, 1966.

Fu, Charles Wei-Hsun. "Confucianism, Marxism-Leninism and Mao: A Critical Study." *Journal of Chinese Philosophy* 1 (1974): 339–71.

Fung Yu-lan, *A Short History of Chinese Philosophy*. New York: The Free Press, 1948.

Gao, Mobo C. F. "Maoist Discourse and Critique of the Present Assessments of the Cultural Revolution." *Bulletin of Concerned Asian Scholars* 26, no. 3 (July–September, 1994): 13–32.

Gayn, Mark. "Mao Tse-tung Reassessed." Pp. 91–107 in *China Readings 3: Communist China*, edited by Franz Schurmann and Orville Schell (Harmondsworth: Penguin, 1967.

Gramsci, Antonio. *Selections from Prison Notebooks*. Edited and translated by Quinton Hoare and Geoffrey Nowell Smith. London: Lawrence and Wishart, 1971.

Gray, J. "History Writing in Twentieth Century China: Notes on Its Background and Development." Pp. 180–203 in *Historians of China and Japan*, edited by W. G. Beasley and E. G. Pulleyblank. London: Oxford University Press, 1961.

———. *Mao Tse-tung*. Guildford and London: Lutterworth Press, 1973.

Gray, Jack, and Patrick Cavendish. *Chinese Communism in Crisis: Maoism and the Cultural Revolution*. London: Pall Mall Press, 1968.

Gurley, John G. *Challengers to Capitalism: Marx, Lenin and Mao*. San Francisco: San Francisco Book Co., 1976.

———. "The Symposium Papers: Discussion and Comment." *Modern China* 3, no. 4 (October 1977): 443–63.

Hak, Han, and Erik Van Ree. "Was the Older Mao a Maoist?" *Journal of Contemporary Asia* 14, no. 1 (1984): 85.

Halfpenny, Peter. *Positivism and Sociology: Explaining Social Life*. London: Allen & Unwin, 1982.

Healy, Paul. "A Paragon of Marxist Orthodoxy: Mao Zedong on the Social Formation and Social Change." Pp. 117–53 in *Critical Perspectives on Mao Zedong's Thought*, edited by Arif Dirlik, Paul Healy, and Nick Knight. Atlantic Highlands, New Jersey: Humanities Press, 1997.

———. "Reading the Mao Texts: The Question of Epistemology." *Journal of Contemporary Asia* 20, no. 3 (1990): 330–58.

Healy, Paul, and Nick Knight, "Mao Zedong's Thought and Critical Scholarship." Pp. 3–20 in *Critical Perspectives on Mao Zedong's Thought*, edited by Arif Dirlik, Paul Healy, and Nick Knight. Atlantic Highlands, New Jersey: Humanities Press, 1997.

Hindess, Barry. *Philosophy and Methodology of the Social Sciences*. Sussex: Harvester, 1977.

Hindess, Barry, and Paul Hirst. *Pre-Capitalist Modes of Production*. London: Routledge & Kegan Paul, 1975.

———. *Mode of Production and Social Formation: An AutoCritique of Pre-Capitalist Modes of Production*. London: Macmillan, 1977.

Hirst, Paul. "The Necessity of Theory." *Economy and Society* 8, no. 4 (November 1979): 417–45.

Hoffheinz, Roy, Jr. *The Broken Wave: The Chinese Communist Peasant Movement, 1922–1928*. Cambridge, Mass.: Harvard University Press, 1977.

Hollingworth, Clare. *Mao and the Men against Him*. London: Jonathan Cape, 1985.

Holubnychy, Vsevolod. "Mao Tse-tung's Materialist Dialectics." *China Quarterly* 19 (1964): 3–37.

Hsiao, Tso-Liang. *Power Relations within the Chinese Communist Movement, 1930–1934: A Study of Documents*. Seattle: University of Washington Press, 1961.

Hsiung, James Chieh. *Ideology and Practice: The Evolution of Chinese Communism*. New York: Praeger, 1970.

Hu Jintao, "Speech at the 2005 Fortune Global Forum." english.peopledaily.com.cn/200505/17/print20050517_185302.htm (17 May 2005).

Huang, Philip C. C. "Mao Tse-tung and the Middle Peasants, 1925–1928," *Modern China* 1, no. 3 (July 1975): 271–96.

Ito Kikazo and Shibata Minoru. "The Dilemma of Mao Tse-tung." *China Quarterly* 35 (July–September, 1968): 58–77.

Jacobs, Dan N., ed. *From Marx to Mao and Marchais.* New York and London: Long-man, 1979.

Jianguo yilai Mao Zedong wengao [Draft documents by Mao Zedong since the establishment of the People's Republic]. Beijing: Zhongyang wenxian chubanshe, 1987–1992. 6 volumes.

Johnson, Chalmers. "The Failure of Socialism in China." *Issues and Studies* 21, no. 1 (July 1979): 22–33.

Joint Publication Research Service, *Miscellany of Mao Tse-tung Thought (1949–1968).* Arlington, Virginia: February 1974.

Joravsky, David. *Soviet Marxism and Natural Science, 1917–1932.* New York: Columbia University Press, 1961.

Karnow, Stanley. *Mao and China: Inside China's Cultural Revolution.* New York: Viking Penguin, 1984.

Kau, Michael Y. M., and John K. Leung, eds. *The Writings of Mao Zedong, 1949–1976 (September 1949–December 1955).* Armonk, New York: M. E. Sharpe, 1986.

———, eds. *The Writings of Mao Zedong, 1949–1976 (January 1956–December 1957).* Armonk, New York: M. E. Sharpe, 1992.

Keith, Ronald C. "The Relevance of Border-Region Experience to Nation-Building in China, 1949–52." *China Quarterly* 78 (1979): 274–95.

Khrushchev, Nikita. *Khrushchev Remembers*, with an introduction, commentary and notes by Edward Crankshaw. London: André Deutsch, 1971.

Kim, Ilpyong J. "Mass Mobilization Policies and Techniques Developed in the Period of the Chinese Soviet Republic." Pp. 78–98 in *Chinese Communist Politics in Action*, edited by A. Doak Barnett. Seattle and London: University of Washington Press, 1969.

———. *The Politics of Chinese Communism: Kiangsi under the Soviets.* Berkeley: University of California Press, 1973.

Knight, Nicholas James. *Mao and History: An Interpretive Essay on Some Problems in Mao Zedong's Philosophy of History.* London: University of London, unpublished PhD thesis, 1983.

Knight, Nick. "Contemporary Chinese Marxism and the Marxist Tradition: Globalisation, Socialism and the Search for Ideological Coherence." *Asian Studies Review* 30, no. 1 (March 2006): 19–39.

———. "From the 2nd Plenum to the 6th NPC: The Retreat Gathers Speed." *The Australian Journal of Chinese Affairs* 12 (July 1984): 177–94.

———. "Herman Gorter and the Origins of Marxism in China." *China Information* XIX, no. 3 (November 2005): 381–412.

———. "Imagining Globalisation: The World and Nation in Chinese Communist Party Ideology." *Journal of Contemporary Asia* 33, no. 3 (2003): 318–37.

———. "The Laws of Dialectical Materialism in Mao Zedong's Thought—The Question of 'Orthodoxy'." Pp. 84–116 in *Critical Perspectives on Mao Zedong's Thought*, edited by Arif Dirlik, Paul Healy, and Nick Knight. Atlantic Highlands, New Jersey: Humanities Press, 1997.

———. "Leninism, Stalinism and the Comintern." Pp. 24–61 in *Marxism in Asia*, edited by Colin Mackerras and Nick Knight. London and Sydney: Croom Helm, 1985.

———. *Li Da and Marxist Philosophy in China*. Boulder, Colorado: Westview Press, 1996.

———. "Lun Mao Zedong yunyong 'fouding zhi fouding' guilü de 'zhengtong-xing'" [The 'orthodoxy' of Mao Zedong's handling of the law of the 'negation of the negation']. Pp. 1549–55 in *Mao Zedong de zhihui* [The Wisdom of Mao Zedong], edited by Zhang Jingru. Dalian: Dalian chubanshe, 1993.

———. "Mao Studies in China: A Review of *Research on Mao Zedong Thought*." *CCP Research Newsletter* 2 (Spring 1989): 13–16.

———, ed. *Mao Zedong on Dialectical Materialism: Writings on Philosophy, 1937.* Armonk, New York: M. E. Sharpe, 1990.

———. "Mao Zedong's *On Contradiction:* An Annotated Translation of the Pre-Liberation Text." *Griffith Asian Papers No. 3.* Nathan: School of Modern Asian Studies, Griffith University, 1981.

———. "Mao Zedong's *On Contradiction* and *On Practice:* Pre-Liberation Texts." *China Quarterly* 84 (December 1980): 641–68.

———. "Mao Zedong's Thought and Chinese Marxism: Recent Documents and Interpretations." *Bulletin of Concerned Asian Scholars* 25, no. 2 (April–June 1993): 54–63.

———. *Marxist Philosophy in China: From Qu Qiubai to Mao Zedong, 1923–1945.* Dordrecht: Springer, 2005.

———, ed. *The Philosophical Thought of Mao Zedong: Studies from China, 1981–1989.* Armonk, New York: M.E. Sharpe, *Chinese Studies in Philosophy*, 1992.

———, ed. *Philosophy and Politics in Mao Texts of the Yan'an Period.* Armonk, New York: M. E. Sharpe, *Chinese Studies in Philosophy*, Winter 1987–88.

———. "Soviet Philosophy and Mao Zedong's 'Sinification of Marxism'." *Journal of Contemporary Asia* 20, no. 1 (1990): 89–109.

Koller, John M. "Philosophical Aspects of Maoist Thought." *Studies in Soviet Thought* 14 (1974): 47–59.

Korsch, Karl. *Marxism and Philosophy.* London: NLB, 1970.

Kuhn, Thomas. *The Structure of Scientific Revolutions.* Chicago and London: University of Chicago Press, 1970, second ed.

Kuo, Warren. *Analytical History of the Chinese Communist Party.* Taipei: Institute of International Relations, 1968, second edition. Volume 2.

Lee, Hong Ying. *The Politics of the Chinese Cultural Revolution: A Case Study.* Berkeley: University of California Press, 1978.

Legge, James. *The Four Books.* Hong Kong: Wei Tung Book Store, 1973.

Lenin, V. I. *Collected Works.* London: Lawrence & Wishart, 1963, 1964.

———. *Selected Works in Three Volumes.* Moscow: Progress Publishers, 1975, 1976.

———. *What is to be Done?* Peking: Foreign Languages Press (hereafter FLP), 1975.

Levy, Richard. "Mao, Marx, Political Economy and the Chinese Revolution: Good Questions, Poor Answers." Pp. 154–83 in *Critical Perspectives on Mao Zedong's Thought*, edited by Arif Dirlik, Paul Healy, and Nick Knight. Atlantic Highlands, New Jersey: Humanities Press, 1997.

Lew, Roland. "Maoism and the Chinese Revolution." *Socialist Register* (1975): 115–59.

Liang Ch'i-ch'ao. *History of Chinese Political Thought During the Early Tsin Period.* London: Kegan Paul, Trench, Trubner and Co. Ltd., 1930.

———. *Intellectual Trends in the Ch'ing Period.* Cambridge, Mass.: Harvard University Press, 1959.

Lichtheim, George. *Marxism: An Historical and Critical Study.* London: Routledge and Kegan Paul, 1961.

Liebman, Marcel. *Leninism under Lenin,* translated by Brian Pearce. London: Jonathan Cape, 1975.

Lifton, Robert Jay. *Revolutionary Immortality: Mao Tse-tung and the Chinese Cultural Revolution.* New York: W. W. Norton and Co., 1976.

Liu Rong. *Mao Zedong zhexue sixiang gaishu* [A commentary on Mao Zedong's philosophical thought]. Guangdong: Guangdong renimin chubanshe, 1983.

Li Zhanping and Li Shuqin. *Mao Zedong lixianji* [A chronicle of dangers experienced by Mao Zedong]. Beijing: Zhongguo shuji chubanshe, 1993.

Li Zhisui. *The Private Life of Chairman Mao.* London: Random House, 1996.

Long Live Leninism. Peking: FLP, 1960.

Lötviet, Trygve. *Chinese Communism, 1931–1934: Experience in Civil Government.* Stockholm: Scandinavian Institute of Asian Studies Monograph Series, 1973.

Lowe, Donald M. *The Function of "China" in Marx, Lenin and Mao.* Berkeley and Los Angeles: University of California Press, 1966.

Lowith, Karl. *Meaning in History.* Chicago: University of Chicago Press, 1949.

Lukács, Georg. *History and Class Consciousness: Studies in Marxist Dialectics.* London: Merlin Press, 1971.

Macfarquhar, Roderick, Timothy Cheek, and Eugene Wu, eds. *The Secret Speeches of Chairman Mao: From the Hundred Flowers to the Great Leap Forward.* Cambridge, Mass.: Harvard Contemporary China Series No. 6, 1989.

Machovec, Milan. *A Marxist Looks at Jesus.* London: Dorton, Longman and Todd, 1976.

Manuel, Frank E. "Introduction." In *Utopias and Utopian Thought,* edited by Frank E. Manuel. Boston: Souvenir Press, 1965, 1966.

Mao Tse-tung. *Basic Tactics.* Translated and with an Introduction by Stuart R. Schram. New York: Frederick A. Praeger, 1966.

———. Mao Tsetung. *A Critique of Soviet Economics,* translated by Moss Roberts. New York: Monthly Review Press, 1977.

———. *Four Essays on Philosophy.* Peking: FLP, 1966.

———. *Selected Works of Mao Tsetung.* Beijing: Foreign Languages Press, 1977. Vol. V.

———. *Selected Works of Mao Tse-tung.* London: Lawrence and Wishart, 1956.

———. *Selected Works of Mao Tse-tung.* Peking: FLP, 1967. Volumes I–IV.

Mao Zedong junshi wenji [Collected military writings of Mao Zedong]. Beijing: Junshi kexue chubanshe, Zhongyang wenxian chubanshe, 1993. 6 volumes.

Mao Zedong. *Report from Xunwu,* translated, with an introduction and notes, by Roger R. Thompson. Stanford: Stanford University Press, 1990.

Mao Zedong shuxin xuanji [Selected letters of Mao Zedong]. Beijing: Renmin chubanshe, 1983.

Mao Zedong sixiang wansui [Long live the thought of Mao Zedong]. N.p.: n.p. 1967.

Mao Zedong sixiang wansui [Long live Mao Zedong Thought]. Taiwan: n.p., 1967.

Mao Zedong sixiang wansui [Long live the thought of Mao Zedong]. N.p.: n.p., 1969.

Mao Zedong wenji [Collected writings of Mao Zedong]. Beijing: Renmin chubanshe, 1993–1999). 8 volumes.

Mao Zedong xinwen gongzuo wenxuan [Selected writings of Mao Zedong on journalism]. Beijing: Xinhua chubanshe, 1983.

Mao Zedong Xuanji [Selected Works of Mao Zedong]. Beijing: Renmin chubanshe, 1966. Volumes I–IV.

Mao Zedong zhexue pizhuji [The philosophical annotations of Mao Zedong]. Beijing: Zhongyang wenxian chubanshe, 1988.

Mao Zedong zhuzuo xuandu [Selected readings from the works of Mao Zedong]. Beijing: Renmin chubanshe, 1986. 2 volumes.

Marchant, Leslie R. *To Phoenix Seat: An Introductory Study of Maoism and the Chinese Communist Quest for a Paradise on Earth.* Sydney: Angus and Robertson, 1973.

Marks, Robert. "The State of the China Field: Or, the China Field and the State." *Modern China* 11, no. 4 (1985): 461–509.

Marx, Karl. *Capital Volume 1.* Harmondsworth: Penguin, 1976.

———. *A Contribution to the Critique of Political Economy.* London: Lawrence and Wishart, 1971.

———. *Early Writings.* Harmondsworth: Penguin, 1975.

———. *The First International and After.* Harmondsworth: Penguin, 1974.

———. *The Poverty of Philosophy.* Moscow: Progress Publishers, 1955.

———. *Pre-Capitalist Economic Formations.* London: Lawrence and Wishart, 1964.

Marx, Karl, and Friedrich Engels. *The German Ideology.* London: Lawrence and Wishart, 1974.

———. *The Holy Family, or Critique of Critical Criticism.* Moscow. Progress Publishers, 1975, second ed.

McBride, William Leon. *The Philosophy of Karl Marx.* London: Hutchinson, 1977.

McDougall, Bonnie S. *"Talks at the Yan'an Conference on Literature and Art": A Translation of the 1943 Text with Commentary*. Ann Arbor: Michigan Papers in China Studies, no. 39, 1980.

Meisner, Maurice. *The Deng Xiaoping Era: An Inquiry into the Fate of Chinese Socialism, 1978–1994*. New York: Hill and Wang, 1996.

———. "Mao and Marx in the Scholastic Tradition." *Modern China* 3, no. 4 (October 1977): 401–6.

———. *Mao's China and After: A History of the People's Republic*. New York: The Free Press, 1977, 1986.

———. *Marxism, Maoism and Utopianism: Eight Essays*. Madison: University of Wisconsin Press, 1982.

Meissner, Werner. *Philosophy and Politics in China: The Controversy over Dialectical Materialism in the 1930s*. London: Hurst and Co., 1990.

Melotti, Umberto. *Marx and the Third World*. London: Macmillan, 1977.

The Ninth National Congress of the Communist Party of China (Documents). Peking: Foreign Languages Press, 1969.

North, Robert. *Moscow and Chinese Communists*. Stanford: Stanford University Press, 1953, 1963.

Ogden, Susanne. *China's Unresolved Issues: Politics, Development, and Culture*. Englewood Cliffs, N.J.: Prentice Hall, 1989.

"On Questions of Party History: Resolution on Certain Questions in the History of our Party since the Founding of the People's Republic of China." *Beijing Review* XXIV, no. 27 (6 July 1981).

"On the Historical Experience of the Dictatorship of the Proletariat." *New China News Agency* 1531 (5 April 1956), supplement 238.

Pang Xianzhi. *Mao Zedong he tade mishu Tian Jiaying* [Mao Zedong and his secretary Tan Jiaying]. Beijing: Zhongguo wenxian chubanshe, 1989.

Paolucci, Henry, ed. *The Political Writings of St. Augustine*. Chicago: Henry Regnery & Co., 1962.

Peking Review 26 (23 June 1967).

Pfeffer, Richard M. "Mao and Marx in the Marxist-Leninist Tradition: A Critique of 'The China Field' and a Contribution to a Preliminary Reappraisal." *Modern China* 3, no. 4 (October 1976): 421–60.

———. "Mao and Marx: Understanding, Scholarship, and Ideology—a Response." *Modern China* 2, no. 4 (October 1977): 379–86.

Plamenatz, John. *German Marxism and Russian Communism*. London: Longmans, 1961.

Plekhanov, George. *The Materialist Conception of History*. New York: International Publishers, 1940.

Pokora, Timoteus. "Book Review of Laurence G. Thompson's *Ta Tung Shu*." *Archiv Orientalni* 29 (1961): 169.

———. "On the Origins of the Notions *T'ai-p'ing* and *Ta-t'ung* in Chinese Philosophy." *Archiv Orientalni* 29 (1961): 448–54.

Popper, Karl R. *The Logic of Scientific Discovery*. London: Hutchinson, 1972.

Pulleyblank, E. J. "Chinese Historical Criticism: Liu Chih-Chi and Ssu-ma Kuang." In *Historians of China and Japan*, edited by W. G. Beasley and E. G. Pulleyblank. London: Oxford University Press, 1961.

Pye, Lucien W. *Mao Tse-tung: The Man in the Leader*. New York: Basic Books, 1976.

———. *The Spirit of Chinese Politics: A Psychocultural Study of the Authority Crisis in Political Development*. Cambridge, Mass.: M. I. T. Press, 1968.

Rabinow, Paul, ed. *The Foucault Reader*. New York: Pantheon Books, 1984.

Reglar, Steve. "Mao Zedong as a Marxist Political Economist: A Critique." *Journal of Contemporary Asia* 17, no. 2 (1987): 208–33.

Resolution on CPC History (1949–81). Beijing: Foreign Languages Press, 1981.

Rice, Edward. *Mao's Way*. Berkeley: University of California Press, 1972, 1974.

Robinson, Joan. *The Cultural Revolution in China*. Harmondsworth: Penguin, 1969, 1970.

Rossanda, Rossana. "Mao's Marxism." *Socialist Register* (1971): 53–80.

Rue, John E. *Mao Tse-tung in Opposition, 1927–1935*. Stanford: Stanford University Press, 1966.

Saich, Tony, ed., with a contribution by Benjamin Yang. *The Rise to Power of the Chinese Communist Party: Documents and Analysis*. Armonk, New York: M. E. Sharpe, 1996.

Salisbury, Harrison E. *The New Emperors: Mao and Deng—A Dual Biography*. London: HarperCollins, 1993.

Sawer, Marian. "The Politics of Historiography: Russian Socialism and the Question of the Asiatic Mode of Production 1906–1931." *Critique* (Winter–Spring 1978–1979): 16–35.

Sayer, Derek. *The Violence of Abstraction: The Analytic Foundations of Historical Materialism*. Cambridge: Basil Blackwell, 1987.

Schaffer, Lynda. *Mao and the Workers: The Hunan Labor Movement, 1920–1923*. Armonk, New York: M. E. Sharpe, 1982.

———. "Mao Zedong and the October 1922 Changsha Construction Workers' Strike: Marxism in Preindustrial China." *Modern China* 4, no. 4 (October 1978): 379–418.

Scharping, Thomas. "The Man, the Myth, the Message—New Trends in Mao-Literature from China." *China Quarterly* 137 (March 1994): 168–79.

Schram, Stuart R. "Chairman Hua edits Mao's Literary Heritage: 'On the Ten Great Relationships'." *China Quarterly* 69 (March 1977): 126–35.

———. "Chinese and Leninist Components in the Personality of Mao Tse-tung." *Asian Survey* III, no. 6 (1963): 259–73.

———. "The Cultural Revolution in Historical Perspective," pp. 1–108 in *Authority, Participation and Cultural Change in China*, edited by Stuart Schram. Cambridge: Cambridge University Press, 1973.

———. "Introduction" to Li Jui, *The Early Revolutionary Activities of Mao Tse-tung*. White Plains, New York: M. E. Sharpe, 1977.

———, ed., *Mao's Road to Power, Revolutionary Writings 1912–1949: Volume I, The Pre-Marxist Period, 1912–1920.* Armonk, New York: M. E. Sharpe, 1992.

———. "Mao Studies: Retrospect and Prospect." *China Quarterly* 97 (March 1984): 95–125.

———. *Mao Tse-tung.* Harmondsworth: Penguin, 1966.

———. "Mao Tse-tung and Secret Societies." *China Quarterly* 27 (July–September 1966): 1–13.

———. "Mao Tse-tung and the Theory of the Permanent Revolution, 1958–1969." *China Quarterly* 46 (1971): 221–44.

———. "Mao Tse-tung as Charismatic Leader." *Asian Survey* VII, no. 6 (June 1967): 383–88.

———. "Mao Tse-tung as Marxist Dialectician." *China Quarterly* 29 (January–March, 1967): 155–65.

———. "Mao Tse-tung's Thought to 1949." In *An Intellectual History of Modern China,* edited by Merle Goldman and Leo Ou-Fan Lee. Cambridge: Cambridge University Press, 2002.

———, ed. *Mao Tse-tung Unrehearsed: Talks and Letters, 1957–71.* Harmondsworth: Penguin, 1974.

———. *Mao Zedong: A Preliminary Reappraisal.* Hong Kong: The Chinese University Press, 1983.

———. "Mao Zedong and the Role of Various Classes in the Chinese Revolution, 1923–1927." Pp. 227–39 in *The Polity and Economy of China: The Late Professor Yuji Muramatsu Commemoration Volume.* Tokyo: Tokyo Keizai Shinposha, 1975.

———. "The Marxist." Pp. 35–69 in *Mao Tse-tung in the Scales of History,* edited by Dick Wilson. Cambridge: Cambridge University Press, 1977.

———. "Modernization and the Maoist Vision." *Bulletin (International House of Japan)* 26 (1979): 1–22.

———. *The Political Thought of Mao Tse-tung.* Harmondsworth: Penguin, 1969, revised ed.

———. "Some Reflections on the Pfeffer-Walder 'Revolution' in China Studies." *Modern China* 3, no. 4 (April 1977): 169–84.

———. *The Thought of Mao Tse-tung.* Cambridge: Cambridge University Press, 1989.

Schram, Stuart R., ed., and Nancy J. Hodes, associate ed. *Mao's Road to Power: Revolutionary Writings 1912–1949: Volume II, National Revolution and Social Revolution, December 1920–June 1927.* Armonk, New York: M. E. Sharpe, 1994.

———, eds. *Mao's Road to Power: Revolutionary Writings, 1912–1949: Volume III—From the Jinggangshan to the Establishment of the Jiangxi Soviets, July 1927—December 1930.* Armonk, New York: M. E. Sharpe, 1995.

———, eds. *Mao's Road to Power: Revolutionary Writings, 1912–1949: Volume IV—The Rise and Fall of the Chinese Soviet Republic.* Armonk, New York: M. E. Sharpe, 1997.

———, eds. *Mao's Road to Power—Revolutionary Writings, 1912–1949: Volume VI—The New Stage, August 1937–1938.* Armonk, New York: M. E. Sharpe, 2004.

———, eds. *Mao's Road to Power: Revolutionary Writings, 1912–1949—Volume VII, New Democracy, 1939–1941.* Armonk, New York: M. E. Sharpe, 2005.

Schrift, Melissa. *Biography of a Chairman Mao Badge: The Creation and Mass Consumption of a Personality Cult.* New Brunswick: Rutgers University Press, 2001.

Schurmann, Franz. *Ideology and Organization in Communist China.* Berkeley: University of California Press, 1971, second edition.

Schwartz, Benjamin I. "China and the West in the 'Thought of Mao Tse-tung'." Pp. 365–79 in *China in Crisis*, edited by Ho Ping-ti and Tsou Tang. Chicago: University of Chicago Press, 1968. Vol. 1, book 1.

———. *Chinese Communism and the Rise of Mao.* Cambridge: Harvard University, 1951.

———. *Communism and China: Ideology in Flux.* New York: Atheneum, 1970.

———. "The Essence of "Marxism Revisited: A Response." *Modern China* 2, no. 4 (1976): 461–72.

———. "The Legend of the 'Legend of "Maoism"'." *China Quarterly* 2 (April–June 1960): 35–42.

———. "On the 'Originality' of Mao Tse-tung." *Foreign Affairs* 34, no. 1 (October 1955): 67–76.

———. "A Personal View of Some Thoughts of Mao Tse-tung." Pp. 352–72 in *Ideology and Politics in Contemporary China*, edited by Chalmers Johnson. Seattle and London: University of Washington Press, 1973.

———. "Presidential Address: Area Studies as a Critical Discipline." *Journal of Asian Studies* 40, no. 1 (November 1980): 15–25.

———. "Thoughts on the Late Mao: Between Total Redemption and Utter Frustration." Pp. 19–38 in *The Secret Speeches of Chairman Mao: From the Hundred Flowers to the Great Leap Forward*, edited by Roderick Macfarquhar, Timothy Cheek, and Eugene Wu. Cambridge, Mass.: Harvard University Press, 1989.

Selden, Mark. *The Yenan Way in Revolutionary China.* Cambridge, Mass.: Harvard University Press, 1971.

Sheridan, James E. *Chinese Warlord: The Career of Feng Yü-hsiang.* Stanford: Stanford University Press, 1966.

Sivin, Nathan. "Chinese Conceptions of Time." *Earlham Review* 1 (1966): 82–92.

Snow, Edgar. *Red Star over China.* Harmondsworth: Penguin, 1972.

Socialist Upsurge in China's Countryside. Peking: Foreign Languages Press, 1957.

Solomon, Richard H. *Mao's Revolution and the Chinese Political Culture.* Berkeley: University of California Press, 1971.

———. "On Activism and Activists: Maoist Conceptions of Motivation and Political Role Linking State to Society." *China Quarterly* 39 (July–September 1969): 76–114.

Stalin, J. V. *Problems of Leninism.* Peking: FLP, 1976.

Starr, John Bryan. "Conceptual Foundations of Mao Tse-tung's Theory of Continuous Revolution." *Asian Survey* XI, no. 6 (June 1971): 610–28.

————. *Continuing the Revolution: The Political Thought of Mao.* Princeton: Princeton University Press, 1979.

————. "'Good Mao,' 'Bad Mao': Mao Studies and the Re-evaluation of Mao's Political Thought." *Australian Journal of Chinese Affairs* 16 (July 1986): 1–6.

————. "Maoism and Marxist Utopianism." *Problems of Communism* (July–August 1977): 56–62.

————. "Mao Tse-tung and the Sinification of Marxism: Theory, Ideology and Phylactery." *Studies in Comparative Communism* 3, no. 2 (April 1970): 149–57.

Sudama, Trevor. "Analysis of Classes by Mao Tse-tung, 1929–39." *Journal of Contemporary Asia* 8, no. 3 (1978): 355–73.

Sung, An Tai. *Mao Tse-tung's Cultural Revolution.* Indianapolis: Pegasus, 1972.

Takeuchi Minoru, ed. *Mao Zedong Ji* [Collected Writings of Mao Zedong]. Tokyo: Hokubasha, 1970–72. Ten volumes.

————, ed. *Mao Zedong Ji. Bujuan* [Supplement to the Collected Writings of Mao Zedong]. Tokyo: Sōsōsha, 1983–1986. Ten volumes.

Tang Tsou. "The Cultural Revolution and the Chinese Political System." *China Quarterly* 38 (April–June, 1969): 63–91.

————. "Mao Tse-tung Thought, the Last Struggle for Succession and the Post-Mao Era." *China Quarterly* 71 (September 1979): 498–527.

Teiwes, Frederick C., with Warren Sun. *China's Road to Disaster: Mao, Central Politicians, and Provincial Leaders in the Unfolding of the Great Leap Forward, 1955–1959.* Armonk, New York: M. E. Sharpe, 1999.

Teng, S. Y. "Wang Fu-chih's Views on History and Historical Writing." *Journal of Asian Studies* XXVIII, no. 1 (November 1968): 111–23.

Terrill, Ross. *Mao: A Biography.* New York: Touchstone, Simon and Schuster, 1980, 1993.

Thompson, Laurence G. *Ta Tung Shu: The One-World Philosophy of Kang Yu-wei.* London: George Allen & Unwin, 1958.

Thornton, Richard C. *China: The Struggle for Power, 1917–1972.* Bloomington and London: Indiana University Press, 1973.

Tillich, Paul. "Critique and Justification of Utopia." Pp. 296–309 in *Utopias and Utopian Thought,* edited by Frank E. Manuel. Boston: Souvenir Press, 1965, 1966.

Townsend, James R. "Chinese Populism and the Legacy of Mao Tse-tung." *Asian Survey* 17, no. 11 (November 1977): 1003–15.

Van der Kroef, Justus M. "Lenin, Mao and Aidit." *China Quarterly* 10 (April–June 1962): 23–44.

Wakeman, Frederic, Jr. *History and Will: Philosophical Perspectives of Mao Tse-tung's Thought.* Berkeley: University of California Press, 1973.

————. "A Response." *Modern China* 3, no. 4 (October 1977): 161–68.

Walder, Andrew. "Actually Existing Maoism." *The Australian Journal of Chinese Affairs* 18 (July 1987): 155–66.

————. "Marxism, Maoism and Social Change." *Modern China* 3, no. 1 (January 1977): 101–18; and 3, no. 2 (April 1977): 125–59.

―――. "A Response." *Modern China* 3, no. 4 (October 1977): 387–89.

Waller, Derek J. *The Kiangsi Soviet Republic: Mao and the National Congresses of 1931 and 1934*. Berkeley: Center for China Studies, University of California, 1973.

Wang Xizhe. "Mao Zedong and the Cultural Revolution." In *On Socialist Democracy and the Chinese Legal System: The Li Yizhe Debates*, edited by Anita Chan, Stanley Rosen, and Jonathan Unger. Armonk, New York: M. E. Sharpe, 1985.

Watson, Andrew, ed. *Mao Zedong and the Political Economy of the Border Region*. Cambridge: Cambridge University Press, 1980.

Watson, Burton. *Ssu-ma Ch'ien: Grand Historian of China*. New York: Columbia University Press, 1958.

Weber, Max. *The Methodology of the Social Sciences*. New York: The Free Press, 1949.

Wetter, Gustav A. *Dialectical Materialism: A Historical and Systematic Study of Philosophy in the Soviet Union*. New York: Praeger, 1958.

Whitehead, Raymond L. *Love and Struggle in Mao's Thought*. New York: Orbis Books, 1977.

Wittfogel, Karl A. "The Legend of 'Maoism'." *China Quarterly* 1 (January–March 1960), part 1: 72–86; and *China Quarterly* 2 (April–June 1960), part 2: 16–34.

―――. "The Marxist View of China (part 2)." *China Quarterly* 12 (1962): 154–69.

Wolf, Eric R. *Peasant Wars of the Twentieth Century*. London: Faber and Faber, 1973.

Wolin, Sheldin S. "Paradigms and Political Theories." Pp. 125–52 in *Politics and Experience*, edited by P. King and B. C. Parekh. Cambridge: Cambridge University Press, 1968.

―――. *Politics and Vision: Continuity and Innovation in Western Political Thought*. Princeton: Princeton University Press, 2004.

Womack, Brantly. *The Foundations of Mao Zedong's Thought, 1917–1935*. Honolulu: University of Hawaii Press, 1982.

―――. "The Historical Shaping of Mao Zedong's Political Thought." Pp. 27–62 in *Contemporary Chinese Philosophy*, edited by F. J. Adelman. The Hague: Martin Nijhoff Publishers, 1982.

―――. "Theory and Practice in the Thought of Mao Tse-tung." Pp. 1–36 in *The Logic of 'Maoism': Critiques and Explication*, edited by James Chieh Hsiung. New York: Praeger, 1974.

―――. "Where Mao Went Wrong: Epistemology and Ideology in Mao's Leftist Politics." *Australian Journal of Chinese Affairs* 16 (July 1986): 23–40.

Womack, John, Jr. *Zapata and the Mexican Revolution*. Harmondsworth: Penguin, 1968.

Wylie, Raymond F. *The Emergence of Maoism: Mao Tse-tung, Ch'en Po-ta and the Search for Chinese Theory, 1935–1945*. Stanford: Stanford University Press, 1980.

―――. "Mao Tse-tung, Ch'en Po-ta and the 'Sinification of Marxism,' 1936–38." *China Quarterly* 79 (September 1979): 447–80.

Zheng Yi and Jia Mei, eds. *Mao Zedong shenghuo shilu* [Records of Mao Zedong's Life]. Nanjing: Jiangsu wenyi chubanshe, 1989.

Zhonggong zhongyang wenxian yanjiushi. *Mao Zedong nongcun diaocha wenji* [Collected rural investigations of Mao Zedong]. Beijing: Zhonggong zhongyang wenxian chubanshe, 1982.

Zhonggong zhongyang wenxian yanjiu shibian. *Mao Zedong nianpu* [Chronology of Mao Zedong]. Beijing: Renmin chubanshe, Zhongyang wenxian chubanshe, 1993.

Zongli Tang and Bing Zuo. *Maoism and Chinese Culture*. New York: Nova Science, 1996.

Index